. Contents .

. Preface .

More than three decades ago Matthew Hodgart's and Mabel Worthington's *Song in the Works of James Joyce* appeared, listing some two hundred fifty allusions to opera in *Finnegans Wake*. Subsequently Professor Hodgart has been occupied in tracing additional opera allusions in James Joyce's last book. In 1988, in connection with an essay I was writing, he kindly sent me his notes on opera for my own use. It was evident, as I examined them, that they constituted a major contribution to understanding *Finnegans Wake*. With Professor Hodgart's permission I undertook to computerize the material, which consisted of some eighty pages of abbreviated notes, typed or in longhand and in page/line order, with additional lists partially alphabetized by opera, character, singer, or aria. After so many years of intense work, Professor Hodgart carried much of the information in his head; but it was necessary for me, approaching them for the first time, to complete the notes from various reference sources.

There were additional materials in the form of drafts of unpublished revisions planned for *Song in the Works of James Joyce* and drafts for Professor Hodgart's *James Joyce: A Student's Guide*. My initial tasks were therefore to collate the Hodgart notes and to devise a computerized format to ease sorting and cross-referencing. In the process of checking the accuracy of my transcriptions against the text of *Finnegans Wake*, I encountered opera allusions not included in the Hodgart notes, and I added these—perhaps 20 percent of the total—to the file.

Beyond cataloging Joyce's allusions to still-current opera repertory, Professor Hodgart and I have included those to operas popular in Joyce's youth in Ireland, although very infrequently performed nowadays, such as Balfe's *Bohemian Girl* or Benedict's *Lily of Killarney*. Joyce was also fond of Gilbert and Sullivan operettas, so his allusions to these are also included, as well as those to light opera or operettas by Rudolf Friml, Franz Lehár, and so on. Because distinctions among operettas, light operas, and musicals are somewhat vague, we have also included such works as Fraser-Simon's *Maid of the Mountain* and Noel Coward's *Bitter Sweet,* both listed as "operettas" by some reference sources.

For greater usefulness, the material in part 2, "Opera in *Finnegans Wake,*" is presented in several formats:

a. chapter 6 is a *page/line list* of opera and light opera allusions in the order in which they occur in *Finnegans Wake;*

b. chapter 7 is an alphabetical *composer list* (including *librettists, conductors, critics, and designers*), including for each composer the titles of his or her operas, arias, themes, or characters mentioned in the *Wake,* with page/line citations;

c. chapter 8 is an alphabetical *finding list* of all *operas, arias, and characters* in the *Wake,* with enough information to find these items in the composer list;

d. chapter 9 is an alphabetical catalog of *opera singers* in the *Wake.*

A detailed explanation of how to use these lists, as well as the abbreviations employed in chapters 6–9, begins on p. 109.

A second task developed as it became evident that all this factual material needed a historical and biographical context. We now know and discuss James Joyce through his writing. In his lifetime friends and family knew him as a multifaceted musician: singer, composer, stage performer, music critic, and patron of singers. In part 1, "Joyce's Opera Worlds," I establish Joyce within that milieu he knew and loved from childhood onward, a world he often recalled in his writings.

Ruth Bauerle

. Acknowledgments .

Many persons and institutions have assisted in this work. Professor Hodgart has shown an admirable patience as I slowly worked my way through his wonderful material. The library staffs of the Ohio State and Ohio Wesleyan Universities, the Delaware County and Columbus Public Libraries, and dozens of institutions reached through interlibrary loan and the Internet aided in reference searches and mail service. I am particularly grateful to the following individuals at Ohio Wesleyan: Elizabeth Barker, Paul Burnam, Marty Chan, Sara Cook, Barbara Deal, Bernard Derr, Denise Green, Thomas Green, Carol Hallenbeck, David Henderson, Helmut Kremling, Eleanor Kroninger, Julie McDaniel, Marilyn Nims, Lois Ward, and Harold Wiebe. Ohio Wesleyan's Theodore Presser Collection was especially helpful. Dawn Moyer did the photography.

Timothy Martin kindly reviewed the Wagnerian allusions and corrected many errors in my transcriptions. William Brockman had useful bibliographical suggestions and put me in touch with Stephen and Nona K. Watt, who generously contributed their notes for the appendix of opera performance in Dublin, 1898–1904. Philip Shields of the Royal Irish Academy of Music and Willis Parker of WOSU-TV answered specific questions. William Russell, the general director of Opera/Columbus, with forty years of varied opera experience, patiently answered technical questions, taught me a tremendous amount in his classes, and read and commented on the introductory chapters. Cheryl Herr, James Hurt, Robert and Donna Janusko, and Timothy Martin read over the full manuscript and improved it by their generous suggestions. Remaining errors are my own responsibility.

Dozens of "electronic friends" on the FWAKE-L and J-Joyce newsgroups commented on ideas as I tried them out via that marvelous year-round Joyce conference. A special acknowledgment should be made to Dublin's Michael O'Kelly, who conceived and manages FWAKE-L; to Karen Lawrence, who initiated J-Joyce;

and to Jorn Barger, Bill Cadbury, Robert and Francie Fuhrel, James LeBlanc, Howard Sage, and Antonio Cobalti, who found the Sinico material in December 1993. Kent Skaar asked a provocative question leading to one identification of Giulia Grisi. Professor Cobalti and Dr. Kathryn Feldman searched Trieste to discover the original of the soprano "La Valanga." Daniel Ferrer helped in obtaining the John Sullivan materials from the archives of the Paris Opéra, and Bernard Derr pardoned my French after I translated those records' legalese. Other e-mail assistance came from Chris Ackersley, Paul Bland, John Church, Liam Greenslade, Peter Hartshorn, Klaus Schwienhorst, and Mark Troy. Catherine Fahy of the National Library of Ireland was also helpful in securing material from the James Joyce–Paul Léon papers there. Other Joyceans who assisted included Morris Beja, Robin Bradford, Vincent Deane, David Hayman, Carol Kealiher, Fritz Senn, and Robert Spoo. Rachel Kalb and Penny Popper aided in translating the Sinico material from Italian. I thank all these colleagues and friends for sharing their time and knowledge with me.

Most important of all these of course is Professor Matthew Hodgart. His notes, made over decades of reading *Finnegans Wake,* were the starting point of the enterprise. Had there been no notes, there would have been no book. For his generosity in sharing those notes, for his patience, and for his kindly support of my work and that of other scholars, I am deeply grateful. I want also to thank Patricia Hodgart, Jeremy Lane, and Angus Ross for sharing their memories of Matthew Hodgart with me.

Judith McCulloh, an executive editor of the University of Illinois Press, has given the book thoughtful, experienced, and appreciative encouragement as it developed. Cynthia Mitchell aided with copyright questions. Theresa Sears, managing editor at the press, was patient with my questions and changes. To Bruce Bethell fell the arduous task of copyediting a manuscript with thousands of details. He succeeded admirably in proving that not only the devil but also God lies in the details, and we are deeply grateful for this expert help.

My family, as always, has been supportive above and beyond the call of duty. All of them—Dick, Jim and Ruthanne, Ellen and David, Philip, Matthew, and Claire—deserve medals.

R.B.

. Abbreviations .

Frequently cited works, given in full in the bibliography, are abbreviated as follows in chapters 1–5, primarily in the notes following them:

CDD	Stanislaus Joyce, *Complete Dublin Diary*
CODO	*Concise Oxford Dictionary of Opera*
D	James Joyce, *Dubliners*
FW	James Joyce, *Finnegans Wake*
GDO	*New Grove Dictionary of Opera*
Grove's (1942)	*Grove's Dictionary of Music and Musicians,* 1942 ed.
JJ	Ellmann, *James Joyce,* 1982
Letters 1	James Joyce, *Letters,* vol. 1, ed. Stuart Gilbert
Letters 2	James Joyce, *Letters,* vol. 2, ed. Richard Ellmann
Letters 3	James Joyce, *Letters,* vol. 3, ed. Richard Ellmann
MBK	Stanislaus Joyce, *My Brother's Keeper*
New Grove	*New Grove Dictionary of Music and Musicians,* 1980
ODO	*Oxford Dictionary of Opera*
P	James Joyce, *A Portrait of the Artist*
SL	James Joyce, *Selected Letters*
U	James Joyce, *Ulysses*

. Matthew J. C. Hodgart .
1916–96

To the great sorrow of his family and his co-author, Matthew Hodgart died of a severe stroke on April 3, 1996, a few months short of his eightieth birthday, just as this volume was to be typeset.

Matthew's fine intellect was evident early, first as a Scholar at Rugby and again as a Scholar during undergraduate days at Pembroke College, where he won a reputation as an outstanding debater and was elected to membership in the Apostles. His graduate studies, begun in 1938 on the Jebb Studentship, were interrupted by the outbreak of World War II. For the next six years Matthew, a Scot, served in the Argyll and Sutherland Highlanders and also in Intelligence, where his work was commended in dispatches. On one occasion he was listed as missing in action or killed, but he endured to serve in North Africa, India, and Italy. At war's end the French government acknowledged his assistance by awarding him the Croix de Guerre and making him a Chevalier de la Légion d'Honneur.

In 1945 Matthew returned to Cambridge as Assistant Lecturer in English and from 1949 to 1964 was Lecturer in English and Fellow of Pembroke College. He was Professor of English at Sussex University for six years and for another six held the same position at Concordia University, Montreal. In these years and again after retiring from Concordia University in 1976 he was a visiting professor at a number of distinguished institutions, including Stanford, Cornell, Johns Hopkins, UCLA, and La Trobe University (Australia). A popular teacher, he took delight in his students' learning and in their later achievements.

Just as military service, teaching, and a love of travel led Matthew to five continents, his scholarly interests resulted in books and articles in varied fields. There were two volumes on English ballads; one on satire; a biography of Samuel Johnson; an edition of Horace Walpole's *Memoirs;* and a novel, *A New Voyage.* His Joycean studies include the ground-breaking *Song in the Works of James Joyce* (with Mabel Worthington) and *James Joyce: A Student's Guide*. His essays and reviews have appeared in many publications on both sides of the Atlantic, and the generous spirit of his reviews encouraged beginning scholars and writers.

As his scholarly work indicates, Matthew had a deep interest in music. He was also drawn to James Joyce's writing by a love of puzzles and problem solving. This talent made him and his wife, Patricia, four-time winners of the *Nemo's Almanac* contests in England.

Matthew Hodgart was a lover of life, with an ironic wit, a joy in books, a taste for good food and good wine, and a delight in tennis, swimming, and walking. In his last months, when age and illness constricted his physical ability to travel, he journeyed nonetheless as he re-read the voyages of Odysseus in Homer's Greek text. Now he has set out on a new voyage of his own, remembered with affection and gratitude by a multitude of colleagues, former students, and friends.

R.B.

Part 1

Joyce's
Opera
Worlds

·

Ruth
Bauerle

A Rich Inheritance from a Bankrupt

Arturo Toscanini and James Joyce learned their first opera arias in the same way: at father's knee. In Parma, Italy, in the early 1870s, Arturo hovered in a kitchen corner to listen with delight as Claudio Toscanini, a tailor, sat at the table with his companions, sipping wine and singing together folksongs, arias, and opera choruses. None was a professional singer; they had learned this music squatting in the cheapest seats at the Teatro Regio, eating bread and cheese during the operas. These spontaneous performances were little Arturo's happiest moments of home life.[1]

Fifteen years later the young Joyce also heard his first opera in his father's voice, although sometimes in a more formal setting. John Stanislaus Joyce sang arias around the home and in neighborhood musicales and concerts, often accompanied by his wife, May Murray Joyce (though one may doubt the recollection of his daughter Eileen that at one time there were seven pianos in the home).[2] Well-known as a singer in two cities, John Joyce began his concert appearances in Cork while still a boy, after voice instruction during a year at St. Colman's College, Fermoy. When he and his mother moved to Dublin about 1875, he studied voice for a time with a teacher who called him the successor to Campanini.[3] Italo Campanini is identified by Gustav Kobbé as "one of the great Edgardos" in *Lucia di Lammermoor.* He sang the tenor roles for an "Italian" company that visited Dublin in September and October 1874, presenting Gounod's *Faust,* Mozart's *Don Giovanni,* and Balfe's *Il talismano.* The company also included soprano Christine Nilsson and young Jean de Reszke, singing baritone roles under the name "Giovanni di Reschi."[4]

Friends heaped praise on John Joyce's music, one assuring him that "If you got three months in jail, you'd sing any of those fellows off the stage," a phrase his son adapted in *Ulysses.*[5] Professional singers also admired his voice: at his farewell party in Cork, a traveling company of opera professionals from England

Italo Campanini, tenor with the Italian Opera Company from London. A Dublin singing teacher proclaimed John Stanislaus Joyce to be Campanini's successor.

joined the guests, and John Joyce sang arias with the company's tenor, who expressed envy of the Joyce talent. Later, in Dublin, Barton M'Guckin, tenor of the Carl Rosa Opera Company, attended an Antient Concert Rooms recital in which John Joyce had a part and called his voice "the best tenor in Ireland." Joyce perceived a continuing envy on M'Guckin's part and reported that the older tenor would "watch and look after me" when they met on the street.[6]

Even the next generation praised John Joyce's singing. James Joyce's university friend C. P. Curran called the elder Joyce "a notable singer, with a wide knowledge of Italian opera," who could "hold the attention of any room all night if there was a piano at which he could sit, play, and sing." Curran added that although James's earliest knowledge of Italian opera came from John Joyce, the son "improved" this knowledge in his years on the Continent. Perhaps the greatest praise came from second son Stanislaus: although he hated his father, he acknowledged that John Joyce had the remnants of the best light English tenor, with an unusual range and tasteful style, that he had ever heard. As for James Joyce, the novelist did not compare his father's voice to that of M'Guckin or some generalized "English tenor"; he declared it equal to that of Jean de Reszke, who had become the great international tenor of the 1890s.[7]

After his eldest son became famous as a writer, John Joyce was interviewed by a reporter who found him to be chiefly interested in reminiscing about concerts and singers, especially Barton M'Guckin.[8] Clearly John Joyce considered himself to be a singer of opera and even, somewhat more professionally, an opera singer. It was a self-conception he passed on to his eldest son.

John Stanislaus Joyce picked up some of his knowledge of opera as casually as did Claudio Toscanini; for with James Gunn, manager of the Gaiety Theatre, he used to watch opera rehearsals of Therese Tietjens and Zélia Trebelli from the back of the theater—a seat even less expensive than the gallery frequented by the elder Toscanini and friends. Like Simon Dedalus singing "M'appari" in *Ulysses'* "Sirens" episode John Joyce preferred to use Italian titles for arias, though he sang them in English. The family remembered the repertory as including "M'appari," from *Martha;* "Ah si, ben mio," from *Il trovatore;* "A te, o cara," from *I puritani;* "Salve dimora" ("Salut, demeure"), from *Faust* (titled in Italian, although Gounod's libretto was in French); and "Di più non lacerarmi," from *La traviata's* third act. To this he added, because he liked to sing the high C, "Yes, let me like a soldier fall," from *Maritana.*[9]

Some of John Joyce's singing appearances were with his wife, May Murray Joyce. Both sang at the Church of the Three Patrons in Dublin, and they appeared together at the Bray Boat Club amateur musicales. Mrs. Joyce also made appearances as a soprano at Mount Argus Church, and when James was six years old, she became a member of the choir in Little Bray Church.[10]

For the Joyces, as for the Toscaninis, opera was not merely for the concert platform or the theater but part of daily life. Stanislaus, James, and Eileen all cherished those evenings of singing among their warmest childhood memories. Thirty years after he left Dublin, James Joyce reminded Alf Bergan of the "merry evenings" they had enjoyed together in the Joyce home. In their new home in Trieste, after 1904, James Joyce and his siblings continued the tradition; there, too, singing was general—Stanislaus in German, James in Italian.[11] The next generation, too—James's daughter and son, Lucia and Giorgio, and his niece Bozena—joined in. Bozena recalls being taught opera arias when quite young.[12] For at least three generations, then, there were good and experienced singing voices in the Joyce home. Although no one, as he himself pointed out, "ever really made a career out of it" (*Letters 3,* 333), Joyce in a very real sense came from a family of opera singers.

James Joyce was known in Dublin even after his death as "Joyce the singer," a title I shall evaluate in my consideration of his choice not to sing professionally. But other Joyces also turned to the possibility of singing careers. His brother Stanislaus studied voice for a time in Trieste, although he found opera itself distasteful because of the "screaming" and the insistence on protecting the singer's voice too confining.[13] Eileen Joyce, whose voice started as a high contralto promising to develop into a soprano,[14] joined her two brothers in Trieste in January 1910, intending to study for a vocal career.[15] Joyce's wife, Nora Barnacle, as part of the family in Trieste, spent her afternoons hard at work practicing the piano.[16] In later years she astonished Maria Jolas by the quantity of music she could sing from opera—including many melodies from operas unknown to Maria herself, although she had studied for a singing career. They had been learned, Nora told her, from the Joyces' almost nightly opera attendance in Trieste.[17]

It was not just that the Joyce family studied for musical careers. Opera provided them with a set of myths for their family life. John Joyce, who had no very high opinion of his wife's family, referred to her sister-in-law, the wife of John Murray, as "Amina" or "La Sonnambula," after the sleepwalker in Bellini's opera. To reconcile with his son, John Joyce sang a melody from *La traviata,* and James responded in kind.[18] Given the operatic quality of the Joyce family life in Dublin—the dramatic dinner-time quarrels over Irish leader Charles Parnell, the stormy scenes created by John Joyce, the agonizing deathbeds of John's son George and his wife, May, the bohemian poverty that more and more characterized the family's life, the occasional celebration over a financial windfall like James's school exhibition prizes, and at last the runaway lovers—these musical myths were an appropriate mode for the Joyces.

Before revisiting the opera worlds Joyce could have experienced in the various cities where he lived, it would be well to review briefly the traditions of performance and audience response that prevailed in Joyce's youth and helped to form his concept of opera. As enjoyed by the Joyce and Toscanini families, nineteenth-century opera was quite different from our conception of the art at the end of the twentieth century. Without digressing into any extended history of opera, I must nevertheless describe some of the changes and development in this musical form to explain Joyce's response to it.

For my purposes opera may be said to have begun in 1597, with Jacopo Peri's *Dafne,* as a small musical entertainment for a private party of nobility. *Dafne,* like most of its immediate successors, was simply a mythological tale set to music and sung as a series of accompanied solos or duets. There was no attempt to act out the story, and the whole performance was closer to what we now consider to be a "concert performance" of opera, or even to an oratorio.

So popular was Peri's invention that it was rapidly copied and by 1637 moved into public theaters in Venice. By 1670 there were opera houses throughout Italy and also many in Germany.[19] By the late eighteenth century these theaters had become a version of modern sports arenas: at the lower levels sat the less affluent members of the community, full of passion about the performance; ranged above and around the theater were the boxes of wealthier music lovers, similar to the special enclosed boxes in American sports stadiums. (In a sense, the Three Tenors concert televised worldwide from Los Angeles' Dodger Stadium in July 1994 was a large-scale return to eighteenth-century opera houses.) In 1770, for example, the Milan theater that preceded the modern La Scala had five rows of one hundred boxes each on either side of the theater. Each box held six persons, who sat along the sides of the box in two rows facing each other, not the stage; at the back of the box, opposite the stage, a broad gallery provided access to the box and from one box to another. Across the gallery each box had a cozy room with a fireplace and facilities for food and cards. The fourth row of boxes on each side of the theater had a common faro table, where play continued throughout the opera. After attending an opera at this theater, Charles Burney complained that "the noise was abominable except while two or three airs and a duet were singing."[20] Clearly, for eighteenth-century Milan, opera was only a part of the evening's entertainment, not the whole focus. The same was true for a substantial portion of the audience in nineteenth-century Paris, where as Charles Baudelaire made clear, members of the Jockey Club, deprived of a chance to see their mistresses dance in the usual ballet, jeered the 1861 staging of Wagner's *Tannhäuser* into inaudibility.[21]

Even where it was taken more seriously, opera was entertainment with the combined functions of a modern *Aïda, Oklahoma,* and *Dallas,* with no distinction of high- or lowbrow;[22] in presenting dramas of human passion, patriotism and betrayal, spies, stolen children, rape, murder, incest, amnesia, and mistaken identity, it was the equivalent of our local movie theaters, television soap operas, or tabloid talk shows. Then as now there were protests that such drama pandered to the lowest in public taste and diverted patrons from worthier cultural pursuits. Taste aside, the sense of opera as entertainment accessible to all social levels continued on the Continent through the nineteenth century. Opera also moved into English music halls in the nineteenth and twentieth centuries, when stars such as Euphrosyne Parepa-Rosa (who sang opera in London,

Malta, and across the United States) and Charles Santley (who had the title role in England's first production of *The Flying Dutchman*) appeared. Gounod's *Faust* was first presented in England in concert form at the Canterbury Music Hall, London. Maggie Teyte, a renowned interpreter of Debussy's music, was the sister of music hall performer James Tate and sister-in-law of music hall star Lottie Collins. Teyte herself made several week-long appearances in music halls.[23] Until the twentieth century, then, opera continued to hold something for everyone, an aspect of the art that Joyce tried to echo in *Finnegans Wake,* with its mélange of allusion to geography, philosophy, history, cricketing, popular songs, opera, and the world of reading.

Quite early in opera history great singers traveled from one opera house to another, so that by 1720 there was a range of international singing stars enjoying a world without boundaries—except in France, where Italian singers were not allowed to perform.[24] Often these singers were Italian castrati (*evirati*); the first who publicly acknowledged that condition were Folignato and Rossini, singing in 1599 in the papal chapel, where both won praise from Pope Clement VIII.[25] Castrati were increasingly popular from the first quarter of the seventeenth century, singing both male and female roles, although sometimes the male roles were sung by female contraltos. Even in male roles the *evirati* sang as sopranos opposite women contraltos. Overall, the "typecasting" of the sexes was rare: Cavalli's *Eliogabalo* had three male soprano roles and one woman's role in the tenor range, Vinci's *Catone in Utica* (1732) cast soprano Lucia Faccinelli as Julius Caesar, Gluck's *Le nozze d'Ercole e d'Ebe* used a woman singer in the part of Hercules, and the San Carlo opera was opened in 1737 with a famous woman contralto, Vittoria Tesi-Tramontini, singing the role of Achilles.[26]

The Roman church threatened with excommunication those who castrated a boy to create a singer; but the same church, following St. Paul's injunction that women should be silent in church, depended on male singers. By the 1780s there were more than two hundred castrati singing in the churches of Rome, including the papal chapel.[27] One such singer in the Vatican chapel late in the nineteenth century was praised by musicologist Enrico Panzacchi as superior to Adelina Patti, the famous soprano.[28] In the eighteenth century as many as 4,000 boys yearly were castrated in the hope of providing them a singing career.[29] To avoid church punishment the family often asserted that the child's voice had been affected by an injury or illness.

Many composers, including Handel and Meyerbeer (as late as 1824 for Giovanni Battisti Velluti), wrote specifically for castrati voices or for a particular castrato. Wagner found the voices intriguing and for a time considered bringing a castrato from Rome to play Klingsor in *Parsifal.*[30]

Composer Gioacchino Rossini, by contrast, disliked using castrati singers because he objected to a technique that was one of their great claims to fame: their command of fioritura, the decoration of the composer's melodic line with improvisations of their own devising.[31] Often fioritura was elaborate and lengthy, with the effect of distracting audience attention from the opera itself to the singer's power of invention. Whatever Rossini's reservations, the castrati bequeathed to nineteenth-century opera production a sense of the singer as a star who, with impunity, could impose his or her concept on that of the composer. They also led to composers' writing "breeches" or "pants" roles for women singers in male attire—Orsini in Donizetti's *Lucrezia Borgia,* Cherubino in Mozart's *Marriage of Figaro,* or Siebel in Gounod's *Faust.*[32]

By the mid-nineteenth century and the day of the Joyces and Toscaninis, these elements were in place: the audience went to hear opera but also to see stars, and the stars were singers with great voices. Audiences had also come to think of themselves as participants in the spectacle, applauding, cheering, booing, or demanding an instant encore of a well-sung or favorite aria. Opera had developed from concerts with a mythic theme to full-scale dramas with music. Singers included both men and women, but as in the days of the castrati, operatic characters were not invariably of the same sex as those who sang the roles, and the sexual identity of a character within an opera was frequently hidden for plot purposes.

For their part, the singing stars had developed a kind of autonomy from the composer to the extent of altering the music not only by adding decorative elements but by changing to a more comfortable key, adding (or subtracting) a high note according to personal ability,[33] dropping difficult arias, or even adding or substituting arias from other operas or songs from no opera at all. They also took advantage of the willingness of the audience to participate by hiring claques to applaud them or anticlaques to boo other singers. One of the most famous claques was apparently voluntary—the Parisian crowd, urged on by the elitist Jockey Club, that booed, whistled, and catcalled through all the 1861 performances of Wagner's *Tannhäuser.* Soprano Maggie Teyte found claques still important on the Paris opera scene just prior to World War I; and Lotte Lehmann, making her Vienna debut in 1916, was visited several times at her hotel by competing heads of the claque, insistent that she hire them to aid her success.[34] Tenor Leo Slezak could still point to the claque's seats at the Metropolitan Opera thirty years after his debut there, and his son asserted that the claque remained in that same location until the company moved to its new house at Lincoln Center in the 1960s.[35]

The hodgepodge that passed for opera in the nineteenth century sometimes had its roots in the confusion of the librettist or composer. Bellini's *I puritani*

(1833), for instance, which has the conflict of the Cavaliers and the Round-heads as its subject, is set in Plymouth because the librettist believed Plymouth to be in Scotland.[36] In 1841 an English manager named Macready, wanting to produce an "English opera," chose Purcell's setting of Dryden's *King Arthur* but arranged for Irish singer and composer Tom Cooke to augment the music by adding sections of Purcell's *Libertine, Indian Queen, Dido and Aeneas,* and *Bonduca,* as well as some music from Arne.[37] Production sites also distracted from the seriousness of the music: at London's St. James's Hall, as Bernard Shaw complained ironically, one of the "well-known attractions" was the odors of fire and cooking food from a restaurant sharing the structure.[38]

Rehearsal seems to have been minimal, so that in a London production of *Don Giovanni,* a Mademoiselle Colombati, attempting "on the most superficial acquaintance" to sing the aria "Batti, batti," got into the second verse first; conductor Luigi Arditi prompted her by bursting into song himself, in a countertenor that Shaw thought had an astonishingly effective "gooselike quality."[39] Taste was also absent from the planning, as when impresario Louis Jullien inserted a pantomime between the acts of Balfe's *Maid of Honour* because he thought that this would please the English public.[40] He was perhaps not far wrong, for Alfred Bunn, who wrote the text for Balfe's *Bohemian Girl,* included a pantomime with his production of Auber's *Fra Diavolo.*[41] Impresario Augustus Harris was not much better in his conceptions: he offered *Carmen* in July 1890 using one conductor for the first and fourth acts and two other conductors for the second and third acts, with a "disastrous" effect on the ensemble effect of the performance.[42] Even Hector Berlioz succumbed to this mixing of music and performers: when he conducted the *Bride of Lammermoor* for Jullien at Drury Lane, he used Beethoven's *Leonora* overture to introduce the Donizetti opera, an action matched in the same production by Jullien's insertion of a minuet into the opera itself.[43] That 1847 event was echoed more than four decades later when, to the dismay of Shaw, the Covent Garden orchestra "eked out" the prelude to Gounod's *Philémon et Baucis* by adding the overture to Wagner's *Tannhäuser.*[44] This casual approach to production lasted into the twentieth century, when John McCormack was astonished by a Covent Garden setting of *La traviata* where Nellie Melba appeared in "modern" (1906) clothing, but Enrico Caruso and Mattia Battistini were in period costumes, including velvet breeches, silk hose, buckled slippers, and plumed hats.[45]

Not only the music but the libretto was mistreated, as when London opera impresarios and audiences divided into two camps, the one favoring opera sung in Italian and the other preferring opera performed in English. As a result the "Royal Italian Opera" often included German or French works translated into

Italian. As late as 1888 Covent Garden presented all operas in Italian, including *The Pearl Fishers* and *Roméo et Juliette.* The pattern began to change in June 1889, when Jean de Reszke sang a French Roméo for the first time in London. But the next month he performed Walther's role in *Die Meistersinger* in Italian, although he felt it an inappropriate language for Wagner's operas. As late as 1930 Covent Garden's French *Pelléas et Mélisande* was offered as part of the "Italian" season, the only other alternative being to include it in the "German" season, where it would have been equally inappropriate.[46]

The libretto was so often set apart from an opera's integrity that it must have strained Covent Garden audiences very little in 1933 when Lauritz Melchior sang Verdi's *Otello* in German while the rest of the cast used the original Italian.[47] Melchior was perhaps following a precedent set on BBC during a 1930 broadcast of *Madame Butterfly.* Soprano Margaret Sheridan became ill after singing the first act in the original Italian; Maggie Teyte rose to the emergency and completed the broadcast, but in English, while the rest of the cast continued in Italian.[48]

Twentieth-century conductors, too, could be as lax as Berlioz; in one under-rehearsed sextet in Mozart's *Marriage of Figaro,* the singers were raggedly out of time with one another. At the conclusion Sir Thomas Beecham smiled and remarked, apparently without irony, "Now there, wasn't that marvellous—we all finished together."[49] With producers and conductors so relaxed, it is little wonder that orchestras sometimes took liberties, as when the Covent Garden orchestra, having reached only the end of act 4 of *Les Huguenots* by 11:55 P.M., packed and went home. Conductor Luigi Mancinelli followed them. As critic Bernard Shaw himself departed, some of the audience were still waiting for act 5.[50]

Following the lead of producers and conductors, the singers, who rightly saw themselves as the stars of the spectacles, took their own liberties. Writhingly angered when Marcella Sembrich dared to alter the ending of Susanna's aria "Deh, vieni non tardar" in *The Marriage of Figaro* from what Mozart had written, Shaw declared himself unable to respond to anything else the soprano sang.[51] Sims Reeves's biographer declared the transposing of the title role of *Don Giovanni* so it could be sung by the tenor Giovanni Mario to be a "re-cooking" of Mozart, even though "hundreds rushed" to hear it.[52] When they were not rewriting or transposing the composers' music, singers often altered the mood of an opera by insertions. Whether a minor singer like the Scots tenor Sinclair or a more prominent one like sopranos Catherine Stephens or Lucia Vestris or tenor John Braham, all apparently felt free to improve on their roles. Braham's conduct was the most egregious in this respect. The final scene of *Guy Mannering* (Boïeldieu's *La Dame blanche* in English translation) takes place in a cave.

Jean de Reszke dressed as Tristan, a tenor role. Earlier he had sung in Dublin as a baritone, using the name Giovanni di Reschi.

There Braham "discovered" a grand piano, remarked "That reminds me of the delightful aria I heard at 'La Scala' the other night," and sat down to accompany himself as he sang the aria—in Italian. Braham responded to the audience's demand for an encore with Handel's "Waft her, angels"; then the cast resumed the confrontation scene in the cave.[53] At best these insertions were by the same composer as the opera itself, as when George Barker introduced Beethoven's "Adelaïde" into *Fidelio* at Liverpool and Manchester.[54] It was worse when the music was, as with the Braham example, wholly extraneous—but at least he was still singing opera. Sometimes, too, the composer (or a publisher or an impresario) was responsible for the interpolations. Sims Reeves found himself assigned to sing a sentimental ballad, "In this old chair," during Balfe's *Maid of Honour* (based on the same story used later by Flotow for *Martha*). Reeves saw no relationship between the song and the opera and concluded that it was introduced to draw it to the attention of music publishers. (It became, ironically, one of his most popular songs, featured for years in his recitals.)[55] Sometimes the interpolations were of text, as when Fyodor Chaliapin, mindful of his travel schedule during a performance in Russian, sang to his servant in the wings, "Go to the hotel immediately. Get the two bottles of good wine I forgot in my room and bring them here, as we leave immediately after this damned opera is over."[56] Adelina Patti, performing Rossini's *Il barbiere di Siviglia* at the Metropolitan Opera, included Echert's "Echo Song" and Payne's "Home, Sweet Home" in the lesson scene; then, as an encore, she had a piano pushed through the curtains so she could sing "Comin' thro' the Rye."[57] That both Melba and Patti are accused of having a piano brought on stage at the end of *Otello* so they might sing "Home, Sweet Home"[58] suggests that the story may be apocryphal about both sopranos; even as myth, however, it symbolizes the looseness of artistic standards during the "golden age of opera."

Occasionally a singer would omit something that seemed too difficult. And composers—if alive—were willing to assist in such a situation, as Mozart added "Dalla sua pace" to *Don Giovanni* because some tenors found "Il mio tesoro" too difficult. Shaw once complained that a tenor named Lestillier ought to have omitted *both* because he did not know the music. In the same performance the baritone Francesco d'Andrade failed to sing the arias as written; Mme Emmy Fursch-Madi omitted "Non mi dir" and reversed the sections of another aria; and Mme Giulia Valda offered "gratuitous B flats."[59] Even very good and very professional singers made such omissions. Jean de Reszke found "Celeste Aïda" inconveniently placed near the beginning of the opera, before his voice was fully warmed up, so he simply omitted it. He told one acquaintance that in some

Sims Reeves, long the leading English tenor, as he looked near the end of his career in the 1880s. He retired officially in 1891 at the age of seventy-three.

nineteen performances as Radamès at the Metropolitan Opera, he had sung this aria only four times.[60]

Sometimes a singer's ability to add, subtract, or improvise proved to be invaluable to a performance. Geraldine Farrar was singing *La bohème* with the tenor Alessandro Bonci when he lost his voice; she sang "a third of his role" for him without the public's noticing anything wrong.[61] Enrico Caruso also saved a colleague in a similar situation; when bass Andrés de Segurola developed hoarseness and could not sing in the last act, Caruso sang both Colline's and Rodolfo's roles to the end of the opera. The conductor was enraged, but again the audience was oblivious.[62] John McCormack also encountered a crisis during *La bohème* when Russian soprano Mlle Axerine (a last-minute replacement for Melba) forgot some lines, and McCormack doubled as Rodolfo and Mimi.[63]

Since the producers and the musicians treated opera so casually on occasion, it is unsurprising that audiences for many decades showed equal unconcern for opera as art. In the early years this disregard was a matter of noise and discourtesy toward musicians performing in Milan or at court functions, where conversation or flirtation might be more significant than the music.[64] Later it might be the operagoers' sense of knowing more about the music than did those on the stage. Tenor Sims Reeves found during his years as a student in Milan that the audience members expressed their reactions all through a solo, applauding one phrase and objecting to the singing of the next. They showed pleasure or displeasure in varied ways: hisses, hoots, laughter, whistles, and applause, always with a vigor proportioned to their emotions.[65] Another audience, after jeering a soprano whose voice cracked, sang her aria in unison from beginning to end in perfect pitch![66] Not all the complaints were musical: at Verona in 1888 when Toscanini was conducting, a soprano was hissed off the stage as insufficiently beautiful to sing the title role in *Lucrezia Borgia*.[67] Most of these audience protests rose from love of the music. Shaw complained about another sort of misconduct—indifference among those who arrived late. As for loud talking during performances, he suggested the extreme measure of moving the soldiers from the lobby to the stalls, where they could shoot noisy patrons.[68]

Dublin audiences tended to be quiet and well-behaved at good performances. Their misconduct inclined toward specific comments on the performance, directed toward the stage, or on the "quality" sitting in the pit. When a tenor reached a high note by using a falsetto, a voice from the "Gods" (the cheapest seats in the fourth tier, or highest balcony) inquired, "Jim! Was that the gas?" As the tenor Tombesi overacted and oversang, a shout advised him in a Dublin pronunciation of his name, "Tom, be aisy!" Adherents of rival singers disputed each other loudly in the Gods. Patrons from the pit shouted for quiet (making the music even more inaudible). One disputant roared at an opponent, "Throw him over! Throw him over!" A comrade added, "Don't waste him, kill a fiddler wid him!"[69]

Plot and action on the opera stage absorbed Dublin audiences. In a production of *Faust*, as Valentine (played by Charles Santley) lay dying in Martha's arms, a gallery voice shouted "Unbutton his weskit!" When Santley, singing Plunkett's role in *Martha*, took up a candle to show Harriet and Nancy to their room, a reproving voice called "Ah, ah! would ye now?"[70]

Dubliners could be generous in their praise, however, as when Trinity students lowered a basket of flowers and doves to Fanny Moody at the conclusion

Therese Tietjens as Lucrezia Borgia in Donizetti's opera of that name. Dubliners said fondly that she had "a heart as big as herself" and pulled her carriage to her hotel after opera performances.

Luigi Arditi, conductor and composer of operas, who conducted several of the companies that appeared in Dublin, where he was "as well-known as the Nelson Pillar."

of *The Bohemian Girl,* or when the city presented an ebony-and-silver baton to conductor Luigi Arditi. Impresario James Mapleson asserted that the habitual occupants of the gallery were medical students, "always without their coats, sometimes without their waistcoats, occasionally without their shirts."[71] Therese Tietjens and Adelina Patti were both visited by mobs of students at their hotels after performances, and both were drawn from theater to hotel by crowds who dragged their carriages, as recalled in Joyce's novella, "The Dead" (199). Patti's experience came at the conclusion of *Martha* in November 1861, and the hotel was Morrison's. The *Irish Times* reported that she was met at the theater door by "a cavalcade of Trinity students—almost all honour men." Tietjens appeared in 1868 in Weber's *Oberon,* and the audience demanded a repetition of the air

"Ocean, thou mighty monster." A great scene ensued, lasting more than fifteen minutes, some demanding a repetition of the aria and others asking instead for various Irish songs; the singer finally compromised by offering "'Tis the last rose of summer." The orchestra lacked music for this song, however, so the tenor Bettini "pulled" a cottage piano from the wings. As Mme Tietjens was helping conductor Arditi climb from the orchestra to accompany her, Bettini accidentally knocked the piano over. Five supers dressed as demons for their roles in the opera rushed from the wings to right the piano, and summer's last rose was heard after a silence so profound that Mapleson was able hear his dropped lapel pin.[72]

A source of conflict between composer and conductor, on one side, and audience and stars, on the other, was the matter of encores within the performance. For the audience, to ask for an encore was a way to show appreciation for a good performance—and perhaps also to get one's money's worth from the opera. For the stars, the audience demand was a proof of success. Caruso, for example, gave five repeats of "La donna è mobile" in a single performance of *Rigoletto* in Rio de Janiero in 1903.[73] For composers like Wagner, who viewed the opera—or at least a given act of the opera—as an integral whole, the applause and the repetition intruded on the concentration of the audience, the singers, and the orchestra.[74] Toscanini held a similar view and went so far as to risk a duel at Casale Monferrato in 1887 during a performance of *La gioconda*. During the third act the audience clamored for an aria's encore. Only twenty years old and in his second conducting job, Toscanini refused. A uniformed man shouted, "You are a fresh young maestro!" Toscanini turned to retort, "You are wrong, you dog!" After the opera concluded, the protester's second challenged Toscanini to a duel. Toscanini laughed it off, and the incident was forgotten.[75] In England Shaw lent his voice to the anti-encore faction, without much success.[76] Joyce, sensitive to artistic integrity, seconds Shaw's motion in *Finnegans Wake* with "passencore" (3.4).

NOTES

1. Taubman, *The Maestro,* 7.
2. Delimata, "Reminiscences of a Joyce Niece," 53.
3. *MBK,* 26. Italian tenor Italo Campanini (1845–96) is mentioned at *FW* 541.7 and in "The Dead," 199. When John Joyce was studying voice in Dublin, Campanini would have been a mere thirty years old, with two decades of his career still ahead—astonishingly early to speak of finding his successor. He had made a fine start as a singer, singing *Lohengrin* in Bologna in 1871 and Gennaro in *Lucrezia Borgia* in London

in 1872. His New York debut came in 1873, and he sang for eleven years (1883–94) at the Metropolitan Opera, beginning with *Faust* in 1883.

4. Gustav Kobbé, *The Complete Opera Book* (1919), 354; Leiser, *Jean de Reszke and the Great Days of Opera*, 25. De Reszke was troubled with stagefright and some uncertainty about his vocal range; he later withdrew from the stage for several years, retrained his voice, and returned as one of the great tenors in opera history.

5. *MBK*, 15. Joyce used this in *Ulysses*, where "base barreltoned" Ben Dollard promises Simon Dedalus that given a week's jail stay on slim rations, "you'd sing, Simon, like a garden thrush" (*U* 11.772–3).

6. *MBK*, 26; *Letters 3*, 333; *JJ*, 15–16.

7. Curran, *James Joyce Remembered*, 70; *CDD*, 6; *Letters 3*, 333, Joyce to Alf Bergan, 20 December 1934.

8. Colum and Colum, *Our Friend James Joyce*, 78.

9. *MBK*, 65.

10. Peter Costello, *James Joyce*, 60, 67, 71, 89, 93.

11. *MBK*, 65; Delimata, 47; *Letters 3*, 333.

12. Delimata, 47.

13. *Letters 2*, 260; *CDD*, 29, 146.

14. *CDD*, 18.

15. Delimata, 45; *JJ*, 308. According to Delimata's recollections, Eileen had been a pianist for Joyce's short-lived Volta Cinema project in Dublin in 1909 and studied for a time with a Triestine teacher named Calazza (Delimata, 45, 47).

16. B. Maddox, *Nora*, 112.

17. Kain, "An Interview with Carola Giedion-Welcker and Maria Jolas," 102.

18. Bauerle, *The James Joyce Songbook*, 68.

19. Heriot, *The Castrati in Opera*, 113.

20. Quoted in Pleasants, *The Great Singers*, 31.

21. Baudelaire, "Richard Wagner and *Tannhäuser* in Paris," 227–29.

22. Heriot, 34.

23. Bauerle, *Picking Up Airs*, 12.

24. Heriot, 13.

25. Ibid., 12.

26. Ibid., 33–34.

27. Ibid., 25.

28. Ibid., 36–37.

29. Koestenbaum, *The Queen's Throat*, 158.

30. Timothy Martin has pointed out to me that Klingsor's castrated state is implicit within the action of *Parsifal.*

31. Heriot, 20–21; Rossini's anger was so aroused by the same Velluti, for whom Meyerbeer had written *Il crociato in Egitto*, that he vowed "never again to let his singers depart from the written notes."

32. Heriot, 22.

33. Rossini so resented tenor Enrico Tamberlik's additions of Cs and C-sharps to Rossini's *Otello* that when Tamberlik called at Rossini's home, he was asked to leave his C-sharp in the vestibule before being admitted to see the composer (Pleasants, 171).

34. Lehmann, *Midway in My Song*, 129–31.

35. Slezak, *What Time's the Next Swan?* 211.
36. Brockway and Weinstock, *World of Opera,* 581.
37. Pearce, *Sims Reeves,* 48.
38. Shaw, *London Music in 1888–89,* 69.
39. Ibid., 217.
40. Pearce, 100.
41. Ibid., 166.
42. Klein, *Thirty Years of Musical Life in London,* 288–89. Hermann Klein was not only music critic of the *Sunday Times* but musical advisor to Augustus Harris, the creator of this somewhat disjointed performance.
43. Pearce, 96. One theory was that Berlioz was eager to show the quality of the orchestra. There were no theories as to the reason for the minuet. The opera was, of course, an English version of *Lucia di Lammermoor.*
44. Shaw, *Music in London, 1890–94,* 1:284.
45. Strong, *John McCormack,* 43. In this matter Melba was in the tradition of the great tenor of the early nineteenth century, Giovanni Rubini, who donned any costume handed to him, whether it fitted his role or not (Pearce, 80).
46. G. O'Connor, *The Pursuit of Perfection,* 171.
47. Covent Garden, 2 June 1933; Brockway and Weinstock, 566.
48. June 1930; G. O'Connor, 170–71.
49. G. O'Connor, 106.
50. Shaw, *London Music in 1888–89,* 153.
51. Ibid., 58.
52. Pearce, 208.
53. Ibid., 30.
54. Ibid., 32.
55. Ibid., 100.
56. Borovsky, *Chaliapin,* 468.
57. Pleasants, 211.
58. G. O'Connor, 107.
59. Shaw, *London Music in 1888–89,* 147. Nor did Shaw like the singers who played Leporello, Masetto, and the Commendatore.
60. Pleasants, 257.
61. D. Caruso, *Enrico Caruso,* 210.
62. Ibid., 208–10.
63. McCormack, *I Hear You Calling Me,* 72. *La bohème* is not a particularly difficult opera to complete, but it is extremely popular, which means singers often find themselves singing it.
64. Pleasants, 32, 34.
65. Pearce, 78.
66. Mordden, *Opera Anecdotes,* 95. The city was Parma, Toscanini's hometown; the date, 1890; the aria, "Gorgheggiate usignoli" ("Warbling nightingales"), from Catalani's *Loreley.*
67. Taubman, 41.
68. Shaw, *London Music in 1888–89,* 142–43.
69. Stanford, *Pages from an Unwritten Diary,* 88.

70. Santley, *Student and Singer,* 223–25.
71. Mapleson, *The Mapleson Memoirs,* 77.
72. Klein, *The Reign of Patti,* 97; Mapleson, *Mapleson Memoirs,* 77.
73. *ODO,* s.v. "Encore."
74. Martin, *Joyce and Wagner,* 3; Kobbé, *The Complete Opera Book* (1919), 91.
75. Taubman, 40–41.
76. Shaw, *London Music in 1888–89,* 372.

Opera Geography

The Joyce family passion grew in a Dublin where opera was enthusiastically received whenever it was available to the public. Dublin's opera tradition reaches back into the eighteenth century, when the second city of the British Empire was an important performance locale for musicians of international reputation. Handel's *Messiah* had its premiere in Dublin in 1742, although his operas were not staged there. As a political capital tied to London, Dublin reflected English musical taste and fashion to a considerable degree. English ballad opera was hugely popular, Gay's *Beggar's Opera* having forty Dublin performances in ten months after its London premiere in 1728. Thomas Arne was a Dublin resident in 1742–44, 1755–56, and 1758–59 and there produced an oratorio, his masque *Comus* (1741, with frequent repetitions over four decades), and several of his operas, including *Artaxerxes* (forty-eight performances between 1765 and 1767). Joyce worked *The Beggar's Opera* and *Artaxerxes,* as well as *Artaxerxes'* star, the castrato Giusto Tenducci, into the text of *Finnegans Wake.*[1]

A number of small theaters presented operas or parts of operas over the years; but the chief stages were the Smock Alley Theatre (1662, reopened 1738, closed 1787), the Crow Street Theatre (closed 1820), the Great Musick Hall (opened in 1741 for Handel's Dublin appearances), and the Fishamble Street Theatre (a 1777 remodeling of the Great Musick Hall, finally closed in 1798). The De Amicis, an Italian traveling company, provided a group of burlettas, or brief satirical pieces, in 1761–64 with little success. A single *opera seria,* or "serious opera," production was the premiere of *L'eroe cinese* by Tommaso Giordano in 1766, in English despite the title. Giordano also managed several of the Dublin theaters for a time: Smock Alley (1761–62) and Crow Street (1766–67), where he produced his comic opera *Love in Disguise* (1766) and another opera, *Phillis at Court* (1767). From 1778 to 1781 he had a small theater in Capel Street in partnership with the singer Michael Leoni. In 1783 he finally settled in Dublin with an Irish wife. The Irish tenor, composer, and opera manager Tom Cooke was one of his students.[2] Later stages were the Theatre Royal in Hawkins Street (opened 1821, burned in 1880, and later rebuilt) and the Gaiety Theatre (1871 to the present).

In 1777 Giuseppe Gazzaniga's *L'isola d'Alcina* became the first opera sung in Italian in Ireland. Gazzaniga was both a prolific and a popular composer of operas, although only a few of them are extant.[3] Works by the well-received eighteenth-century Italian composer Niccolò Piccinni (*FW* 248.5) reached Dublin with traveling opera troupes, and Irish tenor Michael Kelly made his 1779 debut as a boy singer in one, *La buona figliuola*, in the Great Musick Hall.[4] Tenducci staged an English-language version of Gluck's *Orfeo ed Eurydice* (both composer and opera are cited in the *Wake*) in Dublin in 1784, with musical additions by J. C. Bach.

The nineteenth-century dispute over the "proper" language for opera sung in England spilled over into Ireland, with one side arguing for Italian only, no matter what the original language of the libretto. Under this pressure, Meyerbeer's *Les Huguenots*, Gounod's *Roméo et Juliette*, Wagner's *Tannhäuser*, and Flotow's *Martha* were all presented in Italian in London, rather than in the original language. The other side of the controversy argued for creation of "English opera," a term that embraced both opera translated into English for production in the British Isles and opera by English composers. Italian operas on English themes, such as Donizetti's *Anna Bolena* or Bellini's *I puritani*, apparently failed the nationality test. Companies such as the Carl Rosa Opera Company tendered all productions in English, including the British premiere of Puccini's *La bohème*.

In practice this meant that the first operas to reach Dublin in the nineteenth century were either Italian or English in origin or were presented in Italian or English: Mozart's *Così fan tutte*, *Don Giovanni*, and *The Marriage of Figaro* were produced between 1811 and 1820, for instance. Eventually some French operas (still sung in Italian) crept in. After 1820 operas by Rossini, Bellini, and Donizetti began to be heard in Dublin, leading to immense popularity for their composers; Verdi later joined these earlier Italians. Three composers of opera in English were also popular. Although London considered them to be "English," two of these men were Irish, as were the themes of several of their works. Dubliner Michael Balfe's *Bohemian Girl* is often alluded to in *Finnegans Wake*, and a half-dozen other Balfe works are also included. Vincent Wallace was also Irish, and his *Maritana* not only appears in the *Wake* but also lends a major theme to Joyce's *Ulysses*, where the song "There is a flower that bloometh" provides the musical resonance for the conflict of guilt and memory that haunts Bloom, Stephen, and Molly throughout the day. Finally, the German-born Jules Benedict contributed *The Lily of Killarney* to Dublin's—and England's—music.

Although opera is now often thought of as an elitist art, Irish audiences were no more strictly upper class than were those in Italy. The Theatre Royal of the 1860s and 1870s had no stalls—only the pit covering the whole ground floor of the theater. The cheapest seats were in the fourth and uppermost tier, or balcony, the Gods. Buying a ticket meant hours of waiting in the queue or fighting for a place in the pit with the "quality," but the seats in the Gods also filled early. Like the friends of Claudio Toscanini in far-off Parma, these penurious enthusiasts passed the time until the overture by singing the music of the evening's opera—"as well as or better than" it would be sung later on the stage.[5] They were an informed and critical audience, although not rich.

Irish audiences, like those elsewhere in Europe, were boisterous and expressed their opinions freely. In 1849, for instance, two companies appeared almost simultaneously. Willert Beale's group (one of the early traveling companies) included Catherine Hayes, an Irish soprano; all its other singers were foreigners. Its rather short tenor, Paglieri, wore a cloak in *Lucia di Lammermoor* that reached the floor; the effect was heightened by a wide hat that seemed to push him into the floor. The audience's hooting was not lessened after Paglieri sang badly in a duet with Hayes, and tumult ensued. The performance was halted while a new tenor, Damcke, was summoned, but his introduction as "Herr Donkey" increased the merriment. In the audience as Beale's guest that evening was singer Sims Reeves, whose billing in those days was "England's greatest tenor." The crowd began to shout for Reeves to take on the role, but he refused. When he attempted to quiet the audience and speak to them, such an uproar followed that Jules Benedict (future composer of *The Lily of Killarney*) left his conductor's post in disgust, leaving the orchestra leaderless. Beale somehow found yet a third tenor, Lavenu, and the performance continued until a final curtain at 1 A.M.[6] One may question whether this was art or chaos; yet it is remarkable that an impresario could find, even in Dublin, *two* substitute tenors prepared to sing a whole opera on a moment's notice, without calling on the tenor sitting at his side. Dublin audiences were impartial in their rowdiness, however. Two years later, during a performance of *Rob Roy*, Reeves resorted to hiding the words to Moore's "Minstrel Boy" in his hat to aid memory, and the audience booed him.

The distinguished Irish composer Charles Villiers Stanford, three years younger than John Joyce, describes the Dublin opera scene vividly in his *Pages from an*

Unwritten Diary. Born a Dubliner (he left Dublin for Cambridge in 1870), Stanford recalls his first encounters with Wagner's operas as being from private performances, doubtless much like the family musicales the Joyces enjoyed. A "most cultivated tenor singer," Dr. [Sir] William Stokes, returned in 1868 from Dresden, where he had heard the premiere of Wagner's *Die Meistersinger.* Stokes brought with him excerpts from the opera's score, as well as some Wagner songs containing studies for *Tristan und Isolde.*[7] These songs tremendously excited the musical Stanford, and when he later discovered the score of *Lohengrin* in a shop, he found it to be inferior musically to those later Wagner works.[8] So by 1870 early Wagner operas were apparently available in printed score in Dublin, and more recent Wagner was being sung on Dublin's parlor circuit.

Stanford also makes clear that even in the decade or two before John Joyce became a Dubliner, in the 1870s, Dublin enjoyed opera frequently, if irregularly. An opera company from Her Majesty's Theatre, London, gave a season in Dublin every fall at the Theatre Royal. (London opera seasons were usually in spring and summer.) This visit of "the Italian Opera Company" was "one of the chief events of the Dublin year,"[9] and Stanford attended these operas repeatedly, even though that meant hours of queuing at the pit door. Crowds were so large that Stanford had to fight his way through them. A frequent conductor was Luigi Arditi, who became a Dublin landmark, "as well known as the Nelson Pillar."[10] Like John Joyce a few years later at the Gaiety, Stanford also attended rehearsals through connivance with a friend, R. M. Levey, who rehearsed the orchestra.[11]

Among the operas Stanford first heard in Dublin were Mozart's *Don Giovanni,* starring Giovanni Mario, Giulia Grisi (Mario's lifelong companion), and Giuseppe Ciampi,[12] and Beethoven's *Fidelio* in a performance by Carl Formes, Italo Gardoni, Therese Tietjens, and Charles Santley (the "best berrathon sanger in all the aisles," *FW* 254.33), where a very intricate ensemble was so applauded that the performance was halted and the whole movement encored on the spot.[13] In *Fidelio,* too, Stanford heard Tietjens sing the prisoners' chorus and "great concerted pieces" in act 2 that brought tears to his eyes. As a witness to the scene described in chapter 1, when a mob from the Gods pulled Tietjens's carriage to the hotel, Stanford surmised that the triumphant evening was something seldom or never seen elsewhere for *Fidelio.*[14] Of Tietjens Stanford concluded, "A grander voice and a more consummate artist it would be difficult to imagine."[15]

Stanford not only shared John Joyce's memory of Tietjens; the two also held similar opinions about Zélia Trebelli, whom Stanford termed the greatest woman singer he heard in Dublin, saving only Tietjens.[16]

Stanford also was able to hear Mozart's *Marriage of Figaro* and *Magic Flute,* Rossini's *Barber of Seville,* Cherubini's *Les Deux journées,* Meyerbeer's *Robert le diable* and *Les Huguenots,* Weber's *Der Freischütz* and *Oberon* (the latter with Tietjens and Santley), Donizetti's *La Fille du régiment* and *Lucrezia Borgia,* Verdi's *La Traviata* and *Rigoletto,* Thomas's *Hamlet* (with Christine Nilsson), and Gounod's *Faust* and *Mireille.*[17] Probably, following the English pattern, the Cherubini, Meyerbeer, Weber, Thomas, and Gounod works were given in Italian or English, rather than in their original languages. Still, it was a rich operatic diet for a young man not yet eighteen.

Nor were these visiting companies from London second rate. Stanford's biographer, Harry Plunket Greene (himself a gifted singer admired by Joyce),[18] describes Dublin of the 1850s and 1860s as "one of the homes of Grand Opera" and mentions additional singers (Jenny Lind, Adelina Patti, Sofia Scalchi, Trebelli, Pietro Mongini,[19] "and many others") as among the singers Stanford heard there, most of them from Her Majesty's Theatre, London.[20] Of these singers Lind, Patti, Tietjens, Grisi, Mario, Trebelli, Mongini, and Santley figure in *Finnegans Wake.* Tietjens and Trebelli are also remembered in *Dubliners'* "The Dead," and Joyce's friend C. P. Curran recalled that "Tietjens was a superb soprano. Her genius as a singer was equalled by her warm heart and both made her a Dublin idol. . . . Her connection with Dublin lasted fifteen years and more" (*SL* 386).

The other performers referred to but not named by Greene would have included other singers from "The Dead": Georgina Burns (who sang Thomas's *Mignon*), Ilma di Murska, Italo Campanini (to whom John Joyce was the presumed successor), Antonio Giuglini (mentioned by James Joyce also in a letter to Curran); Luigi Ravelli, and Antonio Aramburo. Of these, di Murska and Campanini also appear in the *Wake,* as does Enrico Caruso (whose career had not yet begun when Stanford was in Dublin).

Burns, described as "poor Georgina Burns" in "The Dead" (*D* 199.3), had in fact a reasonably successful career in the United Kingdom. After making her debut at only seventeen in 1877, she went on to roles as Anne Page in *The Merry Wives of Windsor,* Minna in *Nordica,* Isabella in *Robert le diable,* Catherine in *L'Etoile du nord,* and Santuzza in *Cavalleria rusticana* over the next fifteen years. She married Leslie Crotty, a baritone who also sang with the Carl Rosa Opera Company, and together they formed their own traveling company in 1893, although it lasted only a year. William Murray told his nephew, Stanislaus Joyce, that she sang the runs in "I am Titania" (*Mignon*) with great flexibility and hit her high C with "a note like the smashing of thin glass" (*CDD* 36). Not all critics admired her voice, however. Shaw derided her performance as prima donna in

Antonio Giuglini was mad about kites and flew them on the beaches of Dublin when the opera was in town, as Joyce reminded C. P. Curran. He once gestured to conductor Arditi from backstage to hasten a performance of *Don Giovanni* so that Giuglini could get back to his kite flying. This and other obsessions, including fireworks, led to his eventual breakdown while he was singing in St. Petersburg and his lifetime confinement in his Italian villa.

Wallace's *Lurline* (April 1890) in a spangled silk costume "not to be contemplated without amazement and laughter." He acknowledged the power of her voice, which in act 2 was heard despite the blaring of the orchestra brass, and the fact that "Mr Lely roared; Mr Crotty shouted; Mr Eugene bellowed; and the chorus lent a willing hand." Her voice went "ripping, tearing, piercing through the hurly burly until the gallery, astounded and almost hysterical, madly demanded a repetition of the unparalleled sensation. It was magnificent; but it was not singing."[21] "Poor Georgina Burns" indeed!

Although Richard Ellmann suggests that Joyce drew the name for the character Emily Sinico from the family name of his Triestine singing teacher, Giuseppe Sinico, it seems likely that Joyce had first encountered that musical-sounding name in Dublin. The family prima donna was Clarice Sinico, a soprano of some distinction who appeared in London and with "Colonel" James Mapleson's touring Royal Italian Opera Company in the provinces. Mapleson, who traveled with his company, says that Clarice was the wife of a Giuseppe (sometimes called José) Sinico.[22] This was apparently Giuseppe Carlo Sinico, uncle of James Joyce's Triestine singing teacher (see the "Trieste" section of this chapter). After an 1864 debut in Nice, Clarice was hired by Mapleson[23] and appeared frequently at Drury Lane, Her Majesty's Theatre, and Covent Garden from 1865 to at least 1878. Since the Royal Italian Opera Company routinely visited Dublin, Clarice Sinico's fame was Irish as well as English. Harold Rosenthal describes her as part of "a really worthy company" of singers including also Nilsson, di Murska, Trebelli, Santley, A. J. Foli, Mongini, and the bright particular star Tietjens. Clarice's voice was admired by perceptive critics such as Stanford, who termed her "a most finished artist, of the type which Hans von Bülow used to define as a first clarinet: brilliant, incisive, and thoroughly musical."[24] By 1878, during Mapleson's tour of the United States, Clarice Sinico was famous enough to sign endorsements for Steinway pianos.[25]

Also a member of the company for part of the time was Sinico's second husband, Scots baritone Henry McLean Martin, who followed nineteenth-century custom by using an Italian stage name, Enrico Campobello.[26] Records on Campobello are even scantier than for his wife, but they do show that her name became Campobello-Sinico after their 1874 marriage.[27] The couple also performed with the Philharmonic Society in London.[28] Campobello seems later to have joined the Carl Rosa Opera Company: in 1875 he sang Count Almaviva in their London opening-night production of *The Marriage of Figaro*.[29]

Most intriguing of the family for Joyce scholars is Amelia, daughter of Clarice and (presumably) Giuseppe Carlo Sinico. Her name tantalizingly close to Emily Sinico's in "A Painful Case," Amelia is mentioned only once by a critic,

"Colonel" James Mapleson regularly visited Dublin with his Royal Italian Opera Company from London and brought to Ireland de Reszke, di Murska, Trebelli, Nilsson, Hauk, Campanini, Nordica, Clarice Sinico, and others.

when Bernard Shaw complained about her 1890 London debut. At age eighteen she made, he said, "a clever imitation of a prima donna" singing "Ombra leggiera"; but she trusted too fully what she had picked up backstage about the art of singing, instead of applying herself to real study and a proper knowledge of a singer's task.[30] If she continued her singing career with provincial touring companies, or even on the music hall stage, Amelia would have been the right age for Joyce to hear her in Dublin and, with his keen ear, to alter her name to the more musical double-dactyl "Emily Sinico."[31]

Before becoming a London music critic, Shaw was a keen observer of the Dublin opera scene. Seven years younger than John Joyce, four years junior to

Adelina Patti, a "golden" soprano of the nineteenth century, was goddaughter to Giuseppe (José) Sinico, whose nephew of the same name was Joyce's voice teacher in Trieste. Here Patti is shown in her costume as Juliette for Gounod's opera.

Stanford, Shaw was born to a mother who was a singer of some ability, a student—and perhaps more—of Dublin singing teacher George John Vandaleur Lee.[32] From about 1866 to 1873 Lee lived with the Shaw family, an unusual boarder who dissected not only birds but also human corpses in an effort to find out how the voice was produced. He trained Mrs. Shaw's voice and used her "as an amateur prima donna" to illustrate his ideas about singing.[33]

Lee was an enterprising person who as early as 1855 organized Dublin's Amateur Musical Society, which gave three or four concerts yearly, often as benefits for other organizations. Frequently these included excerpts from opera, but never whole operas, although for the 1864 celebration of the Shakespeare tercentenary, the program included "Introductions, Solos, Choruses, &c" from *Macbeth*.[34] This description suggests that the music might have been drawn from Verdi's *Macbeth*, which failed at its Italian premiere in 1847. It was sung in Dublin on 30 March 1859 by Pauline Viardot, in a production conducted by Arditi.[35] The Dublin production was the only one in the British Isles until Covent Garden staged the opera in 1938.

In 1865 Lee's amateur group again performed in the Antient Concert Rooms, this time offering to a large and "fashionable" audience favorites from Donizetti, Meyerbeer, Beethoven, Balfe, and Mozart. The Mozart was an orchestral overture to *Figaro;* "Robert toi que j'aime" from *Robert le diable* served Meyerbeer; and "Lo, the early [beam of] morning" from *The Siege of Rochelle* sufficed for Balfe.[36] In 1866 the group's concerts moved out to the International Hotel, Bray, where Mrs. Shaw sang part of the quartet from *Rigoletto* and the duet, "Quis est homo?" from Rossini's *Stabat Mater* (it was in Molly Bloom's repertory, too; see *U* 5.397–402). She also performed the solo aria "Nobil donna" from *Les Huguenots*.[37] By April 1871 Lee felt confident enough about his "Amateur" Musical Society to offer a commercial concert rather than a charity benefit— and at the capacious Theatre Royal. The program began with "the Gipsy Scene" from *Il trovatore* and concluded with "Mozart's Grand Opera," *Don Giovanni*.[38] This commercial venture produced dissension within the society, apparently from several sources. The first was a quarrel over whether opera should be performed in English or Italian—a reflection of the similar conflict in the London musical world.[39] A second cause seems to have been religion, for Dublin musical organizations—and their audiences—divided rather closely along religious lines. Lee's group had been "Catholic."[40] Indeed, Mrs. Shaw incurred some disfavor from her husband's Protestant family for her involvement with the Catholic group. Even the charities that benefited from Dublin's concerts were separated into Catholic and Protestant. The patrons, too, displayed the religious division, as did, perhaps, the theaters and halls.

Another of Lee's productions, now with a group called the Amateur Musical, Operatic, and Dramatic Society in December 1871, sandwiched selections from *Il trovatore* between a comedy, *The Hunchback,* and a musical burlesque, *Patient Penelope.* Subscribers got good value, however: a one-guinea subscription provided two tickets to the dramatic presentations, to the Italian Opera, and to each concert by the society.[41]

Operas in the repertory of the Amateur Musical Society and its successor included *Il trovatore,* Donizetti's *Lucrezia Borgia,* and probably also Mozart's *Don Giovanni,* and Shaw claimed that by the end of his formal schooling in Dublin, he could "sing and whistle from end to end leading works by Handel, Haydn, Mozart, Beethoven, Rossini, Bellini, Donizetti, and Verdi."[42]

Lee's Dublin career reached its apex when he organized a Dublin Festival in January 1873 at the Dublin Exhibition Palace, with a band and a chorus of more than 500 of his own amateur singers, as well as professional soloists brought to Dublin from the Italian opera in London.[43] No opera was included, but the first program offered Rossini's *Stabat Mater* plus a group of secular pieces; the second program opened with the whole of Handel's *Messiah* followed, again, by secular selections after the interval. The soloists were, indeed, famous: Tietjens, Clarice Sinico, Justine MacVitz from St. Petersburg, Tombesi, Campobello, Borella, and Agnesi. So crowded was the festival that the doors of the hall had to be left open, to allow some of the audience to stand in the outer galleries.[44]

Prior to leaving Dublin Lee staged two more performances of "Italian opera"—these as benefits jointly for himself and for Stanford's friend, conductor R. M. Levey. Again the programming showed the characteristic nineteenth-century style: two acts of Bellini's *La sonnambula* followed by a "slightly compressed" version of Donizetti's *Lucrezia Borgia* formed one evening. The second evening was devoted to Verdi's *Il trovatore,* Azucena's role being sung by Mrs. Shaw.[45]

In addition to mentioning the singers from the Italian Opera in London, and the often talented Dublin amateurs, Shaw names two singers he heard in his childhood: Mario, by then "a toneless baritone with a falsetto C" who had "smoked all the quality out of his voice," and Jean de Reszke, then a baritone singing the roles of Don Giovanni and (in *Faust*) Valentin. Shaw said that de Reszke, in contrast to Mario, was "a godlike juvenile, easily the best I had heard" in both roles. Often a captious critic, Shaw nevertheless added "I have not since heard him surpassed."[46]

It is clear that the Dublin to which John Stanislaus Joyce came about 1875 was full of operatic music, both amateur and professional, although on a basis

The tenor Mario, dressed like Leopold Bloom, with spindle legs and sparrow feet, and the "umbrella sword," though without dark velvet hose or silverbuckled pumps (*U* 15.2480-87, 7.53).

more sporadic than steady. By chance John Joyce arrived in Dublin when a change occurred in opera's presentation there. Previously Dubliners (and residents of Cork, Belfast, and other Irish cities) had mostly depended on opera companies that thought themselves to be situated in London, with temporary tours of the provinces, like the Italian Opera Company, for instance, touring from Her Majesty's Theatre (or occasionally from Drury Lane or the Lyceum, depending on which house the director had leased for his London season). With the formation of the Carl Rosa Opera Company in 1875, however, Ireland began to have opera from a company organized to perform in Dublin and other cities outside London, a company that only irregularly gave a brief season in London itself.

Mario in his prime, with the wavy hair, beard and mustache, and dark eyes attributed to Christ in nineteenth-century religious painting.

Carl Rosa organized the most popular of the traveling English opera companies and won immortality through Corley's tribute to him in Joyce's *Ulysses,* although by 1904 the Carl Rosa Opera Company was under different management.

Another change wrought immediately by the Rosa company involved the language question. The Italian Opera Company performances were almost always given in Italian, whatever the opera. Because Italian is a heavily voweled language, there is a good musical argument for this practice, especially when the original libretto is Italian. Yet this form of presentation also had an element of snobbery, an implication that opera was for those educated enough to know Italian. The Carl Rosa Company, on the other hand, was organized with the express purpose of providing opera in a language everyone could understand—English—and in places where the audience lived—the provinces. (In the nineteenth century, of course, Dublin was, to Londoners, a province.) True, Rosa did want to make a London reputation and regarded some provincial appearances as rather like rehearsals for London. Yet the "rehearsals" constituted most of the company's work, for their London seasons were only a few weeks long.

The idea for the Carl Rosa Opera Company was partly that of Rosa's first wife, Scots soprano Euphrosyne Parepa. Mme Parepa-Rosa was the daughter of Scots singer Elizabeth Seguin and niece of Arthur and Anne Seguin, Londoners who formed the Seguin Opera Company in 1838 and toured the United States and Canada.[47] Parepa-Rosa, nicknamed "The Incomparable," was a soprano of considerable reputation. She made her debut at sixteen in Malta and debuted at Covent Garden five years later. At one concert a man who had been so deaf as to have heard no sound in his whole life claimed that he could hear her high notes.[48] When she toured America the statuesque soprano drew superlatives everywhere. On her American tour in 1867 Parepa-Rosa's concert at the Brooklyn Academy of Music grossed $2,700, the largest receipts to that date at that house for any singer.[49] In San Francisco (1868) she sang Verdi's *Ernani* and Bellini's *Norma,* appearing on stage a remarkable twenty-four nights in the month of August. Appreciative audiences rewarded her with $50,000 net for the several months' appearance. Another six-month American tour in 1868–69 netted another $89,000. She is described as having had a fine voice combining "power and sweetness," with an unusual range of two and a half octaves. Her repertory included both Italian and English opera roles[50] and the then-popular oratorios. A large woman, she had "flutelike" high notes and a "clear, ringing" voice described by one listener as being "five hundred feet long and three hundred feet wide" when it filled the hall at the Boston Jubilee in 1869.[51]

Parepa was en route to an American tour in 1867 when she married a German musician, Carl August Nicolas Rose, who had settled in London and changed his name to Carl Rosa. Rosa was as talented as his wife, but in a different way. A rather small man, a violinist who had studied at the Leipzig and Paris conservatories, Rosa had extraordinary energy and marvelous organizational abilities. Herman[n] Klein, the music critic of *The Sunday Times* from 1881 to 1901, who had studied with the great singer and teacher Manuel Garcia, termed Rosa "energetic and industrious to a fault, an accomplished musician, an excellent conductor, and an experienced operatic manager."[52] Klein also noted Rosa's modesty, describing him as a man who shunned publicity for himself and attempted to focus the attention of the critics on his singers.[53] Wilhelm Kuhe, a pianist who traveled and performed widely in the Victorian period, described Rosa as "a very distinguished wielder of the baton."[54] American music publisher Edward Marks characterized Rosa as a superior conductor. Even Shaw, who had sometimes been sharp in his comments on the company's performance,

Euphrosyne Parepa-Rosa, a statuesque soprano nicknamed "The In-comparable," had already been part owner-manager of a traveling op-era company in the United States when she met and married Carl Rosa and they planned the Carl Rosa organization. A Boston concertgoer credited her voice with restoring his hearing.

wrote at the time of Rosa's death of his "special work" organizing English op-era so well as to leave the company "firmly established in London and the prov-inces," and even with some grudgingly admitted "artistic prestige."[55] But the highest praise came from one best able to judge, a competitor, Arditi, who had conducted many of the Italian Opera Company appearances in Dublin before the Carl Rosa Opera Company was organized. Rosa, said Arditi, was the "shrewdest and cleverest of men, . . . an organizer and conductor *par excellence.* He was animated by high and just principles, as well as by a kind heart."[56] Another tribute of professionals came from the trustees of London's Philharmonic Society, who were pleased to add him as a member of the society in 1881.[57]

After Rosa and Parepa married in 1867, they formed the Parepa-Rosa Opera Company to tour the United States in 1869. Because of her attainments as a singer and his as a conductor, the ensemble of about one hundred persons was able to tour in America for another two years, with the couple serving as codirectors. In England she sang opera at Covent Garden but had more popular success singing in oratorios and at the numerous local festivals that characterized nineteenth-century music.[58]

The Rosas returned to England with the purpose of making the same kind of provincial tours as an opera company, and they did in fact give a production of Wallace's *Maritana* at Manchester in September 1873.[59] The following month at Liverpool they offered the company's "first novelty," Eichberg's *Doctor of Alcantara* in a version entitled *The Village Doctor*.[60] When Mme Parepa-Rosa fell ill, the couple went to Egypt for her health in late 1873, but shortly after their return to England in January 1874, Mme Parepa-Rosa died after bearing a stillborn child. Thereafter the widower reorganized their plans into what was now called the Carl Rosa Opera Company, which made its debut at Dublin on 19 March 1875, at the Gaiety Theatre, probably performing *The Marriage of Figaro,* the opera with which they opened their London season at the Princess's Theatre on 11 September 1875.[61] Other operas given that first season in London by the company included an English premiere of Cagnoni's *Papà Martin,* a revival of *Les Deux journées* by Cherubini, *Faust, The Bohemian Girl, Il trovatore,* and *The Siege of Rochelle*.[62] Almost a half-century later the company's Dublin popularity was immortalized in *Ulysses* by the comment of "Lord John" Corley in "Eumaeus": "God, you've to book ahead, man, you'd think it was for the Carl Rosa" (*U* 16.201–2).

It was characteristic of the Carl Rosa Opera Company to introduce new operas in English to the audiences of the Great Britain and Ireland. In 1876 they brought *The Flying Dutchman;* in 1879 they staged more Wagner with *Rienzi,* a production of which Bernard Shaw said in *The Star,* "Nothing comparable with this achievement has been . . . done here with the exception, perhaps, of the revival of *William Tell* by Mr. Harris last season at Drury Lane."[63]

The company developed a substantial repertory over the years. In 1877 Nicolai's *Merry Wives of Windsor* was a "very great success in Aberdeen," with Georgina Burns ("The Dead," 199.3) making a debut as Anne Page.[64] The 1879 season added Bizet's *Carmen*—for the first time in English—as well as *Rienzi*.[65] When the American soprano Minnie Hauk joined the company in 1880, she sang more Wagner (*Lohengrin*) in English, as well as Verdi's *Aïda,* Thomas's

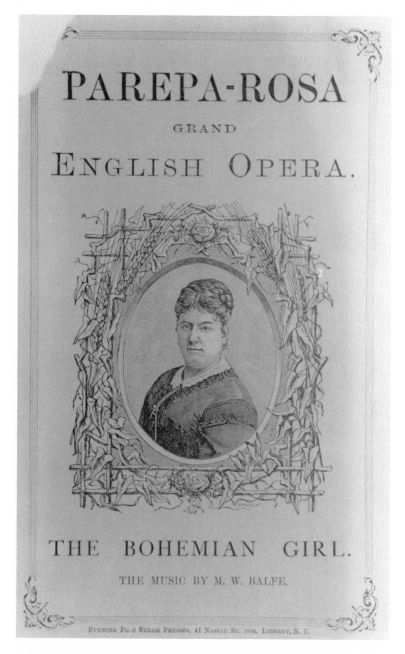

Cover of a libretto for Balfe's *Bohemian Girl,* published by the Parepa-Rosa Opera Company, the American forerunner of the Carl Rosa Opera Company.

Minnie Hauk in costume for her role as Carmen, as described in *Ulysses* 15.2742-49: light-colored, three-quarter-length skirt, edged with fringe, but lacking the black horn fan flirted by Bella Cohen.

Mignon, and Goetz's *Taming of the Shrew.*[66] The company's repertory also included an operetta by Pellegrino titled *Mercedes.*[67]

By the time of James Joyce's birth in 1882, therefore, the Carl Rosa Opera Company was well established and well respected. In 1883 Rosa invited London impresario Augustus Harris[68] to join in managing the company, which then began doing its London seasons at the Theatre Royal, Drury Lane. At the same time, as part of his campaign to bring English opera to the masses, Rosa in 1883 began commissioning operas by English composers. One of the first of these was Arthur Goring Thomas's *Esmeralda,* presented by a "first-rate ensemble" including Georgina Burns, her husband Leslie Crotty, and Barton M'Guckin.[69] Another commission went to Charles Villiers Stanford, whose *Canterbury Pilgrims* the Rosa company produced at Drury Lane in 1884, fourteen years after Stanford left Dublin for Cambridge. The next year M'Guckin sang "splendidly" in Arthur Goring Thomas's *Nadeshda,* also commissioned for the company.[70] It was in 1885, too, that the Carl Rosa company presented the premiere in England of Massenet's *Manon* at Liverpool. M'Guckin also sang a principal role in Frederick Cowen's *Thorgrim* (1890).[71]

Rosa died in 1889, at only forty-seven. His legacy was an active, growing appreciation of opera throughout Great Britain and Ireland. From the memorable moment when the Carl Rosa Opera Company presented its first opera in 1875, he had "sounded the knell of 'ballad-opera'" as standard amusement and brought the public taste to a higher level.[72] Shaw praised him for leaving opera more firmly established in the provinces, and "not without a certain artistic prestige," although the acerbic critic still complained of the welter of Scots, Canadian, Welsh, Irish, and English provincial accents that characterized the company's singing. Wilhelm Kuhe added that Rosa "gave to provincial audiences during a long succession of years lyrical representations, complete and artistically satisfying in every detail, at reasonable and even cheap prices, and in this way popularized works which but for him would rarely have reached the ears of the multitude."[73]

The following year Shaw paid an indirect compliment in the guise of criticism. Expressing a hope that the Carl Rosa Opera Company would get "severe criticism" in quantity during their London season in April 1890, Shaw pointed out that the Italian Opera of Covent Garden was "a class affair at best," with little effect outside London. The Rosa company, by contrast, played "everywhere. They are at it practically all the year round; and the rising generation in the provinces—from which, be it remembered, the future critics and connoisseurs of London will be largely recruited—will have its ideas formed" by the Rosa group's performances. This national responsibility was betrayed, Shaw argued, by a lack of artistic discipline and sham Italianisms of name and accent, leaving the company too often "a fortuitous assemblage of middle-class amateurs."[74] An example of the burden on the Carl Rosa performers would be the claim of principal bass Aynsley Cook that he had a repertory of ninety-two operas, with multiple parts in many of them. In 1889 he told an interviewer that he had sung both *Maritana* and *Faust* that year from memory, not having looked at their scores since he first studied them two decades earlier.[75] This sounds like too many roles and too little study time allowed individual singers.

Of individual performances by the company that spring of 1890, Shaw had a more appreciative view. Their *Mignon* he found "very creditable" and more pleasurable than the production at the Paris Opéra.[76] Meyerbeer's *L'Etoile du nord* was too demanding for their talents, but even so, it never got "quite down to the level of a subscription night" at the Royal Italian Opera during the "regular" season.[77]

To put his critiques of the Carl Rosa company even more in context, one must remember that Shaw in equally scathing tone berated stars of the Royal Italian Opera: he chided Adelina Patti for her willingness to interrupt a death scene on stage so as to rise and take a bow and Christine Nilsson for interrupting a performance of *Il trovatore* to shout "Bravo!" and slap her tenor partner on the back after he sang "Ah sì, ben mio." For Shaw, most opera in England was simply unprofessional well into the 1890s.[78]

After Rosa's death Harris continued briefly as director of the company, but by 1890 he was also managing Covent Garden for the Royal Italian Opera Company and was the lessee of Theatre Royal, Drury Lane. In 1891 he sold the Carl Rosa company to its two managers, T. H. Friend and H. Bruce, who set up three touring companies. They also continued the policy of doing new operas, notably the premieres in England of *Hänsel und Gretel* (1895) and *La bohème* (1897), the latter at Manchester with Puccini's participation.[79] Also at Manchester that year they staged Puccini's one-act *Le Villi*.[80] In the 1890s, too, the company did first productions in English of *Romeo and Juliette, Cavalleria rusticana, L'amico Fritz, Djamileh, Otello, Pagliacci, Faust, Die Meistersinger*, and *Tristan und Isolde*.

Some critics complained that the quality of the Carl Rosa Opera Company productions declined after the death of Rosa and the departure of Harris.[81] But Luigi Arditi, asked by Rosa's widow to conduct the group on a three-month tour in 1894, found merit in chorus voices "exceptionally fresh and young" and remarked on the difficulties under which they labored: regular evening performances plus two matinees weekly, and "continual work" far beyond that demanded of singers at the Royal Italian Opera.[82] His singers on that tour included Barton M'Guckin, who had been so appreciative of John Joyce's voice.

In 1900 the management changed again; from the turn of the century to the beginning of World War I the Carl Rosa Opera Company brought to the British Isles first performances in England of Goldmark's *Die Königin von Saba* and Giordano's *Andrea Chénier,* as well as the first performances in the English language of *Siegfried, La gioconda,* and *La forza del destino.*[83]

The Carl Rosa performances Joyce would have heard in his childhood and early manhood, then, would have been from a company beginning to decline. Still, as Shaw remarked when criticizing their performance of *L'Etoile du nord,* it is better to stage mediocre opera than none at all.

Joyce had a last, faint connection with the Carl Rosa group in the 1930s, when his poem "A Memory" was set by Eugene Goossens III for *The Joyce Book.*[84] Goossens, like his father and paternal grandfather, had worked as a conductor with the Carl Rosa company, and their work was praised by Sir Thomas Beecham.[85] Furthermore, Goossens's maternal grandfather, Aynsley Cook, had been the Rosa company's leading bass for years.

Dublin was not dependent solely on the Royal Italian Opera and the Carl Rosa company for its opera in Joyce's day. At least two other traveling enterprises visited the city: the Arthur Rousbey Company and the Moody-Manners Opera Company. Both were remembered by John McCormack's wife, Lily, as of importance in shaping the musical consciousness of their generation.[86] Two tenors of the Rousbey group are recalled less kindly by Joyce himself in *Ulysses,* where "the usual hackneyed run of catchy tenor solos" are "foisted on a confiding public by Ivan St. Austell and Hilton St. Just" (*U* 16.1850–52). Both are stage names, the first for a singer with the plain English designation of W. H. Stephens; both names come from Cornish towns.[87] In other respects the Rousbey company seems to have been of limited influence. Eugene Goossens III recalls that his father was the company's conductor for about a year, and a harrowing experience it must have been for a good musician. In Goossens's time it traveled with a "skeleton" orchestra, and its advance manager (a businessman, not a musician) hired local musicians to fill in. Goossens II then spent hours every morning rehearsing small groups of these locals, trying—not always successfully—to bring them up to standard. When money was short (as it often was), he had to travel with bone fragments of the skeleton, in one small English town conducting a *Cavalleria rusticana* with a harmonium, two violins, a cornet, and a horn. The next evening he was reduced to a harmonium and two violins for the performance of *Tannhäuser.* The company survived only three or four years, from 1894 to 1898, and Goossens resigned his post in 1898.[88]

The Moody-Manners Opera Company was more successful, especially between 1898 and 1910, although it lasted to 1916. Its founders, singers Fanny Moody and Charles Manners, ran a considerable enterprise. Moody-Manners, like the Carl Rosa company, also gave London seasons; they were the first opera company to present *Madame Butterfly* in English (at the Lyric Theatre, Shaftesbury Avenue, London).[89] The company base was Liverpool, however, where it gave an eight-week season yearly before going on tour. Manners took pride in keeping the singers in employment forty-four to forty-eight weeks per year and providing opera to "the Gods" for a shilling a head.[90] He also maintained a year-round studio to produce stage scenery. Although started with only a single cloth backdrop, at the peak of its success the Moody-Manners company had staged over fifty operas, and the number-one company totaled 175 persons, traveling by special train with their own trucks for costumes and scenery. The directors insisted on separating the sexes on the train, putting the male members of the chorus in the first coaches, the principals in the next coaches, and the female choristers in the last, with the corridor doors locked, resulting in the nickname "The Sunday School on Tour"[91] (*FW* 102.15, "Sunday *Sola*"). The irony of the situation was that although Moody and Manners had both been singing with the Carl Rosa company, they began to get well acquainted only when, leaving Dublin, Manners joined Moody and her sister in their train compartment to admire some doves presented her by students at Trinity College.[92] Perhaps that experience taught them the hazards of propinquity in travel.

Another contributing factor in the Moody-Manners success was their careful development of musicians. They maintained a second, or B, company of only ninety-five persons that toured smaller towns. Talented young singers were assigned to this group, which the directors called their "Academy of Music," to gain experience. (Members referred to this company as "The Nursery.") As they matured, singers were transferred to the number-one company in small roles and gradually promoted to larger parts.

Cornish by birth, Moody was a leading soprano of the Carl Rosa Opera Company from 1887 to 1898. Her career included the role of Tatyana in the first English performance of Tchaikovsky's *Eugene Onegin*, as well as Elsa in *Lohengrin*, Marguerite in *Faust*, Juliette in *Roméo et Juliette*, Leonora in *Il trovatore*, and Santuzza in *Cavalleria rusticana*. Singers with the company recalled her as a "superb Elsa," with a voice comparable to Nellie Melba in timbre or to more recent sopranos such as Isobelle Baillie or Elizabeth Schwarzkopf.[93]

Moody's husband, Charles Manners, was a tall and commanding Irish bass, born Southcote Mansergh, who had studied at the Royal Academy of Music and also in Italy. He sang with the D'Oyly Carte Company for several years, toured with the Carl Rosa company from 1882 to 1890, and sang at Covent Garden in 1890–91 as Bertram in *Robert le diable*. He sang the role of Prince

Gremin in the production of *Eugene Onegin* in which his wife also performed.[94] One of the singers with the Moody-Manners company described Manners's voice as "one of the most glorious . . . I have ever heard, . . . fresh and unimpaired by all his exertions as Producer and Business Manager."[95] Bernard Shaw's evaluation was less favorable; reviewing a concert where Manners sang Schumann's "Two Grenadiers," Shaw complained that Manners's interpolation—meant to be decorative—was in bad taste. Of the same concert Shaw also protested that Manners followed the "custom," singing "Qui sdegno" sharp, and spoiled the end by dropping down to the low E. These, said Shaw, were failings of taste and sense.[96]

Eugene Goossens III recalls the Moody-Manners troupe as having a "long and prosperous existence in friendly rivalry to the Carl Rosa Company."[97] He adds that the prosperity of two companies operating in the same provincial territory (eleven cities plus Dublin, Cork, and Belfast) in the same period indicates the considerable health of opera in English in the quarter-century between 1890 and 1915.

From the vantage point of cities like London, Paris, or New York, where there were resident opera companies, Dublin's dependence on traveling companies might seem to indicate an inferior kind of opera culture. It must be remembered, however, that even London opera seasons in the nineteenth century were relatively short, fitted into the summer months after the Continental seasons had ended and when channel crossings were safer. The Royal Italian Opera at Covent Garden in 1882, the year of Joyce's birth, had a season lasting only three months, from April to July. Londoners had this supplemented by two novelties: a month (called a season) of German opera at Her Majesty's Theatre in May, conducted by Anton Seidl, and six weeks of German opera at Drury Lane, under the direction of Hans Richter. Although Londoners finally had an opportunity to hear much of Wagner in German rather than Italian, all three theaters lost money in 1882.

Eight years later Covent Garden's season was even shorter, from 19 May to 28 July, although the hall was leased by a Signor Lago for a six-week season in October and November with a company that included Fanny Moody and Charles Manners, who had not yet formed their own enterprise. The Carl Rosa Company had also presented a "short season" in early spring of 1890, so London had a total of perhaps twenty weeks of opera that year.[98] A decade later, when James and John Joyce visited London with the money James had received from his *Fortnightly Review* article, Covent Garden's Royal Opera season ("Italian" had been dropped from the company's title) ran from 14 May to the end of July, with twenty-five evenings devoted to Wagner, the premiere of Puccini's

Tosca, the London debut of Alessandro Bonci (a tenor much admired by Joyce), and the last London performances of Jean de Reszke. In the same year Drury Lane presented some opera in English.

These seasons were supplemented, of course, by regular concert series that, as in Dublin, included individual opera arias or choruses. But it was also true that sometimes more than one traveling company visited Dublin in a given year, so that brief as the "season" of a single company might be, there would often have been several such seasons. The Dublin opera offerings may not have equaled those in Europe's capitals, but they were respectable in number and often in the quality of voices and ensemble singing offered music lovers. For comparison, it is safe to say that Dublin in Joyce's day offered more opera than is to be found in any American state capital today, with the possible exceptions of Atlanta and Boston.

As a Dubliner, then, Joyce in his teens and early twenties had access to opera performed by three and perhaps more traveling companies. It was performed in English, and by the 1890s and 1900s the singers were not the stars of the London stage who had visited Dublin in the 1870s and 1880s; but they were hard-working, serious artists nevertheless.

Whatever their quality, these productions drew Joyce. J. F. Byrne recalls their going to "as many operas as we could afford" during the visits of the Rousbey and Carl Rosa companies. In their "very youthful" days they chose to hear *Il trovatore* (a particular favorite of Joyce's among the Carl Rosa company's operas), as well as *Maritana, The Bohemian Girl,* and *The Lily of Killarney.* As they "grew older" they preferred Wagner, particularly *Tristan und Isolde* and *Lohengrin.*[99] C. P. Curran's recollection that by the time he knew Joyce at University College, Wagner had pushed Italian operas off the Dublin stages in the full performances suggests that the shift in taste was in part forced on the young men. Curran adds that excerpts from the earlier Italians were still heard on the concert stages and that Donizetti, Bellini, and Rossini "lived on in the memory of the older generation."[100] Along with Wagner's work, Balfe and Mozart operas were still being produced in Dublin during Joyce's University College years, Curran adds.

In addition to listening to opera, Joyce was himself a singer, as is well known. Prior to his appearance in the 1904 Feis Ceoil singing contest, he studied with two Dublin teachers: Benedetto Palmieri and Vincent O'Brien. There is no record of how many lessons he took from either man or of what musical background he had before working with them. Nevertheless, it seems clear that each was a conscientious and experienced teacher with much to offer an aspiring singer.

Benedetto Palmieri was born in Naples in 1863. Originally a pianist, he taught singing at the Royal College of Music in London in 1885–90. In 1900 he appeared as a teacher at the Royal Academy of Music, Dublin, where he stayed till 1914. During the first two years of World War I he was again in Italy (at more than fifty years of age, he was doubtless too old to be in the army), and in 1916 he returned to London's Royal College of Music.[101] He was also a composer of symphonies, suites, and other orchestral work, as well as of cantatas and chamber music. Joyce had "a few lessons" with Palmieri, then "the best voice teacher in Dublin," at seven shillings each. Then he switched to Vincent O'Brien, "a less expensive teacher," again for just "a few lessons," in Ellmann's phrase (*JJ* 151). The implication is that Joyce changed teachers for financial reasons; but he was doubtless also motivated by the fact that O'Brien, the choral director at the Pro-Cathedral in Marlborough Street, had been the Dublin teacher of both John McCormack and Lily Foley McCormack, and each of them had won a gold medal in the 1903 Feis. Described by L. A. G. Strong as "a figure of power in the Dublin musical world" at the turn of the century,[102] O'Brien had shown himself to be a sympathetic person in preparing John McCormack, donating "all his spare time" to teaching McCormack the test songs: Handel's "Tell Fair Irene" and "The Snowy-Breasted Pearl," an Irish folk melody from Petrie's collection.[103] There is no evidence that O'Brien donated his teaching time to Joyce as well as to McCormack, although he praised Joyce's voice, but Joyce may have been concerned as much with invoking some of O'Brien's musical power on his own behalf as in achieving free tuition. His "few lessons" with O'Brien are remarkably similar to McCormack's "few months" of study with the same teacher: neither pupil seems to have had extensive training by O'Brien.

That price was not the only concern for Joyce in his music studies is demonstrated by his reaction to Palmieri's offer, following the 1904 Feis, of three years of free lessons in return for a share of Joyce's concert fees for a decade.[104] Perhaps it was the thought of ten years of sharing fees or of being tied to Dublin for three years—an eternity at age twenty-two. Joyce refused the offer.

Despite the praise of the judge, Luigi Denza, and the encouragement from Palmieri, Joyce did not win first place in the Feis because he declined to sing the last piece at sight. It is probably not quite accurate to say, as Joyce's friends asserted, that Joyce could not sight-read. There are levels of music-reading skill, as of word-reading skill. Stanislaus Joyce recalled that James spent time studying opera scores.[105] That Stanislaus says "scores" rather than "librettos" suggests that Joyce could indeed read music. Joyce certainly knew enough about musical notation to write out music for himself.[106] Singing at sight professionally in competition, however, demands far more skill than picking out something on a piano in the privacy of home or working one's way studiously through a score. Joyce may well have felt himself unable to read well enough for the Feis.[107]

Even after declining the lessons from Palmieri, Joyce continued to sing in Dublin concerts, including an opera aria, "In her simplicity" ("Elle ne croyait pas") from Thomas's *Mignon*. His performance at this 27 August 1904 concert, in which McCormack also sang, may have been the persuasive touch in winning Nora Barnacle's devotion.[108] Almost three decades later, recommending to Stuart Gilbert synonyms that might be used for the name "Joyce" in Gilbert's *James Joyce's "Ulysses,"* Joyce, in partial self-mockery, suggested "the suburban tenor."[109]

Setting off for the Continent in 1904 with Nora, James Joyce carried with him a background of operatic experience in his family, his own studies, and the varied, if sometimes rather amateurish, offerings of Dublin. In selecting a destination Joyce was thinking of employment, not opera. Nonetheless, one of the attractions of Zurich, toward which he and Nora first fled, would have been its opera house. Chance intervened, however, and the young couple continued their journey to what proved to be an even richer opera environment: Trieste.

TRIESTE

Politically Trieste was part of the Austro-Hungarian empire in 1904. Culturally and musically it was Italian, and opera, the Italian national art born some two hundred miles away in Florence, was available even in small cities. Prima donna Lillian Nordica (née Lillian Norton in Farmington, Connecticut) made her start by singing five performances a week of *La traviata* in a small Italian opera house in the late 1870s; even in a small town it was possible to draw an audience on five successive nights for the same opera.[110] Caruso began his career in 1897 at Livorno, not at Milan's La Scala; and in his youth he sang two operas on Sundays, at the Teatro Mercadante in Naples.[111] John McCormack made his debut at Savona in 1906—a small town on the Gulf of Genoa—and followed that same year with an engagement to sing ten performances of *Faust* at Santa Croce sul Arno, a small town near Florence.[112] Arturo Toscanini, during his student years at the Parma Conservatory, earned money playing cello in a Parma theater orchestra and in five years played the score of about thirty different operas.[113] In his first thirteen years as a conductor, 1886–98, Toscanini led opera at twenty-four theaters in twenty different Italian towns. These included towns with populations of twenty or thirty thousand, as well as major cities such as Rome, Milan, and Turin. Even this "host of smaller communities . . . knew their opera and knew what they liked in a singer. If they were displeased, they made life miserable for the performers," says Howard Taubman.[114] Great operas mingled with unknown titles. Local composers found a hearing for their first compositions; Toscanini conducted seven premieres of new works in those years, as well as the first Italian performance of *Die Götterdämmerung*.[115] For the decade of the 1890s, *New Grove Dictionary of Opera* reports 755 Italian municipalities that together contained more than a thousand theaters doing both drama and opera. Although only eleven were reserved for opera and judged to be first class, the proliferation of small houses not only meant opportunities for hundreds of beginning singers like McCormack to gain experience; it also provided the nineteenth-century equivalent of "Pavarotti in the Park" for thousands of opera lovers in a pretelevision age.

Trieste itself had a strong history of opera performance. *Aïda* was performed in Trieste before it was staged in New York. *Il trovatore* was sung there almost immediately after its Rome premiere, in one of its first three performances outside Italy. *Falstaff* could be heard in Trieste less than a year after its debut at La Scala. The Teatro Comunale (now Teatro Comunale Giuseppe Verdi) also was the site of premieres for works by Mayr, Mercadante, Balfe, Marchetti, Smareglia, Mulè, Camussi, Zanella, and Giuseppe Sinico.[116] Opera lovers in the Istrian city commissioned two works by Verdi: *Il corsaro* (1848) and *Stiffelio* (1850).[117]

Trieste also had a particularly fortunate position geographically, roughly and conveniently between Vienna and Milan. Its opera house, seating 2,000, attracted "the best companies [and] best singers" en route from the Hofopernhaus in the Austrian capital to the major houses in Milan, Venice, and Monte Carlo.[118] The Teatro Comunale offered the first Wagner to Triestines, not only in orchestral concerts but with stagings of *Lohengrin* (1876) and *Tannhäuser* (1878).[119] In addition to boasting the Teatro Comunale, Trieste after 1878 had the Teatro Politeama Rosetti, seating 3,000. The latter house presented Wagner's *Ring* cycle in 1883, directed by Anton Seidl, with an average audience of a thousand each night, more than Wagner had drawn in any Italian city to that date. Also at the Politeama, Enrico Caruso sang two performances of *L'elisir d'amore* in December 1901. Although Caruso had been singing in Italy since 1894, he was relatively unknown until his performance in this same opera at La Scala in 1901. He appeared again in Trieste, this time for two performances of *Rigoletto,* in the same theater in December 1902.[120]

Although indicative of lively opera life in Trieste, these events occurred before Joyce's arrival in that city in 1904. In his eleven years on the Adriatic, however, opera was very much a part of Triestine life. Traveling singers continued to stop there, Amelita Galli-Curci giving five performances in *The Barber of Seville* in September 1913.[121] A few years earlier, when her career was just beginning, she had also sung *Rigoletto* in Pola in 1910, after making her debut in the small Italian town of Trani in 1906.[122]

Nora Barnacle Joyce told Maria Jolas that in Trieste the Joyces had attended opera "almost every evening."[123] Probably this would more accurately be stated as "every evening when an opera was available," for in Trieste, as in Dublin and London, opera was not a year-round affair. And on a good many evenings, Joyce was attending not opera but drama, on free tickets from his friend Alessandro Francini Bruni (*JJ* 265–66). For those months when opera was offered, however, the Joyces were regular in their attendance, as Sylvia Beach confirms.[124] Joyce was absorbing details all the while, as evidenced by his reference to one of the Triestine conductors, Giuseppe Bamboshek (*FW* 527.8, "bombashaw"). The letters indicate at least three operas Joyce heard in Trieste: Massenet's *Werther,* Puccini's *Madame Butterfly* (both before his 1909 trip to Dublin; see *Letters 2,* 253, 255–56, 258), and Rossini's *Barber of Seville* (*Letters 2,* 296). He alluded to *Madame Butterfly* in writing not only to his family but also to students.[125] Puccini's *La fanciulla del west* had its Italian premiere at Rome in 1911, conducted by Toscanini, and by 1913 was popular enough to be sung by Stanislaus and his Triestine friends while they were boating, an event commemorated in "Watching the Needleboats at San Sabba."[126] Probably Joyce himself had also seen the opera performed by then.

Joyce also had opportunities to hear opera in Rome during the nine months the family lived there, from July 1906 to March 1907. He faulted the Roman production of *Die Götterdämmerung,* in his pattern of denigrating Wagner's compositions. It was probably in Rome, too, that Joyce heard the soprano he called "La Valanga" in Verdi's *La forza del destino.* When Joyce returned to Trieste, the staging of Richard Strauss's *Salomé* in April 1909 afforded an opportunity to write on Oscar Wilde for *Il Piccolo della Sera,* and he probably heard the opera performed at that time.[127] By the time Joyce reached Dublin in the fall of 1909, his friends noted that he was constantly singing snatches from Puccini's *Manon Lescaut,* which suggests that he had recently heard it performed, too.[128] Also in the Trieste years Joyce owned librettos of *The Flying Dutchman, Die Götterdämmerung, Das Rheingold,* and *Siegfried;*[129] doubtless he also had the score of *Die Meistersinger* for his use in performance.

The Joyce family also picked up the Italian attitude toward the performers: they were to be judged by a high standard, and as Beach puts it, the Joyces were "relentless toward anyone guilty of shirking the high C."[130] McCormack had discovered this Italian trait while performing in *Faust* at Santa Croce sul Arno:

Johanna Gadski in costume as Brünnhilde, with a horse painted on the backdrop. Joyce despised the type of literal Wagnerian production that cluttered the stage with real horses.

his voice cracked on a high B in act 2, and he fled the stage without waiting for the chorus of whistles and boos.[131]

In Trieste, as in Dublin, Joyce lived among musicians, but these had professional experience, rather than being the devoted amateurs he had known in Ireland. The wife of his colleague Francini had sung in opera before her marriage. To Nora's delight, the Francinis, when they shared an apartment with the Joyces in the early years in Trieste, agreed that James's voice was fine enough for a professional career—and one that would solve the family's financial worries.[132] Joyce's student, Ettore Schmitz (who wrote novels as Italo Svevo), not only had written opera criticism for *L'Indipendent* but was an ardent Wagnerite and the first newsperson in Trieste to write of Wagner.[133] Schmitz, studying his English teacher, noted an "oddly eclectic" musical taste and a comprehension including German classics, old Italian music, Wagner, and opera from Spontini to Debussy.[134]

Within the family, as Eileen Joyce noted, there was constant singing, by James, Stanislaus, Giorgio (James's son), and presumably Eileen herself. In this family vocal circle, James was the star. On warm evenings when the window was open, as Eileen recalled, Triestines would gather outside to listen appreciatively as her oldest brother sang in his sweet Irish tenor.[135]

An even stronger source of opera lore and information for Joyce would have been his voice teacher, Giuseppe Sinico, who came from a family of composers and performers with a distinguished Triestine history. Giuseppe was the son of Francesco Sinico, "a born musician" who in 1833, at only twenty-three, undertook to produce *The Barber of Seville* for the Filarmonico-Drammatica.[136] Most parts were filled by amateurs, but as Count Almaviva, Francesco cast his younger brother, Giuseppe Carlo, a "fresh-faced, golden-voiced" tenor of seventeen who learned the part in just two days. It was the beginning of a substantial career, taking Giuseppe Carlo Sinico to La Scala in Milan and Covent Garden in London, as well as to Paris, St. Petersburg, Vienna, Warsaw, Monaco, and Spain (where he was known as José Sinico). This was apparently the same singer whose adventures included acting as godfather to Adelina Patti in Madrid in 1843, although he probably invented the story that he had actually presided at her birth in the green room of the opera house, tearing up his own costume to provide swaddling clothes.[137] Eventually he seems to have become the husband (in his third and her first marriage) of soprano Clarice Sinico (see chap. 1).

By 1876 the sixty-year-old Giuseppe Carlo Sinico had squandered most of the riches his golden voice had earned, had spent some time teaching voice in London,[138] and was apparently recently divorced from Clarice Sinico; he returned to his native city to manage the Teatro Comunale.[139] His programs there were ambitious: thirteen evenings of *Lohengrin,* then *I puritani, Amleto* [*Hamlet*], *La Muette de Portici,* and *La sonnambula.* Despite fine casts and a municipal subsidy, he met financial disaster. To save the family honor, Francesco's son Giuseppe took over the management from his uncle, Giuseppe Carlo. Francesco, who remained in Trieste while his brother and sister-in-law made successful singing careers abroad, had a busy life as conductor and composer of symphonies, three operas, instrumental music, and concertos. He also founded a program of music instruction in the schools and a music school of his own. In this school, when it was managed by the younger Giuseppe, Joyce studied voice.

In June 1905 Joyce told Stanislaus that Maestro Giuseppe Sinico praised the timbre of his extremely high voice and assured him of success on the stage. Consequently Joyce was "definitely studying for the theatre" (*Letters 2,* 91). The "definitely," however, was diverted to some months in Rome as a bank clerk, followed by a return to Trieste and teaching English. Giuseppe Sinico died on 31 December 1907, shortly after Joyce's return; the music school passed to the management of his son Francesco and his daughter Lidia Sinico-Hermet, a singer recognized at age twenty and for three decades thereafter for the "dolcezza e la freschezza della sua voce" (sweetness and freshness of her voice).[140] However sweet that voice, both James and Stanislaus moved their singing lessons to a Romeo Bartoli, in exchange for English lessons, and both sets of lessons continued into 1909.[141] Nonetheless, Joyce probably paid an ironic tribute to Lidia Sinico-Hermet's sweetness of voice when he created Lydia Douce, the triller of "Oh, my Dolores" in *Ulysses'* "Sirens." Lidia Sinico's name also has the double-dactylic rhythm of Emily Sinico's in "A Painful Case." Like her father's cousin, Amelia, Lidia may have contributed something to that story.

Joyce did venture on stage after the Bartoli lessons—apparently for the first time since leaving Dublin in 1904—as part of the quintet from *Die Meistersinger* (*JJ* 269). The experience seems not to have led him to continue concert appearances. This is the last recorded instance of Joyce's singing publicly for nearly a decade, until he became an off-stage vocalist for the English Players in Zurich.

If he did not sing, Joyce listened. He was keenly aware of opera events in Trieste and elsewhere, as when he inquired of Stanislaus from Dublin in 1909 whether Bartoli's conducting of *L'elisir d'amore* at the Trieste opera had gone well. Also in 1909 he and Nora attended a performance of Massenet's *Werther* together, and from Dublin he wired her, "the beautiful motive . . . you like so much from *Werther,* 'Nel lieto dì pensa a me'" (think of me that joyous day; *Letters 2,* 281). In the same letter he alludes to "Un bel dì" from Puccini's *Madame Butterfly.* The Joyces' emotions were expressed in operatic empathies.

ZURICH

The Joyces' move to Zurich in 1915 was scarcely voluntary. Forced as enemy aliens in World War I to leave an Austrian Trieste, they stopped, said Joyce, at "the first big city after the frontier" (*Letters 1,* 82). But the war provided an indirect benefit in making Zurich an international cultural center, cosmopolitan in feeling, with multiple opportunities for enjoyment. They remained in the city and thus found themselves once again in a locale where opera was a regular part of cultural life.[142] They were, indeed, refugees in the city where Richard Wagner himself had spent nearly a decade of exile in midcentury; Zurich was strongly associated with that composer. During the winter of 1850–51 Wagner had conducted *Der Freischütz, Norma, Fidelio,* and *Don Giovanni* in Zurich. The following year he had also led the first Zurich performance of *Der fliegende Holländer* and three years later conducted *Tannhäuser.* It was also in Zurich that Wagner had a love affair with Mathilde Wesendonck,[143] the wife of his patron; this affair lay behind his *Tristan und Isolde,* whose plot Joyce called one of the few original themes in literature.[144]

Wagner's *Lohengrin* was chosen to open Zurich's new Stadttheater (now called Opernhaus) in October 1891. The *Ring des Niebelungen* had a Zurich premiere in 1900, and the first legitimate *Parsifal* away from Bayreuth was staged in Zurich in 1913. So Joyce came, in 1915, to a city with a strong tradition of Wagner performance, a factor doubtless influencing the large role of Wagner in Joyce's writings.[145]

A series of Wagner operas in Zurich in Joyce's time was conducted by Arthur Nikisch (merged into the *Wake's* allusions to Wagner's "Nixies"), and yet more Wagner was interpreted by Richard Strauss. Indeed, Joyce's friend Otto Luening, who was supporting himself by playing flute in the Stadttheater's orchestra, remembers playing *Tannhäuser* and *Die Walküre* as often as a dozen times per season.[146] Strauss also conducted his own *Elektra* and *Der Rosenkavalier,* as well as some Mozart operas.

Also new was Pfitzner's *Palestrina,* presented in 1917 by a Munich company with Bruno Walter conducting. (The appearance of a Munich opera company in Zurich during the war indicates that neutrality had not completely isolated Switzerland from the rest of Europe.) Another premiere was Ferruccio Busoni's *Turandot,* also in 1917. Busoni's treatment of Gozzi's 1762 drama was comedic; Puccini, a decade later, would make a tragedy of the story. This and other compositions by Busoni in his Zurich years used multiple styles,[147] a technique causing "consternation" among purists, but it was a musical parallel to the multiple styles Joyce was using in *Ulysses* contemporaneously; Joyce, too, would unsettle many early readers. Busoni was also hard at work on another opera, *Doktor Faust*.[148] Othmar Schoeck, a composer whose songs Joyce much admired,[149] had his first great operatic success during Joyce's Zurich years, when *Don Ranudo de Colibrados* was premiered on 16 April 1919.[150] In addition to hearing operas at the Stadttheater, Zurichers could enjoy orchestral concerts at the Tonhalle; and a Viennese operetta company, with Luening as flutist and conductor, shared use of the Kaufleuten with Joyce's English Players and staged *Der Frechling*.[151]

Luening remembers Joyce as "a familiar figure at opera and concert performances."[152] Donizetti, Bellini, Puccini, and Balfe's *Bohemian Girl* were particular favorites (as they had been in the Dublin years), and Verdi was Joyce's favorite opera composer in Zurich. Indeed, Joyce not only praised Verdi but also sang his melodies in snatches and favorite phrases from the operas.[153] Bizet's *Carmen* was also given a number of lively performances.[154] For standard repertory the orchestra was often not rehearsed, leaving it to the younger players to practice the parts at home or, on occasion, sight-read, as Luening did at a production of Gounod's *Faust*.[155] *Le donne curiose* (*Die neugierigen Frauen*) was staged with its composer, Ermanno Wolf-Ferrari, conducting, after a rehearsal that left him in tears.[156] We know that Joyce heard Wagner's *Die Walküre*—though at one performance he walked out when his companion, Ottocaro Weiss, failed to agree that "Sirens" was better (*JJ* 460).

In Zurich, as in Trieste, Joyce associated with musicians. His neighbors, Philipp Jarnach and Charlotte Sauermann, were both professional musicians, the first at the Zurich Conservatory and the second as a singer in the Stadttheater's opera productions. Tristan Rawson, a baritone from the Cologne Opera House, became a member of Joyce's English Players (*JJ* 425). Luening, too, although still a student, was a professional composer and a paid performer in the Stadttheater and Tonhalle orchestras; he often spent evenings in cafés chatting with Joyce about music. He, too, became an active member of the English Players. Joyce and Luening were associated in another sense, for both were beneficiaries of Edith Rockefeller McCormick's financial aid. Through Jarnach Joyce met Ferruccio Busoni, also a Zurich refugee with a Triestine background and at that time a widely renowned pianist, as well as a teacher at the conservatory. The two never became close, however. Joyce found more interest in helping Augustus Milner, an Irish-born baritone who sang, like Sauermann, at the Stadttheater (*JJ* 460). Joyce organized a concert by Milner to further the young singer's career, as a decade later he would enlist himself on behalf of John Sullivan in Paris.

Although Joyce attended performances with his family, his own interests had turned more strongly than ever to the flesh made word. During his decade in Trieste Joyce had found time to study with two singing teachers; in addition to his teaching he prepared *Chamber Music* for publication and completed the writing of *Dubliners, A Portrait of the Artist as a Young Man, Exiles,* and the first two episodes of *Ulysses.* In Zurich, for the first time since he began vocal studies in Dublin in 1904, he seems to have made no effort to train his voice. Even when Charlotte Sauermann offered to arrange an audition for him at the Stadttheater, he declined. Instead he was working intensively on *Ulysses* and helping to organize the English Players, directing and coaching their productions and even serving them as voice coach. He did make a musical appearance with the players, singing offstage Giovanni Stefani's "Amante tradito" in the production of Browning's *In a Balcony.* In fact, it was this performance that led to Luening's association with the dramatic company, for the seventeen year old found it impressive that a mere business manager could sing so well.[157]

At the end of the Zurich years, the Joyces returned briefly to Trieste at the end of 1919. There again the novelist was soon at the opera house. He attempted to lure his Zurich friend Frank Budgen to join him in Trieste by the promise of an approaching production of *Siegfried.*[158] Within eight months, however, the Joyces themselves abandoned Trieste for Paris.

PARIS

For soprano Lotte Lehmann, who had sung successfully in Hamburg, London, Vienna, and Salzburg, to be invited to sing in Paris was to become an international star, to live at the heart of the "great world."[159] Joyce may have tasted some of this greatness during his brief stay in Paris in 1902–3, for Paris between the Franco-Prussian War and the beginning of World War I saw a great unfolding of French music. His only mention of opera in his letters, however, is an urgent request to Stanislaus on 25 January 1903 to send on his copy of Wagner's operas *at once.* The Paris Opéra had added *Siegfried* to the repertory on 3 January 1902, in a French translation by Ernst. In the preceding decade they had produced (always in French) *Les Maîtres Chanteurs de Nuremberg* (1897), *La Walkyrie* (12 May 1893), and *Lohengrin* (16 September 1891). Perhaps it was one of these that Joyce planned to see after he had studied his Wagner. The singers who had recently signed to sing at the Opéra included Nellie Melba, Aïno Ackte, Emma Calvé, and Jean de Reszke, all later memorialized in *Finnegans Wake.* The Opéra-Comique was also active, specializing in works by contemporary composers who had no entrée at the more stately Opéra nearby. There were performances of Reynaldo Hahn's *La Carmélite* on 16 December 1902, Leoncavallo's *Paillasse* on 17 December 1902, Reyer's *La Statue* on 6 March 1903, and Missa's *Muguette* on 18 March 1903 (given eighteen times at the Opéra-Comique—perhaps because one of its librettists was the son of the Comique's director, M. Carré). Certainly Joyce lacked the funds to attend all these performances at both houses, but perhaps he managed one or two.[160]

It may have been partly Joyce's awareness of the richness of opera life in Paris that drew the family, after a nine months' return to a Trieste much changed by World War I, to settle in 1920 in the French capital, their real home for the next twenty years. For though Paris, too, showed the effects of the terrible war, the city still offered probably the richest opera environment in Europe. Not only were the seasons at both the Opéra and the Opéra-Comique longer than those in the other cities where Joyce had lived, but opera was also being offered at many other theaters. The Trianon-Lyrique's operas were subsidized by the Paris city council. There were also the Théâtre des Nations, the Théâtre du Châtelet, and Théâtre des Champs-Elysées for serious opera and another eight houses presenting operetta. Moreover, the great international stars did not just drop in en route elsewhere, as they had in Trieste. They came to give whole seasons, or at least substantial programs over several weeks. And many of them, like Fyodor Chaliapin, made Paris their home.

In Paris, too, opera was available in a multiplicity of languages worthy of *Finnegans Wake:* French, Italian, German, and Russian.[161] With Joyce's wide command of languages, he could respond easily to both libretto and music. In 1922 Tullio Serafin conducted a season of Wagner in Italian, starring Aureliano Pertile as tenor. Two years later the Vienna Staatsoper gave a cycle of Mozart in German and Italian (*Don Giovanni, The Abduction from the Seraglio,* and *The Marriage of Figaro*), followed by another group of Mozart operas performed by a French company in the same theater. Bruno Walter conducted 1928's Mozart: *Figaro, Don Giovanni,* and *Così fan tutte.* Both the Opéra Russe de Monte Carlo and the Opéra Russe de Paris performed in Paris during the 1920s and 1930s. During this period, too, Chaliapin arranged premieres of such Russian operas as *Sadko, Tsar Saltan,* and *The Snow Maiden.* Wagner's *Ring* was heard for the first time in German in Paris in 1929 at the Théâtre des Champs-Elysées. Starring in this production with the ensemble from Bayreuth were Lauritz Melchior, Nanny Larsén-Todsen, and Sigrid Onegin, all mentioned in *Finnegans Wake.*

The regular company of the Opéra was also busy, some of their outstanding presentations including *Les Troyens* of Berlioz in 1921, *Tosca* on 24 November 1925, *Salomé* on 28 April 1927, *La traviata* on 7 June 1927, *Boris Godunov* on

29 May 1929, and a group of Wagner performances in June 1931. The Opéra was closed by fire in 1936 and reopened with Massenet's *Ariane* on 21 February 1937.[162] Also in 1937 Richard Strauss's *Ariadne auf Naxos* and *Der Rosenkavalier* were given in Paris by the Berlin Staatsoper.

In addition to works performed on the giant stage of the Opéra (the largest in Europe), there were galas and concerts by César Franck, Tito Schipa, Lily Pons, Arturo Toscanini, Giacomo Lauri-Volpi, and Marian Anderson.[163]

During the Paris years, even some of Joyce's vacations seem to have been planned to include opera. From 6 August to 27 September 1926 the Joyces visited several Belgian cities, beginning with Ostend, where an August opera season at the Kursaal had been a tradition at least since the opening of the twentieth century, with appearances by performers such as Enrico Caruso, Amelita Galli-Curci, and on the night before World War I broke out in 1914, John McCormack.[164] (August is of course a time for general evacuation of Paris by its inhabitants, and the Kursaal's August season may have been planned to complement the unavailability of opera in Paris and other capitals during that month.) During their trip to Copenhagen (August–September 1936) James and Nora Joyce took the opportunity to see the Royal Danish Ballet performance of Delibes's ballet *Coppélia* at the Royal Opera House (*JJ* 696). The next year, planning a trip to Zurich, he wanted to hear *Don Carlos* and arranged his schedule to be present for its performance about 9 September (*Letters 3*, 406).

In Paris itself one of the first bits of opera Joyce heard was John McCormack's performance of an aria from *Don Giovanni* at a recital in December 1920. (Probably this was "Il mio tesoro"; McCormack's recording of this was considered to be the best performance of it for another twenty or thirty years.) Joyce praised McCormack's singing, with a slight reservation that was characteristic of his relationship with the Great Irish Tenor: "No Italian lyrical tenor that I know (Bonci possibly excepted) could do such a feat of breathing and phrasing." He also commended the beauty of McCormack's tone (*Letters 3*, 32). Not having seen McCormack for sixteen years, Joyce was probably unaware that McCormack disliked Bonci's singing.[165] Bonci being unavailable, Joyce planned to attend a second McCormack recital the following week.

It is difficult to know in detail just what Joyce enjoyed from Paris's rich opera life. Arthur Power remembers a discussion in which Joyce argued that *Carmen* was "the best opera ever written" but does not date the discussion or indicate whether in reaching this "fanatical" opinion, Joyce was influenced by a recent performance of Bizet's masterpiece.[166] Joyce also heard *Siegfried* in his Paris years, "dragging" George Antheil with him to the Opéra.[167] Louis Gillet recalls Joyce as adoring Meyerbeer, Rossini, and Verdi and mentions particularly Rossini's *La gazza ladra* and Meyerbeer's *L'Africaine.* But Gillet also lists among Joyce's enthusiasms Auber's *La Muette de Portici,* and Halévy's *La Juive* (which John Sullivan sang in either 1930 or 1931 in Paris).[168]

For nearly a decade, from late 1929 to 1937, much of Joyce's opera experience in Paris seems to have been associated with the Irish-French tenor John Sullivan. Sylvia Beach reports that Joyce attended the Opéra for every performance of *William Tell* or *Les Huguenots* when Sullivan sang,[169] and as Sullivan was a regular member of the company at the Palais Garnier, Joyce was probably regularly in attendance during his "Sullivan period." His letters indicate that he heard four or five performances of *Tell* in a month's time in 1930—all with Sullivan (*Letters 3,* 204–5). At most of these performances Joyce spent the third act, in which Sullivan had no part, in the foyer or the bar (*JJ* 620). Much as Joyce admired Sullivan's performance as Arnold, he loved *William Tell* also for those themes that paralleled *Ulysses:* the father's search for his son, the son's search for the father, and the powerful love of country.[170] An additional appeal probably lay in Rossini's use of three tenors in the opera.

In addition to performing in *Tell,* Sullivan also sang in 1929, with Joyce attending, *Tannhäuser,* Saint-Saëns's *Samson et Dalila,* and Berlioz's *La Damnation de Faust* (*JJ* 619–20). Another Sullivan performance Joyce attended was a 1934 production of Donizetti's *La favorita* (*Letters 3,* 306). All these appear in the *Wake,* of course.

During these eight years opera without Sullivan seemed to have little value for Joyce. Gillet, who met Joyce in 1931, recalls that the author went by train to Milan, Brussels, and Lyons to hear opera; it seems likely that he was also attending Sullivan performances on these occasions, for Sullivan was invited to sing *Tell* and *Tannhäuser* at La Scala between October 1930 and February 1931 and also to sing in Lyons. And in mid-January 1933 Joyce traveled to Rouen to hear Sullivan sing Reyer's *Sigurd* (*JJ* 663).

Joyce went at least twice to Rimsky-Korsakov's *Invisible City of Kitezh,* the second time with a bass named Zaporoyetz as Prince Yuri.[171] Joyce proclaimed this singer to be the emperor of *basse nobles,* comparable to Sullivan, who "was" (the tense is Joyce's) the king of tenors (*Letters 3,* 345). His interest in this role may also have related to the development of his son's bass voice. At this same period, while Giorgio was seeking to begin a broadcasting career in New York City, his father was busy sending him the music for appropriate bass parts. These included two selections that Joyce attempted to find from *La forza del destino* ("Del mondo i disinganni," a duet; and "Non imprecare, umiliati," a trio; *Letters 3,* 343). He also sent the bass aria "This is no time to dream" from *A Life for the Czar* (*Letters 3,* 343), the aria from the third act of *Kitezh* because Zaporoyetz had sung it "splendidly" (*Letters 1*, 358), an aria of Rodolfo in Puccini's *La bohème,* and an aria for Oroveso in Bellini's *Norma* (*Letters 3*, 346). In this he was carrying on a tradition of a decade, for as early as 8 April 1925, when Giorgio was only nineteen years old, Joyce had asked Robert McAlmon to send from London Holst's one-act opera *At the Boar's Head,* which had just been published (*Letters 3*, 118–19). Indeed, the opera had had its world premiere only on 16 February 1935, at the MacDowell Club in New York City, and its first European performance came on 3 April 1935, in Manchester. Joyce must have been watching opera reviews very attentively to respond so rapidly to Holst's new work. It is, however, one of the rare operas where the bass sings the lead—in this case, the role of Falstaff. Joyce even undertook to manage his son's opera attendance, for from the distance of Paris Joyce noted that Giorgio and his wife, Helen, had apparently enjoyed hearing Lauritz Melchior in *Siegfried* at the Metropolitan Opera, although he remarked on how seldom they attended the opera (*Letters 3*, 344–45). Given his love of opera, this must have seemed a reprimand.

Lucia's illness took the Joyces to Switzerland late in 1934 for her treatment by Carl Jung and later for her hospitalization at a sanatorium in Küsnacht. In late November Joyce, who had a long-standing interest in the plays of Gerhart Hauptmann, took the opportunity to attend Respighi's opera *The Sunken Bell,* based on a Hauptmann play (*Letters 3*, 331). He also wanted Lucia's cure to include opera, for at the end of December he sent her, at Küsnacht, a pair of tickets for a Zurich production of *The Magic Flute* (*Letters 3*, 337–38).

Even the Joyce family's stay-at-home socializing included opera. In July 1935 Sullivan and his wife visited the Joyces to play and sing an aria from Donizetti's *Il duca d'Alba* (*Letters 3*, 364–65). Joyce also used the new channels of radio and film to enrich his opera experiences; he listened to a radio broadcast of *La forza del destino* featuring Ezio Pinza, whom he praised as "pretty good" in an "above average" production, even though he felt Verdi's music to be best suited to a "prestidigitator or for little dancing bears" (*Letters 3*, 379–80). Joyce had never been particularly fond of this Verdi opera. In February 1935 he wrote to Giorgio and Helen that Italians found the work laughable (*Letters 1*, 358), adding that one prima donna who sang it had been nicknamed "La Valanga" ("the avalanche"—remembered in the *Wake* at 240.32 and 406.9).[172] He also recalled for Giorgio a film version of *The Lily of Killarney* that he had seen in London, full of anachronisms of dress and conduct, and perhaps worst of all, with a tenor cast in the baritone's part (*Letters 3*, 379–80). It was a memory at least four years old, for Joyce had last been in London in 1931.

Aside from spending time with Sullivan, Joyce associated with few professional singers in Paris, as compared with his days in Trieste. Musically speaking, Joyce's Paris friends had "almosted it," in Stephen Dedalus's phrase. Maria Jolas had studied for an operatic career in Berlin for a year and then for another five years in Paris; but she interrupted her plans when she married Eugene Jolas, whom she met through his brother, pianist Jacques Jolas.[173] Louis Gillet, whom Joyce knew from 1931 onward, had also trained his deep bass voice for the stage and then given it up for literature, although Joyce still detected in him an "operatic countenance" on occasion (*SL* 386–87). Ford Madox Ford was the son of Dr. Francis Hueffer, who was both a music critic (for London's *Times* in 1882) and a librettist of "elephantine" works.[174] He had collaborated with Alexander C. Mackenzie on the 1883 opera *Columba,* a work that has sunk without many traces, except for several possible allusions to it in *Finnegans Wake.* Even closer to Joyce, within his family circle, his son Giorgio studied voice "for five or six years,"[175] although not very intensively (*JJ* 611). He did, however, have occasional singing engagements in both France and the United States. Lucia also studied music in 1933 with August Suter's wife, who was a singer.[176]

When the approach of World War II and the prospect of German invasion forced the Joyces and the Jolases to leave Paris, they found little opera to divert them in Vichy France. Yet diversion they needed. The friends who had sustained them during the 1930s were scattered, some into the French Resistance, others into concentration camps, a few to America, and others to England or (as in the case of Ezra Pound) to Italy. The war itself brought frantic worry, not only about the threat of violent combat, but about the constrictions of a police state. Food, clothing, fuel, and travel were in short supply. In addition to suffering the pressure from the international conflict, the Joyces worried about Giorgio's military status and Lucia's worsening health. For the year from December 1939 to December 1940, when they finally left France for Switzerland, the Joyces had no opportunity to hear opera unless they could get it by radio or sing the arias with their friends.

It is thus little surprise that when Joyce, in Lausanne en route to Zurich in December 1940, met Jacques Mercanton, "joy dominated his misfortune and suffering" because he had been able to reserve tickets for a Zurich production of *La forza del destino.*[177] It may have been the last opera Joyce heard. Within four weeks he lay dead.

NOTES

1. See also the listing of Dublin theaters in Senn, "Dublin Theatres," 23–26. For the *Wake's* allusions to these works and to Tenducci, see the composer and singer lists in the present volume.

2. *Grove's* (1942), s.v. "Giordani, Tommaso."

3. *New Grove's Dictionary of Opera,* s.v. "Ireland."

4. *ODO,* s.v. "Kelly."

5. Stanford, *Pages from an Unwritten Diary,* 87–88.

6. Pearce, *Sims Reeves,* 142–45.

7. Timothy Martin suggests that these studies might be the group known as the "Wesendonck Lieder."

8. Stanford, 84.

9. Ibid., 88–89.

10. Fitzpatrick, *Dublin: A Historical and Topographical Account of the City,* 267.

11. Stanford, 85–86.

12. Ibid., 89.

13. Ibid., 92.

14. Ibid.

15. Ibid., 89.

16. Ibid., 91.

17. Ibid., 89, 91.

18. Joyce, *Letters 3:* 340, 344; Stanford, 287. Another of Greene's admirers was prima donna Pauline Viardot-Garcia.

19. Young Stanford would have been unaware that on one occasion in Dublin, conductor Luigi Arditi was so irritated by Mongini's drinking, eating, and talking too much before the performance that he bet the singer two bottles of champagne that he would be unable to sing without a "scrog" on his high notes. Arditi won (Arditi, *My Reminiscences,* 176–77).

20. Greene, *Charles Villiers Stanford,* 38; Klein, *Thirty Years,* 25, lists Christine Nilsson, Tietjens, Zélia Trebelli, Ilma di Murska, Pietro Mongini, Gardoni, Joseph-Amédée-Victor Capoul, Theodor Wachtel, Marie Marimon, Louis Agnesi, Charles Santley, A. J. Foli, and Carl Formes as at Her Majesty's in the 1870s. At Covent Garden the leading singers in the same period were Patti, Pauline Lucca, Sophia Scalchi, Enrico Tamberlik, Mario, Alessandro Bettini, Jean-Baptiste Faure, Antonio Cotogni, and Joseph-Dieudonné Tagliafico. Of these at least Scalchi, Mario, and Patti sang in Dublin, although Mario retired in 1871.

21. Shaw, *London Music in 1888–89,* 368–69. Shaw was not always so unkind to her. He described an 1879 production of *Rienzi* in which she appeared with Joseph Maas as the most outstanding opera production done in London, with the possible exception of a staging of *William Tell* by Augustus Harris in 1878 (Shaw, 108).

22. Mapleson, *The Mapleson Memoirs,* 100–101. Mapleson, the impresario at Drury Lane and Covent Garden from the 1860s through the 1880s, was frequently cavalier with his facts, but he had the advantage of knowing the Sinicos personally from business dealings and travel together. Klein, however, says that Clarice Sinico (born 1840) was the daughter of Giuseppe and his second wife (*Reign of Patti,* 6–7). In 1843 Giuseppe Sinico was listed on Adalina Patti's baptismal records as a professor of music from Venice, although he was in fact singing at the Madrid opera. His then wife, Rosa Monara Sinico, gave her birthplace as Cremona, Lombardy. Klein in the same passage describes Giuseppe/José as having later taught singing in London "for some years."

23. Bernard McGinley cites Clarice Sinico as one of the "ghosts" of "A Painful Case" and "The Dead" and suggests that Joyce took Emily Sinico's name from Clarice ("Annotating the Life in *Dubliners,*" 25–26). But see my comments on Amelia Sinico later in this chapter's "Dublin" section.

24. Rosenthal, *Two Centuries of Opera at Covent Garden,* 139; Stanford, 90. Hans von Bülow was the great Wagnerian conductor whose wife, Cosima Liszt von Bülow, became first Wagner's mistress and then his wife.

25. Mapleson, 126.

26. Foster, *History of the Philharmonic Society,* 285.

27. Foster, 285. Italian sources "Italianize" the name even further, to Campobelloni (*Dizionario enciclopedico universale della musica e dei musicisti,* s.v. "Sinico.")

28. Foster, 362.

29. Charles Santley, *Reminiscences of My Life,* 107. Santley wrongly gives Campobello's name as "*né* Campbell."

30. Shaw, *London Music in 1888–89,* 327.

31. Another possibility would be that, after her poor reception in London in 1890, Amelia Sinico joined her seventy-four-year-old father in Trieste for musical study and became associated with the Sinico music school managed by her cousin Giuseppe, Joyce's teacher.

32. On the complex relationships between Lee and the Shaw family, see Rosset's *Shaw of Dublin: the Formative Years,* which argues convincingly that Lee was the father of George Bernard Shaw and possibly of his sister, Elinor Agnes. See also Holroyd, *Bernard Shaw,* 1:24–27.

33. Shaw, *London Music in 1888–89,* 8–11.

34. Rosset, 46–47.

35. Brockway and Weinstock, *World of Opera,* 536.

36. Rosset, 107.

37. Ibid., 108.

38. Ibid., 228–29.

39. Ibid., 230.

40. Ibid.

41. Ibid., 231–32.

42. Shaw, *London Music in 1888–89,* 13.

43. Ibid., 20–21.

44. Rosset, 233–35.

45. Ibid., 235–36.

46. Letter from Shaw to Clara Leiser, in Leiser, *De Reszke,* 88–89. "A smallish boy" suggests that Shaw was perhaps five or six years old, at which time Mario would have been fifty-one or fifty-two. Mario retired in England in 1871, when Shaw was fifteen— hardly a "smallish boy" anymore. In straitened circumstances, Mario toured the United States with Adelina Patti, 1872–73, until he was sixty-three years old.

47. Brockway and Weinstock, 551–52, n. 2.

48. Marks, *They All Had Glamour,* 153. One is reminded of Joyce's claim that John Sullivan's singing restored Joyce's sight (*JJ,* 624).

49. Marks, 162.

50. *Grove's* (1942), s.v. "Parepa-Rosa."

51. Marks, 153.

52. Klein, *Thirty Years,* 48.

53. Ibid., 53.

54. Kuhe, *My Musical Recollections,* 331.

55. Shaw, *London Music in 1888–89,* 107–8.

56. Arditi, 316.

57. Foster, 384.

58. *Grove's* (1942), s.v. "Parepa-Rosa."

59. Loewenburg, *Annals of Opera,* col. 956.

60. Ibid.

61. The 1875 Carl Rosa production of *The Marriage of Figaro* was still being called "the best ever in the English language" by Hermann Klein in 1903. The cast included Charles Santley (Figaro), Campobello (Count Almaviva), Aynsley Cook (Bartolo), Charles Lyall (Antonio), Ostava Torriani (the Countess), Josephine Yorke (Chrubino), and Rose Hersee (Susanna). The public "crowded the house" (Klein, *Thirty Years,* 49).

62. *GDO,* s.v. "Carl Rosa Opera Company."

63. Shaw, *London Music in 1888–89,* 108. *The Star* had been founded in London in 1888 by T. P. O'Connor, who hired Shaw as music critic under the pen name "Corno di Bassetto," or basset horn, a variety of clarinet beloved of Mozart. Both the *ODO* and *CODO* state that Shaw wrote for *The Star* from 1880, but he himself gives the starting date as 1888. The confusion may arise from his obituary for Carl Rosa, which, although published in May 1889, comments on the productions from 1875 to Rosa's death.

64. Klein, *Thirty Years,* 50.

65. Ibid., 101.

66. Ibid., 90; Shaw, *London Music in 1888–89,* 108. Shaw termed Hauk's *Taming of the Shrew* "an excellent performance." Klein called Joseph Maas, in *Mignon,* "the best English stage tenor since Sims Reeves."

67. D. Pellegrino was born ca. 1845 in Italy. I have been unable to find further details about this work, whose title may have reinforced Stephen Dedalus's dream of "Mercedes" in *A Portrait of the Artist as a Young Man* (63–64, 66, 99). Joyce, of course, had been deeply impressed by the Mercedes in Dumas's 1844 novel *The Count of Monte Cristo.* Bizet's *Carmen* (1875), an opera Joyce loved dearly, includes a gypsy girl named Mercedes. The name seems to have been popular and glamorous.

68. Augustus Harris (1852–96) was the son of the Augustus Harris who was stage manager at Covent Garden 1853–73. The younger Harris had a varied experience in theater and opera, including fifteen years (1879–94) as the manager of Drury Lane, during which time he introduced German opera, conducted by Hans Richter, in 1882. At the time of Rosa's death Harris became simultaneously lessee and manager of the Theatre Royal, Drury Lane, manager of the Carl Rosa Opera Company, and impresario of the Royal Italian Opera Company at Covent Garden (Klein, *Thirty Years,* 265). He introduced opera in the original language to Covent Garden and brought such singers as Nellie Melba and the de Reszke brothers (Jean and Edouard) to London (*ODO,* s.v. "Harris").

69. Klein, *Thirty Years,* 141–42.

70. Ibid., 147.

71. Ibid., 146–47, 286.

72. Ibid., 47.
73. Kuhe, 332.
74. Shaw, *London Music in 1888–89,* 370.
75. Goossens, *Overture and Beginners,* 44–45.
76. Shaw, *London Music in 1888–89,* 366.
77. Ibid., 375.
78. Ibid., 371.
79. *GDO,* s.v. "Carl Rosa Opera Company."
80. Brockway and Weinstock, 632.
81. Klein, *Thirty Years,* 295.
82. Arditi, 308–9.
83. *GDO,* s.v. "Carl Rosa Opera Company."
84. Hughes, *The Joyce Book,* 62–67.
85. Beecham, *A Mingled Chime,* 238.
86. McCormack, *I Hear You Calling Me,* 2.
87. Adams, *Surface and Symbol,* 73.
88. Goossens, 27–28. *CODO,* s.v. "Goossens," states that Eugene Goossens II was also at various times conductor for the Carl Rosa, the Burns-Crotty, and the Moody-Manners companies.
89. P. Graves, "The Moody-Manners Partnership," 561.
90. Ibid., 563.
91. Ibid., 561.
92. Ibid., 560.
93. Ibid., 563.
94. *New Grove* (1980), s.v. "Moody, Fanny" and "Manners, Charles."
95. P. Graves, 563.
96. Shaw, *London Music in 1888–89,* 379.
97. Goossens, 38–39.
98. Rosenthal, 204–7, 234–39, 712–13, 720–21.
99. Byrne, *Silent Years,* 65. The time between "youthful days" and growing "older" was six years, from September 1898, when at sixteen and a half Joyce entered University College, to October 1904, when he left Dublin at age twenty-two and a half. There was a hiatus when Joyce was in Paris, December 1902 to April 1903. Timothy Martin suggests the preference for Wagner must have been based chiefly on hearing fragments from these operas in concert performances. Loewenberg's *Annals of Opera* (which lists chiefly first performances at each location) includes for Dublin only *The Flying Dutchman,* 9 August 1877, in Italian, and *Lohengrin,* 11 October 1875, also in Italian (apparently a road version of the London production of May 1875). Both these were before Joyce's birth. There is no indication whether either was ever repeated. *Annals of Opera* is a remarkably full book but not a complete record of opera. It lists not one of Giuseppe or Francesco Sinico's six operas, for instance, although several were performed not only in Trieste but also in other Italian cities. Further, it lists London premieres of opera that may, like *Lohengrin,* have traveled to Dublin:

Tannhaüser	Italian	Covent Garden	6 May 1876
	English	Her Majesty's	14 February 1882
Tristan und Isolde	English	Lyceum	3 February 1899

Meistersinger	Italian	Covent Garden	13 July 1889
	English	Garrick	22 January 1897
Walküre	English	Covent Garden	16 October 1895
	French	Covent Garden	13 June 1896
Siegfried	English	Coronet	31 October 1901
Ring cycle	German?	Her Majesty's	5–9 May 1882
	English	Covent Garden	27 January–1 February 1908
Parsifal	concert	Albert Hall	10 November 1884
	German	Covent Garden	2 February 1914
	English	Covent Garden	17 November 1919
	English	Manchester	12 January 1920

100. Curran, *James Joyce Remembered,* 42.

101. Altmann, *Kurzgefasstes Tonkünstler Lexikon,* s.v. "Palmieri." The Royal College of Music was founded by the Prince of Wales in 1882, the year of Joyce's birth, so when Palmieri joined the faculty, it was a young institution. Negotiations to merge the Royal College of Music (R.C.M.) with the Royal Academy of Music (R.A.M.) came to nothing.

102. Strong, *John McCormack,* 8.

103. McCormack, 2. McCormack's recording of "The Snowy-Breasted Pearl" is available on Murray Hill S-4359, Record 2b. McCormack, like Joyce, had to borrow money to pay the entrance fee for the Feis Ceoil and was the last entrant to qualify: fourteenth out of fourteen. Joyce was the twenty-second of twenty-two contestants (McCormack, 2; Strong, 9).

104. Ellmann, *JJ,* 152. Joyce's singing seems to have won universal praise, for Stanislaus recounts in his *Complete Dublin Diary* (27) that the whore Nellie praised it as the "f——n'est best voice she ever heard."

105. Ulick O'Connor, *The Joyce We Knew,* 42.

106. See Joyce Collection at Olin Memorial Library, Cornell University, item 61, for instance, described in Robert E. Scholes, *The Cornell Joyce Collection,* 27.

107. Timothy Martin, himself a singer, concurs on this point, adding, "It's *very* hard to sing *well* at sight; trained singers need to get a piece 'into' their voices" (to Ruth Bauerle, July 1994).

108. B. Maddox, *Nora,* 39.

109. Gilbert, *Reflections on James Joyce,* 74–75.

110. Kobbé, *Opera Singers: A Pictorial Souvenir,* s.v. "Nordica."

111. D. Caruso, *Enrico Caruso,* 79, 143.

112. McCormack, 17.

113. Taubman, *The Maestro,* 16.

114. Taubman, 38. Toscanini's repertory during this period included operas by Wagner, Meyerbeer, Verdi, Thomas, Rossini, Bizet, Puccini, Mascagni, Giordano, Donizetti, Bellini, Saint-Saëns, Boïto, Catalani, Lozzi, Mancinelli, Franchetti, Apolloni, Peccia, Cagnoni, Ponchielli, Gnaga, Leva, Catalani, Paer, Canti, and Leoncavallo.

115. Taubman, 77–78.

116. Brockway and Weinstock, 422, 624, 483; Loewenburg, cols. 562, 800, 887, 916, 978, 1182–83, 1369, 1382, 1440.

117. *Stiffelio* was performed in March 1994 by the Metropolitan Opera as "Verdi's Lost Opera." In 1850 it was unsuccessful when first presented; Verdi rewrote it several times, once as *Aroldo* and again as *Guglielmo Wellingrode.* The *ODO* says that "many" French and Italian operas had their premieres at Trieste (*ODO,* s.v. "Trieste").

118. Gillet, "The Living Joyce," 194.

119. *GDO,* s.v. "Trieste." *GDO* also lists two men as writing for Triestine newspapers at the time of these Wagner performances: Ettore Schmitz (Italo Svevo), who then used the pen name Ernest Samigli; and Ferruccio Busoni, who signed his pieces with the anagram Bruno Fioresucci. They must have been serving as music critics, or there would be no reason for *GDO* to mention them. Both would later become Joyce's acquaintances. Schmitz, who when Joyce knew him was using the nom de plume "Italo Svevo," served as a model for Leopold Bloom.

120. Enrico Caruso Jr., *My Father and My Family,* 660–61.

121. LeMassena, *Galli-Curci's Life of Song,* 74–75. This soprano, known in opera lore for being almost always slightly flat, was not yet the star she became later as a result of her prolific recordings. Other engagements at the time included the August season at Ostend, the Dal Verme theater in Milan (with Tito Schipa in *La sonnambula*), and the Teatro Massimo Bellini in Catania (seven performances of *I puritani,* also in August).

122. Ibid., 59.

123. B. Maddox, 308.

124. Beach, *Shakespeare and Company,* 187–88.

125. Joyce to Emma Cuzzi, a former student, 7 December 1915, *Letters 2,* 370. Also to Nora Barnacle, 25(?) October 1909, 27 October 1909, 1 November 1909, and 24 December 1909, and to Lucia, 27 April 1935, all in *Selected Letters,* 173, 174, 176, 195, 373.

126. *JJ,* 347. The opera's Italian premiere had been at Rome in June, 1911.

127. James Joyce, "Oscar Wilde: The Poet of *Salomé*," 201–5.

128. Curran, 72.

129. Martin, *Joyce and Wagner,* 16.

130. Beach, 188.

131. Strong, 40.

132. B. Maddox, 61. Maddox gives no source for this.

133. L. Svevo, *Memoir of Italo Svevo,* 14.

134. I. Svevo (Ettore Schmitz), *James Joyce,* 152.

135. B. Maddox, 131.

136. Césari, "I Sinico," 187–97. The information about the Sinicos in the text that follows is drawn from this article, unless otherwise noted.

137. Cone, *Adelina Patti,* 11–12; Klein, *Reign of Patti,* 8.

138. Klein, *Reign of Patti,* 6–7.

139. Clarice Sinico's first husband could have been Giuseppe's son, rather than Giuseppe himself. Giuseppe's return to Trieste so soon after her 1874 remarriage to Henry McLean Martin (Enrico Campobello), however, suggests that it was Giuseppe she divorced.

140. Césari, 197. Césari emphasizes the sweetness of Lidia Sinico-Hermet's voice, repeating the phrase, in quotation marks, twice in a short paragraph, as if it were a verity of Triestine life.

141. *JJ* 269; *Letters 2,* 260, 262, 263, 267, 280, 283, 300. Many of these references to Bartoli in Joyce's letters are concerned with Bartoli's English lessons or with payments from him to Stanislaus, suggesting that his payment was not entirely through trading of English for music lessons. Bartoli was also a conductor, sometimes at the Trieste opera, including a November 1909 performance there of Donizetti's *L'elisir d'amore* (*Letters 2,* 260).

142. Otto Luening describes Zurich in 1917 as a city of about 200,000, "the cultural capital of the world" during the war (Luening, *Odyssey,* 120). See also Dent, *Ferruccio Busoni,* 228.

143. Lernout, "Woman the Inspirer," 1–11.

144. Borach, "Conversations with Joyce," 71.

145. The most profound study of this important area of Joyce's work is Timothy Martin's *Joyce and Wagner,* invaluable for understanding the centrality of Wagner in theory, structure, and technique throughout Joyce's writing.

146. Martin and Bauerle, "A Voice from the Prompt Box," 42.

147. Luening, 181. Elsewhere Luening remarks on Busoni's "impressive" ability to work in different styles—including a parody of an Italian operatic quartet—without losing his own identity (168).

148. Ibid., 174.

149. Ibid., 192; Martin and Bauerle, 42.

150. Loewenburg, col. 1350.

151. Luening, 129, 144.

152. Ibid., 192.

153. Ibid., 192–93. *JJ,* 393, mentions Joyce's and Giorgio's alternating at singing Verdi's "Addio! del passato bei sogni ridenti," from *La traviata,* and Joyce's singing Massenet's "Pourquoi me réveiller, O souffle du printemps," from *Werther.*

154. Luening, 143.

155. Ibid., 157.

156. Ibid., 158.

157. Quoted in Martin and Bauerle, 43.

158. *SL* 252. The production's star was to be an Italian tenor identified in the notes as "Bassi." Victor Gollancz (*Journey toward Music,* 87, 154) mentions an Amadeo Bassi (titled "Commendatore") as singing Dick Johnson in *La fanciulla del west*'s London premiere in May 1911 and *Sigfrido* in Florence in 1926. Given Joyce's handwriting, however, this might be a transcription error for Alessandro Bonci (1870–1940), a leading Italian tenor of his generation considered to be a rival of Caruso. He retired in 1925. Joyce in late 1920 named Bonci as the only Italian tenor who might surpass McCormack in phrasing and breath control (*Letters 3,* 32).

159. Lehmann, *Midway in My Song,* 167.

160. Pitou, *The Paris Opera,* appendix; Loewenburg, col. 1245.

161. Timothy Martin comments that after English, the *Wake*'s most important languages are those of opera. Regrettably, there has not yet been either a French or an Italian lexicon, and the late Brendan O Hehir's *Polyglossary to "Finnegans Wake"* has been delayed by his untimely death.

162. Loewenburg, col. 1274.

163. Labat-Poussin, *Archives du Théâtre National de l'Opéra,* 452–57.

164. McCormack, 92.
165. Ledbetter, *The Great Irish Tenor,* 153.
166. Power, *Conversations with James Joyce,* 108.
167. Antheil, *Bad Boy of Music,* 153.
168. Gillet, "Farewell to Joyce," 168.
169. Beach, 188.
170. Colum and Colum, *Our Friend James Joyce,* 173.
171. Joyce's letter to Giorgio and Helen Joyce describing this performance of *Kitezh* is dated 19 February 1935. Loewenburg says the opera was performed in Paris in concert form at the Opéra on 7 July 1926, staged at the Théâtre des Champs-Elysées on 19 February 1929, and staged again at the Opéra-Comique on 6 March 1935. The latter date would have been several weeks after the date of Joyce's letter. Either the letter is misdated, or Loewenburg errs. I have been unable to identify the bass Zaporoyetz. The *GDO* lists, s.v. "Rimsky-Korsakov," the opera *Zaporozhets za Dunayem* ("A cossack beyond the Danube"). The singer's name may have been a nickname given by the press or by Joyce or a stage name, meaning "cossack." Or it may be faulty transliteration by Joyce or the press of a Russian name.
172. Professors Antonio Cobalti, of the University of Trieste, and Kathryn Feldman, of Nassau Community College, have ascertained that "La Valanga" is not Triestine dialect. This suggests that Joyce may have heard "The Avalanche" sing during his time in Rome in 1906–7.
173. McAlmon and Boyle, *Being Geniuses Together,* 269n.
174. Klein, *Thirty Years,* 132, 148. Hueffer was also an influential Wagnerite, author of *Richard Wagner and the Music of the Future: History and Aesthetics* (London, 1874) and translator of *Correspondence of Wagner and Liszt* (London: H. Grevel, 1888). On his role in the Wagner movement in England, see Martin, *Joyce and Wagner,* 9–10.
175. James Joyce to John McCormack, as quoted in John Scarry, "James Joyce and John McCormack," 535.
176. Suter, "Some Reminiscences of James Joyce," 64–65; *Letters 3,* 294.
177. Mercanton, "The Hours of James Joyce," 248.

· 3 ·

Which Brilliant Career?

In the dazzling light from his accomplishments as a writer, it is easy to view Joyce's choice of a literary career as inevitable. To his wife and his father the choice had no such aura of predestination (*JJ* 169, 611). Nor did it seem fated to Joyce himself at all times, for music was his more natural skill. Explaining to his brother Stanislaus in 1904 why he worked on his novel daily, he asserted that he wanted literary style to become "as easy to him as singing" (*CDD* 52). He studied with at least four singing teachers: two in Dublin and two in Trieste. In 1905 he had fixed intentions of a career in the theater (*Letters 2*, 91), but he changed course, although continuing his voice lessons for a time. Nonetheless, near the end of his life he remarked sadly to Jacques Mercanton, "I could have made a fortune with my voice. And what have I done?"[1] Between youthful intent and middle-aged regret lay a number of missed opportunities as a singer, for his was a voice that impressed everyone who heard him sing, from Nora Barnacle, Luigi Denza, and John McCormack in 1904 to Otto Luening at the English Players in 1918 or Maria Jolas and Ada Macleish in Paris. The acerbic Stanislaus, Padraic and Mary Colum, and Nellie the whore from Nighttown[2] united in praising this voice that stopped people in the street in Trieste in 1907 and brought offers of auditions from Charlotte Sauermann in Zurich in 1918 and of jobs from Tom Rochford in Dublin in 1912 (*Letters 2*, 305). Every teacher with whom Joyce studied thought he could and should sing professionally. During all these years, as Joyce's singing was being praised, his writing was succeeding only against great difficulties. And still he wrote.

When Joyce refused to attempt the sight-reading test at the Feis Ceoil in 1904, acquaintances alleged that he did not know how to read music. This was no permanent obstacle: he could have learned to do so—and probably did. It would not even have been a temporary obstacle, for Renata Tebaldi, Ezio Pinza, and Luciano Pavarotti all achieved success as singers without being able to read music.[3] Joyce apparently had nearly as much musical training as John McCormack. The "Great Irish Tenor" had a winter and spring of study with Vincent O'Brien in Dublin, plus occasional help thereafter. The next year Joyce had a spring and summer of lessons with O'Brien and Benedetto Palmieri. In Italy Joyce began studying music even *before* McCormack did so; for although Richard Ellmann states that McCormack's Feis performance had won him a scholarship to study in Italy (*JJ* 151), McCormack was actually in Dublin in 1903–4, singing in O'Brien's choir but also urging Joyce to enter the Feis. During the summer of 1904 McCormack went to the United States to sing at the Irish exhibit in the St. Louis World's Fair. When he returned to Dublin he gave some concerts to raise money (assisted by Lily Foley McCormack's family in selling tickets and promoting the events), and with the concert proceeds he went to Italy to study with Vincenzo Sabatini sometime in 1905.[4] By Lily's account, he had four or five months of instruction in the spring of 1905 and another few months that fall before his Savona debut on 13 January 1906. L. A. G. Strong and Gordon Ledbetter, depending on McCormack's memory, both date his arrival in Milan as the autumn of 1905, leaving a scant four months of instruction before the debut.[5]

The reasons for Joyce's failure to pursue music were probably more realistic and, in some instances, more prosaic than a mere lack of opportunity or training. Although he loved the show and spectacle of the musical world (especially opera),[6] he was close enough to it to understand its heavy physical and emotional demands on singers. Practice required long hours and constant repetition of effort. Travel was frequent and difficult. Rehearsals and performances were long and fatiguing. Even after one conquered those drawbacks, success depended not only on one's own talent and effort but also on those of other singers, the conductor, the orchestra, and the impresario. In Trieste Joyce doubtless learned, too, of the common practice of Italian opera managers, who hired claques to jeer their own singers so as to be able to invoke a contract clause to lower the artist's pay if the public disapproved the performance.[7]

Joyce was psychologically ill-suited for singing opera, as he doubtless knew. He was essentially a solitary worker, except for needing secretarial or research help. He might dictate to a companion, but he was never, as he would have been in opera, dictated to by a director, a composer, or a fellow-performer. Furthermore, when one of his books succeeded (and Joyce always saw it as a question of when, not whether, success would come), the achievement was his. On an opera stage there were starring roles, and he might soon become a primo tenore, but there would always be with him a prima donna, a basso nobile, another singer or group of singers. A further consideration was that, special though his voice was, the number of starring roles open for a "light Italian" voice (as Luening described it) would have been as limited as they were for McCormack; these were beautiful tenors, but not heroic or dramatic voices.

A further consideration would have been opera's very quality of chance, of miscues, of happy—and unhappy—accidents that Joyce so enjoyed as a spectator. Were he on stage, trying to sing his best, how would he have reacted to an insertion of an aria from another composer simply because a colleague enjoyed the applause it brought her? Would he have tolerated the intrusion of an anticlaque hired by a competitor or the manager? Would he have put up with being booed at, rather than being part of the booing audience? Just as an opera singer's work and successes are public and involved with a group, so that singer's failures are highly public.

In his ventures into theatrical work, Joyce showed himself to be less an actor within an ensemble than a director. With the English Players he was voice coach, director, or prompter, but in Luening's term, "always in charge." With Augustus Milner in Zurich or John Sullivan in Paris, he became again a manager of a career rather than the star performer. Even in the family, as he encouraged his son, Giorgio, to seek a singing career, Joyce was involved as manager: suggesting songs, getting arrangements, and securing introductions.

For himself, Joyce might have avoided some of the problems of ensemble playing by restricting his work to the concert platform, where McCormack had some of his greatest success, drawing as many as 7,000 to a single recital in New York's Hippodrome or filling the Albert Hall. Concert fame came to McCormack after his stunning opera successes, however, and partly because of them.

To achieve even concert success, however, would have required hard work of a kind for which Joyce showed little stomach. As a writer he worked hard and steadily, often hours daily. Except for the time spent on rewriting and revising, a writer starts anew with each sentence or paragraph. A musician, on the other hand, goes over and over the same scales and exercises, even after achieving success. And the best work, the work that brings fame, is repeated almost as often as the scales: did John McCormack tire of "Mother Machree"? Did Jussi Björling want to forget "La donna è mobile"? Would Placido Domingo like to erase "Granada"? Yet the soloist must make each of these, even after hundreds of performances, "the seim anew" (*FW* 215.23).

Writing is not only a more solitary and individual art than singing. It also offered more range to Joyce's subtle genius. A singer interprets another's creation. A writer creates his own art for others to interpret, and for Joyce that art was complex, wide ranging, allusive, rich, and varied.

Even supposing that Joyce had sought a career on the stage in 1905, however, and had succeeded as well as McCormack had, he would have known that he would have less lasting effect on the world's musical arts than he could have had as writer on the literary scene. True, any writer speaks to readers singly, one book, one reader. The single instances must be multiplied into hundreds and thousands. There are rarely—except at an international Bloomsday extravaganza—seven thousand readers at once. But in thousands of rooms, in a thousand places, over hundreds of years, a *Ulysses* could speak to as many people as ever McCormack did.

McCormack could be—and was—paid $500,000 for a single film, *Song o' My Heart* (1929). What remains after six or seven decades is a very fine voice in a very poor and hard-to-find videotape. The warmth and spontaneity of McCormack's smile once reached thousands in an instant, as his voice over radio could reach millions. Now both are memories. But Joyce's smile plays over every page of *Ulysses* and *Finnegans Wake* still. Joyce elected long-range fame and influence over present unimaginable wealth.

A small and prosaic reason probably also influenced Joyce's choice. Although he considered singing to be a supreme art, he also viewed a musical career initially as a potential financial salvation: to win the Feis in 1904 meant a possible ticket out of Ireland to study in Italy. To become a singer in an Italy with scores of opera houses meant a possibility of steady work for pay, as his Trieste friends the Francinis had suggested. By the time he reached Zurich, however, Joyce had new kinds of financial support: some small income from his books; a grant from England's Royal Literary Fund; money from Nora's uncle, Michael Healy; and a generous subvention from Edith Rockefeller McCormick (*JJ* 390, 392, 422). There was no need to sing for his own or anyone else's supper.

NOTES

1. Mercanton, "The Hours of James Joyce," 226.
2. *CDD,* 27.
3. *Pavarotti and the Italian Tenor.*
4. Lily McCormack says that John went to Italy "early in 1905," spent a brief summer vacation in Dublin, returned to Milan in late September 1905, and made his debut in Savona on 13 January 1906 (McCormack, 13–15). Neither she, Strong, nor Ledbetter mentions any scholarship help for McCormack or indicates that he was studying in Italy by 1904; see *JJ* 151.
5. Strong says that McCormack went to Italy in October 1905 (26). Ledbetter says that his 13 January 1906 debut came after "three months' tuition with Sabatini" (45).

6. See, for instance, the comments of Philippe Soupault, "James Joyce," 113; C. P. Curran, *James Joyce Remembered*, 90; and the memories of both Maria Jolas and Carola Giedion-Welcker in Kain, "An Interview with Carola Giedion-Welcker and Maria Jolas," 101.

7. Slezak, *What Time's the Next Swan?* 34–35. The clause was titled "Il protesto del Pubblico o del Maestro" and provided that if either the maestro or the public disapproved of the singer, the manager could cancel the contract. In practice, rather than cancel, the manager would lower the pay because of the claque's booing. As Enrico Caruso put it to Leo Slezak about 1909, explaining why he refused to sing in Italy, "Essere un cantante in Italia è una vergogna" (to be a singer in Italy is a disgrace).

· 4 ·

Two Shems and Two Shauns

The axial poles of Joyce's opera world in his Paris decades were Shem/James and Shaun/John: James Joyce and John McCormack in the 1920s as the good Shem and the evil Shaun; Giacomo/James Lauri-Volpi and John Sullivan in the 1930s as the dark side of Shem and the brightness of Shaun. However certain Joyce was that his own vocation was to write, he followed John McCormack's singing career with an interest that seemed, to his acute publisher, Sylvia Beach, "infatuation."[1] He collected—and persuaded her and Harriet Shaw Weaver, his English benefactor, to collect—McCormack records, and they were many, for McCormack "arrived when everybody had a gramophone and nobody a radio."[2] As it happened, McCormack, too, was fond of his own recordings, especially in retirement, and would remark after playing them, "I was a damned good singer, wasn't I?"[3] He was less successful as an opera singer than as a recitalist and recording artist, for on stage his acting was stiff and his voice not always able to compete with the accompanying orchestra.[4] Like Joyce, however, Mc-Cormack felt the music itself passionately; and when he played Don Ottavio in *Don Giovanni* (his favorite role), he would remain in the wings to hear the other singers rather than return to his dressing room, because he loved the opera.[5]

Joyce kept track of McCormack's development and attempted to maintain contact with the singer when he appeared in Paris. There was good reason for Joyce to feel a kinship with McCormack, who had early encouraged his own singing, shared a concert platform with him, studied music in Italy at the same time Joyce did, and spoke Italian (the only language in which they conversed after 1920).[6] Another connection was Joyce's closest friend from University College days, J. F. Byrne, who had been a schoolmate of McCormack's broth-er-in-law.[7] As Joyce indicated in presenting Shem and Shaun as twins in *Finnegans Wake,* he and McCormack were much alike: both had been stars at school and urged to consider the priesthood; both had studied with Dublin's Vincent O'Brien and been highly praised by singing judge Luigi Denza; both came from families where singing was frequent and spontaneous; and both taught their children opera arias.[8] They loved and sang the same wonderful medley of opera songs and parlor music: "Then You'll Remember Me," *Don Giovanni,* "In her simplicity," "There is a flower that bloometh," "Love's Old Sweet Song," "I'll sing thee songs of Araby," and *Carmen.* Moreover, they had common musical acquaintances. McCormack toured with Ferruccio Busoni in England in 1908–9; Joyce knew Busoni in Zurich in 1918.[9] Both Joyce and McCormack left Ireland to make their careers elsewhere, and both made those careers with the help of patrons. McCormack returned to Ireland to live in the 1930s and to die in 1945.[10] Joyce returned three times in 1909 and 1912, but never thereafter. Yet each man in his own way sang about Ireland all his life. Each was superstitious (McCormack believed the fifteenth of the month to be his lucky day).[11] Ireland attempted to honor both men when they achieved eminence; McCormack was made a freeman of the city of Dublin in 1923, an honorary doctor of music by the National University in Dublin 1927, and vice president of the Royal Irish Academy of Music in 1931.[12] Joyce was invited to join the Academy of Irish Letters but refused.[13] His other honors from his country came only after death.

Both were gregarious (although McCormack was more open with strangers and casual acquaintances than Joyce could ever be). Both loved material comfort and were openhanded with money; McCormack, however, had a horror of borrowing, or of failure to repay.[14] Each was generous to others. In a famous incident, when T. S. Eliot and Wyndham Lewis brought Ezra Pound's parcel of used clothes and secondhand brogues to Paris for the reportedly impecunious Joyce, they were surprised to be taken to dine at an expensive restaurant and to have Joyce (always in charge, as he had been with the English Players) pay for their taxis, tipping cabbie and waiter generously (*JJ* 492–94). McCormack was equally easy about spending. In 1917, the year Joyce published *A Portrait of the Artist as a Young Man,* McCormack became a collector of art (Corot, Rodin, Cuyp, Rembrandt, and others) and violins (both a Stradivarius and a Guarnerius—although he could scarcely play).[15] In 1922, the year Joyce published *Ulysses,* McCormack's stateroom on the voyage from Ireland to New York included a sitting room with a piano.[16] His many homes, always handsome and increasingly spacious, were constantly filled with guests: San Patrizio (in Hollywood); Rocklea (on Connecticut's shore); the Park Avenue apartment in New York; Alton House in London's Hampstead, with a separate wing for the ballroom and billiard room; and Moore Abbey, near Ireland's Curragh—roughly the size of the White House. Guests at Rocklea were shown McCormack's farm (managed by his brother) or taken to New York City for the evening on the McCormack yacht. (The first yacht, the "Macushla," was forty feet long; the second, "Pal O' Mine," was larger.) Moore Abbey being so near the Curragh, there was also a stable of racehorses. In New York, as part of the city's social whirl, the McCormacks arranged their daughter Gwen's debut: dinner at the Park Avenue apartment for about fifty persons, followed by a ball at the Ritz Crystal Room.[17]

All this was paid for by hard work: tours of Australia, Japan, South Africa, the United States, and Europe. Between 15 February and 31 March 1912, for instance, McCormack gave concerts in twenty cities.[18] Travel was by train, often immediately after a concert, sometimes arriving with only enough time to change before singing. Even when not on tour, McCormack moved almost as much as Joyce. In the four decades from 1905 to 1945 he had nineteen homes, not including hotel stays.[19] Almost never did the McCormacks stay for the full length of any lease.

Joyce too was a hard worker, but he was not paid nearly so well. During one thirteen-year period McCormack grossed thirteen million dollars, more than a third from performance fees. In 1918 he made $180,000 from recordings alone, and his total recording income reached several million dollars. At the time income tax in the United States was very small, and millionaires were relatively few.[20] A singing millionaire was a rarity indeed.

It was a rewarding life, but not easy. By 1930 or 1932 McCormack recognized that his voice was diminishing. He continued singing for a while, making his farewell tour of the United States in 1937 and his farewell in England in 1938. When World War II erupted, he came out of retirement to sing concerts in England for the Red Cross. He died of emphysema at his home near Dublin in 1945 at age sixty-one, having become the first international multimedia star of opera, concert stage, recordings, radio, and film. He was even, like Leopold Bloom, a rather marginal salesman, lending his name and photograph to tobacco advertisements and to sheet music covers reading "As sung by John McCormack."

However alike they may have seemed in externals of vocal quality, age, and nationality, Joyce and McCormack had profound differences. Physically Joyce was an ideal example of the ectomorph; McCormack seems to have been about equal parts mesomorph (as an avid tennis and cricket player) and endomorph (explaining a girth that Joyce found comic). Joyce's was a subtle mind, acutely tuned to fine distinctions of gray, alert to every detail around him. McCormack was described by a friend as living in "brilliant colors," with a quick and vio-

John McCormack was a multimedia star whose name sold music and movie tickets, as well as concert seats. This cover from a song in McCormack's 1930 movie *Song o' My Heart* also shows actress Maureen O'Hara in her first film role.

lent temper coupled with a warm friendliness.[21] Joyce was often ill and in pain, so smiling photographs of him are rare; of McCormack they are common.

"What is your father?" Nasty Roche asks Stephen in *A Portrait of the Artist as a Young Man*. And Stephen can at least answer, "A gentleman" (*P* 9). Although John Joyce had fallen in the world, James Joyce, too, could have given that answer; McCormack's father, however, had begun as a laborer and rose to foreman in the Athlone Woolen Mills. McCormack was educated at a Marist Brothers school; Joyce, by Jesuits. The religious instruction of the Marists had a lasting effect, making of the singer not only a devout Christian but a pious Catholic who took seriously the title of papal count given him in 1928 and signed his Christmas cards "John Count McCormack."[22] Although the Jesuits left ineradicable impressions on young Joyce's mind, he could use a nursery rhyme title, "The House That Jack Built," to refer to the Catholic Church (*U* 14.304–5) and parody the mass repeatedly, as at *U* 14.277–312. McCormack had enough worldly experience in the theater to accept the Joyces' then unconventional marriage; he had a harder time accepting the writer's attitudes toward Rome, and at their 1920 meeting he urged Joyce to "get straight with the Church," a bit of preaching that probably irritated Joyce.[23]

McCormack's piety was only strengthened after that 1920 meeting with Joyce, for in April 1922 the singer was stricken with a life-threatening streptococcus infection. He had been given last rites, and the press had gathered for the deathwatch, when Archbishop Patrick Joseph Hayes called and placed in the hands of the unconscious singer what he asserted to be a fragment of Christ's cross. McCormack's fever began dropping at once, and the illness seemed to be conquered from that moment.[24] Both John and Lily McCormack felt that he had been saved by divine intervention. Such piety may have given Joyce pause, but the reputation of Joyce's *Ulysses* after the suppression of the *Little Review* for its publication of the "Nausicaa" episode doubtless made McCormack equally uneasy.

McCormack was also more conventionally patriotic than Joyce, giving concerts that so helped the Allied cause in World War I that France made the tenor a chevalier of the Legion of Honor: he had raised a half-million dollars for the American Liberty Bond drive. (As a biographer points out, McCormack early in his career sang a number of Irish rebel songs, but their occurrence in his programs and recordings fell off after about 1907—the point at which McCormack began to be recognized in the London musical world.)[25] McCormack also made some ripples in the larger world of finance. On New Year's Day 1925 he and soprano Lucrezia Bori made the first celebrity radio broadcast. The radio company's stock rose fourteen points the next day. He edged near politics, too, cruising with Woodrow Wilson on the presidential yacht and in December 1926 appearing as a character witness for Edward L. Doheny, the California oilman accused of bribery in the Teapot Dome scandal of the Harding administration.[26]

Both Irishmen found worldwide fame, although Joyce's came more slowly. Joyce may well have envied some of McCormack's material wealth, although he seems to have had little interest in yachts, Hollywood, racing stables, or papal titles. But another area of inevitable comparison must have hurt Joyce deeply.

The McCormack and Joyce children were very close in age: Cyril McCormack was just three months older than Joyce's daughter, Lucia, and Gwen McCormack was one year younger. When McCormack sang in Paris in December 1920, Gwen, at Joyce's invitation, spent an afternoon with Lucia and found herself uncomfortable.[27] They did not become friends. Later Gwen's life was quite conventional, with a 1926 New York debut (possibly mentioned in the Paris editions of American newspapers), at a time when Lucia, beginning to show signs of the painful mental illness that was to dominate her life, was spending six hours daily practicing rather desperately for a career as dancer. Lucia's emotional balance was further disturbed in 1931 when Samuel Beckett gently detached himself from her. By 2 February 1932, when Lucia threw a chair at her mother and was briefly hospitalized in Paris, the seriousness of her illness was becoming evident. That same spring came her ill-conceived "engagement" to Alex Ponisovsky, followed by a worsening of her illness. Gwen McCormack's well-publicized marriage before two thousand guests in Brompton Oratory, London, in September 1933[28] must have contrasted with the seriousness of Lucia's illness and the growing bleakness of her future.[29]

One of the greatest disparities in Joyce's mind must have been artistic. He and his family liked to remind friends that he had once sung on the same platform with John McCormack. McCormack could easily have reversed the boast: he had once sung on the same platform with the author of *Ulysses*. But the Great Irish Tenor could add that he had shared opera and concert stages with Enrico Caruso, Nellie Melba, Luisa Tetrazzini, Mario Sammarco, Frances Alda, Mary Garden, and Lucrezia Bori. True, Melba would not allow him to take a bow with her, saying, "In this house, nobody takes bows with Melba."[30] That would have been atoned for by the praise of Jean de Reszke, who wrote after hearing McCormack in Monte Carlo, "Bravo, a thousand times Bravo for your *Alma Viva* [*sic*]. You are the true redeemer of Bel Canto."[31] In terms of artistry, fame, financial success, and family happiness, then, McCormack must have seemed to Joyce, repeatedly, the "might he mighthavebeen" (*FW* 52.29).

If Joyce and McCormack were Shem and Shaun, John Sullivan and Giacomo Lauri-Volpi were Shaun and Shem, affording the reversal of roles pointed out by Adaline Glasheen.[32] Most sources agree that Joyce first heard of John Sullivan from Stanislaus, who met the tenor in Trieste and wrote to his brother recommending Sullivan's singing. Stanislaus also recommended to Sullivan (who had been reading *A Portrait of the Artist* when they met) that when the singer returned to Paris, he should call on James (*JJ* 619).[33]

It has been suggested that James Joyce's promotion of Sullivan's singing career was motivated by a desire to surpass McCormack, at least in surrogate fashion.[34] Joyce and McCormack had been in intermittent contact since 1920—Joyce attending McCormack's Paris recitals and urging others to do likewise. He even reminded Harriet Weaver that McCormack would be singing in London in May 1928 (doubtless hoping that she would attend). In 1929 McCormack had made his first film, although it was not released then. Also in that year McCormack had sung "Panis Angelicus" at a mass in Cormack's Chapel on the Rock of Cashel, "over people kneeling in prayer as far around as the eye could reach."[35] In late September he met Joyce in Paris and was given a copy of *Tales Told of Shem and Shaun*. Something may have passed between the two men that aroused Joyce's competitive sense, for in November he began his Sullivanitis in a burst of enthusiasm.[36] Nevertheless, in his letter to McCormack introducing Giorgio Joyce and asking assistance in the young man's singing career, Joyce expresses the hope that "the finest lyrical tenor in the world" still enchants audiences.[37] The genuineness of his admiration for McCormack is confirmed by a letter two weeks later, to Giorgio, in which Joyce notes that Beniamino Gigli's voice, although ampler, was "not so true" as McCormack's (*Letters 3*, 306). McCormack described Giorgio's voice as "a magnificent bass" and confided to his wife that the young Joyce was "another Chaliapin."[38] Had the author known the full impact made by Giorgio's voice on the reigning Irish tenor, the content of *Finnegans Wake* might have been markedly different.

Joyce's promotion of Sullivan eased to a stop in 1937, about the time of McCormack's retirement. By that time, too, *Ulysses* had been admitted to the United States, *Finnegans Wake* was almost completed, and Joyce's sense of his own place in literary history was secure. Sullivan was sixty-one years old, and probably even Joyce could no longer ignore the effects of time on a voice already past its prime when the Sullivan campaign began nearly a decade earlier.

The Sullivan campaign has puzzled Joyce scholars, as it baffled Joyce's friends, nearly all of whom were invited, entreated, commanded, urged, or cajoled into attending the opera when Sullivan was singing. Joyce even tried to summon the

Gormans from London to Paris for a performance to which he had extra tickets. Within the opera house Joyce's behavior was simply a carrying on of the fierce partisanship shown by opera audiences in Dublin and Trieste during his years in those cities. His "Bravo Cork!" and his shouted announcement that Sullivan's singing had restored his sight (*JJ* 624) were also within the tradition—the latter perhaps borrowed from the story of Euphrosyne Parepa-Rosa's giving hearing to a deaf man (see chap. 2). The extra tips to ushers so they would applaud Sullivan were also traditional—a quiet hiring of a claque. His decrying a rival from the audience by shouting "Merde pour Lauri-Volpi" (*JJ* 625) could also be attributed to traditional Irish enthusiasm.

Other parts of Joyce's Sullivan campaign are less traditional but within the patterns of his behavior elsewhere, as when Joyce arranged the recital by Augustus Milner in Zurich to aid that young singer's career. Now he would become Sullivan's impresario and attempt to sway those who could influence appointments: financier Otto Kahn, conductor Thomas Beecham, Lady Maud Cunard, Richard Guinness, and the chef d'orchestre at Zurich's Stadttheater.[39] He sought an Irish government grant, classing Sullivan with Caruso and Lauri-Volpi as a singer famous by his surname only (*Letters 3*, 207). He sent out nearly two dozen recordings of Sullivan singing *William Tell* only to try to recall them after discovering their poor quality (*Letters 3*, 221). He tried to persuade G. P. Putnam's publishing house to include Sullivan's picture in the next edition of the well-known Kobbé's *Complete Opera Book*.[40] He claimed to have won an engagement for Sullivan to sing in Dublin for £120, five times his Paris Opéra remuneration, suggesting that the lead tenor in *William Tell* was being paid only £24—($120 or FF2400) for a five-act opera (*SL* 350). Paris was inexpensive in the 1920s, but this scarcely sounds like adequate support for the eleven people dependent on Sullivan (*JJ* 620). Sullivan's income in the 1920s may have been reduced, as it had a decade earlier, by legal actions against him for bad debts, resulting in the garnisheeing of his Opéra pay. Opéra archives hold pages of legal papers, receipts, and letters concerning Sullivan's nonpayment of rent to at least three landlords.[41] Such debt-juggling would not have offended Joyce (unless the money were owed him); it might even have been quite usual among singers at the Opéra to have their creditors besiege the management about bad debts. The letters do suggest that when Joyce began writing the management to urge better roles for Sullivan, they had already heard of their tenor in a not altogether pleasant way.

Some elements of the Sullivan campaign may puzzle us because they seem to be not quite honorable. Sullivan was already fifty-one years old when Joyce began his crusade, a time when many singers' voices begin to fade. (Soprano Beverly Sills retired at fifty; McCormack began to lose vocal quality by forty-eight, probably the early effects of the emphysema that killed him.) Sullivan acknowledged to Richard Ellmann that his voice was past its prime when Joyce began to lobby on his behalf (*JJ* 698). Yet Joyce began representing other singers at the Opéra as "very old" to make Sullivan's age seem less, even adding more than twenty years to one singer in his thirties.[42] In 1930 Joyce went further by persuading William Bird to write an article for the *New York Sun* asserting falsely that the Boston Opera House had refused to hire Sullivan because of McCormack's jealousy (*JJ* 621). Equally puzzling is the fact that Joyce, having instigated such a lie about McCormack in 1930, would feel no compunction five years later in asking McCormack to aid the career of Giorgio Joyce.

Joyce also ignored the facts of Sullivan's career in what Stuart Gilbert called attacks of "Sullivanitis." Sullivan was hardly a failure, as Sylvia Beach pointed out: to be a leading tenor of the Paris Opéra is to be accounted a success.[43] And Sullivan had many major roles there, not only in *William Tell* but also in *Les Huguenots, Tannhäuser, Samson et Dalila, Il trovatore* (in both Italian and French),[44] *Boris Godunov, La Fille du far-west, Aïda, Les Troyens, Henri VIII, Roméo et Juliette, La Damnation de Faust, La favorita,* and *La Juive.* Apparently from 1912 to 1923 he had the role of Manrico in *Il trovatore* all to himself at Paris.[45]

Nevertheless, Sullivan had experienced some failures. Three years before Joyce's frantic efforts to interest Sir Thomas Beecham in hiring Sullivan for Covent Garden, Joyce's friend had already sung there, with disastrous results. He had been hired to perform Raoul in *Les Huguenots* and the title role in *Otello.* With King George V and Queen Mary in the audience, *Les Huguenots* proved to be "a crushing fiasco—and not least because of [Sullivan]."[46] The king and queen left early, followed by much of the audience. Those who remained booed loudly. The great critic Ernest Newman described the shambles as the kind of performance that made people regard opera as "just one damn sing after another."[47] The next day Sullivan's *Otello* contract was canceled, and the performance itself postponed for a full year. Joyce's only reference to this incident seems to be his explanation that Sullivan had told him the "Italian ring" had prevented his singing at Covent Garden (*JJ* 620). It was probably that *Huguenots* performance only a few years earlier that led the Covent Garden management "mysteriously" to cancel Sullivan's 1932 engagement there (*Letters 3,* 196 n. 3). Sullivan had also blamed the same "Italian ring" for preventing his appearing in Chicago, yet Sullivan did sing in that city in 1919–20, according to the *Oxford Dictionary of Opera.*

In trying to understand almost seventy years later just what kind of singer Sullivan was, one must depend on others' descriptions to supplement Joyce's. By saying little, these say much. Joyce reported that Beecham called Sullivan's tenor "the most amazing" of his experience (*Letters 3*, 203), an ambiguous evaluation that may be more tact than praise. "Amazing" could suggest an indescribably bad tenor as well as a superb one—especially if that tenor's distinguished patron is standing alongside pressing for a good opinion. French opera historian Spire Pitou, although identifying Sullivan in various casts at the Opéra, does not list him among the significant singers.[48] The *New Grove Dictionary of Opera* allots Sullivan only fourteen lines by Elizabeth Forbes (a biographer of Mario and Grisi), listing his roles and his dates of birth and death. (Forbes also asserts that he sang mostly under the name "Sullivan"—rather than O'Sullivan—before he ever met Joyce.) Henry Pleasants's *Great Singers* never mentions Sullivan. No singer in Lanfranco Rasponi's book *The Last Prima Donnas* mentions ever having sung with him, although many of them sang in Europe. Many, by contrast, remember Giacomo Lauri-Volpi, cast by Joyce in the role of opponent and villain. The most positive endorsement of Sullivan, aside from his long association with the Paris Opéra, was his selection by the eminent conductor Tullio Serafin for the cast of *William Tell* when that opera was revived at Naples's San Carlo Theatre in 1923, six years before Sullivan and Joyce met. Serafin was admired for his care in choosing singers, and baritone Tito Gobbi called him "an infallible judge of voice and character."[49] Sullivan, of course, was then only forty-five years old.

Most puzzling of all in evaluating Sullivan as a singer is Joyce's own praise. The novelist had studied voice and knew what was expected of a singer in breathing, diction, tone, agility, and resonance. Herman Klein's slender volume on bel canto technique was in Joyce's library, and Joyce had praised McCormack's phrasing. Yet in Sullivan he praises only high notes, endurance through all five uncut acts of a long opera, and volume, saying inexplicably to Victor Gollancz, "Don't you think the most important thing in a tenor is that he should sing *loud?*"[50] Still praising volume, he compared Sullivan's voice to the "Blessing of the Daggers" scene in *Les Huguenots,* act 4, which Sullivan explained to Ellmann as "a big noise in the fourth act" (*JJ* 620). The nearest approach to mentioning any more valuable quality is the claim that Sullivan's voice synthesized the "principal developments in the tenor tradition" and was a true "survivor" of the golden age of opera (*Letters 3*, 205, n. 6), but these were put forward by Joyce's friend Edgardo Carducci. Joyce himself generalized in calling Sullivan's instrument "incomparably the greatest human voice I have ever heard" (*SL* 351).

Sullivan's own reaction to Joyce's enthusiasm seems to have been embarrassment. He was after all somewhat older than Joyce, and far more experienced in the world of music, yet being advised how to challenge Lauri-Volpi through the newspapers or what to request of opera managers. Padraic and Mary Colum never heard Sullivan, whom they also knew in Paris, mention either Ireland or Joyce, nor did he express any awareness of Joyce's efforts on his behalf.[51] Joyce seemed to be aware of a kind of boorishness, himself describing the tenor to Harriet Shaw Weaver in 1930 as "intractable, quarrelsome, disconnected, contemptuous, inclined to be bullying, undiplomatic, but on the other hand good humoured, sociable, unaffected, amusing and well-informed" (*JJ* 620). To Giorgio Joyce, in June 1935, Joyce wrote of Sullivan as a "rascal" who boorishly "spit in the presence of women and . . . not only fails to pay his own debts but pays nobody anything" (*Letters 3,* 360). In both instances he was probably being ironic—perhaps even paraphrasing criticisms of Sullivan that he had heard in Paris. But if playful, it was rough play.

What of Giacomo Lauri-Volpi, the singer Joyce set up as Sullivan's enemy? Born in Rome in 1892, he made his debut (as Giacomo Rubini) in 1919 and continued as a professional singer until 1959, although he came out of retirement in 1972, at eighty, to sing "Nessun dorma" in a gala concert in Barcelona. When the Paris Opéra chose Sullivan to sing in a centennial production of *William Tell,* Milan's La Scala chose Lauri-Volpi. He sang in one opera at Covent Garden in 1925 and in three more in 1936—almost as brief a career there as Sullivan's. For a decade, 1923–33, he was a member of the Metropolitan Opera, where he sang in twenty-six operas, including Met premieres of *Turandot* and *Luisa Miller.* Like Sullivan he sang in *Il trovatore* and *Les Huguenots.* Harold Rosenthal, writing for the same *New Grove Dictionary of Opera* that merely lists repertory for Sullivan, commends Lauri-Volpi as having a "bright, ringing tone and beautiful legato," qualities that made him "one of the finest lyric-dramatic tenors" of his generation. Two days after Caruso's death in 1921, Lauri-Volpi was one of those tenors nominated by the press as "the new Caruso" (Gigli, Giovanni Martinelli, and Aureliano Pertile were among the others; the British press suggested Edward Johnson, Joseph Hislop, and McCormack).[52] Giulio Gatti-Casazza, the Italian impresario who managed the Metropolitan Opera from 1908 to 1935, praised Lauri-Volpi's singing in the 1926–27 revival of *Norma.*[53] Henry Pleasants in 1966 said that Lauri-Volpi had a voice "less beautiful than Gigli's, but with a persuasive sensual quality and an exultant top" that made his work in *Turandot* and *Andrea Chénier* "unforgettable."[54] Pleasants went on to credit Lauri-Volpi, Martinelli, and Gigli as giving Americans an extended "golden age of opera" in their great tenor roles. The greatest praise, however, came from Giacomo Puccini, who wrote the role of Calaf in his last opera, *Turandot,* with Lauri-Volpi in mind.

Lauri-Volpi was not invariably praised, however. Also speaking of his role as Chénier, Brockway and Weinstock call the soprano in that opera "unlucky" in being paired with him.[55] Arturo Toscanini feuded with him and refused even to consider casting him as Calaf after Puccini's death.[56] Several of those who sang with him complained of his habit of holding a high note in a duet far longer than the score indicated, and therefore longer than his partner. This made him look sensational and them deficient in breath control. Gertrud Grob-Prandl said that he stopped it after she proved that she could hold the note longer than he. Ines Alfani Tellini said that in a Rome production of *Faust,* Lauri-Volpi held his high note "beyond the point of decency." He was enraged at the next performance when she did the same. Adelaide Saraceni also beat him at this vocal arm-wrestling, with the same angry result.[57] During a tour by the La Scala company, Lauri-Volpi held the final note of "Di quella pira" in at least two performances, with Toscanini conducting, and this was apparently the cause of the maestro's lasting rage at the tenor.[58] But these singers also testify to his frequent kindness in performance and to the magnificence of his voice: "like an angel," "magnificent," "a big instrument . . . with a trumpet-like sound," "memorable," "flashes of magic," "riveting." Germana di Giulio said of him, "I have never known anyone who worked so seriously and with such love on his vocal production."[59] This is significant praise, coming from a group of women who often found themselves startled, on stage, to be in a kind of vocal gymkhana with their tenor partner. There is no comparable record of praise for Sullivan that I have been able to find.

One explanation of Joyce's obsession with the singing of both McCormack and Sullivan that has not yet been put forward derives from the erotic nature of the opera experience. The senses are stimulated first of all by the total setting: the auditorium, the crowd, the color and imagination of the costuming, and the general theatricality of the moment. The subject matter of the dramas also feeds erotic fantasy, with tales of love, misunderstanding, separation, disguise, reunion, sexual violation, revenge, injustice, and fallen women. (Fallen women were everywhere in nineteenth-century literature and opera. One of the original aspects of *Finnegans Wake* is that it is about a fallen man.) These themes are powerful even without music. The addition of human voices lifted in song and supported by an orchestra hugely magnifies opera's erotic effect. It is as if there were aural pheromones to affect the listener, provoking a deeply emotional response, for "a singer's voice sets up vibrations and resonances in the listener's body."[60] It is a "contagious" presence, and the listener's existence is "an aftereffect of . . . crescendo."[61]

Stanislaus Joyce suggested something of the sort when he described the young McCormack voice, let out *fortissimo,* as giving "a bang on the ear" (*CDD* 36). Joyce himself indicated an awareness of this response in Bloom's thought in

"Sirens" that "tenors get women by the score" (*U* 11.686)—not merely twenty at a time, as it has been interpreted,[62] but through the medium of the musical score from which they sing. Singer Luciano Pavarotti confirms it, listening to a tape of his predecessor Giuseppe di Stefano and smiling rather fondly as he reminisces that this was the singer who caused a fight between himself and his father, also a vocalist. The elder Pavarotti preferred Beniamino Gigli, on technical grounds; the younger Pavarotti favored di Stefano because there was in his pronunciation something—and here Pavarotti hesitates as he chooses the right word—"sexual."[63]

Victorians were great opera lovers all over Europe, but they did not much discuss eroticism—at least openly. Opera critics have continued the silence, for the most part, except for complaints even in the nineteenth century about divas who had grown too heavy for their romantic roles.[64] This Victorian repression was part of opera's allure for the premoderns: "The operatic voice pretends to be polite but is secretly stressed, huge, exorbitant . . . the furious 'I'-affirming blast of a body that refuses dilution or compromise. This . . . voice is the sound of nineteenth-century sexuality."[65] The opera voice, Wayne Koestenbaum argues, voyages from hiddenness into the world, expressing what is hidden.[66] At the same time that the voice emerges from the hidden, it enters into the hidden part of another self, and there it "exposes the listener's interior, . . . makes me a 'me' . . . by virtue of the fact that I have been entered."[67]

In his analysis of the erotic relationship between singer and audience, Koestenbaum focuses primarily on the responses of homosexual "opera queens." His insights are repeatedly relevant to Joyce's behavior, however, not because Joyce harbored homoerotic feelings toward Sullivan—there is no evidence that he did—but because the singer's voice roused generalized erotic feelings in the listening Joyce. The writer was in love, but with a voice, not a man. The opera aficionado who becomes devoted to a particular singer, Koestenbaum notes, has "reference points" and "a mission," a "timbre against which others would seem too full, too old, too ripe, too controlled."[68] Thus Joyce praised McCormack for having a voice like his own (and by implication, himself for having a voice like McCormack's). He singled out McCormack's phrasing as superior to all (except Bonci's). A McCormack weakness, however, was his lack of volume: one of his patrons urged that the Covent Garden orchestra be restrained so as not to overpower the tenor.[69] Changing his own reference points, Joyce found in Sullivan the sheer force of voice that McCormack—and Joyce himself—lacked.

Joyce's "infatuation" with McCormack and "obsession" with Sullivan also provided him an opportunity for the identification with a singer that Koestenbaum describes. Koestenbaum cites an opera fan who wrote in 1918 of the "sublime heights of ecstasy, generally with a sensual tinge," that he received from voices that sang in "the manner in which I would have wished to sing."[70] In *The Queen's Throat* Koestenbaum speaks also of the effect of high notes Joyce so loved, dominating the rest of the cast and the audience, as when Maria Callas in Mexico City gave forth an unexpected but dazzling high E-flat that thrilled her audience and left her tenor costar, Kurt Baum, furious.[71]

Koestenbaum makes a further point relevant to Joyce, that "opera serves as an erotic go-between: . . . I'm thrilled that . . . we are cohabiting the music."[72] In franker language, this repeats Joyce's urgent pleas to Nora in 1909 to see *Madame Butterfly,* his desire to be *with* her as they listen to that opera's beautiful "Un bel dì," and his sending her a telegram with the words from an aria in *Werther.* Shock has often followed scholars' attention to the grosser qualities of Joyce's 1909 letters to Nora; if we tune our ears aright, we can also hear the sweeter melodies of their passion.

Finally Koestenbaum explains the monomaniacal aspect of Joyce's Sullivanitis. When he fell in love with opera, Koestenbaum failed to find the companionship he expected among other lovers of the form, because each was so devoted to a given star as to be absolutely without any interest in discussing any other performer.[73] So Joyce with Sullivan, beside whom "Chaliapine [*sic*] is braggadocio and McCormick [*sic*] insignificant" (*SL* 351).

Against this background, then, we see that, obsessive as Joyce's behavior about McCormack and Sullivan may seem to those who are not also passionate opera devotees, it was fairly typical of the adoration lavished on a particular star, the sensual reaction to an individual voice, the erotic response to an evening of opera among thousands of other devout enthusiasts.

NOTES

1. Beach, *Shakespeare and Company,* 187. For basic studies of Joyce's relationship to and use of material about John McCormack, see items by John Scarry, Carole Brown, and Leo Knuth in the bibliography to this volume.

2. *Letters 3,* 118; Beach, 186; Pleasants, *The Great Singers,* 334. McCormack was one of the first singers to record, beginning with eight Edison cylinders in 1904, followed by another ten for which he was paid £50. In 1910 Victor paid £2,000 to get McCormack released from his Odeon contract two years early; he recorded for Victor from 1910 to 1938, being paid a $10,000 advance and 10 percent of the list price of the records (McCormack, *I Hear You Calling Me,* 11, 105).

3. Pleasants, 331.

4. Mordden, *Opera Anecdotes,* 168; G. O'Connor, *The Pursuit of Perfection,* 118; Ledbetter, *The Great Irish Tenor,* 49.

5. Strong, *John McCormack,* 71.

6. McCormack, 23. Lily McCormack also says that her husband always wrote to Joyce in Italian, although Joyce's notes to McCormack in the *Letters* are mostly in English.

7. Byrne, *Silent Years,* 6. Lily Foley McCormack's father owned a Dublin pub near what would become the Abbey Theatre. Byrne also recalls Lily acting at the Rotunda in *Little Red Riding Hood.* McCormack borrowed Lily's family name for his debut as Foli at Savona in 1906 (McCormack, 18).

8. McCormack, 120.

9. Strong, 109. Strong reports McCormack as moved to tears by Busoni's playing of Chopin's C-minor Nocturne. Lily McCormack (*I Hear You Calling Me,* 50) says that Mme Emma Albani was included. Dent (*Ferruccio Busoni,* 187) says that Busoni toured the provinces in 1908, but he he makes no mention of McCormack. In 1908 Busoni's reputation was far larger than McCormack's all over Europe. Busoni found provincial touring insufferably bleak.

10. Ledbetter, 105, 135.

11. McCormack, 125.

12. Ibid., 130; Ewen, *Opera,* 485. McCormack won other honors as well.

13. *JJ* 338, 660–61. Although he declined, Joyce let both Harriet Shaw Weaver and Frank Budgen know that he had been asked (*Letters 3,* 259, 261).

14. McCormack, 46, 103.

15. Ibid., 94–96.

16. Ibid., 125. In rough seas the piano came loose from the wall and injured two ladies. Lily raised a question with her husband as to why he had ladies in his sitting room at 2 A.M.

17. For Alton House, see McCormack, 91–93; for Moore Abbey, 139; for the debut, 146–47.

18. The cities were as follows (with the tour sometimes doubling back on itself): Los Angeles, San Diego, Los Angeles, San Francisco, Denver, Omaha, Chicago, St. Louis, Kansas City, Chicago, Detroit, Columbus, Cincinnati, Cleveland, Buffalo, Cleveland, Rochester, Troy, Philadelphia, and Boston (McCormack, 76–77).

19. These included one in Italy, ten in England, five (plus a farm) in the United States, and three (plus a long stay at the Shelbourne Hotel) in Ireland.

20. *The World Almanac and Book of Facts* for 1927 reported government estimates of seventy-four persons in the U.S. in 1924 with *net* incomes of a million dollars annually (155–56). McCormack's was a gross income, from which he would have deducted both the salaries of accompanist, manager, and secretary and those travel expenses paid by him. He was thus probably not among those with net incomes of a million dollars per year, but he probably did belong by the end of the decade to the estimated eleven thousand Americans with a net *worth* of over a million dollars. McCormack's half-million-dollar fee for a film was five times that paid Enrico Caruso a decade earlier. Michael Walsh, commenting on the Three Tenors Concert in Los Angeles (July 1994), asserted that none of these stars is near the earning power of McCormack or Caruso; see M. Walsh, "When Tenors Were Gods," 54.

21. Strong, 271–72.

22. Ledbetter, 140.

23. Scarry, "James Joyce and John McCormack," 529.

24. McCormack, 124.

25. Ledbetter, 105.

26. "Oil Trial Evidence Is Ended Abruptly," *New York Times,* 12 December 1926, p. 1. Doheny, who did business chiefly in Mexico and California, was accused of conspiracy and of bribing President Harding's secretary of the interior, Albert Fall, with $100,000 to win drilling rights in a naval oil reserve. Although Fall was convicted of accepting a bribe, Doheny in a separate trial was acquitted of offering it. Doheny's father was of Irish descent, and the oilman himself was elected president in 1921 of the American Society for the Recognition of an Irish Republic. After the murder of his son in 1929, Doheny gave the University of Southern California a million-dollar library as a memorial to the young man.

27. Scarry, "James Joyce and John McCormack," 530, citing Scarry's interview with Mrs. McCormack in 1965. Scarry says Gwen found Lucia "a very strange girl" and that they spent the afternoon shopping. At the time Lucia was thirteen and a half and Gwen twelve and a half, rather young to be so devoted to "shopping." For teenagers to resist making friends with the children of their parents' friends is not uncommon.

28. McCormack offered to wear his papal count's uniform—scarlet coat, gold lace, plumed cocked hat, and sword—for the wedding. Gwen preferred that he don the conventional cutaway coat and striped trousers. He celebrated the occasion by giving his wife a black, cream, and chromium Rolls Royce (McCormack, 161).

29. "McCormack Is Soloist as Daughter Weds; London Crowds Try to Storm into Church," *New York Times,* 17 September 1933, p. 1. Lily McCormack says that her husband sang "Panis Angelicus" during the service (ibid.). The *New York Times* reports that it was "Ave Maria" (with tears in the tenor's eyes as he finished). Perhaps he sang both. The *Times* reports that many of the 2,000 guests were uninvited, having come for mass earlier and stayed for the wedding. Hundreds more waited outside, since his daughter's wedding was reported as "the only opportunity Londoners would have to hear him this season."

30. Mordden, *Demented,* 71. Joyce would have found this superciliousness intolerable.

31. McCormack, 114, quoting a letter from Jean de Reszke to John McCormack.

32. Glasheen, *Third Census of "Finnegans Wake,"* 262.

33. Beach, 188, has a different account: Joyce had been attending performances of *William Tell* in the early 1920s, but he became distressed by the tenor singing the role of Arnold, who omitted the high Cs Joyce so admired. Then he noted a new tenor's name announced for the role and bought tickets for the whole family. Sullivan, born in 1878, had sung at the Opéra in 1914, 1916–18, and 1922; he was scarcely a "new tenor," although perhaps he was new to Joyce, who came to Paris in 1920 and in 1922 had been preoccupied with the publication of two editions of *Ulysses* and was seriously ill for some time with eye problems. Joyce's count of the notes—actually done by Stuart Gilbert and Giorgio Joyce—was 456 Gs, 93 A-flats, 54 B-flats, 15 Bs, 19 Cs, and 2 C-sharps (JJ 620; S. Gilbert, "Selections from the Paris Diary," 14).

34. Brown and Knuth, *The Tenor and the Vehicle,* 23.

35. McCormack, 150–51.

36. Scarry, "James Joyce and John McCormack," 533–34.

37. 19 May 1934, quoted in Scarry, "James Joyce and John McCormack," 535.

38. Scarry, "James Joyce and John McCormack," 535.

39. *Letters 3,* 204–5; *Letters 3,* 257; *JJ* 625–26.

40. Fahy, *The James Joyce–Paul Léon Papers,* 118.

41. I am greatly indebted to the personnel at the Archives de France for locating and photocopying forty-five pages of these legal papers for me. They were listed under the heading "Opposition sur l'appointement de J. Sullivan" in Labat-Poussin's *Archives du Théâtre National de L'Opéra,* AJ/13 1266.

42. S. Gilbert, *Reflections on James Joyce,* 19.

43. Beach, 189.

44. Brown and Knuth express puzzlement as to why Joyce included *Il trovatore* in *Finnegans Wake* since McCormack had not recorded it (*The Tenor and the Vehicle,* 56). As the present volume demonstrates, many operas in the *Wake* have no association with McCormack. *Il trovatore* is probably there partly as a tribute to Sullivan and partly because Joyce enjoyed the opera and frequently sang its duet, "Ai nostri monti," with Maria Jolas in the 1920s and 1930s.

45. Pitou, *The Paris Opera,* 1335–36.

46. Brockway and Weinstock, *The World of Opera,* 566.

47. Quoted in Rosenthal, *Two Centuries of Opera at Covent Garden,* 450. Rosenthal gives a fairly detailed account of the faults of all the singers, specifying that Sullivan "was in difficulties most of the evening, so much so that his projected appearances as Otello were immediately cancelled," and says *Les Huguenots* was "never again" performed at Covent Garden.

48. This may be because Sullivan sang so little in the period covered by this volume. Volume 4 of the series has not yet been published.

49. *Letters 3,* 200; *ODO,* s.v. "Serafin." Serafin went on to conduct at New York's Metropolitan Opera, from 1924 to 1934, and would have been a natural person to whom to appeal for help in securing a Metropolitan Opera contract—if Sullivan sang well in Naples in 1923. Serafin also conducted at Covent Garden in 1931, but he seems not to have exerted any influence on Sullivan's behalf there to reinstitute the 1930 agreement. He also conducted *William Tell* at the Metropolitan Opera on 21 March 1931, when Arnold's role was sung by Lauri-Volpi. Orchestral conductors of course are not the only influence in casting an opera.

50. Gollancz, *Journey towards Music,* 23.

51. Colum and Colum, *Our Friend James Joyce,* 171, 178.

52. E. Caruso, *Enrico Caruso,* 344. Of these proposed "successors," Edward Johnson was the oldest, at forty-three (Caruso died at age forty-eight). Lauri-Volpi, twenty-nine, was the youngest. The other four were all in their thirties.

53. Gatti-Casazza, *Memories of Opera,* 266.

54. Pleasants, 297.

55. Brockway and Weinstock, 429.

56. Mordden, *Opera Anecdotes,* 73.

57. Rasponi, *The Last Prima Donnas,* 264–65, 273.

58. Ibid., 264–65.

59. Ibid. The preceding quotations come, in order, from pages 204, 273, 282, 300, 358, 392, and 392 again.

60. Koestenbaum, *The Queen's Throat,* 42.

61. Ibid.

62. Brown and Knuth, *The Tenor and the Vehicle,* 35.

63. *Pavarotti and the Italian Tenor.* The program's commentator added that both men were right: Gigli was far better technically, but despite poor technique such as singing all notes as open sounds rather than "covering" any of them, di Stefano had an "artistic energy" lacking in Gigli. The same program indicated that Pavarotti prepares his own roles by hours of listening to recordings of other tenors singing the parts and selecting those effects he wants for himself. A deliberate reproduction of di Stefano's "sexual" quality in his own voice may well contribute to Pavarotti's wide appeal in country after country.

64. Joyce's raillery about McCormack's well-fed look is unusual, for although complaints about hefty prima donnas are a stock opera joke, those against sizeable male singers are rare, except for Luciano Pavarotti, who is built on a different scale from almost everyone else and himself makes jokes about his weight. By contrast, Joyce seems to have found Sullivan's appearance, which he compared to a Dublin policeman, quite pleasing, although Sullivan, too, had a substantial girth.

65. Koestenbaum, 155.

66. Ibid., 155, 159.

67. Ibid., 43.

68. Ibid., 20.

69. Ledbetter, 49.

70. Koestenbaum, 38.

71. Ibid., 137.

72. Ibid., 39–40.

73. Ibid., 34.

· 5 ·

Chapelizod's Opera House

Immersed as he was in opera, James Joyce began incorporating that art into his own work almost from the beginning. Even before *Dubliners* appeared, Joyce's plans for the Volta cinema included an "opera film" in which an opera's complete story would be offered on a special disk, accompanied by an orchestra playing selections from the opera's music.[1] In *Dubliners* "A Boarding House" draws part of its grim effect from its contrast with the radiance of Puccini's *La bohème*.[2] Emily Sinico, the heroine of "A Painful Case," drew her name from a family of opera composers and performers (see chap. 2) and ended her life in the same manner as English opera composer Arthur Goring Thomas (1850–92), who threw himself under the wheels of a train in West Hampstead when he found the pain from an illness unendurable. (He had composed several operas on commission for the Carl Rosa Opera Company: *Esmeralda* [1883], *Nadeshda* [1885], and the posthumously staged *Golden Web* [1893].)[3] Verdi's *Otello* underlies "The Dead," as Lucy B. Maddox has pointed out.[4] *A Portrait of the Artist as a Young Man* draws heavily on Wagner's *Siegfried,* as Timothy Martin has shown.[5] Joyce's *Exiles* is full of Wagner, taking a central theme from that composer's tumultuous relationship with conductor Hans von Bülow and with Bülow's wife, Cosima Liszt von Bülow, who abandoned her husband for Wagner and eventually married the composer. *Carmen* also sounds in the play when Richard Rowan casts the rose at Bertha's feet.[6] *Madame Butterfly* flutters on stage at the moment when Bertha recalls for Rowan the pain of her waiting, with their young son, for his return—like Cio-Cio-San's "Un bel dì" transposed into a different key. The familiar Joycean themes of exile and return recur in *Il trovatore, Mignon, La forza del destino, Tannhäuser,* and many other operas. The infidelities of *Carmen* and *Don Giovanni* haunt *Ulysses.*

It was inevitable, then, that Joyce's last work would incorporate much of what he knew, calling on opera to provide structure, myth, resonance, characters, and plot. It is not the place of this chapter to analyze each opera or composer in the *Wake* in detail, but several longer studies have already begun this work.[7] Certainly the allusions identified in chapter 6 invite future studies of the place of Mozart, Verdi, Puccini, and others in *Finnegans Wake*.

Most important, Joyce seems to have found in the example of Wagner a self-concept as both writer and composer of *Finnegans Wake*. A number of his friends during the shaping of that last work commented on this. Because Joyce scholars are "married to reading and writing" (*FW* 146.22), these remarks have been heard as metaphor rather than factual description. Sylvia Beach, who saw Joyce several times a week in the 1920s and 1930s, compared the *Wake* to "a vast opera . . . a sort of Joycean *Ring*."[8] Parisian literary critic Louis Gillet, himself a singer, heard the *Wake* as "a prodigious *Walpurgis Nacht,* an immense *Götterdämmerung*."[9] Later Gillet returned to this theme, speaking of music in Joyce's writing as "an atmosphere, a condition of thought, an *aura* beyond all words," that was at the same time inside the words, "giving them breath of life. For Joyce, a sentence was not severable from its melodic qualities."[10] The comparison of Joyce's writing to music had been mentioned so often as to become trite, Gillet acknowledged; now, after a half-century, it is time to see that "trite" concept afresh. Journalist Nino Frank, working with Joyce to translate "Anna Livia Plurabelle" into Italian, discovered that "the rhythm, the harmony, the density and consonance of the words were more important to him than the meaning." In this translation Joyce sought a "poetic or metrical" equivalence, even if that meant saying in Italian something "completely different" from the English original.[11] (In some measure Joyce's approach imitated the translators of opera, especially when working from Italian into English; for they strive to preserve the vowel sounds and sequences of the original libretto, even when to do so sacrifices meaning.) The result of their work together was, Frank thought, "richer harmonically" than the original.[12] Jacques Mercanton also turned to musical metaphor, saying that the way in which Joyce described the elements of *Finnegans Wake* designed for cricketers, musicians, the Irish, philosophers, and so on was "handing out parts"—that is to say, it was the action of a conductor or stage manager at an opera.[13]

Even when he heard his own work performed, Joyce responded like an operagoer: he insisted that Nino Frank read aloud their Italian translation of "Anna Livia Plurabelle" at Joyce's 1939 birthday party. At the conclusion Joyce applauded long and enthusiastically and, as if demanding an encore of a singer, insisted that Frank begin again *"da capo."*[14]

Sylvia Beach uses yet another metaphor, without associating it with music, to describe *Finnegans Wake*. Joyce told her that he was "working in layers."[15] In this, too, he was a composer. Although each composer has an individual approach, the following "typical" sequence will serve for illustrative purposes. Maestro Wagnerverdini may begin by selecting a subject, at a very general level—a decision to do an opera about Manon, or Don Quixote, or the Huguenot experience. Or he (typically) may start with a novel (Murger's *Scènes de la vie de Bohème*) or a play (e.g., Shakespeare's *Merry Wives of Windsor,* which furnished material for both Verdi's *Falstaff* and Nicolai's *Die Lustigen Weiber von Windsor*). Occasionally Wagnerverdini begins with a complete libretto but calls in two or three librettists to doctor it up. Sometimes Wagnerverdini even writes his own libretto. With this "little book" the composer begins to work, setting off passages for aria, chorus, or recitative treatment, establishing some melodies and themes, and matching vocal color to the narrative. To the narrative level of the libretto, the music sung by soprano, alto, tenor, bass, and other voices adds several more levels. Thereafter the composer chooses the orchestral instruments to add to or modify the color and sonority of the work, and then he or another orchestrates the whole. Each instrument and every voice has its own musical staff, and these are arranged on the page in "layers."

This is the opera the conductor sees and hears when a performance is being readied. The singers usually work from arrangements indicating only the vocal parts with a reduced-score piano accompaniment. Instrumentalists have their own parts only. The conductor, however, like an experienced reader of *Finnegans Wake,* reads all the "layers" of the score simultaneously. Sometimes a theme will be stated, then dropped for a time, then repeated, perhaps by another voice or instrument. Sometimes singers perform an ensemble—a duet or trio, for example—with the same words for all or one in which each singer has a different text. (One example of the latter from Joyce's own performing experience would be the quintet from *Die Meistersinger.*) The singers may have different melodies as well as different texts to sing. The audience hears the whole, ideally as the composer and the conductor conceive that whole. In something as complex as Richard Strauss's *Salomé,* for instance, the conductor will be reading the music for as many as sixteen singers in seven vocal ranges, plus an orchestra with thirty-five different instruments, sometimes with multiple parts for a given instrument. The audience will hear one unified opera.

Joyce similarly started with relatively small and simple stories, a few pages long, like a composer picking a subject, and constructed enormous underlays and overlays. Like Wagner he was both librettist and composer, adding orchestral effects, creating duets or quartets, and adding "instruments" of all kinds to his own story. A small and early example of this is his treatment of the music-hall song "My Girl's a Yorkshire Girl" in *Ulysses.* Joyce inserts "Baraabum" in the text of the lyric to represent the drumroll of the military band during the two-measure note for singing "through" and "clothes" (10.1253, .1257).[16] Note and drumbeat become the song's motif throughout "Circe" (15.4107, .4133, .4143, .4150), with emphasis shifting to the vulgar from the musical quality. Finally, in "Penelope," the motif reappears most nakedly as "Beerbohm" and "barebum" (18.1042–43).

Ettore Schmitz (Italo Svevo) pointed out as early as 1927 that Joyce "composed" his writing: "When Joyce has written a page of prose he thinks that he has paralleled some page of music."[17] What began with the early writings in Trieste was magnified in the composition of *Finnegans Wake.*

Jacques Mercanton, studying manuscripts for *Work in Progress,* found that a sentence had "been split up by a few new words, which in their turn had engendered a new sentence." Others had been inserted, until two words that had been side by side became separated by a page or more of new text.[18] The idea for the subject had become a libretto, then given a voice, and finally orchestrated. A later music critic writes that Joyce's method enabled "an author who was himself an amateur singer (and patron of singers) to compose, stage, conduct, and sing his own peculiar version of opera, of which [*Finnegans Wake*] constitutes a simulated and overwhelming performance."[19]

In addition to creating a layered "score" in *Finnegans Wake,* Joyce clearly uses opera structurally throughout the book. First, the *Wake* is a complete cycle, deriving as much from Wagner's *Ring* as from Vico in this respect. Like the *Ring,* the *Wake* begins and ends in riverywater. Joyce reinforces this by taking from opera a number of "firsts" for the *Wake's* opening pages: Tristan's first speech from *Tristan und Isolde,* the first aria from Verdi's *Rigoletto,* and the first leitmotif from the *Ring* cycle.[20] Likewise the final words spoken by a number of opera characters fill the last page of Joyce's *Wake:* Madame Butterfly's final word to her son, *gioca* ("play"—or "pray," with the Japanese l/r switch); Gilda's last word, *preghera* ("pray"), from *Rigoletto; Don Giovanni's* last word, *terror;* Desdemona's final *Ave Maria* from *Otello;* Violetta's *gioia* ("joy") from *La traviata;* and Dido's "remember me" from the end of Purcell's *Dido and Aeneas.*[21]

In creating the general operatic structure of his last book, Joyce also used techniques from the music of opera. The "Rossini crescendo," for example, achieves the effect of an increased volume of sound not in the traditional way, with each instrument playing louder, but by starting a theme in one instrument playing at normal volume, then adding another for the same theme, and then another; the final *forte* comes from a multiplication of instruments, not from increasing the loudness of any or all of them.[22] Rossini uses it, for instance, in

Don Basilio's aria in *The Barber of Seville*, "La calunnia è un venticello" (*FW* 199.28–29, *"La Calumnia è un vermicelli"*), where the addition of each instrumental voice epitomizes the addition of another voice to distorting gossip. Joyce does much the same thing by reintroducing a theme repeatedly, so that as the ear-reader hears it repeatedly, it becomes "louder" and moves to the front of consciousness.

Another quality of opera is the sense of costume and disguise. Opera characters are repeatedly hiding from others on the stage, occasionally behind doors or windows, but more often in odd costumes or behind masks. Long before the *Wake,* opera presents Adaline Glasheen's question "Who is who when everybody is somebody else?" Ladies trade places with their maids (as in *The Marriage of Figaro*) or pretend to be boys (*Fidelio*); young lovers pretend to be maids (*Der Rosenkavalier*); gypsies are revealed as the daughters of counts (*Mignon*); nannies are revealed as mothers, and rebel leaders as brothers to the king's general (*Il trovatore*); innocent lovers become sleepwalkers and are blamed for evil intent or action that has never entered their drowsing minds (*La sonnambula*). Listeners who yearn for straightforward plots and characters will find opera fully as confusing as *Finnegans Wake.* The "breeches roles," when a male part is played by a woman singer, antedated—and probably contributed to—the sexual transformations of the music-hall tradition. And Tristan's verbal disguise of inverting his name while in Ireland found its way directly into *Finnegans Wake* as "Tantris" (*FW* 486.7, 571.7) or "Morna" for *Norma* (*FW* 189.25). Opera singers themselves often "disguised" themselves under false names: John McCormack made his debut as Giovanni Foli; Maggie Teyte was born a Tate; Zélia Trebelli anagrammed her birth name, "Le Bert"; and Marie Delna was born "Ledan." Some singers took stage names from their birthplaces, as plain Helen Porter Mitchell of Melbourne, Australia, became Nellie Melba. The whole process of anagramming one name into another was pervasive in opera and gave Joyce thirty years' experience in such wordplay before he ever put it into *Finnegans Wake.*

Another element of nineteenth-century opera production was transferred directly to the *Wake:* the odd mixture of music that so enraged Shaw and other purists and that seemed characteristic not only of after-performance encores but of the presentation itself. The conductor who used the *Tannhäuser* overture to augment the prelude to Gounod's *Philémon et Baucis* at Covent Garden[23] and tenor John Braham, who threw a few of his favorite arias from other works into a scene in *La Dame blanche* (see chap. 1), set a pattern for *Finnegans Wake.* In Joyce's work allusions often squint two or three ways—toward music hall, or

American stage ballads, or opera—all at once. At the top of p. 613, for example, Joyce gives a parodied chorus of

> "God save Ireland!" said the heroes,
> "God save Ireland!" said they all.
> "Whether on the scaffold high
>   or the battlefield we die,
>   Oh what matter when for Ireland dear we fall?"

Buried within Joyce's version is an allusion to the Rheingold ("Goldselforelump!) and Valhalla ("Hailed they. Awed."), and he closes with an allusion to G. F. Root's "Tramp, Tramp, Tramp" (to the same tune as "God Save Ireland"). Three lines along comes an allusion to the Irish traditional song "Savourneen Deelish," followed by an element in a Rossini crescendo, "Pour deday," which has earlier sounded as "Pour le pays" and "Poor the pay." Music from four countries and three languages mingles as easily on Joyce's page as on Braham's stage.

In Trieste's Italian opera culture the tradition of the singer's using fioritura to ornament the composer's music was still strong. Whether Joyce ever attempted such fioritura in his own singing we do not know. Certainly *Finnegans Wake* is built on it, however—passages where the kernel of text has been elaborated repeatedly by Joyce the Singer to dazzle all his aureaders.

The multiple languages of *Finnegans Wake* probably are also rooted in opera, for there were repeated examples of French and German operas performed in Italian in English-speaking Dublin and London or Italian operas in French in Paris. There were even operas, as we have seen, staged with the leading tenor singing in a language different from that used by the rest of the cast or with two sopranos singing successive acts in different languages. The texts were polyglot; the music of the composer was the lingua franca for performer and audience—just as Joyce wished it to happen in *Finnegans Wake*.

The subject matter of *Finnegans Wake* was often drawn from opera themes, as in the case of Wagner's *Ring* or *Tristan und Isolde*. Joyce also borrowed from the biographies of the opera singers, especially if their stories fit his own themes. One such instance from a widely publicized contretemps befalling Enrico Caruso gave Joyce a perfect instance of H. C. Earwicker's misdeed in Phoenix Park. On 17 November 1906, visiting the monkey house at the Central Park zoo in New York City, Caruso was accused by a Mrs. Hannah Graham of touching her on the hip. The incident purportedly occurred in front of the cage of a chimpanzee named "Knocko." A policeman named James Caine or Kane (he used both forms of the name), whose job was to protect women from "mashers" at the zoo, arrested the singer. Reporters discovered that Mrs. Graham and her husband did not live at the address she had given, and she failed to appear in court. There were press reports that the Grahams were friends of Caine. Caruso's associates at the Metropolitan Opera and members of New York's large Italian-American community rallied to the tenor's defense. Mary Garden announced that she and her friends were confident that Caruso "was as far away as possible from being a man of such character." Composer Giacomo Puccini and Jean de Reszke's secretary also supported Caruso, and a resolution of support from a large number of the Met's company was sent to Caruso. At the trial on 21 November the police witnesses gave contradictory testimony, and the defense attorney was able to discredit others. The deputy commissioner of police denounced the large number of Italian-American spectators as "curs and perverts." In this atmosphere Caruso was found guilty of disorderly conduct and given the minimum ten-dollar fine, initiating another storm. A former police chief called the verdict "an outrage." Others described it as "shocking." Despite a large group of supporters, however, Caruso became the subject of disparaging rumors as to his character, his singing, and his future plans.[24] To his embarrassment, the case was widely reported not only in the United States but in his Italian homeland. From Rome Joyce reported to his brother Stanislaus the indignation of the press and a statement from Caruso's manager that the singer had to fend off "shoals of 'offers'" from New York society women (*Letters 2,* 197). Joyce ridiculed the Americans, claiming that it had taken three policemen to arrest the burly tenor, and wondered that they did not also arrest the monkeys at the zoo. Ten days later he commented that half of a letter from Aunt Josephine Murray in Dublin was given over to McCormack's voice and Caruso's trial (*Letters 2,* 199).

Had he written this as fiction, Joyce could hardly have fitted it better to his favorite themes: the tenor unjustly accused of some vague sexual misconduct in the symbolic Eden of a municipal park, the evil but aptly named policeman, the monkeys lending a jungle quality to the setting, the confusion of the witnesses, and the persistence of rumor. The trial thus surfaces early in *Finnegans Wake* as part of "The Ballad of Persse O'Reilly":

> It was during some fresh water garden pumping
> Or, according to the *Nursing Mirror,* while admiring the monkeys
> That our heavyweight heathen Humpharey
> Made bold a maid to woo[.]   (*FW* 46.27–31)

Joyce continues in succeeding stanzas with references to the zoo (47.4) and Cain (47.29). Other allusions appear at 70.8 (one monkey's damages), 139.31 (a magda went to a monkishouse), 193.32 (cannibal Cain), 491.12–18 (tryst, two

Enrico Caruso in costume for *Rigoletto.*

a tutu, Ebell, Kane, Mansianhase parak), 536.25–32 (Kanes nought, Zerobubble Barrentone), and 611.10 (all him monkafellas). The sense that Patrolman Caine/Kane may have "set up" Caruso for the arrest adds to the sense of evil associated with the biblical Cain elsewhere in the *Wake*. The chimp is reborn as H. Chimpden Earwicker, echoing Joyce's charge that Americans would soon be arresting the monkeys themselves for lewd conduct. Finally, Caruso's initials fit Joyce's plan: *E*nrico [*H*enry] *C*aruso.

There are also major opera presences in *Finnegans Wake*. Joyce's criticisms of Richard Wagner (1813–83) are familiar to scholars.[25] Perhaps that very antagonism led Joyce to incorporate, twist, modify, and sometimes subvert Wagner in the *Wake;* but certainly Wagner and his work form the most important

Enrico Caruso at his most dignified, about the time of the anguishing "monkey-house incident" in New York's Central Park.

single opera presence in a book that, like Wagner's *Ring*, is a tale of giants and river maidens, mortals and gods. Joyce also incorporated Wagner's romantic pair, Tristan and Isolde, as protagonists.

Close behind Wagner as an important opera presence in the *Wake* is Giuseppe Verdi (1813–1901); after Verdi comes a later Italian, Giacomo Puccini (1858–1924). If Wagner gave Joyce a northern mythology appropriate to the Viking themes of *Finnegan*, the Italians provided the lyrical melodies so dear to Joyce's ear. Verdi's *Aïda* also contributed a musical undermelody for themes from the Egyptian *Book of the Dead*, as Puccini's *Madame Butterfly* and *Turandot* are musical presences of China and Japan in the *Wake*.[26]

As important as Verdi or Puccini is Wolfgang Amadeus Mozart (1756–91); Professor Hodgart's notes prove that *Don Giovanni* figures as largely in *Finnegans Wake* as in *Ulysses*. *The Magic Flute* is also prominent, and five other Mozart operas have substantial roles: *The Abduction from the Seraglio*, *The Marriage of Figaro*, *Così fan tutte*, *La clemenza di Tito*, and *Bastien and Bastienne*. Nor are other of Joyce's favorite composers neglected. Balfe, Benedict, Bellini, Rossini, Donizetti, Monteverdi, Flotow, Ponchielli—names and music that Joyce's readers will recognize from *Dubliners* and *Ulysses*—still sing in *Finnegans Wake*. Meyerbeer's *Les Huguenots* is accompanied by his *singspiel*, *Das Brandenburgerhor* (1814), an early work but useful to Joyce. Nor were friends forgotten. Geoffrey Molyneux Palmer, whose settings of Joyce poems so pleased the author, is honored in the *Wake* by a reference to his opera *Sruth na maoile*. In all, there are more than 130 composers and nearly 250 operas. The naming of and punning on opera titles and composers' names is part of the fun of *Finnegans Wake*. Its melody, however, comes from allusion to particular arias and themes. Here Joyce drew most often on Mozart's *Don Giovanni*, then (in descending importance) Verdi's *Aïda*, Wagner's *Tristan und Isolde*, and Verdi's *Rigoletto* and *Otello*. Verdi more than any other composer sings in the *Wake*, his arias appearing in at least eighty places. Indeed, we have discovered more arias from Verdi than from all the German and French operas together. To be sure, Verdi was a prolific composer, but it is probable that Joyce was drawn to Verdi's lyricism, as well as by the fact that his own voice was well suited to Italian opera.

The allusion lists in the second part of this volume also demonstrate not only the importance of individual composers or operas but also Joyce's wide range—alphabetical, chronological, and geographical—of opera allusion. Both the first opera composer (Jacopo Peri [1561–1633]) and the first opera (*Dafne*, produced in 1597) are memorialized. So too are operas contemporary with the *Wake* itself: Arnold Schoenberg's *Die glückliche Hand* (1924); Puccini's final, incomplete work, *Turandot* (produced 1926); and probably even the only opera by

Joyce's Zurich friend Otto Luening (*Evangeline* [1932]).[27] Nor is the breadth merely chronological: Joyce managed to include operas from Germany, Italy, France, England, Ireland, the United States, Czechoslovakia, Poland, and Russia, to give his music the same kind of geographical expanse he provided with rivers, cities, historical battles, and so on. Likewise he included composers from Adam to Zingarelli and operas from *Aïda* to *Zàzà*.

More than three hundred singers of the melodies are also commemorated. Since most opera heroines are sopranos, and nearly all heroes are tenors, these dominate the list of singers. Not surprisingly, among the tenors John Sullivan, John McCormack, and two other Irishmen, Michael Kelly and Joseph O'Mara, take pride of place, along with Beniamino Gigli. Caruso is remembered, too, through that monkey-house incident he would have preferred to have forgotten. There are representatives of all other ranges, including the castrati, and a nearly equal division among men and women singers. All three singers from the Hamburg City Opera who created Isolde, Tristan, and King Mark for the first time in England the year Joyce was born (1882) are remembered: Rosa Sucher, soprano; Hermann Winkelmann, tenor; and Eugen Gura, bass-baritone.[28]

Joyce also included considerable opera detail in *Finnegans Wake*. Individual words or phrases, such as "lo zio Bonzo!" ("the Uncle Priest," the crowd's name for Madame Butterfly's uncle, who pronounces the curse in act 1), become part of Joyce's text. Similarly, dozens of opera characters enlarge the crowd of Everybodies at the *Wake*. Several composers' wives (Constanza Mozart, Cosima Wagner, and Giuseppina Strepponi Verdi) are honored, and details of Wagner's attitude toward diet, Jews, and music are also recorded. There are also references to Alfred Lorenz's *Das Geheimnis der Form bei Richard Wagner*,[29] and the Wagnerian tuba, designed by Wagner to get the precise sound he wanted in *Das Rheingold*,[30] is mentioned at several points. At a personal level, the cuckolded von Bülow's modest (or perhaps bitter) self-characterization as "nur der Taktstock Wagners" (only Wagner's baton)[31] underlies the following lines in the *Wake*:

> *"Of my tectucs takestock, tinktact, and ail's weal;*
> . . . . .
> *Your genus its worldwide, your spacest sublime!*
> *But, Holy Saltmartin, why can't you beat time?"* (FW 418.34–419.8)

Von Bülow appears several times in the *Wake*, not only as a conductor and first-rate pianist, but also because he had lived the pattern that so interested Joyce: the husband betrayed by his best friend. For years von Bülow denied his wife's adultery, accepted Wagner's children as his own, and lived in a ménage à trois with Cosima and Wagner, during which time Wagner heaped public denunciation on him during rehearsals. At length he fell ill and was paralyzed physically from the stress of the situation. Eventually he and Cosima were divorced, and he was able to tell a London hostess who asked whether he knew Wagner, "Ah, he married my widow." After his own remarriage he was confined for some time to a mental hospital. Amid all this personal chaos, he made enormous musical contributions, organized two first-rate orchestras, led the premieres of two Wagner operas *(Tristan und Isolde* and *Die Meistersinger)* and a Brahms symphony, encouraged a very young Richard Strauss, and inspired Gustav Mahler's Resurrection Symphony.[32] Through it all he kept the rather mordant wit that pronounced, "A tenor is not a man but a disease" (about which Joyce would have sharply disagreed).[33] After Wagner's death von Bülow had the grace to send a kind note of sympathy to Cosima, who was now not only his widow but Wagner's.[34]

Another bit of opera lore Joyce preserved in the *Wake* was the name of Vittorio Gui, a conductor associated with the revival of bel canto in the twentieth century *(FW* 360.26–27, "O gui, O gui!"). Gui made his debut in Rome in 1907, possibly during Joyce's residence in the Italian capital. Similarly the Swiss artist Adolphe Appia, one of the revolutionary stage designers contemporary with Joyce, found his way into *Finnegans Wake* (297.25, "appia lippia pluvaville"), as well as onto stages at Paris, Dresden, and La Scala. Not only are the usual singing ranges heard ("tenorist voice," *FW* 48.21), but rarer voices like the spinto *(FW* 416.16, "spint"), lying between the lyric and dramatic in character but having something of the qualities of both, also appear. (Spinto roles include the Leonoras of Verdi's *Il trovatore* and *La forza del destino* and tenor parts such as Radamès in *Aïda* or Cavaradossi in Puccini's *Tosca.)*

The initial response to all this opera detail may be that Joyce could not have included so much and that this book must be a case of overannotation. More extensive familiarity with the notes reveals emerging patterns. Joyce was capable of prodigious attention to detail in his own work, and as we have seen, he followed opera assiduously. On 7 May 1939, for instance, in response to a program for the *Maggio Fiorentino* sent him by Jacques Mercanton, Joyced advised Mercanton to see *William Tell* on three nights in a single week; to listen to see whether the Bulgarian tenor sang the opera without cuts; and to spend the third act outside the auditorium, since the character of Arnold did not sing in that portion of the work. He asked Mercanton to send on his own evaluation of the performance and of individual singers, as well as the newspaper reviews. He includes his own opinion of the singers as "good," based on his having heard them on the radio. This is, surely, a remarkable set of instructions.[35] *Tell* was, to be sure, a favorite opera for Joyce, one he had often heard his friend John Sullivan sing. It may be that this "Bulgarian tenor" was Sullivan. Still, we see here the attention to opera detail that reveals itself yet again in the allusions listed in this book.

Finnegans Wake is, indeed, an "aura[l]drama," one that must be heard to be understood.[36] Clearly Joyce hoped that his readers would recognize particular bits of opera music and lore in the same way that, turning on the radio in mid-program, we recognize the voice of Placido Domingo or Luciano Pavarotti, an aria from *La bohème* or a song from George Gershwin. Beyond that, it is nearly impossible to overestimate the significance of Joyce's opera worlds. He did not become a concert artist. Nevertheless, he created a language in *Finnegans Wake* to match his definition of singing as "words with wings," and in writing the *Wake* he played out his own role as the "compositor of the farce of dustiny" (162.02–3), a book mingling all Joyce's musical and linguistic knowledge in a "grand operoar."

NOTES

1. Hutchins, *James Joyce's World,* 80, citing a report in *The Bioscope* for 9 December 1909.

2. Bauerle, *Picking Up Airs,* 6.

3. Joyce would have been ten years old when Thomas died, quite old enough to read news accounts of the event or to hear adult discussions of it.

4. Lucy B. Maddox, "Gabriel and *Otello.*"

5. Martin, *Joyce and Wagner,* particularly chap. 2, "The Artist-hero," 33–53.

6. Martin, "Wagner's *Tannhäuser* in *Exiles,*" 73–76.

7. Hayman, "Tristan and Isolde in *Finnegans Wake,*" 93–112. Hodgart, *James Joyce,* chap. 9, *"Finnegans Wake,"* discusses Wagnerian operas, as well as Puccini's *Turandot,* Verdi's *Il trovatore* and *Otello,* Gounod's *Faust,* and other less prominent works. Timothy Martin's *Joyce and Wagner* is the most thorough study to date of a single composer's relationship to Joyce's writing, including *Finnegans Wake.*

8. Beach, *Shakespeare and Company,* 187.

9. Gillet, "The Living Joyce," 174.

10. Ibid., 196.

11. Frank, "The Shadow That Had Lost Its Man," 97.

12. Ibid. I am grateful to William Russell for explaining opera translation to me. A witty account of the problems may be found in John Mortimer, *Murderers and Other Friends,* 193–201.

13. Mercanton, "The Hours of James Joyce," 235. On Joyce's operatic techniques in *Finnegans Wake* see also Peter Costello, *James Joyce,* 48–49.

14. Frank, 98.

15. Beach, 183.

16. Joyce's addition also changes the meaning of the song's words, "and wears no fancy clothes."

17. I. Svevo, *James Joyce,* 152.

18. Mercanton, 221–22.

19. Lindenberger, *Opera,* 186.

20. Hodgart, 138, and Hodgart notes on opera provided to Bauerle.

21. Hodgart, 186–87.

22. I am grateful to William Russell for explaining the Rossini crescendo to me.

23. Shaw, *Music in London 1890–94,* 1:284.

24. Greenfeld, *Caruso,* 121.

25. See Timothy Martin, "Joyce, Wagner, and Literary Wagnerism," 105–27; Timothy Martin, *Joyce and Wagner.*

26. Cf. Joyce's explanation about juxtaposing Chinese and Japanese words in the *Wake* "as an image for the antagonism that is the permanent background to the history of all men" (Mercanton, 221).

27. *Evangeline* was not given a complete performance till after Joyce's death, but excerpts were performed in Chicago on 29 December 1932, according to H. Earle Johnson, *Operas on American Subjects,* s.v. "Luening." Since the Paris *Tribune* was a branch of the *Chicago Tribune,* the Chicago performance could well have been reported in Paris, and Joyce, whose memory was phenomenal, would have noted the name of his former Zurich friend.

28. Klein, *Thirty Years,* 126; see *FW* 424.28; 435.25; 349.9.

29. Lorenz, *Das Geheimnis der Form bei Richard Wagner.*

30. *New Grove,* s.v. "Wagner tuba."

31. Lebrecht, *The Maestro Myth,* 17. In the American vernacular, of course, Wagner was "beating von Bülow's time" with Cosima von Bülow, and Joyce wrote *Finnegans Wake* in what was often an American milieu.

32. Lebrecht, 17, 23.

33. Mordden, *Opera Anecdotes,* 258.

34. Lebrecht, 22.

35. Mercanton, 247. This card is also printed in *Letters 3,* 441, in the original French and with a slightly different translation, the most important variation being the identification of the tenor as "Bulgarian" by Mercanton and as "Sullivan" by Richard Ellmann. Mercanton does not identify the "Bulgarian" tenor but says that Joyce had spoken of the singer when he and Mercanton met in Paris. Ellmann's transcription as "Sullivan" fits Joyce's well-documented interest in that tenor's career. Willard Potts, in editing the Mercanton piece, agrees that the tenor "would have been Sullivan" but adds that "the context within the letter makes 'Sullivan' an unlikely reading" (Mercanton, 248 n. 46).

36. In this connection, see Stephen Joyce's comment on the extraordinary aural quality in what James Joyce wrote (Paul Doherty, "Q. & A. with Stephen Joyce," 5).

Part 2

Opera in
Finnegans
Wake

.

Matthew J. C.
Hodgart
with
Ruth Bauerle

. Methodology .

Part 2 presents four listings of Joyce's allusions to opera in *Finnegans Wake,* organized in several different ways. In chapter 6, the page/line listing, *Finnegans Wake* is the starting point; readers of that volume will find opera allusions listed page by page and line by line. This list includes all kinds of allusion: to opera composers and their foibles; to individual opera or aria titles; to motifs, themes, key words, or characters in operas; to librettists, conductors, designers and singers of opera; and even to one critic, George Bernard Shaw, writing as "Corno di Bassetto." Bits of opera lore such as the "spinto" voice, Wagner's special tubas, the viola d'amore used by Meyerbeer in orchestrating *Les Huguenots,* and the battle over pitch that raged in English musical circles are also to be found in this chapter.

Other readers may have a particular item of opera lore in mind, however, and wish to discover whether it appears in *Finnegans Wake.* These readers will more easily start with chapter 7, the composer list, which organizes Joyce's opera allusions alphabetically by composer (including librettists, designers, conductors, impresarios, and critics); as subentries under each composer's name are listed, again alphabetically, each opera, aria, character, or theme alluded to in *Finnegans Wake.* For this chapter we have adopted baritone Thomas Hampson's definition of "aria" as "an excerptable moment" of opera music, including in that category solos, duets, ensemble pieces, cavatinas, romances, and so on.

Occasionally readers may want to search out an opera without knowing the composer's name or an aria or character without knowing in which opera it might be found. These researchers will most usefully begin with chapter 8, the finding list, which supplies for each opera title, aria, or character the information needed to find that item in chapter 7.

Finally there is chapter 9, an alphabetical singer list, providing names, dates, nationality, and vocal range for singers alluded to in *Finnegans Wake*, along with the relevant page and line numbers for each allusion.

The pages that follow consist of Matthew Hodgart's edited notes on opera in *Finnegans Wake*, with some additions by Ruth Bauerle. For completeness these have been collated with opera references in other standard listings of allusions in the *Wake* by James Blish, Adaline Glasheen, Clive Hart, Carole Brown and Leo Knuth, Geert Lernout, Roland McHugh, Louis Mink, John Scarry, and Mabel Worthington. To present as complete a picture as possible of Joyce's use of opera in his last book, Ruth Bauerle incorporated opera allusions from these sources in the page/line listing, identifying the source for each (see abbreviations list). Since the references to opera in these sources is only a small part of the original studies, this limited incorporation of other scholars' findings, coupled with credit to them as identifiers, seemed fair. In the instance of Timothy Martin's *Joyce and Wagner*, however, which is devoted solely to Joyce and opera, incorporating all his listed allusions would expropriate a very substantial portion of his book. We have therefore adopted a kind of compromise, using the key "M" to mark an allusion already in the Hodgart notes that Martin had also identified himself and the key "Martin 000" to refer readers to allusions (by page number) in *Joyce and Wagner* but not in the Hodgart or Bauerle notes. This provides readers an index of opera allusions in the *Wake* that is as complete as possible, without infringing on another scholar's work. This cross-reference system also avoids expensive reproduction of material already in print.

Looking for allusions of any sort in *Finnegans Wake* is rather like bird-watching. Many eyes peer into the thicket, and sometimes several watchers spot the bird at the same time. *Wake*-watchers also exchange information quite freely within their community. Consequently it is impossible to establish a "first sighting" of most of these allusions. Rather, the identifier's code after each allusion in the page/line list indicates who *published* an identification of opera in the passage. Some of the allusions listed here also carry several identifier codes. These multiple identifiers do not constitute "endorsement" of an allusion; they merely indicate several spotters. Nor does a single identifier code mean that other scholars disagree about the allusion, although some may—and some will.

Scholars who have read this book in manuscript have reported two conflicting reactions: some thought that not enough allusions were identified; others, that too many were identified, using too loose a definition of "allusion." Since it seems impossible to please all, we have proceeded as we began and present the results here. Those who see gaps are invited to send additional allusions to us or to publish them in relevant journals. Those who fear overannotation may wish to classify some of our identifications as what Clive Hart labeled "overtones" in his *Concordance to Finnegans Wake.*

Throughout these notes opera titles are given in what seemed the most common usage, whether the original language or English. Where Joyce seemed familiar with several titles (as in the Italian *La zingara* for Balfe's *The Bohemian Girl*), both are included and cross-referenced. Titles of arias are in the original language by which they are known, again excepting a few cases where Joyce preferred an Italian title for an aria customarily named in French. Vital dates are provided for persons named and vocal ranges for the singers, except where this information could not be found. More extensive information on any of the allusions may be found in the works listed in the bibliography.

There is some difficulty in distinguishing Joyce's allusive intent when there are works or characters of similar name. Falstaff occurs, for instance, not only in several of Shakespeare's plays but in operas of that name by Verdi, Dittersdorf, Salieri, Balfe, Adam, and Nicolai. It is most probable that Joyce would be familiar with the Verdi *Falstaff,* but he also refers to Nicolai's *Merry Wives of Windsor* in *Finnegans Wake,* and he may have been acquainted, also, with Balfe's work. *Don Quixote* likewise has attracted many composers, and it is difficult to know whether Joyce has in mind Cervantes's text or one of the sixty or more opera versions. In similar fashion, characters with the same or very similar names appear in a number of operas: Rossini's *Barber of Seville* and Mozart's *Marriage of Figaro* share several characters, as do Massenet's *Manon* and Puccini's *Manon Lescaut.* In these instances, both are listed.

One group of allusions in the following list should be pointed out as quite speculative. In *Finnegans Wake* Joyce included more than forty passages of solmization, or solfa syllables. Doubtless for him these represented a melody within his mind as he wrote, but it is well-nigh impossible now to determine exactly which melody that was. What I have done is to identify through the thematic index of Barlow and Morgenstern's *Dictionary of Vocal Themes* the opera arias that begin with the notes supplied by Joyce's *Wake* text. Sometimes several arias begin with the same solfa notes, though in different keys and with different time values. There is of course no certainty that the passages Joyce gives us were heard by him as the opening notes of an aria—they could be a phrase within or concluding an aria, or indeed, from a song outside the opera repertory. These are, therefore, tenuous identifications indeed, included here (for those trying to solve the endless riddles of *Finnegans Wake)* to indicate what Joyce might have had in mind.

ABBREVIATIONS

A	within the page/line list or in the composer list indicates a musical passage that is seen as a unit and may be sung or recorded as such, whether aria, cabaletta, romance, duet, trio, ensemble or chorus
Am.	American
Argen.	Argentinian
Aus.	Austrian
Austral.	Australian
b.	born
B	at end of page/line entry indicates an identification by Ruth Bauerle
Bar	pattern refers to a Wagnerian structure, the *Bar* as explained in *Die Meistersinger: stollen + stollen + abgesang* (stanza + stanza + aftersong)
bar.	baritone
Bel.	Belgian
Blish	at end of page/line entry indicates an identification by James Blish
Bogen-form	refers to a Wagnerian structure, the *archform* or ternary form (ABA)
Boh.	Bohemian
C	within page/line or composer listing indicates a character in an opera
Can.	Canadian
comp.	composer
cond.	conductor
contra.	contralto
Croat.	Croatian
Czech.	Czechoslovakian
Dalton	at the end of page/line entry indicates an identification by Jack Dalton
Dan.	Danish
En.	English
Finn.	Finnish
Fr.	French
Ger.	German
G	at end of page/line entry indicates an identification by Adaline Glasheen in the *Third Census of "Finnegans Wake"*

H   at end of page/line entry indicates an identification by Matthew Hodgart in his previously unpublished notes.

Hart, B   an identification of a solmization passage from Hart's *Structure and Motif in "Finnegans Wake,"* with a subsequent identification by Bauerle of a musical passage from opera represented by these sol-fa notes

H-SG   at end of page/line entry indicates an identification previously published in Hodgart's *James Joyce: A Student's Guide*

Hung.   Hungarian

HW   at end of page/line entry indicates an identification first published in Hodgart and Worthington, *Song in the Works of James Joyce*

HW-SG   at end of page/line entry indicates an identification from Hodgart and Worthington's work that is also discussed in *James Joyce: A Student's Guide*

It.   Italian

K   at end of page/line entry indicates an identification by Carole Brown and Leo Knuth in their studies of Joyce and John McCormack

L   at end of page/line entry indicates an identification by Geert Lernout

M   at end of page/line entry indicates an identification by Timothy Martin

McH   at end of page/line entry indicates an allusion in Roland McHugh's *Annotations to "Finnegans Wake,"* 2d ed.

Martin 000   as a page/line entry refers the user to the page in Timothy Martin's *Joyce and Wagner* where a Wagnerian allusion in this passage of the *Wake* is explained in detail

mezzo-sop.   mezzo-soprano

Mex.   Mexican

Mink   signifies sites associated with opera and identified in Louis Mink's *A "Finnegans Wake" Gazetteer*

New Z.   New Zealander

Nor.   Norwegian

OT   within the page/line list indicates an allusion to an opera title

Port.   Portugese

Prod.   produced

Rom.   Romanian

Russ.   Russian

Scot.   Scottish

Senn	at end of page/line entry indicates an identification by Fritz Senn
sop.	soprano
Sp.	Spanish
Sw.	Swedish
T	within the page/line list or in the composer list indicates a theme, leitmotif, or fragment of libretto from that opera reflected in this passage of *Finnegans Wake*.
ten.	tenor

6

Page/Line List of Opera Allusions
in *Finnegans Wake*

This is a complete record of the allusions to opera and operetta we have identified in Joyce's last work, listed by the page and line number where the allusion occurs in *Finnegans Wake*. The format and punctuation are like the following examples:

FW page/line no., text of *Wake;* nature of allusion, operatic source of allusion.
    Identifier

or, for singers,

FW page/line no., text of *Wake;* singer's name (vocal range). Identifier

Finnegans Wake, Book I.1:
3.1, riverrun; first leitmotiv of Wagner's *Ring* is that of the Rhine, T in Wagner's *Das Rheingold.* H-SG, M
3.4, Sir Tristram; Tristan, C in Wagner's *Tristan und Isolde.* H. Also Lord Tristram (Tristan) de Mikleford, C in Flotow's *Martha.* B
3.4, violer d'amores; viola d'amore, a stringed instrument of five to seven strings, with an equal number of resonance strings, included by Meyerbeer in orchestration of *Les Huguenots.* Joyce's clue early in text that *FW* is a book of multiple resonances. B
3.6, Martin 195
3.11, bland; Maria Theresa Bland (mezzo-sop.). H
3.14, regginbrow; rainbow bridge to Valhalla at end of opera, T in Wagner's *Das Rheingold.* H-SG, M
3.14, ringsome; Ring, T in Wagner's *Ring.* H-SG, M
3.20, Martin 219

3.20–21, sends . . . to the west; "Shade of the Palm" ("Oh, my Dolores,"), A in Stuart's *Floradora. B*

3.21, quest; "Questa o quella," first A in Verdi's *Rigoletto.* H

4.2–3, Ualu Ualu Ualu; "Weia! Waga! Woge, du Welle, walle zur Wiege! Wagalaweia! Wallala weiala weia!" (Rhine Maidens at beginning of opera), T in Wagner's *Das Rheingold.* H

4.6, boomeringstroms; Ring, T in Wagner's *Ring.* H

4.10–11, strawng voice of false jiccup; Giacomo Lauri-Volpi (ten.). B

4.11, false . . . O; "Falstaff O la," T in Verdi's *Falstaff.* H

4.14, was iz? Iseut?; "Was ist? Isolde" (Tristan's first words), T in Wagner's *Tristan und Isolde.* H-SG

4.18, Martin 205

4.24, eviparated; "Evviva!" T in Verdi's *Ernani.* H. Also A, "Evviva!" (shout of chorus at beginning) in Verdi's *Otello. B*

4.35, waalworth; Valhalla, T in Wagner's *Ring.* H, M

5.6, Riesengeborg; castle built by the giants, Valhalla, T in Wagner's *Ring.* H-SG, M

5.9, Hohohoho; Siegfried's forging song, A in Wagner's *Siegfried.* H. Also "Hojohe," T in Wagner's *Flying Dutchman.* H, M

5.22, wesways; first word by sailor—"Frisch weht der Wind der Heimat zu," T in Wagner's *Tristan und Isolde.* H

5.30, wallhall's; Valhalla, T in Wagner's *Ring.* H, M

5.31, tramtrees; Tristan, C in Wagner's *Tristan und Isolde.* H, M

5.31, stonengens; Commendatore, statue, C in Mozart's *Don Giovanni. B*

6.3, fumes; "Nei cieli bigi guardo fumar," A in Puccini's *La bohème.* H

6.11, when a mon merries; "When a man marries," A in Gilbert and Sullivan's *Gondoliers.* H

6.22, Belling; Bellini (comp.). B

6.22, He's stiff; Falstaff, C in Verdi's *Falstaff,* Nicolai's *Merry Wives of Windsor,* and Holst's *At the Boar's Head. G, B*

6.26, fidelios; Beethoven's *Fidelio* (OT). HW

6.35–36, way (a horn!) . . . wail; Weia! Waga! . . . Wagalaweia! (Rhine Maidens at beginning of opera), A in Wagner's *Das Rheingold. B,* H

7.3, O carina! O carina; "Vedrai, carino," A in Mozart's *Don Giovanni.* HW

7.6, Taubling; Richard Tauber (ten.). B

7.9–10, Finfoefom the Fush; giant motif associated with Fafner and Fasolt, T in Wagner's *Ring.* H

7.13, fraudstuff; Falstaff, C in Verdi's *Falstaff,* Nicolai's *Merry Wives of Windsor,* and Holst's *At the Boar's Head. G, B*

7.28–29, Martin 195

7.29–30, reasons, peer yuthner; *Riesen* (Ger.), *jotun* (Nor.) = "giant" motif, T
in Wagner's *Ring*. H

8.4, Martin 219

8.10–10.17, Willingdone; marquess of Willingdone, in Shanghai in 1926 on
Border Indemnity Commission, played tennis with John McCormack at
home of British consul. B; see also G.

8.14, Crossgunn; "Cruiskeen Lawn," A in Benedict's *Lily of Killarney*. B

8.19, dux; Claire Dux (sop.). H

9.32, bissmark; King Mark, C in Wagner's *Tristan und Isolde*. G

11.1, crows have flapped it southenly; ravens of Wotan, C in Wagner's *Ring*. H

11.4, Nixy girls; "He, he! Ihr Nicker!" ("Hey, you nixies," Alberich's first words),
T in Wagner's *Das Rheingold*. H. Also Arthur Nikish (cond.). B

11.5, Neblas; Alberich, C in Wagner's *Ring*. H

11.5–6, gaels of Thon. No nubo no! Neblas on you liv! Her would be too
moochy afreet; Fricka, called by Wotan "Der alte Sturm, die alte Mühe"
(the old storm, the old trouble), C in Wagner's *Die Walküre*. H

11.7, Fe fo fom; giant motif, T in Wagner's *Ring*. H

11.8–9, appear . . . peri; Gilbert and Sullivan's *Iolanthe* (OT). H

11.9, peri; Jacopo Peri (comp.), composer of first opera, *Dafne*. H

11.29–31, How bootifull and how truetowife of her, when strengly forebidden,
to steal our historic presents from the past postprophetical so as to will
make us all lordy heirs; "How beautiful they are, the lordly ones," A in
Boughton's *The Immortal Hour* (opera about Celtic gods and fairies). H

11.34, kickin arias (so sair); arias, T in opera generally. B

11.35, Gricks; des Grieux, C in Puccini's *Manon Lescaut*. H. Also C in Massenet's *Manon*. H

12.11–12, to piff the business on. Paff. To puff the blaziness on. Poffpoff; associated with "I'll huff and I'll puff and I'll blow your house down" to
form giant motif, *FW* 11.7 and 13.32, T in Wagner's *Ring*. H. Also "Piff,
paff," A in Meyerbeer's *Les Huguenots*. H

12.21, collines; Colline, C in Puccini's *La bohème*. H

12.25, Martin 187

13.7, engravure; Louis Greveuse (ten., b. Douthitt). H

13.9, Mitchel; Nellie Melba (sop., b. Mitchell). H

13.13, Lokk; Loge (Loki), C in Wagner's *Ring*. H

13.20, herodotary; Herod, C in Massenet's *Hérodiade*. H. Also R. Strauss's
Salomé. B

13.26–27, Martin 208

13.27, Marchessvan; Mathilde Marchesi de Castrone (mezzo-sop.). H. Also
Salvatore Marchesi (bar.). H. Also Blanche Marchesi (sop.). H. Also Luigi
(Lodovico) Marchesi (male sop.). H

13.32, fassilwise; Fasolt, giant, C in Wagner's *Ring.* H

14.2–3, and be me sawl; as B mi sol, the opening notes of love duet, "Siegmund
heiss' ich, Und Siegmund bin ich," A in Wagner's *Die Walküre.* B

14.6, Martin 187, 219

14.8, *sobralasolas;* A (chorus), as "sol la sol la" this reproduces the opening notes
of "Summ' und brumm'," spinning chorus of Wagner's *Flying Dutchman.*
Also the opening notes of the arias "Era la notte, Cassio dormia" in Verdi's *Otello;* and "Noch ein Weilchen" in Smetana's *Bartered Bride.* B

14.22, marks; King Mark, C in Wagner's *Tristan und Isolde.* G

14.30, Martin 208

14.33, nibbleth; Nibelung, Cs in Wagner's *Ring.* H

14.34–35, skyup is of evergrey; "Nei cieli bigi guardo fumar," A in Puccini's
La bohème. H

15.20, Martin 219

15.33, dragon man; Fafner, C in Wagner's *Ring.* H, M

16.29, One eyegonblack; Wotan's missing eye, T in Wagner's *Ring.* H, M

16.33, wooden; Wotan, C in Wagner's *Ring.* H, M

17.1, Martin 195

17.15, rutterdamrotter; Wagner's *Die Götterdämmerung* (OT). HW, M; see also
Martin 208.

17.30, erde from erde; Erda, C in Wagner's *Ring.* H, M

17.35, drukn; dragon, T in Wagner's *Ring.* H

17.36, iz leebez luv; Isolde, C in Wagner's *Tristan und Isolde.* H, M. Also "Mild
und leise" ("Liebestod"), A in Wagner's *Tristan und Isolde.* HW, M

18.2, Meldundleize; "Mild und leise" ("Liebestod"), A in Wagner's *Tristan und
Isolde.* HW, M

18.11, The gyant Forficules with Amni the fay; Fafner, C in Wagner's *Ring.* H

19.4–5, Right rank . . . rightgorong; "Right Down Regular Royal Queen," A
in Gilbert and Sullivan's *Gondoliers.* HW

19.9, alfrids; Alfred, C in J. Strauss II's *Die Fledermaus.* H

19.25, Martin 208

20.32, .35, frisque . . . Winnie blows; "Frisch weht der Wind," opening T of
Wagner's *Tristan und Isolde.* H

21.2–3, Lissom! . . . Hark, the corne entreats; Brangäne, "Ich höre der Hörner
schall," T in Wagner's *Tristan und Isolde.* H

21.5–23.15, Martin 195

21.6, madameen; "Madamina, il catalogo," A in Mozart's *Don Giovanni*. H

21.12, Martin 195

21.15, prankquean . . . prankquean; Brangäne, C in Wagner's *Tristan und Isolde*. H-SG

21.18, Mark; King Mark, C in Wagner's *Tristan und Isolde*. H, M

21.18–19, why do I am alook alike a poss of porterpease?; love and death potions looked alike, T in Wagner's *Tristan und Isolde*. H

21.21, Martin 195

21.25–26, brannewail . . . prankquean; Brangäne, C in Wagner's *Tristan und Isolde*. B

21.27–28, lovespots; love potion, T in Wagner's *Tristan und Isolde*. H-SG

21.33, pinafrond; Buttercup, C in Gilbert and Sullivan's *H.M.S. Pinafore*. H-SG

21.35, baretholobruised; Bartolo, C in Rossini's *The Barber of Seville*. H. Also C in Mozart's *The Marriage of Figaro*. B. Also C in Luigi and Federico Ricci's *Crispino e la comare*. B

22.4, witter; Donner, C in Wagner's *Das Rheingold*. H

22.5, Martin 195

22.17, Martin 195

22.28, Martin 208

22.29, Martin 195

23.23, Martin 195

23.25, Hairfluke; Alberich's curse ("Verfluch"), T in Wagner's *Das Rheingold*. H

23.36, to make plein avowels; "Faites-lui mes aveux" (Flower Song), A in Gounod's *Faust*. H

24.1, Nilbud; Niebelung, C in Wagner's *Ring*. H

24.5, dragon; Fafner, C in Wagner's *Ring*. H

24.16, Be aisy, good Mr Finnimore, sir; Tombesi, tenor at whom Dublin audience shouted "Tom, be aisy." M

24.33, ring and amberulla, the whole treasure of the pyre; treasure guarded by Fafner and Siegfried's pyre, T in Wagner's *Ring*. H

24.35, Nobucketnozzler; Verdi's *Nabucco* (OT). B

25.9, Your fame is spreading like Basilico's ointment; "La calunnia è un venticello," A sung by Basilio in Rossini's *Barber of Seville*. McH

25.9, Basilico's; Don Basilio, C in Rossini's *Barber of Seville*. H. Also Don Basilio, C in Mozart's *Marriage of Figaro*. H

25.26, Tuskar; Tosca, C in Puccini's *Tosca*. H. Also Puccini's *Tosca* (OT). H

25.30–31, an elmstree twelve urchins couldn't ring round; Wagner's *Ring* (OT). H; see also Martin 195.

26.7, Vestray; Lucia Elizabeth Vestris (contr.). H

26.17, Martin 195

27.1, .22, Tom Bowe . . . Aisy; Tombesi (ten.). B

27.15–16, Merry . . . Purebelle; "Morir! si pura e bella!" A in Verdi's *Aïda*. B

27.15–16, They called her Holly Merry her lips were so ruddyberry; "O ruddier than the cherry" (sung by giant Polyphemus), A in Handel's *Acis and Galatea*. H-SG

28.9, allavalonche; "La Valanga" ("The Avalanche," sop.), *Letters 1, 358*. B

28.26, *Selskar;* Selika, C in Meyerbeer's *L'Africaine*. H

28.31, Worther; Massenet's *Werther* (OT). G, B

29.27, adi and aid; Aïda, C in Verdi's *Aïda*. H

Finnegans Wake, Book I.2:

30.1, Iris; Iris, C in Mascagni's *Iris*. H. Also C in Handel's *Semele*. B

31.31–32, Martin 195

31.35, andrewpaulmurphyc; William Paull (bar.). B

32.8, Donyahzade; Donizetti (comp.). H

32.29, Semperkelly's; Michael Kelly (ten.). H

32.35, *The Bo' Girl;* Balfe's *The Bohemian Girl* (OT). HW. Also Arline, C in Balfe's *The Bohemian Girl*. G

32.35, and *The Lily;* Benedict's *Lily of Killarney* (OT). HW

33.27, Hay, hay, hay! Hoq, hoq, hoq! He! Ho! T in Wagner's *Parsifal*. H

34.17, chin Ted, chin Tam, chinchin; "Chin Chin Chinaman," A in Jones's *Geisha*. B

35.27, tipstaff; Falstaff, C in Verdi's *Falstaff,* Nicolai's *Merry Wives of Windsor,* and Holst's *At the Boar's Head*. G, B

36.20, co-comeraid; KoKo, C in Gilbert and Sullivan's *Mikado*. G

37.17, Martin 208

38.7, a leaman's farewell; Lotte Lehmann (sop.). H. Also Lilli Lehmann (sop.). H

38.34, *The Secret of Her Birth;* "The Secret of My Birth," A from Balfe's *Bohemian Girl*. McH

39.5, Paullock; William Paull (bar.). B

39.23, colleenbawl; Colleen Bawn, C in Benedict's *Lily of Killarney*. G

39.33–34, divers . . . jenny; Jenny Diver, C in Gay's *Beggar's Opera*. G

39.36, the Postboy's Horn; Charles Horn (ten. and bar.). H

40.1–2, the Cup and the Stirrup; "The Stirrup Cup," song by opera conductor Luigi Arditi, 1822–1903. McH, B

40.6, *I come, my horse delayed;* "The Moon Has Raised Her Lamp Above," A from Benedict's *Lily of Killarney.* B

40.7, bussybozzy; Debussy (comp.). H. Also Bizet (comp.). H

40.10, martas; Flotow's *Martha* (OT). HW

40.16, O'Mara; Joseph O'Mara (ten.). H

40.17, Mildew Lisa; "Mild und leise" ("Liebestod"), A in Wagner's *Tristan und Isolde.* HW, M

41.2, Sant Iago; Iago, C in Verdi's *Otello.* H

41.3, Lisa; "Mild und Leise" ("Liebestod"), A in Wagner's *Tristan und Isolde.* G. Also Lisa, the innkeeper in Bellini's *La sonnambula.* B

41.4, Mongan; Pietro Mongini (ten.). H

41.6–7, slept their sleep of the swimborne; Bellini's *La sonnambula* (OT). B

42.17, lubeen; Germaine Lubin (sop.). H

42.17, lieder; Frida Leider (sop.). H

42.26, Ernin; Ernani, C in Verdi's *Ernani.* H

43.17, a fair girl; Colleen Bawn, C in Benedict's *Lily of Killarney.* G

43.18, weaver's; Penelope, C in Fauré's *Penelope.* G, B

43.29, Martin 219

43.31–32, his majesty the flute; Mozart's *Magic Flute* (OT). H; see also Martin 219.

43.34–35, 44.4, a perfect downpour of plaudits among the rapsods, piped out of his decentsoort hat, looking still more like his purseyful namesake . . . *silentium;* tradition of no applause after first act of *Parsifal,* T in Wagner's *Parsifal.* H-SG, M

43.35, purseyful; Parsifal, C in Wagner's *Parsifal.* H, M

44.2–3, hoisted . . . to his companions of the chalice; Grail ritual, T in Wagner's *Parsifal.* H, M

44.4, *silentium in curia;* "Silentium—wach' auf," A (chorus) in Wagner's *Meistersinger.* H-SG, M; see also Martin 205.

44.14, Persse; Parsifal, C in Wagner's *Parsifal.* H

44.19, It's cumming, it's brumming; "Summ' und brumm'," A (chorus) in Wagner's *Flying Dutchman.* H

45.25–26, change that shirt on ye; Berlioz, as opera conductor for Jullien's London productions, worked so vigorously that it was necessary for him to change his shirt while hidden by harp cases during rehearsal. Lernout

46.16, man-o'-war; Josef von Manowarda (bass). H

46.27–31, It was during some fresh water . . . maid to woo; Caruso monkeyhouse incident; see chapter 5. B

47.5, Billing; Elizabeth Billington (sop.). H

47.26–29, And not all the king's . . . raise a Cain; Caruso monkey-house incident; see chapter 5. B

Finnegans Wake, Book I.3:

48.1, Chest Cee; Chest C sound of tenors. McH, B

48.1, Corpo di barragio; Corno di Bassetto, pseud. for Bernard Shaw (critic) as music critic, especially on Italian opera. B

48.11–12, Hilton St Just (Mr Frank Smith), Ivanne Ste Austelle (Mr J. F. Jones); Frank Smith and J. F. Jones sang roles of Vyvyan and S. Vincent in *Maritana* at Theatre Royal Dublin. McH

49.5–6, wild geese, alohned; swan, T in Wagner's *Lohengrin*. H

49.8, Fusilovna; Donizetti's *La Fille du régiment* (OT). B

49.9, marble halls; "I dreamt that I dwelt in marble halls," A in Balfe's *Bohemian Girl*. HW

50.6, druriodrama; Drury Lane Theatre, London, site of much Italian opera in nineteenth century. Mink, B

50.10, austral; Florence Austral (sop.). H

50.19, Martin 196

50.35, nix; Nixies, Cs in Wagner's *Ring*. G, B. Also Arthur Nikisch (cond.). B

51.14, edventyres; Louise Edvina (sop.). H

51.35, Charlotte; Charlotte, C in Massenet's *Werther*. H

53.4, odable; Odabella, C in Verdi's *Attila*. H

53.18–19, *doerehmoose;* as do-re-me-si, possibly first notes of "Dir, hohe Liebe, töne begeistert mein Gesang," A in Wagner's *Tannhäuser*. B and Hart

54.9, dumagirls; Duma, a woman singer with Carl Rosa Company in Dublin, 1894. B. Also Violetta in Verdi's *La traviata,* based on Dumas's *La Dame aux camélias*. B

54.10, minny; Minna, Wagner's first wife. B

54.11, frickans; Fricka, C in Wagner's *Ring*. H

54.11, mladies; Rimsky-Korsakov's *Mlada* (OT). H

55.8–9, Martin 208

55.27–30, Martin 208

56.5–8, Martin 208

57.2, melos; de Mellos, who founded opera on Fishamble Street, Dublin. B

57.2–3, mode the manners; Moody-Manners Opera Company. G. Also Fanny Moody (sop.) and Charles Manners (bass). B

57.3–4, Tsin tsin tsin tsin; "Chin Chin Chinaman," A in Jones's *Geisha*. HW

57.26, bland; Maria Theresa Bland (mezzo-sop.). H

57.27, mild dewed; "Mild und leise" ("Liebestod"), A in Wagner's *Tristan und Isolde.* HW, M

58.3, the part he created; opera term for the first performance of a role, borrowed by Joyce from *Sims Reeves.* Lernout

58.10, sullivans; John Sullivan (ten.). H

58.11, feedailyones; Beethoven's *Fidelio* (OT). H

58.12, Flucher's; "Verfluch" (curse), T in Wagner's *Ring.* H. Also curse in Strauss's *Salomé* (T). B

58.13, ring; Wagner's *Ring* (OT). H

58.13, Chin, chin! Chin, chin; "Chin Chin Chinaman," A in Jones's *Geisha.* HW

58.17, Bugge; Bugge (sop.). H

58.24, Peingpeong; Ping, Pang, Pong, Cs in Puccini's *Turandot.* B

58.32, Marchison; Barbara Marchisio (contr.). H

59.1–2, Halfmoon and Seven Stars; Hoffman and Stella, Cs in Offenbach's *Tales of Hoffmann.* H

59.4, saidaside; Aïda, C in Verdi's *Aïda.* H

60.11, Lynsky; Lenski, C in Tchaikovsky's *Eugene Onegin.* H

60.28, todie; Luisa Todi (mezzo-sop.). B

60.31, turridur's capecast . . . matadear; Turiddu, C in Mascagni's *Cavalleria rusticana.* H. Also "Mamma, quel vino è generoso," A in Mascagni's *Cavalleria rusticana.* H. Also "Voi lo sapete, O mamma," A in Mascagni's *Cavalleria rusticana.* H. Also Toreador's Song, A in Bizet's *Carmen.* H.

61.16, Questa and Puella; "Questa o quella," A in Verdi's *Rigoletto.* HW

61.19, Gobbit; Tito Gobbi (bar.). H

62.5, Mara; Gertrud Mara (sop.). H. Also Joseph O'Mara (ten.). H

62.5, Rahoulas; Raoul, C in Meyerbeer's *Les Huguenots,* a John Sullivan role. H

62.11–12, Emeraldilluim; Arthur Sullivan and Edward German's *Emerald Isle, or The Caves of Carrig-Cleena* (OT). H

62.28, Wednesbury; Valhalla (Wotan's Burg), T in Wagner's *Ring.* H

63.6, wodkar; Wotan, C in Wagner's *Ring.* H

63.6, Thornton; Edna Thornton (contr.). H. Also Thor, C in Wagner's *Ring.* H

63.7, Kane's; Kane, policeman in Caruso (ten.) monkey-house incident. See chapter 5. B

63.8, Midweeks; Mittwoch (Wednesday, Wotan's day), T in Wagner's *Ring.* H

63.12, Martin 208

63.29, falsetook; Falstaff, C in Verdi's *Falstaff,* Nicolai's *Merry Wives of Windsor,* and Holst's *At the Boar's Head.* G, B. Also setup of Caruso (ten.) in monkey-house incident. B

OPERA IN *Finnegans Wake*

64.4–5, he dreamed that he'd wealthes in mormon halls; "I dreamt that I dwelt in marble halls," A in Balfe's *Bohemian Girl.* HW

64.16, knockturn; Knocko, the monkey in front of whose cage Caruso (ten.) was said to have molested a lady. B

64.16, .19–20, reine . . . Rejaneyjailey they were all night; Queen of the Night, C in Mozart's *Magic Flute.* H. Also Caruso (ten.) was briefly jailed after monkey-house incident. B

64.25, Pamintul; Pamina, C in Mozart's *Magic Flute.* H

65.8, papa pals; Papageno, C in Mozart's *Magic Flute.* H

65.28, cherrybum; Cherubino, C in Mozart's *Marriage of Figaro.*

66.9, Exultations'; "Esultate!" A in Verdi's *Otello.* H

66.17, Hyde and Cheek; Walter Hyde (ten.). H

66.21, roger; Gustave Roger (ten.). B

66.21, Martin 196

66.29, tristinguish; Tristan, C in Wagner's *Tristan und Isolde.* H, M; see also Martin 196.

66.30, jubabe from jabule; "Vesti la giubba," A in Leoncavallo's *I pagliacci.* H

67.16, guntinued; Gunther, C in Wagner's *Die Götterdämmerung.* H. Also C in Reyer's *Sigurd.* B

67.33, dilalah; Dalila, C in Saint-Saëns's *Samson et Dalila.* H

68.9, *a la Zingara;* Donizetti's *La zingara* (OT). H. Also Leoncavallo's *I zingari* (OT). B. Also Rinaldo di Capua's *La zingara* (OT). B. Also Balfe's *The Bohemian Girl* (OT) (titled *La zingara* when presented in Italian). B

68.14, dotter of a dearmud; Wagner's *Die Götterdämmerung* (OT). HW, M

68.14–15, her pitch was Forty Steps and his perch old Cromwell's Quarters; arguments within late nineteenth-century English music circles about standard pitch, which was higher in England than on the Continent. See, e.g., *Sims Reeves* (277), which tells how Nilsson and Patti required lowered pitch and specially made instruments tuned lower for a production of *Faust.* Discussion was heated and frequent in the musical press. B

68.15, valkirry; Wagner's *Die Walküre* (OT). HW, M

68.27, Zay, zay, zay; Zàzà, C in Leoncavallo's *Zàzà.* H

69.7–8, Martin 208

69.9–10, horde of orts and oriorts to garble a garthen of Odin and the lost paladays; Valhalla, palace, T in Wagner's *Ring.* H, M. Also "O paradiso," A in Meyerbeer's *L'Africaine.* H

70.4, swobbing broguen eeriesh myth brockendootsch; Brogni, C in Halévy's *La Juive.* H

70.4, Martin 187

70.7–9, and wider he . . . one monkey's damages become; Caruso (ten.) monkey-house incident. See chapter 5. B

72.2, *Twitchbratschballs;* Jemmy Twitcher, C in Gay's *Beggar's Opera.* B

72.4–5, *Wan Wan Wan;* "Wahn! Wahn! überall Wahn," A in Wagner's *Die Meistersinger.* H

72.4, .10, .16, *Number . . . Vindner, . . . In Custody;* "Nume, custode e vindice," A in Verdi's *Aïda.* H

72.35, Martin 219

73.21, Patself on the Bach; Julius Patzak (ten.). H

73.23–24, rochelly . . . siegings; Balfe's *Siege of Rochelle* (OT). HW

74.1–2, he skall wake from earthsleep; Erda wakes, T in Wagner's *Ring.* H. Also Siegfried wakes Brünnhilde, T in Wagner's *Siegfried.* H-SG, M

74.2, valle; Valhalla, T in Wagner's *Ring.* B

74.5, orland; Handel's *Orlando* (OT). H

74.9, faustive; Gounod's *Faust* (OT). H. Also Busoni's *Doktor Faust* and Berlioz's *La Damnation de Faust* (OTs). B. Also Faust, C in Boïto's *Mefistofele.* B

74.9–10, when thy green woods went dry; dry staff goes green, T in Wagner's *Tannhäuser.* H

74.14–15, puff but a piff; "Piff, paff" (associated by JJ with "I'll huff and I'll puff and I'll blow your house down" to form giant motif), T in Wagner's *Ring.* H. Also A in Meyerbeer's *Les Huguenots.* H

Finnegans Wake, Book I.4:

75.8, larcenlads; Nanny Larsén-Todsen (sop.). H

75.8, Zijnzijn Zijnzijn; "Chin Chin Chinaman," A in Jones's *Geisha.* HW

75.10, corngold; Korngold (comp.). H

75.10–11, Martin 196

75.11, Ysit?; Lalo's *Le Roi d'Ys* (OT). H

75.17, a peer saft eyballds; "Take a pair of sparkling eyes," A in Gilbert and Sullivan's *Gondoliers.* HW

75.20, Nash of Girahash; Heddle Nash (ten.). H

76.25, enriched; Enrico, C in Donizetti's *Lucia di Lammermoor.* H. Also C in Haydn's *L'isola disabitata.* B. Also Enrico Caruso (ten.). B

76.27, Wilt; Marie Wilt (sop.). H

78.8, hingeworms; Fafner, C in Wagner's *Ring.* H

78.10, Unterwealth; underworld, Nibelung dwarfs, Cs in Wagner's *Ring.* H

78.11, Uppercrust Sideria; gods in Valhalla, T in Wagner's *Ring.* H

78.13, boughtenland; fairyland, T in Boughton's *Immortal Hour.* H

78.32, Woolwhite's Waltz; Gustavus Waltz (bass and Handel's cook). H

79.18, Venuses; Venusberg, T in Wagner's *Tannhäuser.* H, M

79.18, gigglibly; Beniamino Gigli (ten.). H

79.21, .22, .28, lugod! lugodoo! . . . even . . . glowing; "Morgenlich leuchtend . . . Abendlich dämmernd," A (*Preislied*) in Wagner's *Die Meistersinger.* H

79.28, dreariodreama; Drury Lane Theatre, London, site of much Italian opera in nineteenth-century England. Mink, B

80.21, fidies; Fidès, C in Meyerbeer's *Le Prophète.* B. Also Fidelio, C in Beethoven's *Fidelio.* H

80.21, prey; Gilbert-Louis Duprez (ten.). B

80.36, Martin 196

81.7, Brahm; John Braham (ten.). B

81.22, Parr aparrently; "M'appari," A in Flotow's *Martha.* H

81.31, catching holst; Gustav Holst (comp.). B

81.34, de Razzkias; Jean de Reszke (ten.). H. Also Edouard de Reszke (bass). B

82.12, chew-chin-grin; "Chin Chin Chinaman," A in Jones's *Geisha.* HW

82.16, a woden affair; Wotan, C in Wagner's *Ring.* H, M

83.5, Heart alive; Herzeleide, C in Wagner's *Parsifal.* H

83.29, faust; Faust, C in Gounod's *Faust.* H. Also C in Berlioz's *La Damnation de Faust* and Busoni's *Doktor Faust.* B. Also C in Boïto's *Mefistofele.* B

84.28, Martin 209

84.36, El Don De Dunelli; Dunn, a bass at Theatre Royal, Dublin, who called himself Dunelli. McH. Also Venetian dialect "el don de dunele," "the gift of women," i.e., Mozart's *Don Giovanni* (OT). B

85.5, hyougono; Meyerbeer's *Les Huguenots* (OT). H

86.15, hyacinth; Hyacinth, one name of Octavian, C in R. Strauss's *Der Rosenkavalier.* B

86.18, amadst; Amadis, C in Lully's *Amadis.* H. Also C in Massenet's *Amadis.* B

87.12, Hyacinth; Hyacinth, one name of Octavian, C in R. Strauss's *Der Rosenkavalier.* B

87.29, Martin 196

87.31, the bank from Banagher; Erkel's *Bánk-Bán* (OT). H

87.32, O'Donner; Donner, C in Wagner's *Das Rheingold.* H

88.14, .16, .17, O' Somebody . . . mister . . . murty; "Ocean, thou mighty monster," A in Weber's *Oberon.* H

88.18, twithcherous; Jemmy Twitcher, C in Gay's *Beggar's Opera.* B

88.21, Odin; Wotan, C in Wagner's *Ring.* H, M

88.30, founts of bounty playing; "Then You'll Remember Me," A in Balfe's *Bohemian Girl.* HW

89.10, Crosscann Lorne; "Cruiskeen Lawn," A in Benedict's *Lily of Killarney.* B

91.13, Martin 196

91.30, Warhorror; Valhalla, T in Wagner's *Ring.* H, M

92.7, Martin 196

92.12–18, Martin 219

92.19, pizzicagnoling; "Pizzica, pizzica, pizzica," A (trio) in Verdi's *Falstaff.* H

92.20, dindy dandy; d'Indy (comp.). H

92.25, Gemma; Jemmy, C in Rossini's *William Tell.* H

92.29–32, youthsy, beautsy . . . shayshaun; "Youth's the season," A in Gay's *Beggar's Opera.* HW

93.6, Commodore valley; Commendatore, C in Mozart's *Don Giovanni.* H

93.30, I am the Sullivan that trumpeting tramp; John Sullivan (ten.). H

95.6, Ah dearome forsailoshe; "Caro nome," A in Verdi's *Rigoletto.* H. Also "Ah, fors'è lui," A in Verdi's *La traviata.* H

95.9, Cunningham; Robert Cunningham (ten.). B

95.24, Martin 196

95.25, enrich; Enrico, C in Donizetti's *Lucia di Lammermoor.* H. Also C in Haydn's *L'isola disabitata.* B. Also Enrico Caruso (ten.). B

96.3–4, rogues . . . Lillytrilly; Farinelli ("the rogue," sop.). B

96.5–6, Martin 196

96.11, stuffstuff; Falstaff, C in Verdi's *Falstaff,* Nicolai's *Merry Wives of Windsor,* and Holst's *At the Boar's Head.* G, B

96.12, mushymushy; Musetta and Mimi, Cs in Puccini's *La bohème.* H

96.15, triss; Lord Tristram de Mikleford, C in Flotow's *Martha.* B. See also Martin 196.

96.16, mused her; Musetta, C in Puccini's *La bohème.* H

97.14, volponism; Giacomo Lauri-Volpi (ten.). B

97.14, ravenfed; Anton Raaff (ten.). B

97.17, Mikkelraved; Lord Tristram (Tristan) de Mikleford, C in Flotow's *Martha.* B

98.9, Cornelius; Peter Cornelius (ten.). H. Also Peter Cornelius (comp.). H

98.13, bumbashaws; Giuseppe Bamboschek (cond.). B

98.20, lilypond; Lily Pons (sop.). H

98.30, Hogan; Hagen, C in Wagner's *Die Götterdämmerung.* H. Also C in Reyer's *Sigurd.* B

98.30, punsil; Rosa Ponselle (sop.). H

98.32–33, a wiege n'er a waage is still immer and immor awagering; "Weia! Waga! . . . Wagalaweia!" (Rhine Maidens at beginning of opera), A in Wagner's *Das Rheingold.* H

99.16, svertgleam; gleaming sword, T in Wagner's *Die Walküre.* H

99.16, Valkir; Wagner's *Die Walküre* (OT). B

100.14, Magnifica; Don Magnifico, C in Rossini's *La cenerentola.* H

100.28, tristurned; Tristan, C in Wagner's *Tristan und Isolde.* H, M

100.31, Kurt; Melanie Kurt (sop.). H

101.4, wimdop; Walter Widdop (ten.). H

101.9, mark; King Mark, C in Wagner's *Tristan und Isolde.* G. See also Martin 196.

101.12–13, *Homo Capite Erectus;* "Ho capito, signor," A in Mozart's *Don Giovanni.* H

101.17, colleen bawl; "The Colleen Bawn," A in Benedict's *Lily of Killarney.* HW

101.18, widowpeace; Walter Widdop (ten.). H

102.15, Sunday, *Sola;* Moody-Manner Opera Company was called the "Sunday School on Tour" because it placed male and female members of the opera company in separate cars on the train for decorum's sake. B

102.25, Poppy; Poppea, C in Monteverdi's *L'incoronazione di Poppea.* H

102.26, Marinka; Mařenka, C in Smetana's *Bartered Bride.* H

102.26, Parme; Violetta, C in Verdi's *La traviata.* H

103.8, .11, Nabuch . . . babalong; Verdi's *Nabucco* (OT). B

Finnegans Wake, Book I.5:

104.10, *Treestam and Icy Siseule;* Wagner's *Tristan und Isolde* (OT). H, M

104.11, *mihimihi;* Mimi, C in Puccini's *La bohème.* H

104.20, Cleopater's; Cléopâtre, C in Massenet's *Cléopâtre* (also operas by others with same title). H

105.5, *Boxer Coxer;* Arthur Sullivan's *Cox and Box* (OT). B

105.9, *Taub;* Richard Tauber (ten.). H

105.11, *Minnelisp;* Minnie, C in Puccini's *La fanciulla del west.* H

105.11, *Intimier Minnelisp;* interior monologue of Mime, T in Wagner's *Siegfried.* H-SG

105.15, *Handsel;* Handel (comp.). H

105.20, *Dual of Ayessha;* "Jewel of Asia," A in Jones's *Geisha.* HW

105.27, *Crowalley;* Crow Street Theatre, Dublin. Senn

106.5, *Torsker;* Puccini's *Tosca* (OT). H

106.12, *Siegfield;* Siegfried, C in Wagner's *Siegfried.* H

106.19, *Chee Chee Cheels on their China Miction;* "Chin Chin Chinaman," A in Jones's *Geisha.* HW

106.36, *Tree . . . Stone;* Tristram, C in Wagner's *Tristan und Isolde.* H

107.18, Martin 219

107.36, Martin 209

108.5–6, by a rightdown regular racer; "Right Down Regular Royal Queen," A in Gilbert and Sullivan's *Gondoliers.* HW

108.8–10, patience . . . remember patience is the great thing . . . patience; Gilbert and Sullivan's *Patience* (OT). H

110.10, verdhure's; Verdi (comp.). H

110.35, chalice by another heily innocent; grail, T in Wagner's *Parsifal.* H

112.7, the Zingari; Leoncavallo's *I zingari* (OT). B

112.28, marcella; Marcello, C in Puccini's *La bohème.* H. Also U. Giordano's *Marcella* (OT). H

112.33, fols with her falli-; John McCormack under pseudonym Giovanni Foli (ten.). K

113.11, Silvapais; Silva, C in Verdi's *Ernani.* H

113.12, schwants (schwrites); Weinberger's *Schwanda* (OT). H. Also *Schwanz* (coll. Ger., "penis"), sometimes substituted by sportive tenors in singing "Mein lieber Schwan," T in Wagner's *Lohengrin.* B

113.19, a Treestone with one Ysold; Wagner's *Tristan und Isolde* (OT). H, M. See also Martin 196.

113.21, Martin 192

113.25, ich beam so fresch; "Bin ich nun frei" (Alberich's curse), T in Wagner's *Das Rheingold.* H

114.4–20, Martin 219

115.12, gerontophils; Geronte de Ravoir, C in Puccini's *Manon Lescaut.* H

117.2, Martin 196

117.5–6, Martin 209

117.11, old stoliolum; "E la solita storia," A in Cilea's *L'arlesiana.* H

117.16, nozzy; Mozart's *Marriage of Figaro* (OT). H

117.16, Nanette; Anna Bolena, C in Donizetti's *Anna Bolena,* with ALP. G. Also Nanetta, C in Verdi's *Falstaff.* B

117.18, souffsouff; "Pourquoi me reveiller, O souffle du printemps?" A in Massenet's *Werther.* B

117.24, Paoli's; Alessio de Paolis (ten.). H

117.26–27, a normal Kettlelicker; Bellini's *Norma* (OT). H

117.26–27, Kettlelicker (= "catalogo"); "Madamina, il catalogo," A in Mozart's *Don Giovanni.* H

119.28, marking; King Mark, C in Wagner's *Tristan und Isolde*. G

119.30–31, Martin 196

122.16, O'Mara; Joseph O'Mara (ten.). B

122.19, O'Mara; Joseph O'Mara (ten.). B

123.4, penelopean; Fauré's opera *Penelope* (1913), mentioned in *Letters 3,* 10. B

124.10, .23, *piquéd,* Dame; Tchaikovsky's *Pique Dame* (OT). H

Finnegans Wake, Book I.6:

126.1–3, So? Who do you no tonigh, laxy and gentleman?; as so-do-la-si [laxy], the opening notes of "Un giorno la mano me porse un donzello," A in Donizetti's *La zingara.* B and Hart

126.10–11, Martin 187, 209

126.16, Martin 190

126.23–24, Martin 196

127.11, outharrods; Herod, C in Strauss's *Salomé* and in Massenet's *Hérodiade* (OT). G, B

127.30, commands to dinner; "A cenar teco m'invitasti," Commendatore (statue) invited to supper, A in Mozart's *Don Giovanni.* B, McH

128.1–2, Martin 196

128.2, mildewstaned . . . mouldystoned; "Mild und leise" ("Liebestod"), A in Wagner's *Tristan und Isolde,* with Tristan's name. G, B

128.26, orchistruss; Giusto Ferdinando Tenducci (sop.), nicknamed "Triorchis." B

129.23, homer; Louise Homer (contr.). H

129.30, Giroflee Giroflaa; Lecocq's *Giroflé, Girofla* (OT). H

129.31, Colombo; Mackenzie and Hueffer's *Columba* (OT). B

129.34, oldest creater in Aryania; Monteverdi's *Arianna* (OT). H

130.4–5, Martin 209

131.7, Ostman; Osmin, C in Mozart's *Abduction from the Seraglio.* H

131.8, Paddishaw; Selim Pasha, C in Mozart's *Abduction from the Seraglio.* B

131.12, appauling; William Paull (bar.). B

131.13–14, Martin 209

131.34, chinchin; "Chin Chin Chinaman," A in Jones's *Geisha.* HW

132.25, nibbling; Nibelung, Cs in Wagner's *Ring.* H

133.6, Riesengebirger; "Riesen," T in Wagner's *Ring.* H

133.8–9, Liebsterpet; "Mild und leise" ("Liebestod"), A in Wagner's *Tristan und Isolde.* HW, M

133.19–20, life's eleaxir from the pettipickles of the Jewess; Eléazar, C in Halévy's *La Juive*. H. Also Donizetti's *L'elisir d'amore* (OT). B

133.20, the Jewess; Halévy's *La Juive* (OT). B

133.20–21, ruoulls . . . the Huguenots; Raoul, C in Meyerbeer's *Les Huguenots,* a John Sullivan role. H

133.20–21, ruoulls in sulks if any popeling runs down the Huguenots; Meyerbeer's *Les Huguenots* (OT). H

133.27, one shoebard; Schubert (comp.). H

134.27–28, Martin 196

134.31–32, Martin 196

134.33, Martin 209

134.36–135.2, Martin 196

135.32–33, when older links . . . resemble she; "Then You'll Remember Me," A in Balfe's *Bohemian Girl.* HW

136.1, mursque; Ilma di Murska (sop.). B

136.13, raaven; Anton Raaff (ten.). B

136.21, Timour of Tortur; Timur, C in Puccini's *Turandot.* H

136.34, Martin 196

137.7, Albiony; Emma Albani (sop.). H. Also Marietta Alboni (contr.). H

137.9–10, the Lund's kirk; Louise Kirkby-Lunn (mezzo-sop.). H

138.17, Ivaun the Taurrible; Ivan, C in Bizet's *Ivan IV.* H. Also Ivan, C in Glinka's *Life for the Tsar.* H. Also Ivan, C in Rimsky-Korsakov's *Maid of Pskov* (subtitle: "Ivan the Terrible"). H

139.28, Amin; Amina, C in Bellini's *La sonnambula.* H

139.30–32, where asnake is under clover and birds aprowl are in the rookeries and a magda went to monkishouse and a riverpaard was spotted; Caruso (ten.) monkey-house incident. See chapter 5. B

139.32, Martin 193

141.14, crotty; Leslie Crotty (bar.). B

141.19, Walther; Walther von Stolzing, C in Wagner's *Die Meistersinger.* H

142.12, salés; Albert Saléza (ten.). H

142.26, sullivans; John Sullivan (ten.). H

142.27, Jorn; Karl Jörn (ten.). H

143.3–4, Martin 219

143.15, Hoel; Hoël, C in Meyerbeer's *Dinorah.* H

143.17, gallicry; Amelita Galli-Curci (sop.). H

143.29–148.32, Martin 196

143.36, Perisian; Fanny Persiani (sop.). H

144.6, Prendregast; "Di più non lacerarmi . . . prendi quest'è," A in Verdi's *La traviata*. B

144.10, provencial; "Di provenza il mar," A in Verdi's *La traviata*. B

144.10, Eilish; Colleen Bawn, C in Benedict's *Lily of Killarney*. G

144.10–11, Martin 197

144.30, Mr. Polkingtone; Pinkerton, C in Puccini's *Madame Butterfly*. H

145.1, tutu; "Tu? tu? piccolo iddio!" A in Puccini's *Madame Butterfly*. H

145.14, buttercups; Buttercup, C in Gilbert and Sullivan's *H.M.S. Pinafore*. H. Also Cio-Cio-San, C in Puccini's *Madame Butterfly*. H

145.14–15, Martin 197

145.36–146.1, Martin 197

146.7, Martin 197

146.12, Marguérite; Marguérite, C in Gounod's *Faust*. H. Also C in Berlioz's *La Damnation de Faust* and Meyerbeer's *Les Huguenots*. B Also Margherita, C in Boïto's *Mefistofele*. B

146.17, isabeaubel; Mascagni's *Isabeau* (OT). H

146.33–36, Buybuy! . . . I go you before; "Addio del passato," A in Verdi's *La traviata*. H

146.34, Martin 197

147.6, Mitchells; Nellie Melba (sop., b. Mitchell). H

147.6, Nicholls; Ernest Nicolini (ten.). H. Also Agnes Nicholls (Lady Hamilton Harty, sop.). H. Also Nicolino (male contr.). H

147.10–11, Saint Yves; King Mark, C in Wagner's *Tristan und Isolde*. G

147.12, cough; cough, T in Verdi's *La traviata* and in Puccini's *La bohème*. H

147.12, Gilda; Gilda, C in Verdi's *Rigoletto*. H

147.12, Lou; Louise, C in Charpentier's *Louise*. H

147.13, Poll; Polly Peachum, C in Gay's *Beggar's Opera*. H

147.13, Queeniee; Queen of the Night, C in Mozart's *Magic Flute*. H

147.14, Una, Vela; "Una vela!" (opening words, "A sail!"), T in Verdi's *Otello*. H

147.14, Wanda; C in Doppler's *Wanda*. G. Also C in Offenbach's *La Grand-Duchesse de Gérolstein*. B

147.19, A ring a ring a rosaring; Wagner's *Ring* (OT). H

147.24, chasta dieva; "Casta diva," A in Bellini's *Norma*. HW-SG

147.26, Andrée's; Andrea Chénier, C in U. Giordano's *Andrea Chénier*. H

147.30, my sweet parted lipsabuss; "Water parted from the sea," A in Arne's *Artaxerxes*. B

147.32, Smock Alley; Smock Alley Theatre, Dublin. McH

148.11, Martin 197

148.13, juliettes; Juliet, C in Gounod's *Roméo et Juliette*. G, B

149.13, Martin 187

149.26, *pailleté* with a coat; "Vesti la giubba," A in Leoncavallo's *I pagliacci*. H

150.15, Professor Loewy-Brueller; Hermann Levi (cond.), first conductor of *Parsifal* at Bayreuth. H-SG. Also Hans von Bülow (cond.). H-SG

150.15–159.19, Martin 187

150.17–18, Dr Hydes; Walter Hyde (ten.). H

150.26–28, *Why am I not born like a Gentleman and why am I now so speakable about my own eatables* (Feigenbaumblatt and Father, Judapest, 5688, A.M.); Wagner's (comp.) polemics on Jewish music. H

150.28, takes off his gabbercoat; "Vesti la giubba," A in Leoncavallo's *I pagliacci*. H

151.1, cosm; Cosima von Bülow Wagner (wife of comp.). H-SG, M

151.7, Fairynelly's; Farinelli (male sop.). H

151.10, *parcequeue;* Wagner's *Parsifal* (OT). H-SG, M

151.11, Professor Levi-Brullo; Hermann Levi (cond.), first conductor of *Parsifal* at Bayreuth. Also Hans von Bülow (cond.). H-SG

151.13, Nuremberg; Wagner's *Die Meistersinger* (OT). H-SG, M

151.13, the watches cunldron; Kundry, C in Wagner's *Parsifal*. H-SG. Also Rachel thrown into a cauldron, T in Halévy's *La Juive*. H-SG

151.17, cupolar clods; cupola, T in Wagner's *Parsifal*. H-SG, M. See also Martin 219.

151.19–24, *Mitleid . . . toray;* "Durch Mitleid wissend, der reine Tor" (known through sympathy, the pure fool), T in Wagner's *Parsifal*. H-SG, M

151.32–33, Professor Llewellys ap Bryllars; Hermann Levi (cond.), first conductor of *Parsifal* at Bayreuth. Also Hans von Bülow (cond.). B

152.1–2, where me arts soar . . . where I cling; Klingsor, C in Wagner's *Parsifal*. H-SG

152.15–159.19, Martin 192

152.18–19, Eins . . . onesomeness wast alltolonely; "Einsam in trüben Tagen," A in Wagner's *Lohengrin*. H

152.27, borgeously; Armando Borgioli (bar.). H

152.31, his father's sword; Parsifal's lance, T in Wagner's *Parsifal*. H. Also "Ein Schwert verhiess mir der Vater," A in Wagner's *Die Walküre*. H, M

153.4, colliens; Colline, C in Puccini's *La bohème*. H

153.32, micahlike; Micaëla, C in Bizet's *Carmen*. H

154.20, clement; Edmond Clément (ten.). H

154.20, Martin 192

154.28, *Sancta Patientia;* "O sancta justitia," A in Lortzing's *Zar und Zimmerman.* H

154.31–36, I connow make my submission . . . abler to tell Your Honoriousness; Tell, who would not make his submission, C in Rossini's *William Tell.* H

155.25, Maples; "Col. Mapleson," impresario of Royal Italian Opera in London, whose company toured Dublin annually. B

155.25, lucciolys; Christine Nilsson (sop.), whose Lucia was one of her best roles. B

155.26, Teresa; Therese Tietjens (sop.), member of Mapleson's company. B

155.27, Gresk; Jean de Reszke (ten.). B

155.36, Alldaybrandy's; Frances Alda (sop.). H

156.10, sadcontras; Rimsky-Korsakov's *Sadko* (OT). H

156.25, Vale Hollow; Valhalla, T in Wagner's *Ring.* H, M

156.32–33, Veiled Horror; Valhalla, T in Wagner's *Ring.* H, M. See also Martin 209.

156.34, Elissabed; Elisabeth, C in Wagner's *Tannhäuser.* H, M

157.8, Nuvoletta; Clara Novello (sop.). H. Also Violetta, C in Verdi's *La traviata.* H

157.13, She was alone. All her nubied companions were asleeping; "'Tis the last rose of summer," A in Flotow's *Martha.* B

157.29, .33, spiration! . . . mignons; Sperata, C in Thomas's *Mignon.* H

157.32, .36, *la princesse de la Petite Bretagne* . . . Mrs Cornwallis-West . . . the daughter of the queen of the Emperour of Irelande; Isolde, C in Wagner's *Tristan und Isolde.* H-SG, M

157.33, her mignons arms; Thomas's *Mignon* (OT). B

158.1, Tristis Tristior Tristissimus; Tristan, C in Wagner's *Tristan und Isolde.* H, M

158.9–10, Martin 220

158.25–28, Martin 209

158.31–159.1, Martin 210

159.15, hopeharrods; Herod, C in Strauss's *Salomé* and in Massenet's *Hérodiade* (OT). G, B

159.16–17, Martin 210

159.18, Martin 197

159.19, No applause, please; instruction to audience, end of act 1, Parsifal, T in Wagner's *Parsifal.* H-SG, M

159.32, Tristan da Cunha; Tristan, C in Wagner's *Tristan und Isolde.* H

160.29, faust; Faust, C in Gounod's *Faust.* H. Also C in Berlioz's *La Damnation de Faust* and Busoni's *Doktor Faust* (OTs). B. Also Gounod's *Faust* (OT). H. Also Faust, C in Boïto's *Mefistofele.* B

160.35, 161.16, leisure . . . mildest; "Mild und leise" ("Liebestod"), A in Wagner's *Tristan und Isolde.* H

161.13, Martin 197

161.16, milkstoffs; Falstaff, C in Verdi's *Falstaff,* Nicolai's *Merry Wives of Windsor,* and Holst's *At the Boar's Head.* G, B

161.28, Pedersill; Gianna Pederzini (mezzo-sop.). H

162.2–3, the farce of dustiny; Verdi's *La forza del destino* (OT). HW

162.6, batman; bat theme, T in J. Strauss II's *Die Fledermaus.* H

162.6, soldier . . . commontoryism; Commendatore, C in Mozart's *Don Giovanni.* H

162.22, caviller; Mascagni's *Cavalleria rusticana* (OT). H

162.23, fideism; Fidès, C in Meyerbeer's *Le Prophète.* H. Also Fidelio, C in Beethoven's *Fidelio.* B

162.31, averlaunched; "La Valanga" ("The Avalanche," sop.), *Letters 1,* 358. B

163.17, Cusanus; Giovanni Carestini, sometimes called "Cusanino" (male contr.). B

164.14, 19–20, Margareen . . . *Sweet Margareen,* and the more hopeful *O Margareena! O Margareena;* Marguérite, C in Gounod's *Faust.* H. Also C in Berlioz's *La Damnation de Faust* and Meyerbeer's *Les Huguenots.* B. Also Margherita, C in Boïto's *Mefistofele.* B

164.31, Harlene; Arline, C in Balfe's *Bohemian Girl.* H

164.34, *aria;* aria, T in opera generally. B

165.2, Maace; Joseph Maas (ten.). H

165.7, true Bdur; Verdi's *Il trovatore* (OT). H

165.9, tonehall; Zurich's Tonhalle, site of opera productions. B

165.29, *boîte;* Boïto (comp.). H

166.24–26, more mascular personality by flaunting frivolish finery over men's inside clothes, for the femininny of that totamulier will always lack the musculink of a verumvirum; Wagner's fondness for fancy clothes (comp.). H

166.30, Margareena; Marguérite, C in Gounod's *Faust.* H. Also C in Berlioz's *La Damnation de Faust* and Meyerbeer's *Les Huguenots.* B. Also Margherita, C in Boïto's *Mefistofele.* B

166.34, cleopatrician; Cléopâtre, C in Massenet's *Cléopâtre* (also operas by others with same title). H

167.32, ring; Wagner's *Ring* (OT). H

Finnegans Wake, Book I.7

169.18, manroot; Paderewski's *Manru* (OT). H

169.20, tristended; Tristan, C in Wagner's *Tristan und Isolde*. H, M

170.7, bittersweet; Coward's *Bitter Sweet* (OT). B

170.10, Bohemeand lips; Puccini's *La bohème* (OT). H. Also Balfe's *Bohemian Girl* (OT). H

170.10, when Bohemeand lips; "Then You'll Remember Me," A in Balfe's *Bohemian Girl*. HW

170.34, Grex's . . . greasilygristly; Giulia Grisi (sop.). H. Also Giuditta Grisi (mezzo-sop.). H. Also Massenet's *Grisélidis* (OT). B

171.14, gulletburn; Ellen Gulbranson (sop.). H

171.15, the tragic jester sobbed himself; Rigoletto, C in Verdi's *Rigoletto*. H-SG. Also Canio (Pagliaccio), C in Leoncavallo's *I pagliacci*. H-SG

172.1–2, Patatapapaveri's, fruiterers and musical florists; Papageno, C in Mozart's *Magic Flute*. H

172.13, .23, hereditary . . . asylum; "Asile héréditaire," A in Rossini's *William Tell*. H-SG

172.22, Guardacosta; Sir Michael Costa (cond.). B

172.22–23, Guardacosta leporello?; "Guardate ancor, padrone," A in Mozart's *Don Giovanni*. H

172.23, leporello; Leporello, C in Mozart's *Don Giovanni*. HW

173.4, troubadouring; Verdi's *Il trovatore* (OT). H

173.10, pensile; Rosa Ponselle (sop.). B

173.12, Jansens Chrest; Herbert Janssen (bar.). H

174.14, apasafello; Wagner's *Parsifal* (OT). H

175.12, *Sachsen;* Hans Sachs, C in Wagner's *Die Meistersinger*. H

175.16, *Peacepeace;* "Pace, pace," A in Verdi's *La forza del destino*. H

175.17, *Hempal must tumpel;* Frieda Hempel (sop.). H

175.17, *Gardener's bound;* Mary Garden (sop.). H

175.23, Martin 197

176.18, Raimbrandt; Raimbaut the minstrel, C in Meyerbeer's *Robert le diable*. H

176.22, marshalaisy; Marzelline, C in Beethoven's *Fidelio*. H. Also prison + Marzelline in *Fidelio* = Marshalsea prison, T in Beethoven's *Fidelio*. H

176.36, telemac; Telemann (comp.). H

177.14, cherubum; Cherubino, C in Mozart's *Marriage of Figaro*. H

177.14, Nero; Boïto's *Nero* (OT). H

177.14, Nobookisonester; Verdi's *Nabucco* (OT). H

177.18, gunnard; Gounod (comp.). H

177.18, Martin 210

177.25, thair's; Massenet's *Thaïs* (OT). H

178.9, Lucalizod; Isolde, C in Wagner's *Tristan und Isolde*. H. Also Lucia, C in Donizetti's *Lucia di Lammermoor,* Rossini's *La gazza ladra,* and Ponchielli's *I promessi sposi.* B

178.10, cobbleway; Giuseppina Cobelli (sop.). H

178.17, *O pura e pia bella;* "Morir! sì pura e bella!," A in Verdi's *Aïda.* HW

178.24, sevenspan ponte *dei colori;* rainbow bridge, T in Wagner's *Das Rheingold.* H, M. Also da Ponte, comp. and librettist. G. Also Lily Pons (sop.). B

179.32, a roseschelle cottage by the sea; "My love and cottage near Rochelle," A in Balfe's *Siege of Rochelle.* HW

179.34–35, sickcylinder; "Siciliana," A in Mascagni's *Cavalleria rusticana.* H. Also Verdi's *I vespri siciliani* (OT). B

179.35, operahouse; any opera house. B

180.6, soap ewer; "M'appari," A in Flotow's *Martha.* HW. Also "Morir! sì pura e bella!" A in Verdi's *Aïda.* HW

180.8, Baraton McGluckin; Gluck (comp.). B. Also Alma Gluck (sop.). G. Also Barton M'Guckin (ten.). H

180.10, handle side; Handel (comp.). H

180.12, (*Alfaiate punxit*); Alfio stabs Turiddu, T in Mascagni's *Cavalleria rusticana.* H

180.13–14, Lindundarri; Jenny Lind (sop.). H

180.17–30, but what with . . . a word a week; "Lord Chancellor's Song" ("When you're lying awake"), A in Gilbert and Sullivan's *Iolanthe.* H

181.16, an epical forged cheque; Siegfried forges Nothung, T in Wagner's *Ring.* B, H-SG

182.4–7, phantastic . . . beerlitz; Berlioz (comp.). H

182.28, boric; Lucrezia Bori (sop.). H

183.20–21, twisted quills; "Questa o quella," A in Verdi's *Rigoletto.* HW

183.25–28, schoolgirls', young ladies', . . . godmothers' garters; "Madamina, il catalogo," A in Mozart's *Don Giovanni.* H

184.19, *Mas blanca que la blanca hermana;* "Plus blanche que la blanche ermine," A in Meyerbeer's *Les Huguenots.* H

184.23, Pinkingtone's; Pinkerton, C in Puccini's *Madame Butterfly.* H

184.23, patty; Adelina Patti (sop.). H

184.27, Gabrielle; Adriana Gabrieli (sop.). H

185.5, romeruled; Emma Romer (sop.). H

185.20, Martin 197

185.25, O'Ryan's; Le Comte Ory, C in Rossini's *Le Comte Ory.* H

186.10, dal dabal dab aldanabal; Frances Alda (sop.). H. Also Mafalda Favero (sop.). B

186.11, arklast fore arklyst; Arkel, C in Debussy's *Pelléas et Mélisande.* H

186.19, Kruis-Kroon-Kraal; "Cruiskeen Lawn," A in Benedict's *Lily of Killarney.* B

186.28, Arcoiris; André d'Arkor (ten.). H. Also rainbow bridge to Valhalla, T in Wagner's *Das Rheingold.* B

186.31, grazious; Francesco Graziani (bar., first Don Carlo in Verdi's *La forza del destino*). H. Also Lodovico Graziani (ten., first Alfredo in Verdi's *La traviata*). H

186.36, Purtsymessus and Pertsymiss; Bizet's *La Jolie Fille de Perth* (OT). H

187.18, Putterick O'Purcell; Purcell (comp.). H

189.5, a philtred love; love philter, T in Wagner's *Tristan und Isolde.* H, M. See also Martin 197.

189.5, trysting by tantrums; Tristan, C in Wagner's *Tristan und Isolde.* B, M

189.8, strabismal; Stravinsky (comp.). H

189.12, minneful; Minne (ten.). H. Also Minnie, C in Puccini's *La fanciulla del west.* H

189.12, Martin 188

189.17–19, Martin 197

189.25, Hail! Hail! Highbosomheaving Missmisstress Morna; "Heil dir, Sonne! Heil dir, Licht!" T in Wagner's *Siegfried.* H

189.25, Morna; Bellini's *Norma* (OT). B

190.18, do your little thruppenny bit; Weill's *Die Dreigroschenoper* (OT). Janusko

191.35, Martin 205

191.36, wishywashy sank; "Chin Chin Chinaman," A in Jones's *Geisha.* B

192.5, Malingerer; Mathilde Mallinger (sop.). H

192.14, Reynaldo; Handel's *Rinaldo* (OT). H

193.32 cannibal Cain; Caruso (ten.) monkey-house incident. See chapter 5. B

194.4, mimine; Mimi, C in Puccini's *La bohème.* H

194.4–9, mimine . . . so . . . for . . . millimetre; read as mi-mi-so-fa-mi, this suggests "A Vesta, portez vos offrandes; devant elle je vais m'incliner," A in Gounod's *Polyeucte;* also "Turn, turn in this direction, Shed, o shed a gentle smile" from Gilbert and Sullivan's *Patience.* B and Hart

194.12–14, la . . . dominate . . . me . . . dogstar; read as la-do-mi-do, the opening notes of the apprentices' chorus, "Das Blumenkränzlein aus Seiden fein, wird das dem Herrn Ritter," A in Wagner's *Die Meistersinger.* B and Hart

Finnegans Wake, Book I.8:

196.1–2, O tell; Verdi's *Otello* (OT). H

196.1–2, O tell me all; "Ah! Dite alla giovine," A in Verdi's *La traviata.* B

196.1–3, O tell me all about Anna Livia; "Parle-moi de ma mère," A (duet) in Bizet's *Carmen.* H

196.2, tell; Rossini's *William Tell* (OT). B

196.17–18, Martin 197

197.1, Reeve Gootch . . . Reeve Drughad [Reeve + Reeve = Reeves]; Sims Reeves (ten.). H

197.6, swank; swan, T in Wagner's *Lohengrin.* H

197.8, Huges Caput Earlyfouler; Henry the fowler, C in Wagner's *Lohengrin.* H

197.17–18, Martin 194

197.26, quaggy waag; "Weia! Waga! . . . Wagalaweia!" (Rhine Maidens at beginning of opera), A in Wagner's *Das Rheingold.* H

197.36, the whale's away with the grayling; grail, T in Wagner's *Parsifal.* H

198.13, Gota; Duke Gottfried, C in Wagner's *Lohengrin.* H

198.17, in passession, the proxenete! Proxenete and phwhat is phthat?; "Possente Phtha," T in Verdi's *Aïda.* H

199.4–5, Martin 210

199.9–10, he durmed adranse in durance vaal; "I dreamt that I dwelt in marble halls," A in Balfe's *Bohemian Girl.* B

199.12, Wendawanda; Wanda, C in Doppler's *Wanda.* G. Also C in Offenbach's *La Grand-Duchesse de Gérolstein.* B

199.19, .26, sukry . . . tawe; Suky Tawdry, C in Gay's *Beggar's Opera.* B

199.22, russ; Russ (sop.). H

199.23, vivers; Jenny Diver, C in Gay's *Beggar's Opera.* B

199.27–28, *The Heart Bowed Down;* "The heart bowed down," A in Balfe's *Bohemian Girl.* HW

199.28, Chelli Michele's; Michael Kelly (ten.). H

199.28, Michele's; Michele, C in Puccini's *Il tabarro.* H

199.28–29, *La Calumnia è un Vermicelli;* "La Calunnia è un venticello," A in Rossini's *Barber of Seville.* HW

199.29, balfy; Balfe (comp. and bar.). H

199.29, *Robidson;* Paul Robeson (bar.). H

200.4, porpor; Nicola Porpora (comp.). H

200.4, brahming; John Braham (ten.). H

200.9, glucks; Gluck (comp.). H. Also Alma Gluck (sop.). G

200.9, Madame Delba; Nellie Melba (sop.). H. Also Marie Delna (contr.). H

200.9, Madame Delba to Romeoreszk; A (duet) in Gounod's *Roméo et Juliette.*
H

200.9, Romeoreszk; Jean de Reszke (ten.). H

200.24, benders; Paul Bender (bass). H

200.35, flut ye, pian piena; "Pian, pianin" (act 4 finale), A in Mozart's *Marriage of Figaro.* H. Also Mozart's *Magic Flute* (OT). B

201.3–4, Martin 210

201.8, Martin 197

201.33, Martin 220

201.35, O loreley; Catalani's *Lorelei* (OT). H. Also Mendelssohn's *Lorelei* (OT).
H

201.35–36, Martin 210. Also Hagen, C in Reyer's *Sigurd.* B

202.8, diveline? Casting; "Casta diva," A in Bellini's *Norma.* HW

202.19, Nieman from Nirgends found the Nihil; Albert Niemann (ten.). H.
Also "Nirgends ein Grab! Niemals der Tod!" (Nowhere a grave! Never death!), T in Wagner's *Flying Dutchman.* H

202.20, Albern; Alberich—encounter with Rhine Maidens, C in Wagner's *Ring.*
H, M. See also Martin 210.

203.8–9, Wasut? Izod?; "Was ist? Isolde" (Tristan's first words), T in Wagner's
Tristan und Isolde. H, M

203.13, leandros; Leandro, C in Busoni's *Arlecchino.* B

203.20, venersderg in junojuly; Venusberg, T in Wagner's *Tannhäuser.* H, M

203.20, oso sweet and so cool and so limber; "M'appari," A in Flotow's *Martha.* B

203.21, Nixie; Rhine daughters, Cs in Wagner's *Das Rheingold.* G, McH. Also
Arthur Nikisch (cond.). B

203.21, Nanon L'Escaut; Massenet's *Manon* (OT). H. Also Puccini's *Manon
Lescaut* (OT). H

203.26–27, Vale Vowclose's . . . reignbeau's heavenarches; rainbow bridge to
Valhalla, T in Wagner's *Ring.* B

203.27, reignbeau's heavenarches; Alfredo, C in Verdi's *La traviata.* H

203.29, vierge violetian; Violetta (associated in *FW* with Manon as two prostitutes), C in Verdi's *La traviata.* H

203.31, Maass; Joseph Maas (ten.). G

204.2, ruz; Marie Roze (sop., sang *Manon* with Joseph Maas). G

204.10, laida; Aïda, C in Verdi's *Aïda.* H

204.30, Veronica's wipers; Messager's *Véronique* (OT). H

204.30, rancing; Jack Rance, C in Puccini's *La fanciulla del west.* H

205.10, diabolo; Fra Diavolo, C in Auber's *Fra Diavolo.* H

205.16, Well; Wellgunde, C in Wagner's *Ring.* H. Also "Welle" (waves), T in Wagner's *Das Rheingold.* H

206.9, .11, bergened . . . Shaun; Berg (comp.). H. Also Schoenberg (comp.). H

206.14, in the mascarete; Verdi's *Un ballo in maschera* (OT). H

206.15–16, Minneha, minnehi, minaaehe, minneho; Minnie, C in Puccini's *La fanciulla del west.* H

206.15–16, Martin 188

207.3–6, of fallen griefs of weeping willow. Then she made her bracelets and her anklets and her armlets and a jetty amulet for necklace of clicking cobbles and pattering pebbles and rumbledown rubble; Desdemona's death, T in Verdi's *Otello.* H-SG

207.7, rhunerhinerstones; Rhine, T in Wagner's *Das Rheingold.* H, M

207.12, Ciliegia Grande; Francesco Cilea (comp.). H

207.12, Ciliegia; "Scuoti quella fronda di ciliego" (Flower Duet), A (duet) in Puccini's *Madame Butterfly.* H

207.26, Bon a ventura; Bonaventura, one name of Octavian, C in R. Strauss's *Der Rosenkavalier.* B

208.19, swansruff; swan, T in Wagner's *Lohengrin.* H

208.30–31, Missus be good and don't fall in the say; as mi-do-fa-si, opening notes of "O Dieu, Dieu," A in Halévy's *La Juive.* B

209.18, Well, . . . waveney lyne; "Welle" (waves), T in Wagner's *Das Rheingold.* H

209.18, Well; Wellgunde, C in Wagner's *Ring.* H

209.24, Isolabella; Giuseppe Gazzaniga's *L'isola d'Alcina* (OT, first complete Italian opera performed in Ireland). B. Also Giuseppe Scarlatti's *L'isola disabitata* (OT). B. Also Joseph Haydn's opera of same title (OT). B. Also Isola, codirector of Opéra-Comique. B. Also Anna Isola (sop.) or Gaetano Isola (comp.). B

209.24, Martin 197

209.34, Annchen; Aennchen, C in Weber's *Der Freischütz.* H-SG

210.9, cough; cough, T in Puccini's *La bohème* and Verdi's *La traviata.* H

210.28, reiz; Albert Reiss (ten.). H. Also Mark Reyzen (bass). B

210.30, Eva Mobbely; "La donna è mobile," A in Verdi's *Rigoletto.* H

210.30, Eva; Eva, C in Wagner's *Die Meistersinger.* H

211.4, frey; Freia, C in Wagner's *Ring.* H, M

211.8, Lena Magdalena; Maddalena, C in Verdi's *Rigoletto.* H. Also C in Donizetti's *Linda di Chamounix.* B

211.8, Camilla (Dumas's story was *La Dame aux camélias*); Violetta, C in Verdi's *La traviata*. B

211.8, Ludmilla; Ludmila, C in Glinka's *Russlan and Ludmila*. H. Also C in Smetana's *Bartered Bride*. B

211.11, Wally Meagher; Catalani's *La Wally* (OT). H

211.12, Elsie; Elsa of Brabant, C in Wagner's *Lohengrin*. H

211.14, Bellezze; Vincenzo Bellezza (cond.). H

211.14, *Missa pro Messa;* Mimi, C in Puccini's *La bohème*. H

211.16, Rogerson Crusoe; Enrico Caruso (ten.). H

211.17–18, revery warp in the weaver's woof for Victor Hugonot; Meyerbeer's *Les Huguenots* (OT). H

211.26, Tristram; Tristan, C in Wagner's *Tristan und Isolde*. H. Also Lord Tristram (Tristan) de Mikleford, C in Flotow's *Martha*. B

211.32, a stonecold shoulder for Donn Joe Vance; Mozart's *Don Giovanni* (OT). H

211.35, Ida Ida; Gilbert and Sullivan's *Princess Ida* (OT). H

211.35, Elletrouvetout; Verdi's *Il trovatore* (OT). B

212.6, Selina; Selika, C in Meyerbeer's *L'Africaine*. H

212.8, Maassy; Joseph Maas (ten.). H

212.9, Melissa; Mélisande, C in Debussy's *Pelléas et Mélisande*. H. Also C in Dukas's *Ariane et Barbe-bleu*. B. Also Melissa, C in Gilbert and Sullivan's *Princess Ida*. H

212.10, Penelope; Fauré's *Penelope,* 1913 (OT). B

212.11, Rohan; Maria di Rohan, C in Donizetti's *Maria di Rohan*. H

212.13, Foyle; John McCormack (ten.) under pseudonym Giovanni Foli. K

212.13, Irmak; Ilma di Murska (sop.). B

212.14, Lily; Benedict's *Lily of Killarney* (OT). B. Also Lily Foley McCormack, John's (ten.) wife. B

212.27, lohaned; Lohengrin, C in Wagner's *Lohengrin*. H

213.1, Sheridan's; Margaret Sheridan (sop.). H

213.2–3, *Floss* . . . flossies; Flosshilde, Wellgunde (Rhine Maidens), Cs in Wagner's *Ring*. H

213.5–7, that piece . . . lost it; "Rhinegold," T in Wagner's *Das Rheingold*. H

213.6, Hoangho; Brünnhilde, cry of the Valkyrie, C in Wagner's *Ring*. H, M

213.11, Well; "Welle," waves, T in Wagner's *Das Rheingold*. H. Also Wellgunde, C in Wagner's *Ring*. H

213.25, Else; Elsa of Brabant, C in Wagner's *Lohengrin*. H

214.18, Maria; Maria, one name of Octavian, C in R. Strauss's *Der Rosenkavalier*. B

214.19–23, Madammangut! . . . Amn't I up since the damp dawn, marthared mary allacook; LeCocq (comp.). H. Also Lecocq's *La Fille de Madame Angot* (OT). H

214.21, Carrigacurra; Edward German and Arthur Sullivan's *Emerald Isle, or The Caves of Carrig-Cleena* (OT). H

214.23, marthared; Flotow's *Martha* (OT). H

214.24, Alice; Alice, Ford's wife, C in Verdi's *Falstaff.* H. Also C in Rossini's *Le Comte Ory* and Meyerbeer's *Robert le diable.* B

214.30, Carlow; Don Carlos, C in Verdi's *Don Carlos.* H

215.4, .6, .10, love . . . you'll find . . . way; "Love will find a way," A in Fraser-Simon and Tate's *Maid of the Mountains.* H

215.22, Elvenland; Elvino, C in Bellini's *La sonnambula.* H. Also in Bellini's *Il pirata.* B

215.23, Ordovico or viricordo; Riccardo, C in Verdi's *Un ballo in maschera.* H

215.26, .28, eure, orphans; Orfeo and Euridice, Cs in Gluck's *Orfeo ed Euridice.* H

215.31–32, Flittering bats; J. Strauss II's *Die Fledermaus* (OT). H

Finnegans Wake, Book II.1:

219.1–259.10, Martin 220

219.3, gads; Johanna Gadski (sop.). H

219.5, massinees; Angelo Masini (ten.). H. Also Galliano Masini (ten.). H. Also Massenet (comp.). H

219.9, Archimimus; Archibald Grosvenor, C in Gilbert and Sullivan's *Patience.* H

219.18, *Mime;* Mime, C in Wagner's *Siegfried.* H-SG

219.23, robot; Meyerbeer's *Robert le diable* (OT). H-SG. Also W. S. Gilbert's *Robert le Diable* (OT). B

220.3, THE FLORAS; Fiora, C in Montemezzi's *L'amore dei tre re.* H. Also Floria Tosca, C in Puccini's *Tosca.* H

220.3, Martin 220

220.3, Bride's; T in ending of Weber's *Der Freischütz.* H-SG

220.5–6, valkyrienne; Wagner's *Die Walküre* (OT). HW, M

220.7, IZOD; Isolde, C in Wagner's *Tristan und Isolde.* H, M

220.8, blonde; Blonde, C in Mozart's *Abduction from the Seraglio.* H

220.24, Makeall Gone; Michael Gunn (impresario). McH

220.25, Martin 190

220.26, magical helmet . . . cap-a-pipe; Tarnhelm, T in Wagner's *Ring.* H, M. Also magic flute, T in Mozart's *Magic Flute.* H-SG

221.4–5, quest . . . final; "Questo è il fin," A in Mozart's *Don Giovanni*. H

221.8, Glen; Wolf's Glen, T in Weber's *Der Freischütz*. H-SG

221.9, lokistroki; Loge (Loki), C in Wagner's *Ring*. H, M

221.11, Martin 197

221.12, Rachel; Rachel, C in Halévy's *La Juive*. H

221.13, Madam d'Elta; Nellie Melba (sop.). H. Also Marie Delna (contr.). H

221.15, whorts; Ortrud, C in Wagner's *Lohengrin*. H

221.24, Berthe; Bertram the unknown (the devil), C in Meyerbeer's *Robert le diable*. H

221.25, Harley Quinn and Coollimbeina; harlequin, T in Leoncavallo's *I pagliacci*. H

221.25, Quinn; Quinquin, nickname of Octavian, C in R. Strauss's *Der Rosenkavalier*. B

221.27, R.I.C. Lipmasks; Riccardo, C in Verdi's *Un ballo in maschera*. H

221.29, Pedersen; Gianna Pederzini (mezzo-sop.). H

221.29, Pine; Louisa Pyne (sop.). H

221.34, Shop-Sowry; J. Strauss II's *Die Fledermaus* (OT). H

221.36, Martin 210

222.5, chorale; T, ending of Weber's *Der Freischütz*. H-SG

222.7–8, Joan MockComick, male soprano; John McCormack (ten.). H-SG

222.8, Jean Souslevin; John Sullivan (ten.). H-SG

222.10, Der Rasche; Jean de Reszke (ten.). H

222.10–11, Rasche . . . Nitscht; "Der Holle Rache," A in Mozart's *Magic Flute*. H-SG

222.10–11, Oh Off Nunch Der Rasche Ver Lasse Mitsch Nitscht; "Komm', Hoffnung, lass den letzten Stern," A in Beethoven's *Fidelio*. H

222.17, a Magnificent Transformation Scene; transformation scene, act 2, T in Wagner's *Parsifal*. H

222.17, Magnificent; Don Magnifico, C in Rossini's *La cenerentola*. H

222.18, Neid; Queen of the Night, C in Mozart's *Magic Flute*. H

222.18, Moorning; Monostatos the Moor, C in Mozart's *Magic Flute*. H-SG

222.22, his soard fleshed light; Nothung, T in Wagner's *Siegfried*. H

222.27, eyesoult; Isolde, C in Wagner's *Tristan und Isolde*. H, M

222.29–30, To part from these, my corsets, is into overlusting fear; Siegfried (only mortal without fear), C in Wagner's *Siegfried*. H

222.32, Aminxt; Amina, C in Bellini's *La sonnambula*. H

222.32, evelings; Eva, C in Wagner's *Die Meistersinger*. H

222.32–33, evelings . . . girly; Ladies of the Town, collectively, in Gay's *Beggar's Opera*. B

222.32–33, pierceful in their sojestiveness were those first girly stirs, with zit-
terings; "Zitti, zitti, piano, piano," A (trio) in Rossini's *Barber of Seville*.
H

222.32–36, Martin 220

222.34, twitchbells; Jemmy Twitcher, C in Gay's *Beggar's Opera*. B

222.36, Sammy; Samiel, C in Weber's *Der Freischütz*. H-SG. Also Slippery Sam,
C in Gay's *Beggar's Opera*. B

223.2, Louisan Shousapinas; Charpentier's *Louise* (OT). H

223.2, Louisan; Louise, C in Charpentier's *Louise*. H

223.3, agnols from the wiles of willy wooly woolf; Agnes, wolf glen, C in Weber's *Der Freischütz*. H-SG

223.3, woolf; Giacomo Lauri-Volpi (Ital ten.). B

223.6, Rose, Sevilla; Rossini (comp.) and his opera *The Barber of Seville* (OT).
H

223.6–7, brideness . . . Esmeralde; Esmeralda, C in Smetana's *Bartered Bride*.
H. Also *The Bartered Bride* (OT). B

223.7, Esmeralde; Arthur Goring Thomas's *Esmeralda* (OT) (1883), featuring
Georgina Burns in the title role. B

223.7, Viola; Violette, C in Leroux's *La Reine Fiammette*. B. Also Violetta, C
in Verdi's *La traviata*. H. Also duchess of Parma, C in Busoni's *Doktor
Faust*. B

223.11, Isot; Isolde, C in Wagner's *Tristan und Isolde*. H, M

223.18, O'Sheen ascowl; "Signore, ascolta," A in Puccini's *Turandot*. H

223.19, evangelion; Eva, C in Wagner's *Die Meistersinger*. H. Also Luening's
Evangeline (OT). B

223.19–21, Arrest thee, scaldbrother! . . . ill s'arrested; "Arrêtez, O mes frères,"
A in Saint-Saëns's *Samson et Dalila*. H-SG

223.21, s'arrested; Sarastro, C in Mozart's *Magic Flute*. H-SG

223.24, queen; Queen of the Night, C in Mozart's *Magic Flute*. H

223.31, Martin 197

223.25–26, Seeks . . . feinder; Siegfried, C in Wagner's *Siegfried*. H

224.11, colline; Colline, C in Puccini's *La bohème*. H

224.11, colline born; "The Colleen Bawn," A in Benedict's *Lily of Killarney*. HW

224.19, vogalstones; Heinrich Vogl (ten.). H. Also bird, T in Wagner's *Siegfried*.
H

224.22–23, The youngly delightsome frilles-in-pleyurs are now showen drawen,
if bud one, or, if in florileague; Flower Maidens, Cs in Wagner's *Parsifal*.
H, M

224.23, florileague; Fiordiligi, C in Mozart's *Così fan tutte*. H

224.25, trapadour; Verdi's *Il trovatore* (OT). H

224.28, ba; Pooh-Bah, C in Gilbert and Sullivan's *Mikado*. H

224.28, Quanty purty bellas; Dorabella, C in Mozart's *Così fan tutte*. H. Also "Quanto è bella," A in Donizetti's *L'elisir d'amore*. HW. Also "Morir! sì pura e bella!" A in Verdi's *Aïda*. HW

224.29–30, Madama Lifay! . . . Madama; Puccini's *Madame Butterfly* (OT). H

224.30, Cinderynelly; Rossini's *La cenerentola* (OT). H. Also Farinelli (male sop.). B

224.30–31, cho chiny; Cio-Cio-San, C in Puccini's *Madame Butterfly*. H

224.30–35, do say? . . . Mi, O la; as do-si-mi-la, the opening notes of "Ah! tu dei vivere! Sì, all'amor mio vivrai," A sung by Amneris to Radamès in act 4, sc. 1, of Verdi's *Aïda;* in scene 2 Radamès sings "Morir! sì pura e bella!" [*FW* 224.28] to Aïda. B and Hart

224.35, thong off his art; *Song o' My Heart,* John McCormack's (ten.) first film. K

225.1, tittertit; town of Titipu, T in Gilbert and Sullivan's *Mikado*. H

225.2, ringsoundinly; Wagner's *Ring* (OT). H, M. See also Martin 220.

225.11, muffinstuffinaches; Méphistophélès, C in Gounod's *Faust*. H-SG. Also C in Berlioz's *La Damnation de Faust,* Busoni's *Doktor Faust,* and Boïto's *Mefistofele*. B

225.13–14, worrawarrawurms; Fafner, C in Wagner's *Ring*. H

225.15–17, what she meaned he could not can. All she meaned was golten sylvup, all she meaned was some Knight's ploung jamn; Nedda (= not); Silvio (= sylvup); Canio (= can), Cs in Leoncavallo's *I pagliacci*. H

225.20, Mitzymitzy; Mimi, C in Puccini's *La bohème*. H

225.21–22, .24, .26, I'm not the bogdoxy, ... monbreamstone . . . Hellfeuersteyn . . . coral pearl; Jewel Song ("Ah, je ris"), A in Gounod's *Faust*. H

225.30, Ring we round; Wagner's *Ring* (OT).

225.35, flossies; Flosshilde, C in Wagner's *Ring*. H

226.1, pearlagraph, the pearlagraph; Lisa Perli (sop., b. Dora Labette). H

226.1–2, Martin 220

226.4, Isa; Isolde, C in Wagner's *Tristan und Isolde*. H, M. See also Martin 197.

226.4–5, tincelles a . . . swan's; Elsa of Brabant, C in Wagner's *Lohengrin*. H. Also Swan, T in Wagner's *Lohengrin*. H

226.4–15, Martin 210

226.5, tarnished; Tarnhelm, T in Wagner's *Ring*. H

226.7, beauman's; Belmonte, C in Mozart's *Abduction from the Seraglio*. H

226.9, France's; Zandonai's *Francesca da Rimini* (OT). H

226.13, Eve's; Eva, C in Wagner's *Die Meistersinger*. H

226.14, tryst and; Tristan, C in Wagner's *Tristan und Isolde.* H, M. See also Martin 197.

226.14–15, Mammy was, Mimmy is; Mamma Lucia, C in Mascagni's *Cavalleria rusticana.* H

226.15, Mimmy; Mime, C in Wagner's *Siegfried.* H-SG. Also Mimi, C in Puccini's *La bohème.* H

226.25, Pennyfair . . . pinnyfore; Gilbert and Sullivan's *H.M.S. Pinafore* (OT). H

226.25, ring; Wagner's *Ring* (OT). H

226.25–29, ring . . . link . . . a lessle, a lissle. Then rompride; "Israël, romps ta chaîne," A in Saint-Saëns's *Samson et Dalila.* H

226.29, a lessle, a lissle; Jean Lassalle (bar.). H

226.30–31, cadenzando coloratura! . . . A is Arancia; Giannina Arangi-Lombardi (sop.). H

226.30–33, Martin 220

226.31, A is Arancia, Y is for Yilla and N for greeneriN; "Gli aranci olezzano sui verdi margini," A (chorus) in Mascagni's *Cavalleria rusticana.* H

226.31, Y is for Yilla and N for greeneriN; greenery-yallery, T in Gilbert and Sullivan's *Patience.* H-SG

226.36, Eons; eons theme, T in Puccini's *Turandot.* H

227.1–2, The many wiles of Winsure; Nicolai's *Merry Wives of Windsor* (OT). H

227.3, haricot; Harriet, C in Flotow's *Martha.* H

227.7, harrier; Harriet, C in Flotow's *Martha.* H

227.14, Ida; Princess Ida, C in *Princess Ida* (Gilbert and Sullivan). H

227.14–18, Winnie, Olive and Beatrice, Nelly and Ida, Amy and Rue. Here they come back, all the gay pack, for they are the florals, from foncey and pansey to papavere's blush, foresake-me-nought, while there's leaf there's hope, with primtim's ruse and marry-may's blossom, all the flowers of the ancelles' garden; Flower Maidens, Cs in Wagner's *Parsifal.* H-SG, M

227.17, hope; riddle (hope), T in Puccini's *Turandot.* H

227.18, garden; Mary Garden (sop.). H-SG

227.21, tornaments; "Tornami a dir," A (duet) in Donizetti's *Don Pasquale.* H

227.23, oathword; oath, sword, Ts in Wagner's *Ring.* H

227.30, Gillie; Dinh Gilly (bar.) and Renée Gilly (sop.). H

227.34, nothing; Nothung, T in Wagner's *Siegfried.* H

227.35, Tartaran tastarin; Timur, C in Puccini's *Turandot.* H-SG

228.3, preying; Gilbert-Louis Duprez (ten.). B

228.5, Cross; Joan Cross (sop.). H

228.14, schlucefinis; Heinrich Schlusnus (bar). H

228.14, Gelchasser; riddle (ice = *gel*), T in Puccini's *Turandot*. H

228.16, Dora; Dorabella, C in Mozart's *Così fan tutte*. H

228.19, Martin 198

228.22–23, Paname . . . tarry easty; Therese Malten (sop., debut as Pamina). B

228.24, Roder; Wilhelm Rode (bass-bar.). H

228.26, cashel; Casilda, C in Gilbert and Sullivan's *Gondoliers*. H

228.29, fuyerescaper; riddle (fire), T in Puccini's *Turandot*. H

229.7, scribenery; Scribe (librettist). H. Also Scriabin (comp.). H

229.14, A Wondering Wreck; Wanderer (Wotan), C in Wagner's *Siegfried*. H-SG, M. See also Martin 190.

229.16, Walpurgas Nackt; Queen of the Night, C in Mozart's *Magic Flute*. H. Also Walpurgis Nacht, T in Gounod's *Faust*. H

229.19, sabbatarian; Victor de Sabata (cond.). H

229.22, gummer; Gama, C in Gilbert and Sullivan's *Princess Ida*. H. Also Vasco da Gama, C in Meyerbeer's *L'Africaine*. H

229.23, malters; Therese Malten (sop.). H

229.33, heldin; Fanny Heldy (sop.). H. Also Heldentenor, or heroic tenor roles in Wagner operas. B

229.33–35, Martin 188

229.34, Boyrut season; Bayreuth (Wagner festival), T in Wagner's (comp.) life. H

229.35, ottorly . . . her husband; Otto Wesendonk, whose wife, Mathilde, was Isolde to Wagner's (comp.) Tristan. McH

230.6, .13, osco de basco de pesco de bisco . . . Parisise; Vasco da Gama, C, and "O paradiso," A, in Meyerbeer's *L'Africaine*. H

230.10, schortest; Friedrich Schorr (bass-bar.) and Anton Schott (ten.). H

230.10, caughtalock; "Madamina, il catalogo," A in Mozart's *Don Giovanni*. H

230.12, wagoner . . . mudheeldy wheesindonk; Wagner (comp.) and his mistress Mathilde Wesendonk. G, H, M

230.13, trist in; Tristan, C in Wagner's *Tristan und Isolde*. H, M

230.13, tourments of tosend years; eons theme, T in Puccini's *Turandot*. H-SG. See also Martin 198.

230.15, Casanuova; Lortzing's *Cazanova* (OT). H

230.15, Neblonovi's; Nibelung, Cs in Wagner's *Ring*. H

230.17, si through severalls of sanctuaries; eons theme, T in Puccini's *Turandot*. H

230.21, foil the fluter; John McCormack (ten.) under pseudonym Giovanni Foli. K

230.21, g.s.M; manuscript of prelude to *Die Walküre* was inscribed "G.s.M." or "Gesegnet sei Mathilde" ("Blessed be Mathilde [Wesendonk]," Wagner's [comp.] mistress). McH

230.22, rickwards; Riccardo, C in Verdi's *Un ballo in maschera*. H

230.26, Martin 198

230.26, treetrene; Montemezzi's *L'amore dei tre re* (OT). H

230.29–30, Avus and Avia; Avito, C in Montemezzi's *L'amore dei tre re*. H

230.30, veloutypads; Giovanni Battista Velluti (male sop.). H

230.32, Martin 198

230.32, .33, .34, patriss . . . germane faces . . . patruuts; Germont, C in Verdi's *La traviata*. H

230.34, archimade; Archibald Grosvenor, C in Gilbert and Sullivan's *Patience*. H. Also Archibaldo (one of the three kings), C in Montemezzi's *L'amore dei tre re*. H

230.34, patruuts to a man; Manfredo (one of the three kings), C in Montemezzi's *L'amore dei tre re*. H

230.35–36, Martin 198

231.3, gussies; Gustavus, C in Verdi's *Un ballo in maschera*. H

231.6, *preyed;* Gilbert-Louis Duprez (ten.). B

231.7, *verdigrassy;* Lodovico Graziani (ten., first Alfredo in Verdi's *La traviata;* "especially successful in Verdi repertory"—CODO). B. Also Verdi (comp.). H. Also Francesco Graziani (bar., first Don Carlo in Verdi's *La forza del destino*). B

231.7, *vallsall;* Valhalla, T in Wagner's *Ring*. H

231.9, ecstasy; "La rivedrà nell' estasi," A in Verdi's *Un ballo in maschera*. H

231.10–11, Timor . . . herepong . . . pinging; Ping, Pang, Pong, Cs in Puccini's *Turandot*. H. Also Timur, C in Puccini's *Turandot*. H-SG

231.13, freytherem; Freia, C in Wagner's *Ring*. H-SG

231.16, sanguish blooded; riddle (*sangue* = "blood"), T in Puccini's *Turandot*. H

231.19, millions of years a life of billions of years; eons theme, T in Puccini's *Turandot*. H

231.20, violast; Violetta, C in Verdi's *La traviata*. H

231.20–22, he shall not forget . . . gnawthing unheardth; Siegfried forges Nothung, forgets Brünnhilde, T in Wagner's *Siegfried*. H-SG

231.21, pucking; Puccini (comp.). H

231.21, Holihowlsballs and bloody acres; Valhalla, T in Wagner's *Ring* cycle. B

231.23, Summ; "Summ' und brumm'," A (chorus) in Wagner's *Flying Dutchman.* H

231.23–25, Martin 211

231.27, richt; Hans Richter (cond.), first good Wagnerian conductor in England. B

231.32, locofoco . . . redhot; riddle (fire), T in Puccini's *Turandot.* H

231.36, Seekeryseeks; Siegmund and Siegfried, Cs in Wagner's *Ring.* H

232.10–11, herzian waves; Herzeleide, mother of Parsifal, C in Wagner's *Parsifal.* H

232.11, a butterfly; Puccini's *Madame Butterfly* (OT). H

232.11, Martin 192

232.13, Martin 198

232.23, Satanly, lade; Balfe's *Satanella* (OT). H

232.27, to her dot; Puccini's *Turandot* (OT). H-SG

232.36–233.2, Martin 190

233.5, Angelinas; Angelina, C in Rossini's *La cenerentola.* H. Also Angelica, C in Puccini's *Suor Angelica.* H. Also Angelina, C in Gilbert and Sullivan's *Trial by Jury.* H

233.8, haunting; Hunding, C in Wagner's *Die Walküre.* H

233.11, guessing; Gessler, C in Rossini's *William Tell.* H

233.11, seagoer; Siegfried, C in Wagner's *Siegfried.* H. Also Siegmund, C in Wagner's *Ring.* H. Also Vanderdecken, C in Wagner's *Flying Dutchman.* B

233.13, .14, can . . . know; Canio, C in Leoncavallo's *I pagliacci.* H

233.21, jaoneofergs; Janáček's *Jeňfa* (OT). H

233.23, mayjaunties; Mařenka, C in Smetana's *Bartered Bride.* H

233.25, nunsibellies; Nancy, C in Flotow's *Martha.* H. Also Nun's Chorus, A in Lortzing's *Cazanova.* H

233.27, Micaco; Gilbert and Sullivan's *Mikado* (OT). H

233.28, Ping an ping nwan ping pwan pong; Ping, Pang, Pong, Cs in Puccini's *Turandot.* H-SG

233.31, segur; Reyer's *Sigurd* (OT). H

233.32, yallah; greenery-yallery, T in Gilbert and Sullivan's *Patience.* H

233.33, skarp; Scarpia, C in Puccini's *Tosca.* H

233.34, tartatortoise; Timur, C in Puccini's *Turandot.* H. Also Calaf, C in Puccini's *Turandot.* H

233.36, Gelagala; riddle (*gel* = "ice"), T in Puccini's *Turandot.* H

234.2, bedizzled; Bizet (comp.). H

234.3, debuzzled; Debussy (comp.). H

234.3, tristiest; Tristan, C in Wagner's *Tristan und Isolde*. H, M

234.3, cabaleer on; Mascagni's *Cavalleria rusticana* (OT). H

234.4, donkey shot at; Massenet's (and other composers') *Don Quixote* (OT). B

234.4–5, Or a peso; Oroveso, C in Bellini's *Norma*. H

234.5, besant; Gabriella Besanzoni (mezzo-sop.). H

234.6, Sin Showpanza; Sancho Panza, C in Massenet's (and other composers') *Don Quixote*. B

234.16, dandypanies; Dandini, C in Rossini's *La cenerentola*. H

234.18, suessiest; Ina Souez (sop.). H

234.20, .36, pilgrim . . . neuchoristic . . . chant en chor; Pilgrim's Chorus, A in Wagner's *Tannhäuser*. H

234.20–21; prinkips . . . neuchoristic congressulations; McCormack's singing at Eucharistic Congress, Phoenix Park, as papal count. B

234.23, dulsy nayer; Dulcinea, C in many versions of *Don Quixote*. McH

234.26, t'rigolect; Verdi's *Rigoletto* (OT). HW

234.28, safras; Saphir, C in Gilbert and Sullivan's *Patience*. H

234.33, gust of his gushy old; Gustavus, C in Verdi's *Un ballo in maschera*. H

234.35, Adelphus; Adèle, C in J. Strauss II's *Die Fledermaus*. H. Also in Rossini's *Le Comte Ory*. B

234.36, come; "Komm!" (Flower Maidens' Song), T in Wagner's *Parsifal*. H

234.36, chor; T, ending of Weber's *Der Freischütz*. H-SG

235.4, hope; riddle (hope), T in Puccini's *Turandot*. H

235.6, Osman; Osmin, C in Mozart's *Abduction from the Seraglio*. H

235.7–8, wasteward . . . allahlah lahlah lah; "Weialala leia / Wallala leialala," Rhine Maidens' Song quoted by T. S. Eliot in "Waste Land," ll. 277–78, T in Wagner's *Das Rheingold*. H, M

235.8, turquewashed; Turk, C in Mozart's *Abduction from the Seraglio*. H. Also Puccini's *Turandot* (OT). H-SG

235.10, innocent; Parsifal, C in Wagner's *Parsifal*. H-SG

235.10–11, Should in ofter years it became about you; "Then You'll Remember Me," A in Balfe's *Bohemian Girl*. B

235.13, mobility; "La donna è mobile," A in Verdi's *Rigoletto*. H

235.13, Roseraie, Ailesbury; "D'amor sull'ali rosee," A in Verdi's *Il trovatore*. H

235.21–22, palypeachum; Lucy Lockit and Polly Peachum, Cs in Gay's *Beggar's Opera*. H

235.26, garden; Mary Garden (sop.). H. Also Klingsor's garden, T in Wagner's *Parsifal*. H

235.27, T . . . I; Tristan and Isolde, Cs in Wagner's *Tristan und Isolde.* McH

235.29, Percy; Parsifal, C in Wagner's *Parsifal.* G, H

235.32, Tintin tintin; "Chanson bohème" ("Les tringles des sistres tintaient"), A in Bizet's *Carmen.* H

235.35, caramel dancings; Caramello, C in J. Strauss II's *Eine Nacht in Venedig.* H. Also Carmen dancing, T in Bizet's *Carmen.* H

236.4, Cococream; Koko, lord high executioner, C in Gilbert and Sullivan's *Mikado.* H-SG

236.5–6, sticksword . . . Headiness; Koko, lord high executioner, C in Gilbert and Sullivan's *Mikado.* H

236.6, Luisome; Liù, C in Puccini's *Turandot.* H. Also Verdi's *Luisa Miller* (OT). H

236.8, Easter; Florence Easton (sop.). H

236.9–10, A paaralone! A paaralone; "A paradox? A paradox!" A (trio) in Gilbert and Sullivan's *Pirates of Penzance.* H

236.10, adin; Adina, C in Donizetti's *L'elisir d'amore.* H

236.17–18, Anneliuia; Liù, C in Puccini's *Turandot.* H-SG

236.30, the bedeafdom of po's taeorns; eons theme, T in Puccini's *Turandot.* H-SG

236.35–36, and is tournesoled straightcut or sidewaist; Turandot, C in Puccini's *Turandot.* B. Also C in Busoni's *Turandot.* B

237.6, bridawl; T, ending of Weber's *Der Freischütz.* H-SG

237.8–9, Martin 198

237.9, elixir. Lovelyt; Donizetti's *L'elisir d'amore* (OT). H

237.11, Enchainted; Balfe's *Enchantress* (OT). H

237.12, aboutobloss; Emma Abbott (sop.). H

237.15, barnaboy; Barnaba, C in Ponchielli's *La Gioconda.* H

237.15, pampipe; Pamina, C in Mozart's *Magic Flute.* H. Also Papageno's pipes, T in Mozart's *Magic Flute.* H

237.22, loki; Loge (Loki), C in Wagner's *Ring.* H

237.22, blanched; Lady Blanche, C in Gilbert and Sullivan's *Princess Ida.* H

237.25, pure . . . pure . . . puerity; "If you're anxious for to shine in the high aesthetic line" ("a most particularly pure young man this pure young man must be"), A in Gilbert and Sullivan's *Patience.* H

237.26, Elleb [= Belle]; Ella, C in Gilbert and Sullivan's *Patience.* H

237.31, Siker of calmy days; Siegfried, C in Wagner's *Siegfried.* H. Also Siegmund, C in Wagner's *Ring.* H

237.33, Labbeycliath; Luigi Lablache (bass). H

237.36–238.1, magdelenes; Magdalene, C in Wagner's *Die Meistersinger.* H

238.1, dot; Puccini's *Turandot* (OT). H-SG

238.3, an isaspell; Isolde, C in Wagner's *Tristan und Isolde*. B

238.3, dandydainty; Dandini, C in Rossini's *La cenerentola*. H

238.5, wayward [= *traviata*, literally, "gone off the way, astray"]; Violetta, C in Verdi's *La traviata*. H

238.10–11, Angèles . . . Angèle's; Angelina, C in Rossini's *La cenerentola*. B

238.11, constant; Constanze, C in Mozart's *Abduction from the Seraglio*. H. Also Mozart's (comp.) wife, Constanza. B

238.13, heing; Ernestine Schumann-Heink (contr.). H

238.17, idolhours; "Shade of the Palm" ("Oh, my Dolores"), A in Stuart's *Floradora*. B. Also reference to this A in "Sirens." B

238.23, List; Liszt (comp.). H. Also Emanuel List (bass). H

238.23, Bianca Mutantini; Bianca Bianchi (sop.). H. Also Balfe's *Bianca* (OT). H

238.26, weothers; Massenet's *Werther* (OT). B

238.26, Bohnaparts; Bohnen, Michael (bass-bar.). H

238.32, iris; Mascagni's *Iris* (OT). H. Also C in Handel's *Semele*. B

238.33, .35, Caro . . . Teomeo; "Caro nome," A in Verdi's *Rigoletto*. H

238.34, mellisponds; Mélisande, C in Debussy's *Pelléas et Mélisande*. H. Also in Dukas's *Ariane et Barbe-bleu*. B

238.34, minnies; Minnie, C in Puccini's *La fanciulla del west*. H. Also Minna, Wagner's (comp.) first wife. B

238.36, Gizzygazelle; Gizziello (male sop.). H

239.11, come; "Komm," said by Flower Maidens, T in Wagner's *Parsifal*. H

239.24, Carminia; Bizet's *Carmen* (OT). H

239.26, ringing; Wagner's *Ring* (OT). H

239.27, gyrogyrorondo; Puccini's *La rondine* (OT). B

239.28, waltzing; Volsung, T in Wagner's *Ring*. H

239.29, angeline; Angelina, C in Gilbert and Sullivan's *Trial by Jury*. H. Also Angelina, C in Rossini's *La cenerentola*. H. Also Angelica, C in Puccini's *Suor Angelica*. B

239.34, lucisphere; Mamma Lucia, C in Mascagni's *Cavalleria rusticana*. H. Also Lucia, C in Donizetti's *Lucia di Lammermoor*. H. Also Lucia, C in Rossini's *La gazza ladra* and Ponchielli's *I promessi sposi*. B

239.36, ring; Wagner's *Ring* (OT). H

239.36, rund; Puccini's *La rondine* (OT). B

240.1, sassage; Marie-Constance Sass (sop.). H

240.10, Experssly; Wagner's *Parsifal* (OT). H

240.18, bianconies; Bianca Bianchi (sop.). H. Also Balfe's *Bianca* (OT). H

240.21, Calembaurnus; Calaf, C in Puccini's *Turandot.* H

240.24, calaboosh; Calaf, C in Puccini's *Turandot.* H-SG

240.25, mussymussy; Mimi and Musetta, Cs in Puccini's *La bohème.* H

240.25, calico; Calaf, C in Puccini's *Turandot.* H-SG

240.26, what name; riddle, T in Puccini's *Turandot.* H-SG

240.30, peachskin; Pekin, T in Puccini's *Turandot.* H. See also 241.5.

240.32, avalunch; "La Valanga" ("the Avalanche," sop.), *Letters 1,* 358. B

241.1, akter; Aïno Ackte (sop.). H

241.2, coaxyorum; Mrs. Coaxer, C in Gay's *Beggar's Opera.* B

241.2, pennysilvers; Gay's *Beggar's Opera* (OT, in Weill and Brecht's *Die Drei-groschenoper,* or *Threepenny Opera,* as title was translated). Janusko, B

241.5, pollygameous; Polly Peachum, C in Gay's *Beggar's Opera.* B

241.6, heather; Captain Macheath, C in Gay's *Beggar's Opera.* B

241.8, rhodomantic; Rodolfo, C in Puccini's *La bohème.* H. Also C in Verdi's *Luisa Miller.* B. Also Radamès, C in Verdi's *Aïda.* H

241.8, wert; Massenet's *Werther* (OT). H

241.9, walk in her sleep; sleepwalking, T in Bellini's *La sonnambula.* H

241.20, farrer; Geraldine Farrar (sop.). H

241.22, benighted queendom; Queen of the Night, C in Mozart's *Magic Flute.* H-SG

241.23, aidant; Verdi's *Aïda* (OT). H

241.24, ameltingmoult; Amelita Galli-Curci (sop.). H

241.25, tammy ratkins; Tamino, C in Mozart's *Magic Flute.* H

241.25, Martin 220

241.26, Martin 188

241.32, liarnels; Lionel, C in Flotow's *Martha.* HW

241.33, Lotta; Charlotte, C in Massenet's *Werther.* H

241.33, Whore affirm is agains sempry; "Ora e per sempre addio," A in Verdi's *Otello.* H

242.12, .14, .34, vittles . . . julias . . . flamen; Vittoria, Giulia, Fiametta, Cs in Gilbert and Sullivan's *Gondoliers.* H

242.14, .21, .27, trial by julias . . . By a jury . . . judges; Gilbert and Sullivan's *Trial by Jury* (OT). HW-SG

242.14, celestial; "Celeste Aïda," A in Verdi's *Aïda.* H

242.17, rhainodaisies; Flower Maidens, Cs in Wagner's *Parsifal.* B. Also Rhine/Rhein, T in Wagner's *Ring.* H

242.20, Samhar; Samiel, C in Weber's *Der Freischütz.* H-SG

242.27, judges; Judge, C in Gilbert and Sullivan's *Trial by Jury.* H

242.30, Psing . . . psexpeans; Lady Psyche, C in Gilbert and Sullivan's *Princess Ida.* H. Also Pitty Sing, C in Gilbert and Sullivan's *Mikado.* B

242.33, Howarden's; Kathleen Howard (contr.). H

243.6, .15, Schi schi . . . giantar; Puccini's *Gianni Schicchi* (OT). H

243.7, pignpugn . . . pan; Ping, Pang, Pong, Cs in Puccini's *Turandot.* H

243.7–8, pialabellars in their pur war; "Morir! sì pura e bella!" A in Verdi's *Aïda.* HW

243.10, zoravarn; "O souverain, ô juge," A in Massenet's *El Cid.* H

243.10–11, zoravarn lhorde and givnergenral, and led her in antient consort ruhm; Zorah and Ruth, Cs in Gilbert and Sullivan's *Ruddigore.* H. Also Ruth, C in Gilbert and Sullivan's *Pirates of Penzance.* B

243.15, giantar; Gianetta, C in Gilbert and Sullivan's *Gondoliers.* H. Also giants, Mime's riddle, T in Wagner's *Ring.* H

243.16, Signur; Siegfried, C in Wagner's *Siegfried.* H-SG, M. See also Martin 188, 211.

243.16, Foli Signur's; A. J. Foli (Foley) (bass). H. Also John McCormack (ten.) under pseudonym of Giovanni Foli. B

243.17, ladwigs out of his lugwags; William Ludwig (bar., b. Ledwidge). H

243.17, Martin 188

243.18, favourites; Donizetti's *La favorita* (OT). H

243.22, kip; Alexander Kipnis (bass). H

243.25, dinars; Meyerbeer's *Dinorah* (OT). H

243.26, Berenice; Berenice, C in Handel's *Berenice.* H. Also C in Rossini's *L'occasione fa il ladro.* B

243.26, Mayde Berenice; Meyerbeer (comp.). B

243.34, Sant; Santuzza, C in Mascagni's *Cavalleria rusticana.* H

243.34, wop mezzo; Montemezzi (comp.). H

243.34–35, Sant Pursy Orelli that gave . . . their loyal devouces to be offered up missas; Mass scene, T in Wagner's *Parsifal.* B

243.35, Luiz-Marios Josephs; William Ludwig (bar., b. Ledwidge) and Joseph Maas (ten.). H. Also Giovanni Mario (ten.). H. Also Joseph O'Mara (ten.). G. Also Luiz, Marco, and Giuseppe, Cs in Gilbert and Sullivan's *Gondoliers.* H. Also three kings, Cs in Montemezzi's *L'amore dei tre re.* H-SG. Also Josephine, C in Gilbert and Sullivan's *H.M.S. Pinafore.* H

244.4, .22, lolave, . . . lolling; Lola, C in Mascagni's *Cavalleria rusticana.* H

244.13, darkles; Hariclea Darclée (sop.). H

244.14–15, Alvemmarea; *Ave Maria,* A in Verdi's *Otello.* H. Also Almaviva, C in Mozart's *Marriage of Figaro* and Rossini's *Barber of Seville.* H

244.18–20, Where is our highly honourworthy salutable spousefounderess? The foolish one of the family is within. Haha! Huzoor, where's he? At house, to's pitty; parody of polite Japanese constructions, T in Gilbert and Sullivan's *Mikado*. H-SG

244.20, pitty; Pitty Sing, C in Gilbert and Sullivan's *Mikado*. H-SG

244.20, Nancy; Nanki-Pooh, C in Gilbert and Sullivan's *Mikado*. H-SG

244.24–25, rambling . . . What era's o'ering?; Where'er you walk, A in Handel's *Semele*. H

244.26, Sillume, see lo! Selene, sail O; Salomé, C in R. Strauss's *Salomé*. H

245.1, tusker; Tosca, C in Puccini's *Tosca*. H

245.1, Salamsalaim; Salomé, C in R. Strauss's *Salomé*. B

245.1, Rhinohorn; Rhine and Siegfried's horn, Ts in Wagner's *Siegfried*. H, M

245.1, .10, Rhinohorn . . . toran; "reine Tor" (pure fool), *Parsifal* motif, Ts in Wagner's *Parsifal*. H-SG, M. Also Holst's *Perfect Fool* (OT). B

245.3, muzzing; Claudia Muzio (sop.). H

245.5–6, When otter leaps in outer parts then Yul remembers Mei; "Then You'll Remember Me," A in Balfe's *Bohemian Girl*. HW

245.6, Yul; Liù, C in Puccini's *Turandot*. H

245.6, Mei; Medea Mei-Figner (mezzo-sop.). H

245.8, siemens; Margarethe Siems (sop.). H

245.10, toran; Siegfried's horn, T in Wagner's *Siegfried*. H-SG

245.10, toran and knots; Puccini's *Turandot* (OT). H

245.10, Martin 220

245.18, Rosimund; Rosina, C in Rossini's *Barber of Seville*. H. Also Siegmund, C in Wagner's *Die Walküre*. H. Also Schubert's *Rosamunde* (OT). H

245.21, cieclest; La Cieca, C in Ponchielli's *La gioconda*. H

245.22, waltzers; Walther von Stolzing, C in Wagner's *Die Meistersinger*. H. Also Volsung, C in Wagner's *Ring*. H

245.24, wenderer; Wanderer (Wotan), C in Wagner's *Siegfried*. H-SG, M

245.29, Martin 198

245.27, lack mulsum; Delibes's *Lakmé* (OT). H

245.33, Watsy Lyke; Berg's *Wozzeck* (OT). H

246.2, Jug and Chambers; Judge in chambers, C in Gilbert and Sullivan's *Trial by Jury*. H

246.3–5, war's alull . . . starfort . . . castle; Valhalla, palace and fort, T in Wagner's *Ring*. H

246.4, Gorey; jury, T in Gilbert and Sullivan's *Trial by Jury*. H

246.6–7, Brandenborgenthor. At Asa's arthre. In thundercloud periwig; Thore, C in Meyerbeer's *Les Huguenots*. B. Also Meyerbeer's *Das Brandenburg-*

ertor (OT). B. Also the gods Thor (thunder, *Donner*) and Aesir and burg
(= Valhalla), Ts in Wagner's *Ring*. H

246.10, Ansighosa; Siegmund, C in Wagner's *Ring*. H. Also Siegfried, C in
Wagner's *Siegfried*. H

246.13, ring; Wagner's *Ring* (OT). H-SG

246.13–15, joyous guard . . . palashe . . . wonner; Valhalla (palace), T in Wagner's *Ring*. H-SG

246.15, wonner; "Der Wonne, seligen Saal" ("the wondrous heavenly hall,"
Wotan's first words, addressing Valhalla), T in Wagner's *Das Rheingold*.
H-SG

246.16, Leonie; Leonore, C in Beethoven's *Fidelio*. H. Also Michael Leoni
(Meyer Lyon, alto). B

246.17, Josephinus and Mario-Louis; Joseph Maas (ten.), William Ludwig (bar.,
b. Ledwidge), and Giovanni Mario (ten.). H. Also Joseph O'Mara (ten.).
G. Also Luiz, Marco, and Giuseppe, Cs in Gilbert and Sullivan's *Gondoliers*. H. Also three kings, Cs in Montemezzi's *L'amore dei tre re*. H. Also
Josephine, C in Gilbert and Sullivan's *H.M.S. Pinafore*. B

246.18, Florestan; Florestan, C in Beethoven's *Fidelio*. H

246.18, lily of Bohemey, Florestan; Florestein, C in Balfe's *Bohemian Girl*. H

246.18, lily of Bohemey; Balfe's *Bohemian Girl* and Benedict's *Lily of Killarney*.
(OTs). HW

246.18, Thaddeus; Thaddeus, C in Balfe's *Bohemian Girl*. H

246.18, Hardress; Hardress Cregan, C in Benedict's *Lily of Killarney*. HW

246.18–19, lily . . . Myles; Myles na Coppaleen, C in Benedict's *Lily of Killarney*. HW

246.20, Icy-la-Belle; riddle (ice), T in Puccini's *Turandot*. H. Also Isolde, C in
Wagner's *Tristan und Isolde*. H

246.22, vamp, vamp, vamp; "Stride la vampa," A in Verdi's *Il trovatore*. H

246.26, fray; Freia, C in Wagner's *Das Rheingold*. H

246.27, bartrossers; Bartolo, C in Luigi and Federico Ricci's *Crispino e la comare*. B. Also C in Rossini's *Barber of Seville*. H. Also C in Mozart's *Marriage of Figaro*. B. Also Smetana's *Bartered Bride* (OT). H

246.32, healing and Brune; Brünnhilde, C in Wagner's *Ring*. H-SG, M

246.32, Jour d'Anno; Umberto Giordano (comp.). H. Also Tommaso Giordano
(comp.). B

246.33, Bettlimbraves; Donizetti's *Betly* (OT). H

246.34, Teaseforhim; Tessa, C in Gilbert and Sullivan's *Gondoliers*. H

246.35, Else; Elsa of Brabant, C in Wagner's *Lohengrin*. H

247.4, Martin 198

247.6, ramming; Ramiro, C in Rossini's *La cenerentola.* H

247.7, for getting; forge, T in Wagner's *Siegfried.* H

247.10, ruffo; Titta Ruffo (bar.). H

247.10, Barto; Bartolo, C in Luigi and Federico Ricci's *Crispino e la comare.* B. Also Bartolo, C in Rossini's *Barber of Seville.* H. Also C in Mozart's *Marriage of Figaro.* B. Also Smetana's *Bartered Bride* (OT). H

247.10, mor; Otello, C in Verdi's *Otello.* H

247.18, Highly Momourning he see the before him; "Eily Mavourneen," A in Benedict's *Lily of Killarney.* B

247.19, Melained; Zinka Milanov (sop.). H

247.20, Santalto . . . saint; Charles Santley (bar.). H. Also Santuzza, C in Mascagni's *Cavalleria rusticana.* H

247.21, margary; Marguérite, C in Gounod's *Faust.* H. Also C in Berlioz's *La Damnation de Faust* and Meyerbeer's *Les Huguenots.* B. Also Margherita, C in Boïto's *Mefistofele.* B

247.22–23, Martin 198

247.34, dandymount; Dandini, C in Rossini's *La cenerentola.* H

247.34, .36, Prettimaid . . . mimosa; Mimosa-san, C in Jones's *Geisha.* B

247.36, lucile, mimosa; Mimi (named Lucia, but called Mimi), C in Puccini's *La bohème.* H. Also "Mi chiamano Mimi," A in Puccini's *La bohème.* H

247.36, mimosa; Mime, C in Wagner's *Siegfried.* H-SG

248.2, zaza; Leoncavallo's *Zázá* (OT). H

248.5, piccions; Nicola Piccini (comp.). H. Also Puccini (comp.). H

248.7, .33, Turn . . . Turnagain; Eva Turner (sop.). H

248.9, tambourine; Antonio Tamburini (bar.). H

248.12, vulser . . . valsed; Volsunge, T in Wagner's *Ring.* H

248.13, flower that stars the day; "E lucevan le stelle ed olezzava la terra," A in Puccini's *Tosca.* B

248.13, stars the day; "O Abendstern," A in Wagner's *Tannhäuser.* H

248.13–14, pilger's fahrt; Pilgrim's Chorus, A in Wagner's *Tannhäuser.* H

248.23, swanwater; swan, T in Wagner's *Lohengrin.* H

248.32–33, Blanche de Blanche's; Lady Blanche, C in Gilbert and Sullivan's *Princess Ida.* H. Also "Plus blanche que la blanche ermine," A in Meyerbeer's *Les Huguenots.* B

248.34, Max; Max, C in Weber's *Der Freischütz.* H-SG. Also C in Donizetti's *Betly.* B

249.3, Martin 198

249.4, Valentine; Valentin, C in Gounod's *Faust.* H. Also Valentine, C in Meyerbeer's *Les Huguenots.* B. Also Valentini (Valentino Urbani, castrato,

contra./ten.). H. Also Francesco Valentino (bar.). H. Also Henri Justin
A. J. Valentino (cond., premiere of *William Tell*). H

249.7, rubinen; Giacomo Lauri-Volpi (ten.), who made debut as Giacomo
Rubini. B. Also Giovanni-Battista Rubini (ten.). B

249.12, uniomargrits; Marguérite, C in Meyerbeer's *Les Huguenots*. B. Also
Marguérite, C in Gounod's *Faust* and Berlioz's *La Damnation de Faust*,
and Margherita, C in Boïto's *Mefistofele*. H-SG

249.13, avowals; "Faites-lui mes aveux" (Flower Song), A in Gounod's *Faust*.
H-SG

249.18–20, gander . . . Oh backed von dem zug! Make weg for their tug; arrival of swan, T in Wagner's *Lohengrin*. Blish, H, M

249.19, The boy which she now adores. She dores; Mimi knocking on Rodolfo's door and then falling in love with him, T in Puccini's *La bohème*. B

249.20–21, Oh backed von dem zug! Make weg for their tug! With a ring ding;
"Zurück vom Ringe!" (Back from the ring; last sentence, spoken by
Hagen), T in Wagner's *Die Götterdämmerung*. H-SG

249.29, My name is Misha Misha but call me Toffey Tough; "Mi chiamano
Mimi" ("My name is Lucia, but they call me Mimi"), A in Puccini's *La
bohème*. H

249.30, .31, Mettenchough. . . . Ogh! Ogh; Mimi's cough, T in Puccini's *La
bohème*. H

249.30–31, It was her, boy the boy that was loft in the larch; Rodolfo, the "boy
in the loft," lifting the latch for Mimi, T in Puccini's *La bohème*. B

249.32, reverence; reverenza, T in Verdi's *Falstaff*. H

249.35, noth . . . Not; Nothung, T in Wagner's *Siegfried*. H

250.1, 11–12, Avis was there and trilled her about it. . . . cleany fuglers; Siegfried understands the forest bird, who tells him of Mime's murderous
intentions, T in Wagner's *Siegfried*. H

250.3, rossy; Countess Rossi (sop.). H

250.4, ribbings; Count Ribbing, C in Verdi's *Un ballo in maschera*. H

250.5, Swarthants; Gladys Swarthout (mezzo-sop.). H

250.12, Grandicellies; Margherita Grandi (sop.). H

250.12, zitty; "Zitti, zitti, piano, piano," A (trio) in Rossini's *Barber of Seville*.
H

250.16–18, For a burning would . . . leap no more; Macbeth's regicide, T in
Verdi's *Macbeth*. B

250.16–18, Glamours hath moidered's lieb and herefore Coldours must leap
no more; Liù's last aria, "Tu, che di gel sei cinta," A in Puccini's *Turandot*, and Turandot's last aria about love, A in Puccini's *Turandot*. H

250.19, .21, Lolo Lolo . . . Lala Lala; Lola, C in Mascagni's *Cavalleria rustica-na*. H

250.19–21, liebermann . . . loved to be leaving . . . Liber Lord. . . . Leapermann; "Mein lieber Schwan" (Lohengrin's farewell), T in Wagner's *Lohengrin*. H

250.19–22, L words; Liù, C in Puccini's *Turandot*. H

250.21, Lala Lala; Rhine Maidens, T in Wagner's *Ring*. H

250.27, Aghatharept; Agathe, C in Weber's *Der Freischütz*. H-SG

250.29, prunktqueen; Brangäne, C in Wagner's *Tristan und Isolde*. H

250.29–30, prunktqueen . . . heeling; Brünnhilde, C in Wagner's *Ring*. H

250.32, where air she went; "Where'er you walk," A in Handel's *Semele*. B

250.33, Martin 220

250.35, sward; Nothung, T in Wagner's *Siegfried*. H

250.35, incoronate; Monteverdi's *L'incoronazione di Poppea* (OT). H

251.1, Attilad! Attattilad; Verdi's *Attila* (OT). H

251.14, pierce; Jan Peerce (ten.). H

251.15, murkery; Ilma di Murska (sop.). B

251.15–17, murkery . . . wishmarks; King Mark, C in Wagner's *Tristan und Isolde*. G

251.17, Martin 198

251.17, imogenation; Imogene, C in Bellini's *Il pirata*. H

251.23, .26, .28, Turning . . . Turn . . . Eva; Eva Turner (sop.). H. Also Puccini's *Turandot* (OT). H

251.28, Eva; Eva, C in Wagner's *Die Meistersinger*. H

252.2, fausties; Gounod's *Faust*, Berlioz's *La Damnation de Faust*, and Busoni's *Doktor Faust* (OTs). B. Also Faust, C in Boïto's *Mefistofele*. B

252.13, Grassy ass ago; "Di grazia, mi" ("Excuse me"), T in Puccini's *La bohème*. B

252.15, bivitellines; Colline, C in Puccini's *La bohème*. B

252.15, Metellus; Marcello, C in Puccini's *La bohème*. B

252.16, biekerers; Rodolpho gives Mimi water in a "bicchiere" (a glass), act 1, T in Puccini's *La bohème*. B

252.17, superfetated; Conchita Supervia (mezzo-sop.). H

252.21, shyly bawn; Colleen Bawn, C in Benedict's *Lily of Killarney*. G

252.24, hope dashes hope; riddle (hope), T in Puccini's *Turandot*. H

252.31, Ange; Angelina, C in Rossini's *La cenerentola*. B. Also Angelina, C in Gilbert and Sullivan's *Trial by Jury*. B. Also Angelica, C in Puccini's *Suor Angelica*. B

252.31, Fleur; Fiora, C in Montemezzi's *L'amore dei tre re*. B

252.32, Gardoun; Mary Garden (sop.). H-SG

253.5, mappamund; "M'appari," A in Flotow's *Martha*. H

253.8, no thing making newthing; Nothung, T in Wagner's *Siegfried*. H

253.11, regionals; Reginald, C in Gilbert and Sullivan's *Patience*. H

253.12, sammarc; Mario Sammarco (bar.). H

253.17, come into the garner mauve; Flower Maidens, Cs in Wagner's *Parsifal*. H

253.20, patenly; Mary Ann Paton (sop.). H. Also Gilbert and Sullivan's *Patience* (OT). H

253.23–24, gossan; Eugene Goossens I and II (conds. of Carl Rosa Opera Company). B

253.24, pomelo; Pamina, C in Mozart's *Magic Flute*. H

253.27, scarf; Scarpia, C in Puccini's *Tosca*. H

253.28, .32, Myama's . . . Lucanhof; Mimi (Lucia, called Mimi), C in Puccini's *La bohème*. H. Also "Mi chiamano Mimi," A in Puccini's *La bohème*. H

253.32, Lucanhof; Lucia, C in Donizetti's *Lucia di Lammermoor*. B. Also C in Rossini's *La gazza ladra* and Ponchielli's *I promessi sposi*. B

253.33, vrayedevraye; Freia, C in Wagner's *Das Rheingold*. H

254.8, sulpicious; Sulpice, C in Donizetti's *La Fille du régiment*. H

254.11, archers; Archibald Grosvenor, C in Gilbert and Sullivan's *Patience*. H

254.12 fish; Ludwig Fischer (bass), who sang Sarastro in Mozart's *Magic Flute*. B

254.12, Sara's drawhead; Sarastro, C in Mozart's *Magic Flute*. H-SG

254.13, butt; Clara Butt (contra.). H

254.13, minnelisp extorreor; Mime's interior monologue, T in Wagner's *Siegfried*. H

254.14, Perrichon; Offenbach's *La Périchole* (OT). H

254.14, Bastienne; Bastienne, C in Mozart's *Bastien and Bastienne*. H

254.19, Only the caul knows his thousandfirst hame; riddle (Calaf's name), T in Puccini's *Turandot*. H-SG

254.23, Lollapaloosa; Lola, C in Mascagni's *Cavalleria rusticana*. H

254.25, .28, Jane . . . Groceries; Lady Jane Grosvenor, C in Gilbert and Sullivan's *Patience*. H-SG

254.26, cycloannalism; eons theme, T in Puccini's *Turandot*. H

254.33, the best berrathon sanger in all the aisles; Charles Santley (bar.). B

254.35, prince; Calaf, C in Puccini's *Turandot*. H-SG

254.35–36, Bunnicombe . . . herblord; Bunthorne, C in Gilbert and Sullivan's *Patience*. H-SG

254.36, herblord; Parsifal, C in Wagner's *Parsifal*. H

254.36, gillyflowrets; Dinh Gilly (bar.). H. Also Renée Gilly (sop.). H. Also Flower Maidens, Cs in Wagner's *Parsifal*. H

254.36, Artho; Désirée Artôt (mezzo-sop.). H

255.1, name is on the hero, Capellisato; riddle (Calaf's name), T in Puccini's *Turandot*. H-SG

255.4, Tamor; Timur, C in Puccini's *Turandot*. H-SG. Also riddle (*amor* = "love"), T in Puccini's *Turandot*. H-SG

255.9, storks; Rosina Storchio (sop.). H

255.10, wot; Wotan, C in Wagner's *Ring*. H-SG

255.14, Calavera; Calaf, C in Puccini's *Turandot*. H-SG

255.23, winkel; Hermann Winkelmann (ten., b. Winckelmann). H

255.32, spanning; Hina Spani (sop.). H

256.11, oddmund; Siegmund, C in Wagner's *Ring*. H

256.12, barkes; Edmund Arbrickle Burke (bass). H

256.12, cease your fumings; "Cease your funning," A in Gay's *Beggar's Opera*. H-SG

256.12–13, sherrigoldies; Margaret Sheridan (sop.). H

256.21, Marusias; King Mark, C in Wagner's *Tristan und Isolde*. G

256.33, nibulissa; Nibelung, Cs in Wagner's *Siegfried*. H

256.35, Caspi; Caspar, C in Weber's *Der Freischütz*. H-SG

257.6, jeerilied; Maria Jeritza (sop.). H

257.11, blondes; Blonde, C in Mozart's *Abduction from the Seraglio*. H

257.23, ponch in jurys; Ponchielli (comp.). H

257.23, crabeyes; Armand Crabbé (bar.). H

257.27–28, doerendunandurra . . . toory; Puccini's *Turandot* (OT). H-SG

257.31, schouwburgst; Schubert (comp.). H

257.34, Gonn the gawds; Wagner's *Die Götterdämmerung* (OT). B, M. Also the "Gods," or topmost balcony in Michael Gunn's Gaiety Theatre in Dublin. B

257.34, Gunnar; Gunther, C in Wagner's *Die Götterdämmerung*. H, M. Also Gunther in Reyer's *Sigurd*. B

257.36, snorres; Ludwig Schnorr von Carolsfeld (ten., sang first Tristan). H. Also Malvina Schnorr von Carolsfeld (sop., sang first Isolde). B

258.2, gttrdmmrng; Wagner's *Die Götterdämmerung* (OT). HW, M

258.2, Hlls vlls; Valhalla, T in Wagner's *Ring*. H, M

258.3, lammalelouh; Donizetti's *Lucia di Lammermoor* (OT). H

258.34, cheeryboyum; Cherubino, C in Mozart's *Marriage of Figaro*. H

259.1–2, tree from tree, tree among trees, tree over tree become stone to stone, stone between stones, stone under stone; Tristan, C in Wagner's *Tristan und Isolde.* H, M

259.6, gomeet madhowiatrees; Tristan, adultery, C in Wagner's *Tristan und Isolde.* B

Finnegans Wake, Book II.2:

260.11, Crescent; Girolamo Crescentini (male sop.). B. See also 260.F2.

260.17, Montan; Manon (prostitute, associated in *FW* with Violetta), C in Massenet's *Manon.* H. Also Manon, C in Puccini's *Manon Lescaut.* H

260.F2, Nipples; Naples, where Girolamo Crescentini (see 260.11) taught during his last decade. B

261.2, voylets; Violetta (associated in *FW* with Manon), C in Verdi's *La traviata.* H

261.12, cacchinated; Giulio Caccini (comp.). H. Also Francesca Caccini (comp.). H

261.F2, Martin 198

262.3, .5, .11–12, This bridge is upper. . . . Thus come to castle. . . . Hoo cavedin earthwight At furscht kracht of thunder; rainbow bridge to Valhalla, T in Wagner's *Das Rheingold.* H

262.8–9, Martin 220

262.12, furscht; Emma Fürsch-Madi (sop.). H

262.13, shoo, his flutterby; Cio-Cio-San, C in Puccini's *Madame Butterfly.* H

262.15, Martin 211

262.18, Martin 220

262.F4, amat; Pasquale Amato (bar.). H

263.18, Gunne's; Michael Gunn (impresario). McH

264.5–6, Horn of Heatthen; Charles Horn (ten. and bar.). H

264.25–26, Orchards here are lodged; sainted lawrels evremberried; Orfeo and Euridice, Cs in Gluck's *Orfeo ed Euridice* and in Monteverdi's *Favola d'Orfeo.* B, H

264.29, Norman; Bellini's *Norma* (OT). H

264.F2, When you dreamt that you'd wealth in marble arch; "I dreamt that I dwelt in marble halls," A in Balfe's *Bohemian Girl.* HW

264.F 3, rose marines; "Rose Marie," title A from Friml's operetta, recorded by John McCormack. K

265.12, cobbeler; Hans Sachs, C in Wagner's *Die Meistersinger.* H

265.13, brandnewburgher; Hans Sachs, C in Wagner's *Die Meistersinger.* H

265.13, Martin 198

265.23, .28, wine, . . . generous; "Mamma, quel vino è generoso," A in Mascagni's *Cavalleria rusticana.* H

266.8, Schore; Friedrich Schorr (bass-bar.). H

266.9–10, Martin 198

266.24–25, catalaunic; Angelica Catalani (sop.). H. Also Alfredo Catalani (comp.). H

266.25, Attil's; Verdi's *Attila* (OT). H

266.27, O june of eves; "O Abendstern," A in Wagner's *Tannhäuser.* H

266.27, O june of eves the jenniest; Schumann's *Genoveva* (OT). H

267.2, Maidadate, Mimosa; Mimosa-san, C in Jones's *Geisha.* B

267.7, gael, gillie, gall; Dinh Gilly (bar.). B. Also Renée Gilly (sop.). B

267.17, trebly; Zélia Trebelli (mezzo-sop.). H

267.19, Martin 198

267.22, Vetus may be occluded behind the mou; "O Abendstern," A in Wagner's *Tannhäuser.* B

268.1, fleur; Flower Maidens, Cs in Wagner's *Parsifal.* B

268.2, ringrang; Wagner's *Ring* (OT). B

268.3, conchitas; Conchita Supervia (mezzo-sop.). H. Also Zandonai's *Conchita.* (OT). H

268.3, sentas; Senta, C in Wagner's *Flying Dutchman.* H-SG, M

268.14, on solfa sofa; as so-fa-so-fa, opening notes of "Légères hirondelles, oiseaux bénis de Dieu," A in Thomas's *Mignon.* B and Hart

268.14–15, Stew of the evening, booksyful stew; "O Abendstern," A in Wagner's *Tannhäuser.* B

268.18, mascarine; Verdi's *Un ballo in maschera* (OT). B

269.F3, maledictions; "la maledizione," T in Verdi's *Rigoletto.* H

270.L2, *O'Mara;* Joseph O'Mara (ten.). B

270.F3, Martin 198

271.19, jennings; Jenny Diver, C in Gay's *Beggar's Opera.* B

271.24, Coax; Mrs. Coaxer, C in Gay's *Beggar's Opera.* B

271.20, Martin 220

272.30, Gringrin gringrin; "Chin Chin Chinaman," A in Jones's *Geisha.* B

273.4–5, Martin 211

274.15, datetree doloriferous; "Shade of the Palm" ("Oh, my Dolores"), A in Stuart's *Floradora.* B

274.L 4, *As Shakefork might pitch it;* nineteenth-century dispute over pitch. B

275.14, Airyanna and Blowyhart; Dukas's *Ariane et Barbe-bleu* (OT). B

275.F5, hairyoddities; Herod, C in Strauss's *Salomé* and in Massenet's *Hérodiade* (OT). G, B

276.6, jilldaws; Gilda, C in Verdi's *Rigoletto*. H

276.19, dawnsong; Peter Dawson (bar.). H

276.F6, lisplips; "Then You'll Remember Me," A in Balfe's *Bohemian Girl*. B

277.3–5, Martin 211

277.11, Toft; Catherine Tofts (sop.). H

277.23, Martin 190

278.7–8, Fanciulla's heart, the heart of Fanciulla; Puccini's *La fanciulla del west* (OT). B, H

278.25–26, Martin 198

279.1–2, treebark . . . rainstones; Tristan, C in Wagner's *Tristan und Isolde*. B, M. See also Martin 211.

279.F1.21–22, d'Oyly and Winnie Carr; Richard d'Oyly Carte, founder of D'Oyly Carte Opera company. G

280.22–23, Martin 198

280.24, peethrolio; Pedrillo, C in Mozart's *Abduction from the Seraglio*. H

280.28, Pious and pure fair one; "Morir! sì pura e bella!" A in Verdi's *Aïda*. B

281.6, .14, *marguerite,* . . . Margaritomancy; Marguérite, C in Gounod's *Faust*. H. Also C in Berlioz's *La Damnation de Faust* and Meyerbeer's *Les Huguenots*. B. Also Margherita, C in Boïto's *Mefistofele*. B

281.14, Hyacinthinous; Hyacinth, one name of Octavian, C in R. Strauss's *Der Rosenkavalier*. B

281.16, Cassio; Cassio, C in Verdi's *Otello*. H

281.17, 'tis demonal; Desdemona, C in Verdi's *Otello*. McH, B

281.18–19, il folsoletto nel falsoletto col fazzolotto dal fuzzolezzo; "Il fazzoletto" (handkerchief), T in Verdi's *Otello*. H-SG

281.20–23, Sickamoor's . . . Sieger; Siegfried, C in Wagner's *Siegfried*. H-SG, M

281.21, moor's; Otello, C in Verdi's *Otello*. McH and B

281.21, moor's . . . Ancient's; Iago (listed in cast as "Ancient to Otello"), C in Verdi's *Otello*. H-SG

281.21, sally; "Salce, Salce" (Willow Song), A in Verdi's *Otello*. McH

281.22–23, Martin 211

281.F1, Valsing-; Volsung, T in Wagner's *Ring*. H, M

281.F1, Valsinggiddyrex and his grand arks day triump; Wälse (Wotan and rainbow bridge), C in Wagner's *Ring*. B

281.F4, niggar; Otello the Moor, C in Verdi's *Otello*. B

281.L2, *Dons Johns;* Mozart's *Don Giovanni* (OT). B

281.L4, *nothums;* Nothung, T in Wagner's *Siegfried.* B

282.26, quickmarch; March, a male singer with Carl Rosa Opera Company in Dublin (1894). B

282.30–32, puff pive piff . . . poopive; "Piff, paff," A in Meyerbeer's *Les Huguenots.* B

282.F4, waltz; Gustavus Waltz (bass and Handel's cook). H

282.L1, Martin 198

283.1–2, Foughty Unn, Enoch Thortig, endso one, like to pitch of your cap; nineteenth-century dispute over pitch. B

283.L2, *Dondderwedder;* Donner, C in Wagner's *Das Rheingold.* B

284.F4, Braham Baruch . . . Braham the Bear; John Braham (ten.). H

285.27, Iris; Iris, C in Mascagni's *Iris.* H. Also C in Handel's *Semele.* B

285.F6, Quinceys; Quinquin, nickname of Octavian, C in R. Strauss's *Der Rosenkavalier.* B

287.25, *tute fluvii modo mundo;* Toti dal Monte (sop.). H. Also "Tutto nel mondo," A in Verdi's *Falstaff.* HW

287.31, pizdrool; Pizarro, C in Beethoven's *Fidelio.* H

288.2, tropadores; Verdi's *Il trovatore* (OT). H

288.9, faust; Gounod's *Faust* (OT). H. Also Berlioz's *La Damnation de Faust* and Busoni's *Doktor Faust* (OTs). B. Also Faust, C in Boïto's *Mefistofele.* B

288.13, Martin 199

288.15, *Eva;* Eva, C in Wagner's *Die Meistersinger.* H

288.22, Martin 199

289.22–23, *disparito, duspurudo, desterrado, despertieu;* Dapertutto, C in Offenbach's *Tales of Hoffmann.* H

289.25, page Ainée; Anna Page, C in Nicolai's *Merry Wives of Windsor.* G

289.26, Lady Elisabbess; Elisabeth de Valois, C in Verdi's *Don Carlos.* B. Also Elisabeth, C in Wagner's *Tannhäuser.* B, M

289.27, trueveres; Verdi's *Il trovatore* (OT). B

289.27–28, the Ides of Valentino's; Valentin, C in Gounod's *Faust.* H. Also Valentine, C in Meyerbeer's *Les Huguenots.* B. Also Valentini (Valentino Urbani, castrato contra./ten.). H. Also Francesco Valentino (bar.). H. Also Henri Justin A. J. Valentino (cond., premiere of *William Tell*). H

289.28, Isolade; Isolde, C in Wagner's *Tristan und Isolde.* B, M. Also Gazzaniga's *L'isola d'Alcina* (OT). B. Also Giuseppe Scarlatti's *L'isola disabitata* (OT). B. Also Joseph Haydn's opera of same title (OT). B. Also Isola, codirector of Opéra-Comique, Paris, 1914–25. B. Also Anna Isola (sop.). B

290.2, trysting; Tristan, C in Wagner's *Tristan und Isolde.* B, M

290.2, belle of La Chapelle, shapely Liselle; Isolde, C in Wagner's *Tristan und Isolde.* B, M

290.11, .18, F6, Douge . . . douche . . . *O alors!* . . . Miss Dotsh; "Shade of the Palm" ("Oh, my Dolores"), A in Stuart's *Floradora,* and Miss Douce, who sings the aria in "Sirens." B

290.12–13, Martin 199

290.15–17, Martin 199

290.19, Martin 199

290.21, tubatubtub; Wagner (comp.) designed and had built special tubas for his orchestras. B

290.28, Nash; Heddle Nash (ten.). H

291.1, .9, Saint Yves . . . ives of Man; King Mark, C in Wagner's *Tristan und Isolde.* G

291.1–2, Martin 199

291.5, Martin 199

291.12, juwelietry . . . madornaments; Wolf-Ferrari's *I gioiella della Madonna* (OT). K

291.19, Folly; John McCormack (ten.) under pseudonym of Giovanni Foli. K

291.F3, dido; Dido, C in Purcell's *Dido and Aeneas.* G, B. Also in Berlioz's *Les Troyens.* B

291.F4, Mester Bootenfly; Cio-Cio-San, title C in Puccini's *Madame Butterfly.* G

292.1, lamoor; Donizetti's *Lucia di Lammermoor* (OT). B

292.4, mark; King Mark, C in Wagner's *Tristan und Isolde.* G

292.12, *la gonna è mobile;* "La donna è mobile," A in Verdi's *Rigoletto.* HW

292.22, faustian fustian; Faustina Bordoni (sop.). H. Also Gounod's *Faust.* H. Also Berlioz's *La Damnation de Faust* and Busoni's *Doktor Faust* (OTs). B. Also Faust, C in Boïto's *Mefistofele.* B

293.F1, betterlies; Cio-Cio-San, C in Puccini's *Madame Butterfly.* H

294.6, noth and; Siegfried's sword Nothung, T in Wagner's *Siegfried.* G

294.25, magmasine; Massenet (comp.). G

295.18, nothung; Nothung, T in Wagner's *Siegfried.* B, M

295.20, Luccan; Pauline Lucca (sop.). H

295.28, handel; Handel (comp.). H

297.12, nadir; Nadir, C in Bizet's *Pearl Fishers.* H

297.24, fiho miho; "Di provenza il mar," A in Verdi's *La traviata.* HW

297.25, appia; Adolphe Appia (designer). B. Also Giuseppe Appiani (Appianino, probably castrato). B

297.28–29, the lass that lured a tailor; Gilbert and Sullivan's *H.M.S. Pinafore* (subtitle: "The Lass That Loved a Sailor" [OT]). B, H

298.6, smarket; King Mark, C in Wagner's *Tristan und Isolde.* G

299.1–2, Martin 199

299.8, quincidence; Quinquin, nickname of Octavian, C in Strauss's *Der Rosenkavalier.* B

300.F2, Stephens; Catherine Stephens (sop.). H

301.8, Martin 199

301.15, waggy; "Weia! waga! . . . Wagalaweia!" (Rhine Maidens at beginning of the *Ring*), A in Wagner's *Ring.* H. See also Martin 188.

301.15–18, Martin 199. Also Lord Tristram (Tristan) de Mikleford, C in Flotow's *Martha.* B

301.16–18, trieste, ah trieste . . . steifel; Triestine premiere of Verdi's *Stiffelio,* 1850. B

301.17, harriot; Harriet, C in Flotow's *Martha.* H

301.17, *trovatore;* Verdi's *Il trovatore* (OT). HW

301.19, purate out of pensionee; Gilbert and Sullivan's *Pirates of Penzance* (OT). HW

301.22, twitches; Jemmy Twitcher, C in Gay's *Beggar's Opera.* B

302.6–9, Martin 199

303.21, woodint; Wotan, C in Wagner's *Ring.* H, M

304.3, Formalisa. Loves deathhow; "Mild und leise" ("Liebestod"), A in Wagner's *Tristan und Isolde.* HW, M

304.4, Slutningsbane; Twilight of the Gods, T in Wagner's *Die Götterdämmerung.* H

304.9, rayingbogeys rings; rainbow, T in Wagner's *Ring.* H, M

304.20–22, Martin 199

304.F2, Chinchin Childaman! Chapchopchap; "Chin Chin Chinaman," A in Jones's *Geisha.* HW

305.3–4, sickenagiaour . . . Forge; Siegfried on forge, T in Wagner's *Siegfried.* H

305.20, Quin; Quinquin, nickname of Octavian, C in Strauss's *Der Rosenkavalier.* B

305.32, mark; King Mark, C in Wagner's *Tristan und Isolde.* G

305.L1, *Orexes;* Orest, C in R. Strauss's *Elektra.* H

306.20–21, Martin 212

306.L3, *Homer;* Louise Homer (contra.). H

306.F1, The divvy wants that babbling brook. Dear Auntie Emma Emma Eates; Emma Eames (sop.). G

307.L, *Samson;* Samson, C in Saint-Saëns's *Samson et Dalila.* G, B

307.L, *Cain;* accusing policeman in Caruso's monkey-house incident; see chapter 5. B

308.L, *Boox and Coox;* Sullivan's *Cox and Box* (OT). G, B

Finnegans Wake, Book II.3

309.19, Bellini; Bellini (comp.). G, McH

309.21, woman formed mobile; "La donna è mobile," A in Verdi's *Rigoletto.* HW

310.8, serostaatarean; Sarastro, C in Mozart's *Magic Flute.* H

310.15, Ropemakers; Norns, winding the skein of life, T in Wagner's *Die Götterdämmerung.* H

310.15–16, Barringoy Bnibrthirhd; blood-brotherhood, T in Wagner's *Die Götterdämmerung.* H

311.5, lealand in the luffing; Daland, C in Wagner's *Flying Dutchman.* H-SG, M

311.5–332.9, Martin 190

311.31, faist; Gounod's *Faust* (OT). H. Also Berlioz's *La Damnation de Faust* and Busoni's *Doktor Faust* (OTs). B. Also Faust, C in Boïto's *Mefistofele.* B

312.5–8, Martin 190

312.7, Franz; Paul Franz (ten.). H. Also Ferdinand Frantz (bass-bar.). B

312.8, evenstarde; "O Abendstern," A in Wagner's *Tannhäuser.* H, M

312.19–20, Martin 190

312.27, pilerinnager's grace; pilgrimage, T in Wagner's *Tannhäuser.* H

313.1, weavers; Penelope, C in Fauré's *Penelope.* G, B

313.20, velut; Giovanni Battista Velluti (male sop.). H

313.23, Martin 212

313.24, coppels token; Coppelius, C in Offenbach's *Tales of Hoffmann.* H. Also Myles na Coppaleen, C in Benedict's *Lily of Killarney.* B

313.29 a bullyon; Anna Bolena, C in Donizetti's *Anna Bolena.* G

314.22, Martin 190

314.34, Martin 199

315.16–18, Martin 193

315.26, wigger on a wagger; "Weia! Waga! . . . Wagalaweia!" (Rhine Maidens at beginning of opera), A in Wagner's *Das Rheingold.* H

316.8, eric; Erik, C in Wagner's *Flying Dutchman.* H, M

316.15–16, Martin 190

316.17, doomering; Wagner's *Die Götterdämmerung* (OT). H, M. See also Martin 212.

317.15, gombolier; Gilbert and Sullivan's *Gondoliers* (OT). B, H

317.18, Maldemaer; Walter Malde, C in Verdi's *Rigoletto*. H

317.35–36, do you kend yon peak with its coast so green?; "Connais-tu le pays?" ("Kennst du das Land?"), A in Thomas's *Mignon*. B

317.36, trystfully; Tristan, C in Wagner's *Tristan und Isolde*. H, M

318.3–10, Martin 190

318.13–14, Martin 212

318.17, Martin 188

318.31, coldtbrundt; Isabella Colbran (sop.). H

318.32, Alpyssinia . . . nihilnulls; conflict of Egypt and Abyssinia, T in Verdi's *Aïda*. B

318.32–319.1, Martin 212

319.7, gnir; Wagner's *Ring* (OT). H

319.16–17, Martin 190

319.20, gobbos; Rigoletto as hunchback, C in Verdi's *Rigoletto*. H

319.27, Martin 212

320.20, .23, Fellagulphia . . . Stuff, Taaffe, stuff; Falstaff, C in Verdi's *Falstaff*, Nicolai's *The Merry Wives of Windsor*, and Holst's *At the Boar's Head*. G, B

321.9, bianconi; Bianca Bianchi (sop.). H

321.16, buttercup; Buttercup, C in Gilbert and Sullivan's *H.M.S. Pinafore*. G

322.2, Boildawl; Adrien Boïeldieu (comp.). H

322.32, Nilsens; Christine Nilsson (sop.). H. Also Alice Nielsen (sop.). B. Also Hans Hermann Nissen (bass-bar.). B

323.1, bugganeering wanderducken; Vanderdecken, C in Wagner's *Flying Dutchman*. H, M

323.1–8, Martin 191

323.4, bloodooth; blood-brotherhood, T in Wagner's *Die Götterdämmerung*. H, M

323.9, Donnerbruch; Donner and the bridge, T in Wagner's *Das Rheingold*. H

323.32, Toni; Tonio, C in Leoncavallo's *I pagliacci*. H. Also in Donizetti's *La Fille du régiment*. B

324.16, allohn; Lohengrin, C in Wagner's *Lohengrin*. H

325.14, Martin 199

325.16, gosse and bosse; Sullivan's *Cox and Box* (OT). B

325.25 Martin 212

325.25–26, brothers Coathes; John Coates (ten.). H. Also Edith Coates (mezzo-sop.). H

325.26, blooders' oathes; blood-brotherhood, T in Wagner's *Die Götterdäm-merung.* H, M

325.31, wutan; Wotan, C in Wagner's *Ring.* H, M

325.33, Neddos; Nedda, C in Leoncavallo's *I pagliacci.* H

326.3–4, the lollies off the foiled; John McCormack (ten.) under pseudonym of Giovanni Foli. K. Also Mrs. McCormack, b. Lily Foley. B

327.5, eslucylamp; Lucia, C in Donizetti's *Lucia di Lammermoor.* H. Also C in Rossini's *La gazza ladra* and Ponchielli's *I promessi sposi.* B

327.11, rheadoromanscing; Radamès, C in Verdi's *Aïda.* H

327.12, Lavinias; Lavinia Fenton (sop.). H

327.16, tubas tout for the glowru of their god; Wagner (comp.) designed and had built special tubas for his orchestras, first put into the revised score for *Das Rheingold* in 1854 for the Valhalla motif in scene 2. B

327.18, marchadant; Mercadante (comp.). G

327.22–26, Martin 191

327.23, flyend of a touchman; Wagner's *Flying Dutchman* (OT). HW, M

327.27, wrecker; Ethel Smyth's *Wreckers* (OT). H

327.30, mireiclles; Gounod's *Mireille* (OT). H

327.30, Norgeyborgey; Donizetti's *Lucrezia Borgia* (OT). H

327.34, aiden; Verdi's *Aïda* (OT). H

328.1, pool roober; Macheath the highwayman, C in Gay's *Beggar's Opera.* B

328.4–5, coaxfonder; Mrs. Coaxer, C in Gay's *Beggar's Opera.* B

328.26, Fuchs; Marta Fuchs (sop.). H

328.31, fiery quean; Purcell's *The Fairy Queen* (OT). H

328.36, Martin 193

329.10, a chenchen for his delight time and a bonzeye nappin; "Lo zio Bonzo," C, and Nippon (Japan), T, in Puccini's *Madame Butterfly.* B. Also Cio-Cio-San, C in Puccini's *Madame Butterfly.* B

330.21, .29, zig . . . mundom; Siegmund, C in Wagner's *Ring.* H

330.24, Klein . . . ; Peter Klein (ten.). H

330.25, Norening; Eidé Norena (sop.). H

331.21, tofts; Catherine Tofts (sop.). H

331.26, cinderenda; Rossini's *La cenerentola* (OT). B

332.5, appar; "M'appari," A in Flotow's *Martha.* B

332.5, Pappappapparras; Papageno and Papagena, Cs in Mozart's *Magic Flute.* H

332.15, reining; Maria Reining (sop.). H

332.18, O gué, O gué; Vittorio Gui (cond.). B

332.29, Martin 199

333.5, szszuszchee is slowjaneska; Suzuki, C in Puccini's *Madame Butterfly.* B

333.9, wally; Catalani's *La Wally* (OT). H

333.18, Bullingdong; Anna Bolena, title C in Donizetti's *Anna Bolena.* G, B

333.23, tubtail of mondayne; Toti Dal Monte (sop.). H. Also "Tutto nel mondo," A in Verdi's *Falstaff.* H

334.17, reverence; *reverenza,* T in Verdi's *Falstaff.* H

334.31, Martin 188, 221

334.36, Martin 199

335.6, hyacinths; Hyacinth, one name of Octavian, C in R. Strauss's *Der Rosenkavalier.* B

335.15, frey; Freia, C in Wagner's *Das Rheingold.* H, M

335.16–17, .23, A lala! laleish! Ala lala! A lala; Rhine Maidens' song, T in Wagner's *Das Rheingold.* H, M. See also Martin 212.

336.13–14, Martin 191

336.20, Shinshin. Shinshin; "Chin Chin Chinaman," A in Jones's *Geisha.* HW

336.23, mark; King Mark, C in Wagner's *Tristan und Isolde.* G

337.8, annapal; Domenico Annibali (male sop.). B

337.9, semeliminal; Handel's *Semele* (OT). H

337.28, Heyday too; "Heda! Hedo!" T in Wagner's *Das Rheingold.* H

337.29, hahititahiti; "Heiaha," T in Wagner's *Die Walküre.* H

337.35–36, Tancred; Rossini's *Tancredi* (OT). H

337.36, Artaxerxes; Arne's *Artaxerxes* (OT). B

338.3, Germanon; Germont, C in Verdi's *La traviata.* H

338.3, Ehren; Ehrenreich, one name of Octavian, C in R. Strauss's *Der Rosenkavalier.* B

338.9, blurty moriartsky blutcherudd; blood-brotherhood, T in Wagner's *Die Götterdämmerung.* H

338.11, .17, .21, *mottledged,* . . . jubalant . . . palignol; "Vesti la giubba," A in Leoncavallo's *I pagliacci.* H

338.12, *sorry dejester;* Rigoletto as jester, C in Verdi's *Rigoletto.* H. Also Canio (Pagliaccio), C in Leoncavallo's *I pagliacci.* B

338.16–17, Humme to our mounthings; "Ai nostri monti" ("Home to Our Mountains"), A in Verdi's *Il trovatore.* HW-SG

338.17, jubalant tubalence; Wagner (comp.) designed and had built special tubas for his orchestras. B

338.20, amaltheouse; Paul Althouse (ten.). H

338.20, leporty hole; Leporello, C in Mozart's *Don Giovanni.* H

338.20, langdwage; William Ludwig (bar., b. Ledwidge). B

338.30–31, the morn hath razed out limpalove; "The Moon Has Raised Her Lamp Above," A in Benedict's *Lily of Killarney.* McH, B

339.1–2, *lipponease longuewedge . . .* Sehyoh narar, pokehole sann; "Un bel dì," A in Puccini's *Madame Butterfly.* B

339.23, mangraphique; Count (Graf) di Luna merged with Manrico, Cs in Verdi's *Il trovatore.* H-SG

340.1, Scutterer; "Scuoti quella fronda di ciliego" (Flower Duet), A in Puccini's *Madame Butterfly.* H

340.4, pinkpoker; Pinkerton, C in Puccini's *Madame Butterfly.* H

340.22–23, lelias . . . samp; Saint-Saëns's *Samson et Dalila* (OT) G, B

340.25, *psychophannies;* Rimsky-Korsakov's *Maid of Pskov* (OT). H

340.32, luna; Count di Luna, C in Verdi's *Il trovatore.* H

341.1, polecad; Polkan (Russian general), C in Rimsky-Korsakov's *Golden Cockerel.* H

341.9, balacleivka! Trovatarovitch! I trumble; count hears lute (balaleika), T in Verdi's *Il trovatore.* H-SG. Also "Il trovatore! Io tremo" (The troubador! I tremble), T in Verdi's *Il trovatore.* H-SG. Also Verdi's *Il trovatore* (OT). HW

341.12, Mortar martar tartar wartar; "Martern aller Arten," A in Mozart's *Abduction from the Seraglio.* H

341.16–17, Piff paff for puffpuff and my pife; "Piff, paff," A in Meyerbeer's *Les Huguenots.* H

341.17, my pife for his cgar; Glinka's *Life for the Tsar* (OT). HW

341.36, *Slippery Sam;* thieving tailor, C in Gay's *Beggar's Opera.* McH

342.5, *Samael;* Samiel, C in Weber's *Der Freischütz.* H

342.33, *Loundin Reginald;* Reginald, C in Gilbert and Sullivan's *Patience.* H

342.35, *tiomor;* Timur, C in Puccini's *Turandot.* H

343.1, pognency; Pogner, C in Wagner's *Die Meistersinger.* H

343.3, corsar; Verdi's *Il corsaro* (OT). H

344.4, *lean o'er;* Leonore, C in Beethoven's *Fidelio.* G

344.4, not athug; Nothung, T in Wagner's *Siegfried.* B

344.22–23, pagne pogne; Ping, Pang, Pong, Cs in Puccini's *Turandot.* H. Also Pogner, C in Wagner's *Die Meistersinger.* H

344.32, Deer Dirouchy; Jean de Reszke (ten.), who made Dublin debut as Jean or Giovanni di Reschi. B

345.1, Irmenial; Delius's *Irmelin* (OT). H

345.4, *waldmanns;* Maria Waldmann (mezzo-sop.). H

345.21, *norms;* Bellini's *Norma* (OT). H. Also Norns, T in Wagner's *Die Götterdämmerung.* H

346.4, *antigreenst;* Antigone, C in multiple operas (multiple composers). H. Also rivalry of Wagner's followers with Verdi (comp.). B

346.4–7, *How Alibey Ibrahim . . . jehumispheure;* entombment scene, T in Verdi's *Aïda.* B

346.5, *Bella Suora;* Angelica, C in Puccini's *Suor Angelica.* B

346.9–11, *selleries . . . soulleries . . . sulleries . . . silleries;* Antonio Salieri (comp.). G. Also "Sull'aria" (Letter Duet), A (duet) in Mozart's *Marriage of Figaro.* H

346.20, rosing; Vladmir [*sic*] Rosing (ten.). H

347.4, Nemorn; Nemorino, C in Donizetti's *L'elisir d'amore.* H

347.29, Boxerising and coxerusing; Sullivan's *Cox and Box* (OT). H

348.7, medears; Medea, C in a number of operas with that title. G, B

348.10, waulholler; Valhalla, T in Wagner's *Ring.* H, M

348.12, wody; Wotan, C in Wagner's *Ring.* H

348.23–24, Martin 199

348.29–30, Martin 212

348.36, ohosililesvienne biribarbebeway; Rossini's *Barber of Seville* (OT). H

349.4, For zahur and zimmerminnes; Lortzing's *Zar und Zimmermann* (OT). HW

349.9, *guranium;* Eugen Gura (bar). B

349.22, Martin 199

350.13, *marking;* King Mark, C in Wagner's *Tristan und Isolde.* G

350.17, chaste daffs; "Casta diva," A in Bellini's *Norma.* B

350.21, askormiles' eskermillas; Escamillo, C in Bizet's *Carmen.* HW

350.22, rawmeots and juliannes; Gounod's *Roméo et Juliette* (OT). McH, B. Also Louis Julienn (comp. and cond.). B

350.25, preying players; Gilbert-Louis Duprez (ten.). B

350.27, Spence of Parishmoslattary; Sparafucile, C in Verdi's *Rigoletto.* H. Also Spalanzani, C in Offenbach's *Tales of Hoffmann.* H

350.27, Parishmoslattary; "Pari siamo," A in Verdi's *Rigoletto.* H

350.27–28, Parishmoslattary to go and leave us; "Parigi, o cara," A in Verdi's *La traviata.* H

350.29, huguenottes; Meyerbeer's *Les Huguenots* (OT). B

350.29–32, huguenottes . . . sand us and saint us and sound as agun; "La Causa è santa" ("Pour cette cause sainte"), A in Meyerbeer's *Les Huguenots.* B

350.30, spalniel's; Spalanzani, C in Offenbach's *Tales of Hoffmann.* H. Also Sparafucile, C in Verdi's *Rigoletto.* H

351.8, waynward; Violetta, C in Verdi's *La traviata.* H

351.10, jiggilyjugging; Beniamino Gigli (ten.). H

351.12, tsingirillies; Niccolò Zingarelli (comp.). B

351.13, poppyrossies; Nicola Porpora (comp.). B. Also Rossini (comp.). B

351.13–14, Choplain . . . Bissbasses; Fyodor Chaliapin (bass; also spelled Shalyapin). H

351.25, preyers; Gilbert-Louis Duprez (ten.). B

352.2, nemcon enchelonce; "Nemico della patria," A in U. Giordano's *Andrea Chénier.* H

352.8, maddeling; Maddalena, C in Verdi's *Rigoletto.* H. Also C in Donizetti's *Linda di Chamounix.* B

352.25, Martin 212. Also Hagen, C in Reyer's *Sigurd.* B

353.2, Martin 199

353.19, Igorladns; Borodin's *Prince Igor* (OT). H

353.24, *ivanmorinthorrorumble;* Rimsky-Korsakov's *Maid of Pskov* (OT). B, H-SG

353.24, .26, *Parsuralia . . . perceivable;* Wagner's *Parsifal* (OT). H-SG, M

354.14, *Cicilian;* "Siciliana," A in Mascagni's *Cavalleria rusticana.* K

354.29, traublers; Helen Traubel (sop.). H

355.22, Amelakins; Amelia, C in Verdi's *Simon Boccanegra.* H. Also Amelia in Verdi's *Un ballo in maschera.* H. Also C in Mercadante's *I brigante.* B

355.33–35, Martin 212

356.1, faust; Gounod's *Faust,* Berlioz's *La Damnation de Faust,* and Busoni's *Doktor Faust* (OTs). B. Also Faust, C in Boïto's *Mefistofele.* B

356.5, hummley; Johan Nepomuk Hummel (comp.). B. Also Humming Chorus, A in Puccini's *Madame Butterfly.* B

356.6, orofaces; Oroveso, C in Bellini's *Norma.* H

356.17, Martin 213

357.9, perssian; Fanny Persiani (sop.). H

357.15, *Dido;* Purcell's *Dido and Aeneas* (OT). B

357.19, cobbler; Hans Sachs, C in Wagner's *Die Meistersinger.* H

358.3, renations; Renato, C in Verdi's *Un ballo in maschera.* H

358.12, colombophile; Mackenzie and Hueffer's *Columba* (OT). B

358.20, Martin 221

358.34, slammocks; Mrs. Slammekin, C in Gay's *Beggar's Opera.* B

359.14, Danelope; Penelope, C in Fauré's *Penelope.* G, B

359.14, laurettas; Lauretta, C in Puccini's *Gianni Schicchi.* H

359.19–20, the oldcant rogue; Farinelli (It. for "rogue"), stage name of Carlo Broschi (male sop.). B

359.24–25, Tales of . . . hofdking or a hoovthing; Offenbach's *Tales of Hoffmann* (OT). H

359.26, Eeric; Erik, C in Wagner's *Flying Dutchman*. B

359.26, pinginapoke; Ping, Pang, Pong, Cs in Puccini's *Turandot*. B

359.28–29, Lhirondella, jaunty lhirondella! With tirra lirra rondinelles; Puccini's *La rondine* (OT). H

359.32, naughtingels; bird, T in Wagner's *Siegfried*. H-SG

359.32, .35, naughtingels . . . Jinnyland; Jenny Lind (sop.). HW

359.33, rosescenery; Rossini (comp.). HW

359.33–34, haydyng; Haydn (comp.). HW

359.34, waldalure; Wagner's *Die Walküre* (OT). H. Also Valhalla, T in Wagner's *Ring*. HW, M. See also Martin 213.

359.35, duskfoil; John McCormack (ten.) under pseudonym of Giovanni Foli. K

359.35, Moore-; Grace Moore (sop.). H

359.35–36, Mooreparque; conflation of two McCormack homes, Moore Abbey and Esher Park. K

360.1–2, Martin 221

360.2, sweetishsad lightandgayle; bird, T in Wagner's *Siegfried*. H-SG. Also Jenny Lind (sop.). HW

360.2–3, twittwin twosingwoolow; "Willow, Tit-Willow, Tit-Willow," A in Gilbert and Sullivan's *Mikado*. HW

360.3, Let everie sound of a pitch keep still in resonance; nineteenth-century battle over pitch in England. B

360.7, pere Golazy; Pergolesi (comp.). HW

360.7, mere Bare; Meyerbeer (comp.). HW

360.7, Bill Heeny; Bellini (comp.). HW

360.8, Smirky Dainty; Mercadante (comp.). HW. Also anagram of first part of Rimsky-Korsakov (comp.), G

360.8, beethoken; Beethoven (comp.). HW

360.8–9, wheckfoolthenairyans; Wagner (comp.). HW, M

360.9–10, gluckglucky; Alma Gluck (sop.). B. Also Gluck (comp.). HW. Also Schoenberg's *Die glückliche Hand* (OT). B

360.11–12, inchimings . . . clinkars; "Klinget, Glöckchen" (ring, bells), T in Mozart's *Magic Flute*. H

360.11, ceased to the moment; "Ai nostri monti" ("Home to Our Mountains"), A in Verdi's *Il trovatore*. Blish

360.12, clinkars; Glinka (comp.). HW

360.12, nocturnefield; John Field (comp.). HW

360.12, sweetmoztheart; Mozart (comp.). HW

360.12–13, night's . . . queen; Queen of the Night, C in Mozart's *Magic Flute.* HW-SG

360.13, Carmen; Bizet's *Carmen* (OT). HW

360.13, Carmen Sylvae; "Care selve," A in Handel's *Atalanta.* HW

360.13, my quest, my queen; "Questa o quella," A in Verdi's *Rigoletto.* HW

360.13–16, Martin 213

360.24, youd remesmer; "Then You'll Remember Me," A in Balfe's *Bohemian Girl.* HW

360.25, Holy moon priestess; Norma, druid priestess, C in Bellini's *Norma.* H

360.26, Pschtt! Tabarins; Puccini's *Il tabarro* (OT). H

360.26–27, O gui, O gui; Vittorio Gui (cond.). B

360.27, Salam, salms, salaum; R. Strauss's *Salomé* (OT). H

360.34, Wee wee; "Wie, wie, wie," T in Mozart's *Magic Flute.* H

360.34, anthill; Antheil (comp.). H

360.36, Panchomaster; Don Quixote, C in Massenet's (and other composers') *Don Quixote.* B

361.1, colombinations; Mackenzie and Hueffer's *Columba* (OT). B

361.21, Lodewijk; William Ludwig (bar., b. Ledwidge). B

361.21, onongonamed; Tchaikovsky's *Eugene Onegin* (OT). H

362.8–9, Martin 191

362.16, .19, generose . . . hould the wine; "Mamma, quel vino è generoso," A in Mascagni's *Cavalleria rusticana.* H

362.17, umbrasive of yews all; "Ombra mai fù" (Largo), A in Handel's *Serse.* H

363.9, hoax . . . exexive; Mrs. Coaxer and Mrs. Vixen, Cs in Gay's *Beggar's Opera.* B

363.10, rosing; Vladmir [*sic*] Rosing (ten.). H

363.15, Martin 199

363.15, foil the flouter; John McCormack (ten.) under pseudonym of Giovanni Foli. K

363.18, suked; Suky Tawdry, C in Gay's *Beggar's Opera.* B

363.20, Guilty but fellows culpows; Coppelius and Giuletta, Cs in Offenbach's *Tales of Hoffmann.* H

363.24, Martin 199

363.26, Martin 199

363.28, Martin 200

363.33, upfallen girls; the Ladies of the Town, Cs in Gay's *Beggar's Opera.* B

364.27, Y; Lalo's *Le Roi d'Ys* (OT). H

365.1, mircles; Doctor Miracle, C in Offenbach's *Tales of Hoffmann*. H. Also Bizet's *Le Docteur Miracle* (OT). B

365.1, Martin 213

365.6, Bacchulus; Baculus, C in Lortzing's *Der Wildschütz*. H

365.16, Martin 213

365.28, Nessies; Giuseppe Nessi (ten.). H

365.28, Nixies; Nixies, Cs in Wagner's *Ring*. G, B. Also Arthur Nikisch (cond.). B

366.22, bramblers; Brambilla family (singers). H

366.23–24, trovatellas; Verdi's *La traviata* (OT). H. Also Verdi's *Il trovatore* (OT). HW

366.30, Fall stuff; Verdi's *Falstaff* (OT). H. Also C in Verdi's *Falstaff*, Nicolai's *Merry Wives of Windsor*, and Holst's *At the Boar's Head*. B

367.8–14, Martin 200

367.33, calif; Calaf, C in Puccini's *Turandot*. H

368.8, gianerant; Gennaro, C in Donizetti's *Lucrezia Borgia*. H. Also Gennaro in Wolf-Ferrari's *I gioiella della Madonna*. B

368.9, murketplots; King Mark, C in Wagner's *Tristan und Isolde*. G

368.10, .15, belloky . . . bellock; Teresa Belloc-Giorgi (mezzo-sop.). H

368.33, Leonocopolos; Coppelius, C in Offenbach's *Tales of Hoffmann*. H. Also Leoncavallo (comp.). H

369.9, Carolan Crescent; in association with another singer, Carolan, a reference to Girolamo Crescentini (male sop.). B

369.11, Rode; Wilhelm Rode (bass-bar.). H

369.17, Fidelisat; Beethoven's *Fidelio* (OT). H

369.19, perchypole; Offenbach's *La Périchole* (OT). B

369.26, Paullabucca; William Paull (bar.). B

370.7, cavaliery; Lina Cavalieri (sop.). H. Also Mascagni's *Cavalleria rusticana* (OT). H

370.8, Trouvas; Verdi's *Il trovatore* (OT). B

370.13, Fool step; Falstaff, C in Verdi's *Falstaff*, Nicolai's *Merry Wives of Windsor*, and Holst's *At the Boar's Head*. G, B

370.23, oddstodds on bluebleeding; Dukas's *Ariane et Barbe-bleu* (OT). B

370.23, boarhorse; Holst's *At the Boar's Head* (OT), which JJ ordered for Giorgio Joyce, the lead role—Falstaff—atypically being for bass. B

370.36, Capolic; Joseph-Amédée-Victor Capoul (ten.). H

371.6, sieguldson; Siegfried, C in Wagner's *Siegfried*. H

371.6–9, 19–20, 31–32, Dour Douchy . . . wather parted from the say; "Water parted from the sea," A in Arne's *Artaxerxes*. HW. Also Tenducci (sop.). Senn

371.15, the last dropes of summour down through their grooves of blarneying; "'Tis the last rose of summer" (air: "The Groves of Blarney"), A in Flotow's *Martha*. B

371.36, hugon; Meyerbeer's *Les Huguenots* (OT). H

372.4, Martin 200

372.7, barttler; Bartolo, C in Luigi and Federico Ricci's *Crispino e la comare*. B. Also Bartolo, C in Rossini's *Barber of Seville*. H. Also in Mozart's *Marriage of Figaro*. B

372.8, frankling; David Franklin (bass). H

372.9, Raoul; Raoul, C in Meyerbeer's *Les Huguenots* (a John Sullivan role). H

372.26–27, By wather parted from the say; "Water parted from the sea," A in Arne's *Artaxerxes*. HW

372.28, Martin 200

372.28, Free rogue Mountone; Farinelli (It. for "rogue"), stage name of Carlo Broschi (male sop.). B

372.32, O'Ryne; Le Comte Ory, C in Rossini's *Le Comte Ory*. H

373.4, sailalloyd; Edward Lloyd (ten.). B

373.4, donggie; Mozart's *Don Giovanni* (OT). H. Also Damcke (ten.). B

373.5, Moherboher; Meyerbeer (comp.). H

373.10–11, O'er wather parted from the say; "Water parted from the sea," A in Arne's *Artaxerxes*. HW

373.12, ebblynuncies; Princess Eboli, C in Verdi's *Don Carlos*. H

373.15, Roger; Gustave Roger (ten.). H

374.21, one hyde; Walter Hyde (ten.). H

374.21, Two stick holst; Gustav Holst (comp.). B

375.23, Don Gouverneur; Mozart's *Don Giovanni* (OT). H

376.1, Ineen MacCormick; John McCormack (ten.). H

376.1, O'Puckins; Puccini (comp.). H

376.2, MacKundred; Kundry, C in Wagner's *Parsifal*. H. Also MacCunn (comp.). H

376.16–17, Aunt . . . unclish . . . Neffin; Isolde, King Mark, and Tristan, Cs in Wagner's *Tristan und Isolde*. G.

376.18, Gunting; Gunther, C in Wagner's *Die Götterdämmerung*. H. Also in Reyer's *Sigurd*. B

376.36, soullfriede; Siegfried, C in Wagner's *Siegfried*. H

377.13, Welsey Wandrer; Wanderer (Wotan), C in Wagner's *Siegfried*. H. Also Wälse (Wotan), C in Wagner's *Ring*. H

377.31–32, Mr. Justician Marks; King Mark, C in Wagner's *Tristan und Isolde*. G

377.32–33, Johnston-Johnson; Edward Johnson (ten.; became manager of the Metropolitan Opera). H, B. Also Johnson, C in Puccini's *La fanciulla del west.* H

378.14, Martin 200

378.26, frayshouters; Weber's *Der Freischütz* (OT). H

378.31, vulsyvolsy; Volsung, T in Wagner's *Ring.* H

379.10, Carlow; Verdi's *Don Carlos* (OT). H

379.12, volleyholleydoodlem; Valhalla, T in Wagner's *Ring.* B

379.12, .18, Fall of Toss . . . Fell stiff; Falstaff, C in Verdi's *Falstaff,* Nicolai's *Merry Wives of Windsor,* and Holst's *At the Boar's Head.* G, B

379.16, Nessies; Giuseppe Nessi (ten.). H

379.17, rheinbok; the Rhine, T in Wagner's *Ring.* H

379.20, pappappoppopcuddle; Papageno, C in Mozart's *Magic Flute.* H

379.21, sord, fathe; Nothung, T in Wagner's *Siegfried.* B

379.23–24, fortycantle glim lookbehinder; candles and lamp, T in Bellini's *La sonnambula.* B

379.24, rubiny; Giovanni-Battista Rubini (ten.), who sang Elvino in *La sonnambula.* B. Also Giacomo Lauri-Volpi (ten.), who debuted as Giacomo Rubini. B

379.24, leeses; Lisa, the innkeeper, C in Bellini's *La sonnambula.* B

379.30, B E N K B A N K B O N K; Ping, Pang, Pong, Cs in Puccini's *Turandot.* B

379.33–35, Martin 213

380.4–5, Martin 200

380.12, polemarch; March, a male singer with Carl Rosa Opera Company in Dublin, 1894. B

380.24, comicsongbook; John McCormack (ten.). H

380.25, pallyass; Pelléas, C in Debussy's *Pelléas et Mélisande.* H. Also Leoncavallo's *I pagliacci* (OT). H

381.10–11, right royal round rollicking toper's table; "Right Down Regular Royal Queen," A in Gilbert and Sullivan's *Gondoliers.* HW

381.19, *Adams;* Suzanne Adams (sop.). H

381.27–28, he could not tell what he did ale; Tenducci (male sop.). M

382.2, brindishing; brindisi, any drinking song in opera. See in chapter 8 under "Brindisi." McH

382.13, Litvian; Félia Litvinne (sop.). H

Finnegans Wake, Book II.4
383.1–399.36, Martin 200

383.1, .8, *Mark!... Mark;* King Mark, C in Wagner's *Tristan und Isolde*. H, M

383.3, Martin 200

383.11, *Tristy's;* Tristan, C in Wagner's *Tristan und Isolde*. H, M

383.14, Martin 200

383.15, song sang seaswans; Swan, T in Wagner's *Lohengrin*. B

383.18, Trustan with Usolde; Wagner's *Tristan und Isolde* (OT). H-SG, M

384.6, maaster; Joseph Maas (ten.). G

384.8, .11, Marcus Lyons... Marcus; King Mark, C in Wagner's *Tristan und Isolde*. B, M

384.10, Miracle; Doctor Miracle, C in Offenbach's *Tales of Hoffmann*. H. Also Bizet's *Le Docteur Miracle* (OT). B

384.21, colleen bawn; Colleen Bawn, C in Benedict's *Lily of Killarney*. G

384.31, Isolamisola; Gazzaniga's *L'isola d'Alcina* (OT). B. Also Giuseppe Scarlatti's *L'isola disabitata* (OT) and Joseph Haydn's opera of same title (OT). B. Also Isola, codirector of Opéra-Comique, Paris, 1914–25. B. Also Anna Isola (sop.). B

384.31–32, Isolamisola, and whisping and lisping her about Trisolanisans; as so-la-mi-so-la, opening notes of "Mein lieber Schwan," A in Wagner's *Lohengrin*. B

384.31–32, Martin 200

385.1, Cullen's barn; "The Colleen Bawn," A in Benedict's *Lily of Killarney*. HW

385.19, Marcus; King Mark, C in Wagner's *Tristan und Isolde*. H, M

385.26–27, .36, revelling... Ossian; "Pourquoi me réveiller" (Werther's song from Ossian), A in Massenet's *Werther*. H

386.8–9, Martin 200

387.14, Martin 200

387.28, Martin 200

388.2–4, Kram... Llawnroc... gink... yord... Wehpen... luftcat revol ... natsirt.... Tuesy; series of references, spelled mostly backward, to Mark, Cornwall, king, dory, nephew, tactful lover, Tristan, and Yseut, Ts and Cs in Wagner's *Tristan und Isolde*. H, McH, M, B

388.4, mild aunt Liza; "Mild und leise" ("Liebestod"), A in Wagner's *Tristan und Isolde*. HW-SG, M. See also Martin 200.

388.10, Martin 200

388.33, 389.27 Bockleyshuts... rodolling; Rudolf Bockelmann (bass-bar.). H

388.34, Marcus Lyons; King Mark, C in Wagner's *Tristan und Isolde*. H, M

389.3, pioja at pulga bollas; "Morir! sì pura e bella!" A in Verdi's *Aïda*. B

389.24, Martin 200

389.27, rodolling; Rodolfo, C in Puccini's *La bohème*. H. Also Rodolfo, C in Verdi's *Luisa Miller*. B

389.28, Cornelius; Peter Cornelius (ten.). H

390.6, turner; Eva Turner (sop.). H

390.7, Skelly, with the lether belly; Michael Kelly (ten.). Lernout

390.22, .28, .33, they parted, raining water . . . And so they parted, . . . Part. Ay, Ay; "Water parted from the sea," A in Arne's *Artaxerxes*. B

391.8, maasters; Joseph Maas (ten.). G

391.14, Martin 200

391.21, Roneo to Giliette; Gounod's *Roméo et Juliette* (OT). K

391.28, Davies; Edward Davies (ten.), appeared in *Faust* in Dublin, 1903–4. B

392.2–3, he was only funning; "Cease your funning," A in Gay's *Beggar's Opera*. B

392.10, the poor old coax; Mrs. Coaxer, C in Gay's *Beggar's Opera*. B

392.14–15, Abbotabishop; Emma Abbott (sop.). B. Also Anna Bishop (sop.). B

392.32, alfred; Alfred, C in J. Strauss II's *Die Fledermaus*. H

393.5, Cunningham; Robert Cunningham (ten.). B

393.30, ys! ys; Lalo's *Le Roi d'Ys* (OT). H

394.9, rancers; Jack Rance, C in Puccini's *La fanciulla del west*. H

394.20, Martin 200

394.23–25, Martin 200

394.30, Martin 201

395.1–2, murky . . . Narsty . . . Idoless; Mark, Tristan, and Isolde, Cs in Wagner's *Tristan und Isolde*. McH

395.1–2, Martin 201

395.29, Martin 201

395.32, queeleetlecree of joysis crisis; "Des cris joyeuse," A in Massenet's *Werther*. H

396.7–10, strapping modern old ancient Irish prisscess, . . . red hair and solid ivory; Isolde, C in Wagner's *Tristan und Isolde*. H-SG

396.11, a firstclass pair of bedroom eyes; "Take a pair of sparkling eyes," A in Gilbert and Sullivan's *Gondoliers*. B

396.31, Martin 201

397.3, .21, Mar . . . Marcus Lyons; King Mark, C in Wagner's *Tristan und Isolde*. G

397.5, girleen bawn; Colleen Bawn, C in Benedict's *Lily of Killarney*. G

397.10, mousework; huge, ungainly concert organized at Her Majesty's Theatre, fall 1850, described as "mousework" by the *Athenæum*, with Sims Reeves as participant. Lernout

397.10, making it up; phrase used from the "Gods" to Reeves and Calcraft after performance of *Lucia di Lammermoor* in Dublin, 1849, wherein Reeves was forced to substitute for two tenors (Damcke and Pagleri), resulting in conductor Jules Benedict's leaving theater in a temper, orchestra proceeding without conductor, and Reeves barely speaking to the soprano (Catherine Hayes) and the manager (Calcraft). Lernout

397.12, follies; A. J. Foli (bass, b. Foley). H. Also John McCormack (ten.) under pseudonym of Giovanni Foli. G

397.16, materny; Amalie Materna (sop.). H

397.18–19, Martin 201

397.21, Martin 201

398.2, Martin 201

398.10, death and the love embrace; "Mild und leise" ("Liebestod"), A in Wagner's *Tristan und Isolde*. HW, M

398.18, Martin 201

398.29, Iseult la belle! Tristan; Wagner's *Tristan und Isolde* (OT). H-SG, M

399.4, Martin 213

399.31, Martin 201

Finnegans Wake, Book III.1:

403.1, .3, Hark! . . . Hork; "Horch" (listen), T in Wagner's *Tristan und Isolde* (Isolde speaking). H-SG

403.1–22, chimes; "Hört ihr Leut' und lasst euch sagen, Die Glock' hat Zehn geschlagen," A in Wagner's *Meistersinger*. H-SG. Also church bells, T in Wagner's *Tannhäuser* (while in Venusburg, Tannhäuser hears church bells). H-SG

403.2, sax; Marie-Constance Sass (sop.). H

403.2, .4, Tolv two elf kater ten (it can't be) sax. . . . Pedwar pemp foify tray (it must be) twelve; "Cinque—dieci—venti—trenta—trenta sei—quaranta tre," A in Mozart's *Marriage of Figaro*. H-SG

403.6, fogbow . . . arch; rainbow bridge to Valhalla, T in Wagner's *Ring*. B, M

403.6, Mark; King Mark, C in Wagner's *Tristan und Isolde*. H, M

403.9, Titubante of Tegmine; Mozart's *La clemenza di Tito* (OT). H

403.9–10, mobiling so wobiling; "La donna è mobile," A in Verdi's *Rigoletto*. H

403.11, Anastashie; Anastasia Robinson (sop.). H

403.11, green; Verdi (comp.). H

403.13, becco; Verdi's *Nabucco* (OT). H-SG

403.13, .17, 404.19, becco, . . . Black! . . . lacers; "Il lacerato spirito," A in Verdi's *Simon Boccanegra*. H

403.14–16, Pensée . . . aal in her dhove's; "Va pensiero, sull' ali dorati," A (chorus of Hebrew slaves) in Verdi's *Nabucco.* H-SG

403.15, veilch veilchen veilde; Violetta, C in Verdi's *La traviata.* H

403.20, vixen's laughter; Mrs. Vixen, C in Gay's *Beggar's Opera.* B

403.22, violet; Violetta, C in Verdi's *La traviata.* H

404.1, darkling; Hariclea Darclée (sop.). H

404.19, ferrier; Kathleen Ferrier (contra). H

404.19, mereswin; Wladyslaw Mierzwinski (Polish ten.). H-SG

404.21, sparable; Sparafucile, C in Verdi's *Rigoletto.* H

404.24, krasnapoppsky; Otakar Kraus (bar.), debuted 1935. H. Also Felix von Krauss (bass). B. Also Gabrielle Krauss (sop.). B. Also Ernst Kraus (ten.). H

404.26, Tamagnum; Tamino, C in Mozart's *Magic Flute.* H. Also Francesco Tamagno (ten.). H-SG

404.26, loud boheem; Puccini's *La bohème* (OT). H

404.26, boheem toy; Balfe's *Bohemian Girl* (OT). H-SG

405.6–7, I, poor ass, am . . . dunkey; "Dunque io son," A (duet) in Rossini's *Barber of Seville.* H. Also Massenet's (and other composers') *Don Quixote* (OT). B

405.7, messonger; Messager (comp.). H

405.7, angels; Nazareno de Angelis (bass). H

405.13, fellow . . . stuff; Falstaff, C in Verdi's *Falstaff,* Nicolai's *Merry Wives of Windsor,* and Holst's *At the Boar's Head.* G, B

405.20, rool; Raoul, C in Meyerbeer's *Les Huguenots,* a John Sullivan role. H

405.21, immense; "Già la mensa è preparata" (the table is laid), T in Mozart's *Don Giovanni.* H

405.23, matters; Arnold Matters (bar.). H

405.24, Lawzenge; Marjorie Lawrence. H

405.27, .30, queen . . . spadefuls; Tchaikovsky's *Queen of Spades* (OT). H

405.32, pranzipal; Wagner's *Parsifal* (OT). H

406.6, wolp; Giacomo Lauri-Volpi (ten.). H-SG

406.7–8, Margareter, Margaretar, Margarasticandeatar; Marguérite, C in Gounod's *Faust.* H. Also C in Berlioz's *La Damnation de Faust* and Meyerbeer's *Les Huguenots.* B. Also Margherita, C in Boïto's *Mefistofele.* B

406.9, avalunch; "La Valanga" ("the Avalanche," sop.), *Letters 1,* 358. B

406.13, .27, Boland's . . . Anne; Anna Bolena, C in Donizetti's *Anna Bolena.* H

406.15, carusal; Enrico Caruso (ten.). H-SG

406.17, hotted; Hans Hotter (bass-bar.). H

406.18, veal more; "Veau d'or," A in Gounod's *Faust*. H

406.18, stuffed following; Falstaff, C in Verdi's *Falstaff,* Nicolai's *Merry Wives of Windsor,* and Holst's *At the Boar's Head*. G, B

406.22–23, aman, . . . the best of the wine *avec*. For his heart was as big as himself, so it was, ay, and bigger; "Mamma, quel vino è generoso," A in Mascagni's *Cavalleria rusticana*. B. Also Therese Tietjens (sop.), described in Dublin as having a "heart as big as herself." McH

406.23–24, While the loaves are aflowering and the nachtingale jugs; "E lucevan le stelle ed olezzava la terra," A in Puccini's *Tosca*. B

406.24, Jilian's; Beniamino Gigli (ten.). H

406.25, Mabhrodaphne; Jacopo Peri's *Dafne* (OT), the first opera (1597). B

406.31, nourritures; Louis Nourrit (ten.). H-SG. Also Adolphe Nourrit (ten.). H-SG

406.35, prelove appetite; "Ah, che barbaro appetito," A in Mozart's *Don Giovanni*. H

407.10, Overture and beginners; Giuseppina Ronzi de Begnis (sop.). H. Also Giuseppe de Begnis (bass). H. Also callboy shouts this backstage at dressing rooms when performance is to begin. McH

407.13, .20, .21, .24, voice . . . softly . . . open . . . heart; "Mon coeur s'ouvre à ta voix," A in Saint-Saëns's *Samson et Dalila*. H

407.13–14, voice, the voce of Shaun, vote of the Irish, voise from afar; "Una voce poco fà," A in Rossini's *Barber of Seville*. H

407.14–15, Martin 221

407.16, Michaeleen Kelly; Michael Kelly (ten.). H

407.16, Mara; Gertrud Mara (sop.). H. Also Joseph O'Mara (ten.). H

407.16, O'Mario; Giovanni Mario (ten.). H

407.18–19, from Inchigeela call the way; "From Inchigela all the way," A in Benedict's *Lily of Killarney.* HW-SG

407.19, morepork! morepork; Grace Moore (sop.). H. Also conflation of two McCormack homes, Moore Abbey and Esher Park. B

407.19–20, to scented nightlife as softly; "E lucevan le stelle ed olezzava la terra," A in Puccini's *Tosca*. B

407.23–24, handshell cupped, his handsign pointed, his handheart mated; Humperdinck's *Hänsel und Gretel* (OT). H

407.27, aladdin; Dalila, C in Saint-Saëns's *Samson et Dalila*. B

407.27–28, Does she lag soft fall means rest down?; as do-si-la-sol-fa-me-re-do, this approximates the opening notes of "Ah! réponds à ma tendresse" (following immediately after "Mon coeur s'ouvre à ta voix"), A in Saint-Saëns's *Samson et Dalila*. B

407.31, 'stuesday's shampain; "Finch'han dal vino" (Champagne Aria), A in Mozart's *Don Giovanni.* H

407.31–32, the memories of the past; "There is a flower that bloometh," A in Wallace's *Maritana.* HW-SG

407.32–33, the musics of the futures; *Zukunftsmusik,* Wagner's "music of the future" (T). H, M

407.35–36, houseful of deadheads; Janáček's *From the House of the Dead* (OT). H

408.2, manducators; Duke of Mantua, C in Verdi's *Rigoletto.* H

408.4, to resk at once; Jean de Reszke (ten.). H-SG

408.4, .10, .11, dowanouet . . . mere mailman . . . principot of Candia; Giovanni Mario, count of Candia (ten.). H, B

408.11–12, the first degree, the principot of Candia, no legs and a title, for such eminence; John McCormack (ten.), whom Joyce mocked for being fat (principot = small fat prince) and pigeon-toed (he wasn't particularly so), whose first papal title was later raised to higher ones. He was no cardinal (eminence), but his papal uniform had scarlet trim, and he was a friend of several cardinals in both Ireland and the United States. K, B

408.21–22, Sim . . . reeve; Sims Reeves (ten.). H

408.23, Tune in, tune on, old Tighe; "Turn on, old time," A in Wallace's *Maritana,* a favorite encore for Sims Reeves. HW-SG

408.26, Bonzeye; Alesandro Bonci (ten.). H-SG. Also "Lo zio Bonzo," C in Puccini's *Madame Butterfly.* B

408.32, old Madre Patriack; "O patria mia . . . O cieli azzurri," A in Verdi's *Aïda.* H

409.1, Wouldndom; Wotan, C in Wagner's *Ring.* H

409.4, recitativer; recitative, element in opera generally. B

409.8, But have we until now ever besought you; "Shall I never more behold thee?" A in Donizetti's *Lucia di Lammermoor.* B

409.12–13, catlik . . . candylock; Ann or Anne Catley (sop.). JJ has merged "Catley" and "cowlick." B, H-SG. Also "Madamina, il catalogo," A in Mozart's *Don Giovanni.* H

409.12, in echo rightdainty; "Ecco ridente in cielo," A in Rossini's *Barber of Seville.* HW-SG

409.14, Athiacaro; "A te o cara," A in Bellini's *I puritani.* H-SG

409.14, Comb his tar odd gee sing your mower O meeow?; "Come sta oggi signor moro mio," A in Verdi's *Otello.* H

409.15, Greet thee Good?; "Dich, teure Halle, grüss' ich wieder, froh grüss' ich dich," A in Wagner's *Tannhäuser.* H

409.16, Fatiguing, very fatiguing; "Notte e giorno faticar," A in Mozart's *Don Giovanni.* H-SG

409.17, Poumeerme; "Pour me rapprocher de Marie, je m'ensolai pauvre soldat," A in Donizetti's *La Fille du régiment.* H

409.28, Colleenkiller's; Benedict's *Lily of Killarney* (OT). G, B

409.30, Tilvido; Georges Thill (ten.). H-SG

409.35, Books . . . Cooks; Sullivan's *Cox and Box* (OT). B

410.2, hairydittary; McCormack's (ten.) hereditary papal countship. McH

410.9, grizzild; Giuditta Grisi (mezzo-sop.). H. Also Giulia Grisi (sop.). H

410.14, ponteen; da Ponte (comp. and librettist). H

410.23, Emailia; Amelia, C in Verdi's *Simon Boccanegra.* H. Also C in Verdi's *Un ballo in maschera.* H. Also C in Mercadante's *I brigante.* B. Also Emilia, C in Verdi's *Otello.* B, H

410.23, Speak to us of Emailia; "Parle-moi de ma mère," A in Bizet's *Carmen.* H

410.26, Barbe, that is a lock; Rossini's *Barber of Seville* (OT). H

410.29, moreboy; Otello, C in Verdi's *Otello.* H

411.12, in my simplicity; "Elle ne croyait pas" (sung by JJ in recital as "In her simplicity"), A in Thomas's *Mignon.* B

411.17, bonzar; "Lo zio Bonzo," C in Puccini's *Madame Butterfly.* B

411.18–19, Martin 221

411.20, Maria; *Ave Maria,* A in Verdi's *Otello.* H

411.20–21, I believe. Greedo; "Credo in un dio crudel," A in Verdi's *Otello.* H

411.27–28, The gloom hath rays, her lump is love; "The Moon Has Raised Her Lamp Above," A in Benedict's *Lily of Killarney.* HW-SG

411.29, Thrubedore; Verdi's *Il trovatore* (OT). H

411.31, coat's wasting after striding on the vampire; Edith Coates (mezzo-sop.). H. Also "Stride la vampa," A in Verdi's *Il trovatore.* HW

412.1, grandiose; Margherita Grandi (sop.). H

412.5–6, Moyhard's daynoight; "You Are My Heart's Delight" ("Dein ist mein ganzes Herz"), A in Lehár's *Land of Smiles.* McH. Also "The Moon Has Raised Her Lamp Above," A in Benedict's *Lily of Killarney.* B

412.7, bel chant; bel canto style of singing, as well as Wyndham Lewis's name for JJ. McH

412.7–8, Martin 213

412.8, *tuba;* Wagner designed and had built special tubas for his orchestras. B

412.8, *Buccinate;* Puccini (comp.). H

412.8, *Emenia;* Emma Eames (sop.). H

412.9, phausdheen; Faust, C in Gounod's *Faust,* Busoni's *Doktor Faust,* Berlioz's *La Damnation de Faust,* and Boïto's *Mefistofele.* B

412.11, .33, verdure, verdigrease; Verdi (comp.). H. Also Giulia Grisi (sop.). B

412.22, purcell's; Purcell (comp.). H

412.23, Miss Enders; Marian Anderson (sop.). B. Also Sybil Sanderson (sop.).
B

412.23–24, .29, Miss Enders . . . Men's . . . *apartita;* "Già la mensa è preparata . . . appetito" (the table is laid . . . appetite), A in Mozart's *Don Giovanni.* H-SG

412.24, Scotic; Antonio Scotti (bar.). H

412.29, *Becco;* Verdi's *Nabucco* (OT). H

412.36, Nickil; Ernest Nicolini (ten.). B. Also Nicolino (male contra.). H

413.1, force of destiny; Verdi's *La forza del destino* (OT). HW

413.1, destiny; Emmy Destinn (sop.). H

413.5, .14, .15, Mrs Sanders . . . sweet Standerson . . . Mevrouw von Andersen; Marian Anderson (sop.). H. Also Sybil Sanderson (sop.). H

413.8, Easther's; Florence Easton (sop.). H

413.15, Andersen; Ivar Andrésen (bass). H. Also Mary Anderson, actress and close friend of John McCormack (ten.). McH

413.16, .19, Honour . . . honour; "l'honore," T in Verdi's *Falstaff.* H

413.34, paste; Giuditta Pasta (sop.). H

413.34, rubiny; Giacomo Lauri-Volpi (ten.), who made debut as Giacomo Rubini. B. Also Giovanni Battista Rubini (ten.). H

413.34, winklering; Hermann Winkelmann (ten.; b. Winckelmann). H

414.1, rhino, rhine, O joyoust rhine; Felix Weingartner (cond.). B. Also Wagner's *Das Rheingold* (OT). H, M

414.2, Miss Anders; Marian Anderson (sop.). H. Also Sybil Sanderson (sop.).
H

414.13, andrainit; Francisco d'Andrade (bar.). H

414.27, orefice; Oroveso, C in Bellini's *Norma.* H. Also Orfeo, C in Gluck's *Orfeo ed Euridice,* in Offenbach's *Orfée aux enfers,* and in Monteverdi's *Favola d'Orfeo.* H

414.30, melissciously; Mélisande, C in Debussy's *Pelléas et Mélisande.* H. Also C in Dukas's *Ariane et Barbe-bleu.* B

414.35, Or, if he was always striking up funny funereels; Orfeo, C in Gluck's *Orfeo ed Euridice,* Monteverdi's *Favola d'Orfeo,* and Offenbach's *Orfée aux enfers.* B

415.9, tambarins; Antonio Tamburini (bar.). H

415.10, rockcoach; Rocco, C in Beethoven's *Fidelio.* H

415.11–12, the ra, the ra, the ra, the ra; "La rà, la rà, la rà, la rà," A in Verdi's *Rigoletto.* H

416.9–10, Martin 201

416.16, spint; spinto voice, a voice lying between lyric and dramatic, with qualities of both. B

416.25, ternitary; Milka Ternina (sop.). H

416.29, grillies; "Amore o grillo," A in Puccini's *Madame Butterfly.* H

416.30–32, Martin 191

416.31, trestraversed; Verdi's *La traviata* (OT). H

417.4, smetterling; Smetana (comp.). H

417.4–5, nissunitimost; Hans Hermann Nissen (bass-bar.). H

417.19, cosy fond tutties; Mozart's *Così fan tutte* (OT). HW

417.21, pinchably; Ezio Pinza (bass). H

417.27, formicolation; Cesare Formichi (bar.). H

417.27, allallahbath; Rhine Maidens, T in Wagner's *Ring.* H, M

417.28, crabround; Armand Crabbé (bar.). H

417.30, jucking Vespatilla jukely; Emma Juch (sop.). H

417.32, imago; Iago, C in Verdi's *Otello.* B

417.34, journeeys; Marcel Journet (bass). H

418.1, Let him be Artalone; "Yours is my heart alone" ("Dein is mein ganzes Herz"), A in Lehár's *Land of Smiles.* H-SG

418.1, Weeps with his parisites; "O paradiso," A in Meyerbeer's *L'Africaine.* H-SG

418.3–4, Conte Carme makes the melody that mints the money (JMc's fees); John McCormack (ten.). H-SG, K

418.11, *fauces;* Helen Faucit (sop.?). B

418.13, *sukes;* Suky Tawdry, C in Gay's *Beggar's Opera.* B

418.16, *count;* John McCormack (ten.). G

418.17, *saida;* Verdi's *Aïda* (OT). H

418.34–419.8, *Of my tectucs takestock . . . beat time?;* von Bülow's (cond.) self-characterization as "nur der Taktstock Wagners" (only Wagner's baton). B

419.13, *vive sparanto qua muore contanto;* "Con onor muore chi non può serbar vita con onore" (who cannot live with honor can die with honor), T in Puccini's *Madame Butterfly.* H

419.16, Corneywall; King Mark, C in Wagner's *Tristan und Isolde.* G

419.16–17, Martin 201

419.21, quistoquill; "Questa o quella," A in Verdi's *Rigoletto.* HW

419.22, nobly . . . Pope; McCormack (ten.) made a count by pope. McH

419.24, Oscan; Oscar, C in Verdi's *Un ballo in maschera.* H

419.30, Gay; John Gay (comp.). H. Also Maria Gay (mezzo-contra.). H

420.9, Francie; Benvenuto Franci (bar.). H

420.9, Fritzie; Mascagni's *L'Amico Fritz* (OT). H

420.9–10, figgers . . . Hair's; Figaro, C in Mozart's *Marriage of Figaro*. H

421.2, Lemmas; Helen Lemmens-Sherrington (sop.). H

421.4, Butt; Clara Butt (contra.). H

421.7, Desert it; "Deserto sulla terra," A in Verdi's *Il trovatore*. H

421.10, Destinied; Verdi's *La forza del destino* (OT). H. Also Emmy Destinn (sop.). H

421.22, vigorously; Mozart's *Marriage of Figaro* (OT). H

421.30, high Gee; high G. B

421.31, fagroaster; Figaro, C in Mozart's *Marriage of Figaro*. H

421.32, Gilligan's; Beniamino Gigli (ten.). H-SG

422.3, fleischcurers; Katherina Fleischer-Edel (sop.). H

422.13, Hisstops; Joseph Hislop (ten.). H

422.22, esiop's foible; "Si può?" A (prologue) in Leoncavallo's *I pagliacci*. H

422.23, partly; Aureliano Pertile (ten.). H

422.24, hunger; Georg Unger (ten.; first "Heldentenor," created Siegfried at Bayreuth, 1876). H

422.26, Braham; John Braham (ten.). H. Also Sims Reeves (ten.). Lernout

422.26, Melosedible; de Mellos, who founded opera on Fishamble Street, Dublin. B

422.33, Nickies; "He, he! Ihr Nicker!" (He, he! You Nixies!; Alberich's first words), T in Wagner's *Ring*. H. Also Arthur Nikisch (cond.). B

422.33, Folletta; John McCormack (ten.) under pseudonym of Giovanni Foli. K

423.2, garcielasso; Pauline Viardot-Garcia (mezzo-sop.). H. Also Eugenia Garcia (sop.). H. Also Joaquina Garcia (range unknown). H. Also Maria-Felicita Garcia (mezzo-contra.). H

423.3. Martin 201

423.8, Horrid; Herod, C in Strauss's *Salomé* and in Massenet's *Hérodiade* (OT). G, B

423.22–23, Martin 191

424.4–5, eyes of the Hooley Fermers; "En fermant les yeux," A in Massenet's *Manon*. H-SG

424.5–6, Martin 201

424.6, .10, squeaked . . . Chaka; Tchaikovsky (comp.). H-SG

424.9, .10, Conshy! . . . Chaka; Konchak, C in Borodin's *Prince Igor*. H-SG

424.12, cooked; Tom Cooke (ten.). H

424.12, cram; King Mark, C in Wagner's *Tristan und Isolde*. G

424.18, crawsbomb; Otakar Kraus (bar.). H. Also Gabrielle Krauss (sop.). H. Also Felix von Krauss (bass). H. Also Ernst Kraus (ten.). H

424.28, treestem; Tristan, C in Wagner's *Tristan und Isolde.* H, M

424.28, sucker; Rosa Sucher (sop., first Isolde in England). H

424.28, Mildbut likesome; "Mild und leise" ("Liebestod"), A in Wagner's *Tristan und Isolde.* HW, M

424.29, tibbes; Lawrence Tibbett (bar.). H

424.34, Martin 201

424.34, monothong; Nothung, T in Wagner's *Siegfried.* B

424.35–36, rightdown lowbrown schisthematic robblemint; "Right Down Regular Royal Queen," A in Gilbert and Sullivan's *Gondoliers.* HW

425.18, badily; Ernesto Badini (bar.). H

425.18, pinsel; Rosa Ponselle (sop.). B. Also Ezio Pinza (bass). H

425.25–26, one of these fine days; "Un bel dì," A in Puccini's *Madame Butterfly.* H-SG

425.29–30, Martin 201

426.3–4, set ever annyma roner moother of mine on fire; set my mother on fire, T in Verdi's *Il trovatore.* H

426.7–15, he virtually broke down on the mooherhead . . . overpowered by himself with the love of the tearsilver that he twined through her hair . . . showchest . . . loads of feeling . . . a wipe at his pudgies; John McCormack (ten.), who wept at his own singing, and JJ's disdain for McCormack's girth. B, K

426.8, mooherhead; Otello, C in Verdi's *Otello.* H

426.13, calef; Calaf, C in Puccini's *Turandot.* H

426.16–17, no belong sollow mole pigeon. Ally bully. Fu Li's gulpa; "Non piangere Liù" ("Sorrow no more"), A in Puccini's *Turandot.* H-SG

426.18, halk; Halka, C in Moniuszko's *Halka.* H

426.21, pansiful; Wagner's *Parsifal* (OT). H, M. See also Martin 221.

426.26, the mansions of the blest turning on old times; "Turn on, old time," A in Wallace's *Maritana,* one of tenor Sims Reeves's favorite encores. HW. Also "Alas, those chimes so sweetly stealing," A in Wallace's *Maritana.* HW

426.30, careened; "Vedrai, carino," A in Mozart's *Don Giovanni.* H

426.32, asterisks betwink themselves; "E lucevan le stelle ed olezzava la terra," A in Puccini's *Tosca.* B

427.10–11, And the stellas were shinings. And the earthnight strewed aromatose; "E lucevan le stelle ed olezzava la terra," A in Puccini's *Tosca.* HW-SG

427.13, O dulcid dreamings languidous! Taboccoo; "O dolce bacio," A in Puccini's *Tosca.* H

427.17–18, dall and; Daland, C in Wagner's *Flying Dutchman*. H. Also "Dalla sua pace," A in Mozart's *Don Giovanni*. H

427.22, Tuskland; Puccini's *Tosca* (OT). H

427.23, Amiracles; Doctor Miracle, C in Offenbach's *Tales of Hoffmann*. B. Also Bizet's *Le Docteur Miracle* (OT). B

427.23, toll stories; tall stories, T in Offenbach's *Tales of Hoffmann*. B

427.25, manomano; "O dolci mani," A in Puccini's *Tosca*. H

427.29, pittites; used in biography of Sims Reeves to describe those with seats in the pit. Lernout

427.29, Countenance; John McCormack (ten., papal count). H

427.32–33, Martin 205

428.3, marking; King Mark, C in Wagner's *Tristan und Isolde*. G

428.3, jornies; Karl Jörn (ten.). H

428.8, saling moonlike; "The Moon Has Raised Her Lamp Above," A in Benedict's *Lily of Killarney*. B

428.8, Slyly mamourneen's; "Eily Mavourneen, I See Thee before Me," A in Benedict's *Lily of Killarney*. McH

428.21, Moylendsea; Palmer's *Sruth na maoile* (OT). H

428.27, battercops; Buttercup, C in Gilbert and Sullivan's *H.M.S. Pinafore*. G

Finnegans Wake, Book III.2

429.1, Jaunty Jaun; Mozart's *Don Giovanni* (OT). H

429.6, Lazar's; Sylvio Lazzari (comp., JJ's contemporary in Paris), composer of *Le Sauteriot*. B. Also Hippolito Lazaro (ten.). H. Also Virgilio Lazzari (bass). H

429.19, butterblond; Buttercup, C in Gilbert and Sullivan's *H.M.S. Pinafore*. G

429.19, Sigurdsen; Sigurd, C in Reyer's *Sigurd*. B. Also Siegmund, C in Wagner's *Ring*. H-SG. Also Siegfried, C in Wagner's *Siegfried*. H

429.22, Osbornes; Hannah Osborne (sop.). H

430.7–8, his knave we met on the moors; Iago (knave) and Otello, Cs in Verdi's *Otello*. B

430.9, pedalettes; Mariano Padilla (bar.).

430.10, jouay; Etienne Jouy (librettist for *William Tell*). B

430.15, trove; Verdi's *Il trovatore* (OT). B

430.22, pellmale; Debussy's *Pelléas et Mélisande* (OT). H

430.35, Agatha's; Agathe, C in Weber's *Der Freischütz*. H

431.3, fricky-; Fricka, C in Wagner's *Ring*. B, M. Also Antonietta Fricci (sop.). H

431.11, Martin 188

431.12, Sampson's tyke; Samson and Dalila, Cs in Saint-Saëns's *Samson et Dalila.* H

431.12–13, Jones's . . . King; Gruenberg's *Emperor Jones* (OT). B. Also Parry Jones (ten.). H

431.17, forget her so tarnelly easy; tarnhelm, T in Wagner's *Ring.* H-SG, M. Also Siegfried forgets Brünnhilde, T in Wagner's *Ring.* H-SG, M

431.18, benedict; Benedict (comp.). B

431.27, journey; Marcel Journet (bass). H

431.32, derringdo . . . daddyho; "O terra addio," A in Verdi's *Aïda.* H. Also Francesco Daddi (ten.). H. Also João Guilherme Daddi (comp.). B

432.4, I rise; Jewel Song ("Ah, je ris"), A in Gounod's *Faust.* H

432.11, teat-a-teat; Therese Tietjens (sop.). H. Also Maggie Teyte (sop.). H

432.21, Dellabelliney; Dalila, C in Saint-Saëns's *Samson et Dalila.* H. Also Bellini (comp.). B

432.25, furtive; "Una furtiva lagrima," A in Donizetti's *L'elisir d'amore.* H

432.26–27, commandments; Commendatore, C in Mozart's *Don Giovanni.* H

432.30, pasqualines; Donizetti's *Don Pasquale* (OT). H

432.30, verdidads; Verdi (comp.). H

432.31, voyoulence; Violetta, C in Verdi's *La traviata* (associated with Manon). H

432.32, besant; Gabriella Besanzoni (mezzo-sop.). H

433.3, she's, is a bell; Isolde, C in Wagner's *Tristan und Isolde.* B

433.3–4, Undetrigesima, vikissy manonna; rhythm of "La donna è mobile," A in Verdi's *Rigoletto.* B

433.4, manonna; Manon, C in Massenet's *Manon* and Puccini's *Manon Lescaut* (also OTs). H

433.4, Doremon's; Do-re-mi, opening notes of "Infelice cor tradito . . . per angoscia" (these notes are sung by Gilda, who is later joined by Maddalena, Duca, Rigoletto), A (quartet) in Verdi's *Rigoletto;* also of "Si può," the tenor prologue to Leoncavallo's *I pagliacci.* B

433.5, Gay; John Gay (comp.). B. Also Maria Gay (mezzo-contra). H

433.6, Gwenn du Lake; Gilda (g-d-l), C in Verdi's *Rigoletto.* H. Also C in Chabrier's *Gwendoline* (OT). H

433.6, Manducare; Duke of Mantua, C in Verdi's *Rigoletto.* H

433.7, farrier's; Geraldine Farrar (sop.). H

433.10–11, lostsomewhere . . . butrose; "'Tis the last rose of summer," A in Flotow's *Martha.* B

433.11, butrose to brideworship; Smetana's *Bartered Bride* (OT). H

433.13, linen of Killiney; Benedict's *Lily of Killarney* (OT). HW

433.25, buttoncups; Buttercup, C in Gilbert and Sullivan's *H.M.S. Pinafore.* G

433.31, ern; Ernani, C in Verdi's *Ernani.* H

433.36, despyneedis; Despina, C in Mozart's *Così fan tutte.* H

434.3, frem; Olive Fremstad (sop.). H

434.7, Daradora; Dorabella, C in Mozart's *Così fan tutte.* B

434.7, gerils; Franz Xaver [*sic*] Gerl (bass). H

434.8, playing breeches parts; women playing men in opera—sometimes cast that way, as with Prince Orlofsky in *Die Fledermaus,* or because the part requires them to pretend to be men, as Leonore is disguised as Fidelio in the opera of that name. Lernout

434.12, Hayes; Roland Hayes (ten.). H. Also Catherine Hayes (sop.). H

434.12, Conyingham; Robert Cunningham (ten.). B

434.12, Erobinson; Paul Robeson (bar). H

434.17, Martin 201

434.21–23, Martin 188

434.23, Lola; Lola, C in Mascagni's *Cavalleria rusticana.* H-SG

434.23, Scenta; Santuzza, C in Mascagni's *Cavalleria rusticana.* H-SG. Also Senta, C in Wagner's *Flying Dutchman.* H-SG, M

434.24, stiffstuffs . . . full; Falstaff, C in Verdi's *Falstaff,* Nicolai's *Merry Wives of Windsor,* and Holst's *At the Boar's Head.* G, B

434.29, Ulikah's; Ulrica, C in Verdi's *Un ballo in maschera.* H

434.31, darkled; Hariclea Darclée (sop.). H

435.3, *Venus;* Venusberg, T in Wagner's *Tannhäuser.* B

435.10, volses; Volsung—brother-sister incest, T in Wagner's *Ring.* H

435.18, oval . . . paravis; "O paradiso," A in Meyerbeer's *L'Africaine.* H

435.22, bondman; Balfe's *Bondman* (OT). H

435.25, Winkyland; Hermann Winkelmann (ten., b. Winckelmann). B

435.29, Sully van; John Sullivan (ten.). H

435.30, hailies; Valhalla, T in Wagner's *Ring.* B

435.30, fingringmaries; Wagner's *Ring* (OT). B

436.6, *Ragazza ladra;* Rossini's *La gazza ladra* (OT). HW. Also *Il Ragazzo,* or "the boy," nickname for Farinelli (Carlo Broschi, male sop.). B

436.14–16, Martin 213

436.27, billing; Elizabeth Billington (sop.). H

436.29, goby; Tito Gobbi (bar.). B

436.35, raise; Rosa Raisa (sop.). H

437.7, handelbars; Handel (comp.). H

437.7, go-be-dee; Tito Gobbi (bar.). H

437.7, your airs of go-be-dee; "Si può?" A (prologue) in Leoncavallo's *I pagliacci* (starting on notes G, B, D). B

437.11, vinvin, vinvin; "Viva il vino," A in Mascagni's *Cavalleria rusticana*. H. See also "Brindisi" in chapter 8.

437.16, skip; Tito Schipa (ten.). H

437.33, Melosiosus; de Mellos, impresario who founded opera on Fishamble Street, Dublin. B

438.2, calfloving; Calaf, C in Puccini's *Turandot*. H. Also Emma Calvé (sop.). H. Also "Veau d'or," A in Gounod's *Faust*. B

438.30, Luca-; Pauline Lucca (sop.), Giuseppe de Luca (bar.), and Fernando de Lucia (ten.). H

438.34, colleen bawns; Colleen Bawn, C in Benedict's *Lily of Killarney*. G

438.36, lindsays; Jenny Lind (sop.). H

439.6, maledictions; "Maledizione," T in Verdi's *Rigoletto*. H

439.9, trumpadour; Verdi's *Il trovatore* (OT). H

439.17, valiantine; Valentin, C in Gounod's *Faust*. H. Also Valentine, C in Meyerbeer's *Les Huguenots*. B. Also Henri Justin A. J. Valentino (cond. at premiere of *William Tell*). H. Also Valentini (Valentino Urbani, castrato, contra./ten.). H. Also Francesco Valentino (bar.). H

439.20, Daddy; João Guilherme Daddi (comp.). B. Also Francesco Daddi (ten.). H

440.2, *Miracula;* Doctor Miracle, C in Offenbach's *Tales of Hoffmann*. H. Also Bizet's *Le Docteur Miracle* (OT). B

440.4, cathalogue; "Madamina, il catalogo," A in Mozart's *Don Giovanni*. H

440.12, *licet;* Miriam Licette (sop.). H

440.15, Gillydehooly's; Renée Gilly (sop.) and Dinh Gilly (bar.). H

440.17, Loper; Leporello, C in Mozart's *Don Giovanni*. B

440.17, Figas; Figaro, C in Mozart's *Marriage of Figaro*. H

440.19–20, scentaminted . . . *Send;* Senta, C in Wagner's *Flying Dutchman*. H

440.21, *Fanciesland;* Giuseppe Fancelli (ten.). H

440.22, vignettes; Francisco Vignas (ten.). H

440.27, Cinderella; Rossini's *La cenerentola* (OT). H

440.27–28, robbing . . . Polly; Polly Peachum, C in Gay's *Beggar's Opera*. H

440.30, lass that toffs a tailor; *The Lass That Loved a Sailor*, subtitle of Gilbert and Sullivan's *H.M.S. Pinafore*. B

440.35, mozzed; Mozart (comp.). H

441.2, Faminy; Faninal, C in R. Strauss's *Der Rosenkavalier*. H

441.6, knot; Heinrich Knote (ten.). H

441.8–10, You can down all the dripping you can dumple to, and buffkid scouse too ad libidinum, in these lassitudes; Wagner on diet: Wagner (comp.). H-SG

441.9, libidinum; brindisi (drinking song, "Libiamo, libiamo"), A in Verdi's *La traviata*. H. See also "Brindisi" in chapter 8.

441.11–12, Mavis Toffeelips; Méphistophélès, C in Gounod's *Faust*. H. Also C in Berlioz's *La Damnation de Faust* and Busoni's *Doktor Faust*. B. Also Boïto's *Mefistofele* (OT). B

441.16, rose marine; "Rose Marie," title A from Friml's operetta, recorded by John McCormack. K

441.18, guard that gem; guarding the treasure, T in Wagner's *Ring*. H-SG, M. See also Martin 213–14.

441.19, jewel; Jewel song ("Ah, je ris"), A in Gounod's *Faust*. H-SG

441.21, ring; Wagner's *Ring* (OT). H-SG, M. See also Martin 213–14.

441.25, Brahaam; John Braham (ten.). H

441.28–29, there must have been a power of kinantics in that buel of gruel he gobed at bedgo; love potion, T in Wagner's *Tristan und Isolde*. B

442.1, fremdling; Olive Fremstad (sop.). H

442.1, Martin 201

442.3, tammany; Tamino, C in Mozart's *Magic Flute*. H-SG

442.5, constantineal namesuch; Constanza Mozart (comp.'s wife). H-SG. Also Constanze, C in Mozart's *Abduction from the Seraglio*. H-SG

442.15, March's; King Mark, C in Wagner's *Tristan und Isolde*. G

442.18, Martin 201

442.24, Gaylad; Julia Gaylord (sop.?), singer with Carl Rosa Opera Company. B

442.27, Blonderboss; Blonde, C in Mozart's *Abduction from the Seraglio*. H-SG

442.34, grand operoar; grand opera. H

443.3, manners; Charles Manners (bass). H

443.5, Dora's; Dorabella, C in Mozart's *Così fan tutte*. H-SG

443.7–12, wind . . . pitch in . . . gleeful men; battle over pitch in nineteenth-century England. B

443.14, federal; U. Giordano's *Fedora* (OT). H

443.16, burkes; Edmund Arbrickle Burke (bass). H

443.21, Gunger; Mozart (comp.). H-SG

443.22, Arnolff's; Arnold, C in Rossini's *William Tell*. H. Also Sigrid Arnold-son (sop.). H

443.26, beard; John Beard (ten.). H

443.35, angeleens; Angelina, C in Rossini's *La cenerentola*. B. Also Angelina, C in Gilbert and Sullivan's *Trial by Jury*. B. Also Nazareno de Angelis (bass). H

444.3, stale cough; cough, T in Puccini's *La bohème* and Verdi's *La traviata*. B

444.4, favourite; Donizetti's *La favorita* (OT). H

444.8, fluther's; Mozart's *Magic Flute* (OT). H-SG

444.17, butthering; Clara Butt (contra.). H

444.19, straphanger; Giuseppina Strepponi (sop.; became Verdi's wife). H

444.26, minners, tip; miners and mine tip (Minnie runs a gold-rush saloon), T in Puccini's *La fanciulla del west*. B. Also Minnie, C in Puccini's *La fanciulla del west*. H. Also Charles Manners (bass). H

444.29, Rosemiry; "Rose Marie," title A from Friml's operetta, recorded by John McCormack. K

444.31, Annybettyelsas; Elsa, C in Wagner's *Lohengrin*. H, M

444.32, Wolf the Ganger; Mozart (comp.). H-SG

444.34, isod; Isolde, C in Wagner's *Tristan und Isolde*. H, M

445.8, partial's; Aureliano Pertile (ten.). H

445.9, rodeo; Wilhelm Rode (bass-bar.). H

445.10, lecit; Miriam Licette (sop.). H

445.14, mikely; Michael Kelly (ten.). B

445.17, papapardon; Papageno, C in Mozart's *Magic Flute*. H-SG

445.19, bussycat; Debussy (comp.). H

445.24, bullin heifer; title C in Donizetti's *Anna Bolena*. G, B

445.26–27, ire turn o'er see . . . return here; "Il mio tesoro," A in Mozart's *Don Giovanni*. K

445.32, homerole; Louise Homer (contra.). H

445.32, Ostelinda; Jenny Lind (sop.). H. Also Eva von der Osten (sop.). H

446.2, melittleme were wonderful so; "Mir ist so wunderbar," A in Beethoven's *Fidelio*. H. Also Friar Melitone, C in Verdi's *La forza del destino*. H

446.3, Martin 221

446.6–7, Martin 201

446.13, daddyoak; João Guilherme Daddi (comp.). B. Also Francesco Daddi (ten.). H. Also "Addio del passato," A in Verdi's *La traviata*. B. Also "Addio senza rancor," A in Puccini's *La bohème*. B. Also "Addio fiorito asil," A in Puccini's *Madame Butterfly*. B

446.17, marks; King Mark, C in Wagner's *Tristan und Isolde*. H, M

446.24, Coppal; Myles na Coppaleen, C in Benedict's *Lily of Killarney*. B. Also Coppelius, C in Offenbach's *Tales of Hoffmann*. H

446.25, noreland; Eidé Norena (sop.). H

446.28, sales; Albert Saléza (ten.). H

446.31, O'Dwyer; Robert O'Dwyer (comp.). H

446.34, garden; Mary Garden (sop.). H

447.2, Meliorism; Lauritz Melchior (ten.). H

447.6, Armourican's iron core; Balfe's *Armourer of Nantes* (OT). H

447.8, mortinatality; Giovanni Martinelli (ten.). H. Also Caterina Martinelli
(sop.). H

447.13, .33, jubilee . . . vestee; "Vesti la giubba," A in Leoncavallo's *I pagliacci.*
H

447.22–23, Jno . . . Pierce; Jan Peerce (ten.). H

447.27–28, black coats of Spaign; Edith Coates (mezzo-sop. who sang role of
the countess in Tchaikovsky's *Queen of Spades*). H

447.35, Aston's; Florence Easton (sop.). B

448.7, slush; Heinrich Schlusnus (bar.). H

448.8, cross; Joan Cross (sop.). H

448.9, Capels; Gertrude Kappel (sop.). H

448.11, Troia; Berlioz's *Les Troyens* (OT). H

448.12, Carmen; Bizet's *Carmen* (OT). H

448.19, Bailey; Isobel Baillie (sop.). H

448.23, tippers; Lawrence Tibbett (bar.). H

448.23, flags; Kirsten Flagstad (sop.). H

448.34–35, voise somewhit . . . fa; "Una voce poco fà," A in Rossini's *Barber
of Seville.* H-SG

449.6, ducks; Claire Dux (sop.). H

449.7, tristys; Tristan, C in Wagner's *Tristan und Isolde.* H, M

449.10, the nippy girl . . . Toutou; Cio-Cio-San, C in Puccini's *Madame Butterfly.* B. Also "Tu? tu? piccolo iddio!" A in Puccini's *Madame Butterfly.*
B. Also Mimosa-san, Japanese girl in Jones's *Geisha.* B

449.15, Pershawm; Fanny Persiani (sop.). H

449.18–19, I'll dreamt . . . my sigh hiehied; "I dreamt that I dwelt in marble
halls," A in Balfe's *Bohemian Girl.* HW

449.31–32, moor . . . moor; Otello, C in Verdi's *Otello.* B

450.2–3, .5, riverside . . . swansway; swan, T in Wagner's *Lohengrin.* B

450.7, pursewinded; Parsifal, C in Wagner's *Parsifal.* B

450.9, .31, logansome, . . . logans; Loge (Loki), C in Wagner's *Ring.* H

450.10, solfanelly; Farinelli (male sop.). B

450.12, heart's deelight; "The Moon Has Raised Her Lamp Above," A in Benedict's *Lily of Killarney.* McH

450.12, .24, saptimber . . . voicical; "Voi, che sapete," A in Mozart's *Marriage of Figaro.* H-SG

450.16, L'Alouette's; Lalo (comp.). H

450.17, naughtingerls; Jenny Lind (sop.). B

450.17, juckjucking; Emma Juch (sop.). B

450.22, I give to me alone I trouble give; as do-me-sol-do', opening notes of "Di piacer me balza il cor, ah bramar di più non so," A in Rossini's *La gazza ladra;* and of "Gross Glück und Heil lacht nun dem Rhein, da Hagen, der Grimme," A in Wagner's *Die Götterdämmerung;* and of "Haste, haste to town," A in Purcell's *Dido and Aeneas.* B, Hart

450.23, lamagnage; Francesco Tamagno (ten.). H

450.24, Nomario; Giovanni Mario (ten.). H

450.25, .28, whatyoumacormack . . . athlone; John McCormack (ten., b. in Athlone). H

450.28–29, I'm athlone in the lillabilling of killarnies; "I'm Alone," A in Benedict's *Lily of Killarney.* McH. Also Benedict's *Lily of Killarney* (OT). HW

450.30, garden; Mary Garden (sop.). H

450.30–32, Lethals lurk heimlocked in logans. Loathe laburnums. Dash the gaudy deathcup! Bryony O'Bryony, thy name is Belladama; poisons and death cup, T in Wagner's *Tristan und Isolde.* H-SG, M

450.31, laburnums. Dash the gaudy; Gilda (G-l-d), C in Verdi's *Rigoletto.* H

450.32, Belladama; Hypolite Belhomme (bass). B

450.32, O'Bryony; Weber's *Oberon* (OT). H

451.3, mesdamines; "Madamina, il catalogo," A in Mozart's *Don Giovanni.* McH

451.6, fish; Ludwig Fischer, Ger. bass who sang Sarastro in Mozart's *Magic Flute* in the comp.'s day. B

451.7, erbole; Karl Erb (ten.). H

451.8, magic fluke; Mozart's *Magic Flute* (OT). HW

451.8, fair; Musorgsky's *Sorochintsi Fair* (OT; McCormack's last opera appearance). K

451.9, mart as a; Flotow's *Martha* (OT). K

451.24–25, shake a pale of sparkling ice; "Take a pair of sparkling eyes," A in Gilbert and Sullivan's *Gondoliers.* HW-SG

451.29, nevers; Comte de Nevers, C in Meyerbeer's *Les Huguenots.* H

451.30, Gizzygay; Gizziello (male sop.). H

452.17, benedictine; Benedict (comp.). B

452.20, pharoph; St. Phar, pseudonym of Chappelou, C in Adam's *Le Postillon de Longjumeau.* H

452.20–21, dead . . . ramescheckles; Radamès, C in Verdi's *Aïda*. B

452.26, to be going to meet a king; "Right Down Regular Royal Queen," A in Gilbert and Sullivan's *Gondoliers*. B

452.34, 453.31–34, Annanmeses . . . hooked and happy, . . . among the field-nights eliceam, *élite* of the elect, in the land of lost of time. . . . die; Amneris, C in Verdi's *Aïda*. H

453.3, primmafore's wake; Gilbert and Sullivan's *H.M.S. Pinafore* (OT). H

453.14–15, Jaun Dyspeptist; Jochanaan (John the Baptist), C in R. Strauss's *Salomé*. B

453.15, .18, wood . . . robbing; Weber's *Der Freischütz* (OT). H

453.17–18, voiceyversy it's my gala bene fit; custom in nineteenth-century English and Irish musical life of doing a concert or opera, all proceeds of which went to the singer, prima donna, or manager whose "benefit" it was. Lernout

453.22, eastern; Florence Easton (sop.). H

453.22, hummingsphere; Humming Chorus, A in Puccini's *Madame Butterfly*. H

453.33, Johannisburg's; Johannistag, T in Wagner's *Die Meistersinger*. H-SG

453.36, postilium; Adam's *Le Postillon de Longjumeau* (OT). H

454.7, Shorn; Friedrich Schorr (bass-bar.). H

454.16–18, Thou pure! Our virgin! . . . O salutary; "Salut, demeure, chaste et pure," A in Gounod's *Faust*. H. Also "M'appari," A in Flotow's *Martha*. HW

454.18–19, salutary! . . . solitude . . . strokest; "È la solita storia," A in Cilea's *L'arlesiana*. H

454.18–20, when suddenly . . . suddenly; "La donna è mobile," A in Verdi's *Rigoletto*. B

454.21, Rizzies; Gilda Dalla Rizza (sop.). H

454.30, gardens; Mary Garden (sop.). B

454.33, Shunt us! shunt us! shunt us; Sanctus from the Mass in Wagner's *Parsifal*. McH, B

455.7, avider; Avito, C in Montemezzi's *L'amore dei tre re*. H

455.7, Saffron buns or sovran; "O souverain, ô juge," A in Massenet's *El Cid*. H

455.11, Joe Hanny's; Don Giovanni, C in Mozart's *Don Giovanni*. McH

455.14, Bouncer; Alesandro Bonci (ten.). H

455.14, Naster; Nast (sop.). H

455.17, destined; Emmy Destinn (sop.). H

455.26, Royal Revolver; Theatre Royal, Dublin, site of Dublin opera, 1821–80; rebuilt later. Mink, B

455.28–29, SPQueaRking Mark; King Mark, C in Wagner's *Tristan und Isolde.* B, M

455.36, Santos; Santuzza, C in Mascagni's *Cavalleria rusticana.* H

455.36, Mozos; Mozart (comp.). H

456.3–4, boiled protestants (allinoilia allinoilia!); Protestant martyrs, T in Meyerbeer's *Les Huguenots.* B

456.10, Oliviero; Magda Olivero (sop.). H

456.14–15, Huguenot; Meyerbeer's *Les Huguenots* (OT). H

456.22, nabocs; Verdi's *Nabucco* (OT). H

456.22, erics; Erik, C in Wagner's *Flying Dutchman.* B, M

456.25, ryuoll; Raoul, C in Meyerbeer's *Les Huguenots,* a Sullivan role. H

456.30, Thaddeus; Thaddeus, C in Balfe's *Bohemian Girl.* H

456.30, Kellyesque; Michael Kelly (ten.). H

456.31, Kelly-Cooks; Tom Cooke (ten.). B. Also Clara Louise Kellogg (sop.). H. Also Thomas Aynsley Cook (bass with Carl Rosa company). B. Also Michael Kelly (ten.). B

456.32, marshalsea; Marzelline, C in Beethoven's *Fidelio.* H. Also Marschallin, C in R. Strauss's *Der Rosenkavalier.* H

456.33, Offenders; Offenbach (comp.). H

457.3, Ferdinand; Ferrando, C in Mozart's *Così fan tutte* and in Verdi's *Il trovatore.* B. Also Don Fernando, C in Beethoven's *Fidelio.* H

457.7, hunger's; Georg Unger (ten.). H

457.7, anger's; Florence Austral (sop.). B

457.13, tethera; Luisa Tetrazzini (sop.). H

457.14, manners; Charles Manners (bass). H

457.20, Look for me always at my west; "Shade of the Palm" ("Oh, my Dolores"), A in Stuart's *Floradora.* B

457.29, sweet nunsongs; Nun's Chorus, A in Lortzing's *Casanova.* H

457.34–35, memento . . . allathome I with grief can call my own; "The heart bowed down," A in Balfe's *Bohemian Girl.* HW

457.36, Jaunick; Leoš Janáček (comp.). H

457.36, witwee's mite; Franz Lehár's *Merry Widow* (OT [*Die lustige Witwe*]). H

458.2, valentino; Valentin, C in Gounod's *Faust.* H-SG. Also C in Meyerbeer's *Les Huguenots.* B. Also Henri Justin A. J. Valentino (cond. at premiere of *William Tell*). H. Also Valentini (Valentino Urbani, castrato, contra./ten.). H. Also Francesco Valentino (bar.). H

458.3, Fr Ml; Rudolf Friml (comp.). H

458.10, Maggy; Marguérite, C in Gounod's *Faust*. H-SG. Also C in Berlioz's *La Damnation de Faust* and Meyerbeer's *Les Huguenots*. Also Margherita, C in Boïto's *Mefistofele*. B

458.14, floralora; Stuart's *Floradora* (OT). HW

458.14, veronique; Véronique, C in Messager's *Véronique*. H

458.29, ans; Giuseppe Anselmi (ten.). H

458.34, Cheveluir; R. Strauss's *Der Rosenkavalier* (OT). H

459.2, ringarosary; R. Strauss's *Der Rosenkavalier* (OT). H. Also Wagner's *Ring* (OT). B

459.5, sleeptalking; sleepwalking, T in Bellini's *La sonnambula*. H

459.6, mudstuskers; Puccini's *Tosca* (OT). H

459.20–22, betrue . . . betrue . . . betreu . . . . betray; "Betrug! Betrug! Schänd-lichster Betrug!" (Deceit! Shameful deceit!), T in Wagner's *Die Götterdäm-merung*. H

459.26, cordon; Norman Cordon (bass). H

459.27, Obealbe myodorers; Dorabella, C in Mozart's *Così fan tutte*. B

459.31–32, Martin 202

459.34, donkeys; Massenet's (and other composers') *Don Quixote* (OT). B

459.36, whot a tell; Rossini's *William Tell* (OT). B

460.17, elmoes; Cloe Elmo (mezzo-sop.). H

460.17, stele; Sophie Stehle (sop.). H

460.17, A'Mara; Joseph O'Mara (ten.). H

460.17, Mara; Gertrud Mara (sop.). H

460.26, Margrate; Marguérite, C in Gounod's *Faust*. H-SG. Also C in Berlioz's *La Damnation de Faust* and Meyerbeer's *Les Huguenots*. Also Margherita, C in Boïto's *Mefistofele*. B

460.32, Thingavalla; Valhalla, T in Wagner's *Ring*. H, M

460.34, till you'll resemble me; "Then You'll Remember Me," A in Balfe's *Bohe-mian Girl*. HW

460.36, evernew; Tristan, as nephew of King Mark, was nephew also of Mark's wife, Isolde. McH

461.9, dusess; Sophia Dušsek (mezzo-sop., b. Corri). H

461.10, me laughing; Jewel Song ("Ah, je ris"), A in Gounod's *Faust*. H-SG

461.13, pussiness; Puccini (comp.). H

461.15, calvescatcher; Emma Calvé (sop.). H

461.15, Pinchapoppapoff; Popov, C in Lehár's *Merry Widow*. H. Also Ezio Pinza (bass). H

461.17–18, violents; Violetta, C in Verdi's *La traviata*. H. Also duchess of Parma, C in Busoni's *Doktor Faust*. B

461.26, whesen with other lipth; "Then You'll Remember Me," A in Balfe's *Bohemian Girl*. HW

461.28, thildish; Georges Thill (ten.). H

461.31, .33, Juan; . . . Juan; title C in Mozart's *Don Giovanni*. G

461.32, ah ah ah ah; Bell Song, A in Delibes's *Lakmé*. H-SG. Also Laughing Aria, A in Lehár's *Merry Widow*. H-SG

461.35, 462.2–3, chalished drink . . . brindising brandisong; brindisi, any drinking song in opera. H. See "Brindisi" in chapter 8.

462.7, Doris; Julie Dorus-Gras (sop.). H

462.11, pearlies; Lisa Perli (sop., b. Dora Labette). H

462.11, pearlies in their sparkling; "Take a pair of sparkling eyes," A in Gilbert and Sullivan's *Gondoliers*. B

462.22, me O treasauro; "Il mio tesoro," A in Mozart's *Don Giovanni*. HW

462.24–25, Leperstown; Leporello, C in Mozart's *Don Giovanni*. H

462.25–26, Lumtum lumtum; sound of lute, T in Verdi's *Il trovatore*. H-SG

462.26, The froubadour! I fremble; "Il Trovatore! Io tremo" (The troubador! I tremble), T in Verdi's *Il trovatore*. H-SG

462.27, Eccolo me; "Ecco il leone," A in Verdi's *Otello*. H

462.28, Jaunstown; Johnson, C in Puccini's *La fanciulla del west*. H

462.32, coming home to mourn mountains; "Ai nostri monti" ("Home to Our Mountains"), A in Verdi's *Il trovatore*. HW

462.34, quinquisecular; Quinquin, nickname of Octavian, C in R. Strauss's *Der Rosenkavalier*. B

462.36, suicide; "Suicidio!" A in Poncielli's *La gioconda*. H

463.3, orf; Orfée, C in Offenbach's *Orfée aux enfers*. B. Also Orfeo, C in Gluck's *Orfeo ed Euridice*, and in Monteverdi's *Favola d'Orfeo*. B. Also Carl Orff (comp.). B

463.5, Figura; Figaro, C in Mozart's *Marriage of Figaro*. H

463.8, Romeo; Roméo, C in Gounod's *Roméo et Juliette*. B

463.11, unpeppeppedi-; Papageno, Papagena, Cs in Mozart's *Magic Flute*. H

463.16, twitch; Jemmy Twitcher, C in Gay's *Beggar's Opera*. B

463.21, pirates; Bellini's *El pirata* (OT). H

463.21, quinconcentrum; Quinquin, nickname of Octavian, C in R. Strauss's *Der Rosenkavalier*. B

463.22, Basilius; Don Basilio, C in Mozart's *Marriage of Figaro* and in Rossini's *Barber of Seville*. H

463.22, O'Cormacan MacArty; John McCormack (ten.). H

463.24, in Alba; Emma Albani (sop.). H

464.3, Mark; King Mark, C in Wagner's *Tristan und Isolde.* B

464.5, foil; John McCormack (ten.) under pseudonym of Giovanni Foli. K. Also
A. J. Foli (bass, b. Foley). B

464.7, O'Loonys; Count di Luna, C in Verdi's *Il trovatore.* H-SG

464.11, sansa pagar; Sancho Panza, C in various operas titled *Don Quixote.* G, B

464.24, dapper dandy; Dapertutto, C in Offenbach's *Tales of Hoffmann.* H

464.27, Auster; Florence Austral (sop.). H

464.28, Hungrig; Georg Unger (ten.). B

464.29, greas; Giulia Grisi (sop.). B

464.30, Freeshots; Weber's *Der Freischütz* (OT). H

464.30, garden; Mary Garden (sop.). H. Also Covent Garden. B

464.30, costard; Sir Michael Costa, (cond. and dir. of Royal Italian Opera,
Covent Garden). B

464.32, Geesyhus; Jones's *Geisha* (OT). B

464.35, landskip; Lenski, C in Tschaikovsky's *Eugene Onegin.* H

465.1–3, Martin 202

465.7, Weih; "Weia! Waga! . . . Wagalaweia!" (Rhine Maidens at beginning of
opera), A in Wagner's *Das Rheingold.* H

465.15, stablelads; Mariano Stabile (bar.). H

465.16, hungry (with "boyrun to" = Bayreuth at *FW* 465.17); Georg Unger
(ten.). B

465.16, angry; Florence Austral (sop.). B

465.16, cavileer; Mascagni's *Cavalleria rusticana* (OT). H

465.17, boyrun to; Bayreuth (with "hungry and angry" in previous line, refer-
ring to Wagnerian singers Unger and Austral), T in Wagner's life. B

465.18, pinchme; Ezio Pinza (bass). H

465.21, county de Loona; Count di Luna, C in Verdi's *Il trovatore.* H-SG

465.28, Chink chink; "Chin Chin Chinaman," A in Jones's *Geisha.* HW

465.29–30, tich to the tissle; Joseph Tichatschek (ten.). H

465.30, rossy; Rossini (comp.). B. Also Countess Rossi (sop.). H

465.31, bloodysibby; blood-brotherhood, T in Wagner's *Die Götterdämmerung.*
H

465.36, The leady on the lake; Rossini's *La donna del lago* (OT). H

466.6, love potients; love potion, T in Wagner's *Tristan und Isolde.* H, M

466.6, king; King Mark, C in Wagner's *Tristan und Isolde.* G

466.9, pyre; "Di quella pira," A in Verdi's *Il trovatore.* H-SG

466.9, Turn; Eva Turner (sop.). H

466.18, jubalharp; "Vesti la giubba," A in Leoncavallo's *I pagliacci.* H-SG

466.18, Jinglejoys; Beniamino Gigli (ten.). H-SG

466.19–20, .21, .24, .27, *il diavolo . . .* Dauber Dan *. . .* priesty *. . . fra! . . . Diavoloh;* Daniel François Esprit Auber's *Fra Diavolo* (OT). HW. Also Daniel François Esprit Auber (comp.). B

466.20, Dauber; Richard Tauber (ten.). H

466.24, coloraturas; coloratura (from Ger. *Koloratur*), elaborate ornamentation of the melody; also a voice, not necessarily a soprano, that can do such ornamentation. B

466.25–26, My loaf and pottage neaheaheahear Rochelle; "My love and cottage near Rochelle," A in Balfe's *Siege of Rochelle.* HW

466.26, fiddeley fa; Beethoven's *Fidelio* (OT). G

466.29, betrayal buy jury; Gilbert and Sullivan's *Trial by Jury* (OT). HW

466.30, mind uncle Hare?; "Gott! Welch Dunkel hier" (God! What darkness here), T in Beethoven's *Fidelio.* H-SG

466.32, *Miserere mei;* "Miserere," A in Verdi's *Il trovatore.* H

466.32, *mei;* Medea Mei-Figner (mezzo-sop.). H

467.6–7, behind the curtain . . . worrid; Turiddu begins by singing behind the curtain, T in Mascagni's *Cavalleria rusticana.* H-SG

467.8, octavium; Octavian, C in R. Strauss's *Der Rosenkavalier.* H. Also Don Ottavio, C in Mozart's *Don Giovanni.* H

467.8, Martin 202

467.15, Woodenbeard; Wotan, C in Wagner's *Ring.* H

467.19, miracle; Doctor Miracle, C in Offenbach's *Tales of Hoffmann.* H. Also Bizet's *Le Docteur Miracle* (OT). B

467.25, beurlads; Berlioz (comp.). H

467.26, chaplan; Fyodor Chaliapin (bass; also spelled Shalyapin). H

467.27, allemanden; Pauline l'Allemand, woman singer with Carl Rosa Opera Company in Dublin, 1894. B

467.33, ancomartins; Mario Ancona (bar). H

467.34, Pernicious; André Pernet (bass). H

468.20, Echo, read ending; "Ecco ridente in cielo," A in Rossini's *Barber of Seville.* HW

468.27, moore; Otello, C in Verdi's *Otello.* H. Also Grace Moore (sop.). B

468.28, Farewell but whenever; "Ora e per sempre addio," A in Verdi's *Otello.* H-SG

468.31, corthage; Antonio Cortis (ten.). H

468.33–469.23, shack's . . . Bennydick; Benedikt Schack (ten.). H

468.34–469.1, Martin 221

468.36, 'Bansheeba; Alesandro Bonci (ten.). H

469.2, turnabouts; Eva Turner (sop.). B

469.19–20, Martin 191

469.21, Linduff; Lindorf, C in Offenbach's *Tales of Hoffmann.* H

469.23, Bennydick; Benedict (comp.). H

469.34–35, cherubs in the charabang; Cherubino, C in Mozart's *Marriage of Figaro.* H

470.1, nada; Jean Nada, French professor at Zurich Conservatory 1917, flutist, teacher of Joyce's friend Otto Luening; played principal flute in Stadttheater orchestra. B

470.11, favours, a favourable; Mafalda Favero (sop.). H. Also Donizetti's *La favorita* (OT). H

470.13–14, dosiriously . . . to-marionite's; Mario Cavaradossi, C in Puccini's *Tosca.* H-SG. Also Dosifey or Dositheus, C in Mussorgsky's *Khovanschina.* H

470.13, 15–20, dosiriously . . . Oasis, . . . Oisis, ... Oasis, . . . Oisis, . . . Oasis, . . . Oisis; "O, Isis and Osiris," A in Mozart's *Magic Flute.* H

470.24–25, 471.28, gentlest weaner among the weiners . . . statuemen; "O statua gentilissima," A in Mozart's *Don Giovanni.* H

470.33, Juan; title C in Mozart's *Don Giovanni.* G

471.5, Solyma! Salemita; Selim Pasha's palace, T in Mozart's *Abduction from the Seraglio.* H. Also R. Strauss's *Salomé* (OT). H

471.11, easting; Florence Easton (sop.). H

471.24, seraph's; Tullio Serafin (It. cond. 1878–1968). B

471.28, statuemen; Commendatore, statue, C in Mozart's *Don Giovanni.* H

471.30, Sickerson; Siegfried, C in Wagner's *Siegfried.* H

471.30, bjoerne; Jussi Björling (ten.). H-SG

472.5, Mint; Mat of the Mint, C in Gay's *Beggar's Opera.* B

472.6, Coax; Mrs. Coaxer, C in Gay's *Beggar's Opera.* B

472.15, Joss-El; José, C in Bizet's *Carmen.* H. Also Jussi Björling (ten.). H-SG

472.20, .34, victorihoarse . . . retourneys; "Ritorna vincitor," A in Verdi's *Aïda.* H-SG

472.32, 473.18, pray to the spirit above . . . spirt; "Spirto gentil," A in Donizetti's *La favorita.* H

473.2–3, withering . . . . Walker; "Where'er you walk," A in Handel's *Semele.* H-SG

473.3, Walker; Edyth Walker (mezzo-sop.). H

473.4, Waltzer; Walther von Stolzing, C in Wagner's *Die Meistersinger.* H-SG, M

473.5, flagway; Kirsten Flagstad (sop.). H-SG

473.7, nomore cares; "Caro nome," A in Verdi's *Rigoletto*. H

473.17, Bennu; Francesco Benucci (bass). H

473.17, .19–20, *faotre!* . . . flambe. Ay . . . sombrer; "Ombra mai fù" (Largo), A in Handel's *Serse*. H

473.18–19, spyre . . . flambe; Siegfried's pyre, T in Wagner's *Siegfried*. H-SG. Also "Di quella pira," A in Verdi's *Il trovatore*. H-SG

473.19, stride the rampante; "Stride la vampa," A in Verdi's *Il trovatore*. HW-SG

473.24, morroweth; "con onor muore chi non può serbar vita con onore" (who cannot live with honor can die with honor), T in Puccini's *Madame Butterfly*. H

Finnegans Wake, Book III.3:

474.10, treble; Zélia Trebelli (mezzo-sop.). H

475.2, aggala; "Weia! Waga! . . . Wagalaweia!" (Rhine Maidens at beginning of opera), A in Wagner's *Das Rheingold*. H

475.11, waltzing; Volsung, T in Wagner's *Ring*. B

475.11, gardenfillers; Mary Garden (sop.). B. Also Covent Garden opera house. B

475.11, puritan; Bellini's *I puritani* (OT). B

475.22, Mallinger; Frank Coningsby Mullings (ten.). H. Also Mathilde Mallinger (sop.). B

475.34, bawl of a mascot; Verdi's *Un ballo in maschera* (OT). McH

476.4, .9, Walker . . . wheresoever; "Where'er you walk," A in Handel's *Semele*. H-SG. Also Edyth Walker (mezzo-sop.). H

476.8, the hand making silence; prohibition against applause at performances, T in Wagner's *Parsifal*. B. Also "Silentium—wach' auf," A (chorus) in Wagner's *Die Meistersinger*. B

476.11, .35, curtsey, . . . curchycurchy; Amelita Galli-Curci (sop.). H

476.24, Lord Lumen; Count di Luna, C in Verdi's *Il trovatore*. B

476.26, Marcus; King Mark, C in Wagner's *Tristan und Isolde*. B

477.22, puisny donkeyman; Massenet's and other composers' *Don Quixote* (OT). B

477.23, slipping beauty; Brünnhilde, C in Wagner's *Ring*. B, M

477.25, planckton; Pol Plançon (bass). H

477.27, mazing hour; Margarete Matzenauer (sop.). H

477.29, moor; Otello, C in Verdi's *Otello*. B

477.30, mellifond; Mélisande, C in Debussy's *Pelléas et Mélisande*. H. Also C in Dukas's *Ariane et Barbe-bleu*. B

477.33, .34, Ecko! . . . lions'; "Ecco il leone," A in Verdi's *Otello.* H-SG

478.21, trouvay; Verdi's *Il trovatore* (OT). B

478.21, .28, .34, *champs . . . fatherick . . . padredges;* "Champs paternels," A in Méhuel's *Joseph.* B

478.26, Martin 202

478.30, Martin 202

478.34, O mis padredges; "O patria mia . . . O cieli azzurri," A in Verdi's *Aïda.* B

479.21, vixens; Mrs. Vixen, C in Gay's *Beggar's Opera.* B

479.28–29, knowest thout the kind? . . . Weissduwasland; "Connais-tu le pays? ("Kennst du das Land?"), A in Thomas's *Mignon.* HW-SG

479.36–480.1, Conning two lay payees; "Connais-tu le pays?" ("Kennst du das Land?"), A in Thomas's *Mignon.* HW

480.3–4, Martin 202

480.11, mark; King Mark, C in Wagner's *Tristan und Isolde.* G

480.27, lyceum; London Lyceum, where the Carl Rosa Opera Company sometimes had its seasons, also called the English Opera House. B

480.28, volp volp; Giacomo Lauri-Volpi (ten.). B

480.36, Wolfgang; Mozart (comp.). H

481.10, tristich; Tristan, C in Wagner's *Tristan und Isolde.* H, M

481.16, Romeo; Roméo, C in Gounod's *Roméo et Juliette.* B

482.14, donkeyschott; Massenet's and other composers' *Don Quixote* (OT). B

482.17, Hayden; Haydn (comp.). B

483.9, bonze; "Lo zio Bonzo," C in Puccini's *Madame Butterfly.* B

483.11, Borsaiolini's; Francesco Borosini (ten.). B

483.16–17, Martin 202

483.34, Martin 202

484.5, eyesalt; Isolde, C in Wagner's *Tristan und Isolde.* B, M

484.15, meer hyber; Meyerbeer (comp.). B

484.19, rancer; Jack Rance, C in Puccini's *La fanciulla del west.* B, H

484.21, bland; Maria Theresa Bland (mezzo-sop.). H

484.25, Lazary; Virgilio Lazzari (bass). H

484.26–27, Washywatchywataywatashy! . . . Watacooshy; "Chin Chin Chinaman," A in Jones's *Geisha.* B

484.33, Kelly; Michael Kelly (ten.). H

484.35, Pappagallus; Papageno, C in Mozart's *Magic Flute.* H

485.1, Catlick's; Ann or Anne Catley (sop.). B

485.2, .17, tripenniferry. . . . thruppenny croucher; Weill's *Die Dreigroschenoper* (OT). H. Also Gay's *Beggar's Opera,* on which Weill's work was based (OT). H

485.20, peachumpidgeonlover; Polly Peachum, C in Gay's *Beggar's Opera*. H

485.28, .36, Ho ha hi he hung! Tsing tsing! . . . chinchin; "Chin Chin China-man," A in Jones's *Geisha*. HW

485.29, Me no angly mo, me speakee Yellman's lingas; Chinese pidgin, T in Puccini's *Turandot*. H

485.30, Lu; Liù, C in Puccini's *Turandot*. H

485.36–486.1, chinchin chat with nipponnipers; Cio-Cio-San, C in Puccini's *Madame Butterfly*. B, H

486.4, .7, *tryst* . . . Tantris, . . . tryst; Tristan, C in Wagner's *Tristan und Isolde*. B, H-SG, M

486.7, Martin 193

486.14, Tuttu; "Tu? tu? piccolo iddio!" A in Puccini's *Madame Butterfly*. H

486.20, tistress isoles; Wagner's *Tristan und Isolde* (OT). B, M

486.23–24, Martin 202

486.26, Purely, in a pure manner; "Morir! sì pura e bella!" A in Verdi's *Aïda*. B

487.9–10, Martin 214

487.15, Martin 191

487.23, Martin 202

487.26, Martin 202

487.32, Martin 202

489.32, Alibany; Emma Albani (sop.). H

490.24, Martin 202

490.25–26, Jenny Rediviva; Jenny Diver, C in Gay's *Beggar's Opera*. H. Also Jenny Lind (sop.). H

491.12, tryst; Tristan, C in Wagner's *Tristan und Isolde*. H, M

491.12–13, 16–18, a tryst too, two a tutu . . . Kane. . . . *Mansianhase parak*; Caruso (ten.) monkey-house incident. See chapter 5. B

491.13, too, two a tutu; "Tu? tu? piccolo iddio!" A in Puccini's *Madame Butterfly*. H

491.15, Demaasch; Joseph Maas (ten.). H

491.17, *Marak! Marak! Marak;* King Mark, C in Wagner's *Tristan und Isolde*. H, M

491.29, Maomi, Mamie; Mimi, C in Puccini's *La bohème*. H

491.30, drary lane; Drury Lane Theatre, London, site of much Italian opera in the nineteenth century. Mink and B

492.8, Anna Delittle; Dalila, C in Saint-Saëns's *Samson et Dalila*. H

492.30, orpentings; Sir William Orpen (1878–1931), painted McCormack's favorite portrait of McCormack. B

493.3, Martin 221

493.28, Irise, Osirises; Iris, C in Mascagni's *Iris* and in Handel's *Semele*. B. Also Jewel Song ("Ah, je ris"), A in Gounod's *Faust*. B. Also "O, Isis and Osiris," A in Mozart's *Magic Flute*. B

493.29, pont; da Ponte, comp. and librettist. G. Also Lily Pons (sop.). B

493.29–30, Martin 214

493.31, Nu-Men; "Nume, custode e vindice," A in Verdi's *Aïda*. H

494.1–4, Martin 214

494.14, Noth; Nothung, T in Wagner's *Ring*. H

494.29, melbaw; Nellie Melba (sop.). H

495.1–2, .7, Sully . . . Shovellyvans . . . Sulleyman; John Sullivan (ten.). H

495.1–3, The said Sully, a barracker associated with tinkers, the blackhand, Shovellyvans, wreuter of annoyimgmost letters; Caruso (ten.) in New York was troubled by anonymous extortion letters police later traced to the Black Hand gang. B

495.15, pallyass; Pelléas, C in Debussy's *Pelléas et Mélisande*. H. Also Leoncavallo's *I pagliacci* (OT). H

495.16, holy poly; Golaud (Golo), C in Debussy's *Pelléas et Mélisande*. H

495.18, Quink; Quinquin, nickname of Octavian, C in R. Strauss's *Der Rosenkavalier*. B

495.19, hiding under my hair; hair of Mélisande, T in Debussy's *Pelléas et Mélisande*. H

495.24, Shadow La Rose; Dalua, Shadow God, C in Boughton's *Immortal Hour*. B

495.24, Shadow; Shadow Song, A in Meyerbeer's *Dinorah*. H

495.25, Elsebett; Elsa, C in Wagner's *Lohengrin*. H, M. Also Elisabeth, C in Wagner's *Tannhäuser*. H, M

495.30, margey; Marguérite, C in Gounod's *Faust*. H. Also C in Berlioz's *La Damnation de Faust* and Meyerbeer's *Les Huguenots*. B. Also Margherita, C in Boïto's *Mefistofele*. B

495.33, Amn; Amneris, C in Verdi's *Aïda*. H

495.35–36, *patrona . . . silvanes . . . salvines*; Pergolesi's *La serva padronna* (OT; an intermezzo). H

495.36, silvanes; Silvano, C in Verdi's *Un ballo in maschera*. B. Also Silva, C in Verdi's *Ernani*. B

495.36, salvines; Fanny Salvini-Donatelli (sop.). B

496.4–5, show-the-flag flotilla; American fleet arrives, T in Puccini's *Madame Butterfly*. B

496.23, margery; Marguérite, C in Gounod's *Faust*. H. Also C in Berlioz's *La Damnation de Faust* and Meyerbeer's *Les Huguenots*. B. Also Margherita, C in Boïto's *Mefistofele*. B

496.32, Crow; Crow Street Theatre, Dublin. B

496.36–497.1, *quinnigan . . . Quinnigan's;* Quinquin, nickname of Octavian, C in R. Strauss's *Der Rosenkavalier*. B

497.15, kraal; Grail (Ger., *Gral*), T in Wagner's *Parsifal*. H

497.18, Luccanicans; Pauline Lucca (sop.). H

497.27, Persee; Wagner's *Parsifal* (OT). H

497.28, Rinseky Poppakork; Rimsky-Korsakov (comp.). H

497.32, queen of knight's; Queen of the Night, C in Mozart's *Magic Flute*. H

497.33, salaames; R. Strauss's *Salomé* (OT). H

498.7, halle of the vacant fhroneroom; Castle of Montsalvat, T in Wagner's *Parsifal*. H-SG. See also Martin 221.

498.13, gemmynosed sanctsons; Jemmy, C in Rossini's *William Tell*. H

498.15, -taya . . . kovskva; Tchaikovsky (comp.). H

498.18, a'mona; Amonasro, C in Verdi's *Aïda*. H

498.18, oels a'mona; Desdemona, C in Verdi's *Otello*. B

498.18–19, beers o'ryely; Parsifal, C in Wagner's *Parsifal*. B, H-SG

498.19, o'ryely; Le Comte Ory, C in Rossini's *Le Comte Ory*. H

498.26–27, ringcampf, circumassembled by his daughters in the foregiftness; Amfortas, T in Wagner's *Parsifal*. H-SG

498.28–29, he lay in all dimensions, . . . of his swathings; Amfortas's bandages, T in Wagner's *Parsifal*. H-SG

498.30, cummulium of scents; communion of saints, T in Wagner's *Parsifal*. H

498.33, serafim; Tullio Serafin (cond.). B

498.36, healed cured; Amfortas, T in Wagner's *Parsifal*. H-SG

499.8, Woh Hillill! Woe Hallall; Valhalla, T in Wagner's *Ring*. H, M. See also Martin 214.

499.15, Muster of the Hidden Life; Lord of the Hidden Way, C in Boughton's *Immortal Hour*. H

499.30, *Tris tris;* Tristan, C in Wagner's *Tristan und Isolde*. H, M

499.31, Wonted Foot; Amfortas's wounds, T in Wagner's *Parsifal*. H

499.33, Donnerbruck; rainbow bridge created by Donner's storm, T in Wagner's *Das Rheingold*. H

500.1, dead giant; Fafner slays Fasolt, T in Wagner's *Das Rheingold*. H

500.4, ring; Wagner's *Ring* (OT). H

500.21, .22, .27, Brinabride, . . . Brinabride; Brünnhilde, C in Wagner's *Ring.* H, M. See also Martin 214.

500.21, .23, .24, am . . . Us! . . . Fort! Fort; Amfortas, C in Wagner's *Parsifal.* H

500.22, .25, I sold! . . . Isolde; Isolde, C in Wagner's *Tristan und Isolde.* B, M. See also Martin 202.

500.24, Bayroyt; Bayreuth (Wagner festival), T in Wagner's life. H, M. See also Martin 188.

501.4, Iss? Miss?; Isolde, C in Wagner's *Tristan und Isolde.* B, M

501.7, Martin 221

501.19, Penzance; Gilbert and Sullivan's *Pirates of Penzance* (OT). B

502.9, Martin 202, 214

502.36, Paronama; "Caro nome," A in Verdi's *Rigoletto.* B

503.7, Martin 214

503.28, sigeth; Siegfried, C in Wagner's *Siegfried.* H

503.28, Woodin; Wotan, C in Wagner's *Ring.* H, M

503.28, Warneung; Erda's warning, C in Wagner's *Das Rheingold.* H

503.30, .32, eshtree . . . . Ashe's; Wotan's *Weltesche*, T in Wagner's *Ring.* H, M

504.20, Corcor; Captain Corcoran, C in Gilbert and Sullivan's *H.M.S. Pinafore.* H

504.20, *Udi, Udite;* "Udite, udite, o rustici," A in Donizetti's *L'elisir d'amore.* H

504.28, charlotte; Charlotte, C in Massenet's *Werther.* H

505.11, Martin 203

505.13, Odd's end; Wotan's end, T in Wagner's *Die Götterdämmerung.* H

505.16–21, Martin 203

505.21, law indead; "Mild und leise" ("Liebestod"), A in Wagner's *Tristan und Isolde.* H

505.25, Martin 214

506.15–18, Martin 214

506.24, Martin 203

508.5, *Yule Remember;* "Then You'll Remember Me," A in Balfe's *Bohemian Girl.* HW

508.18, leidend; Frida Leider (sop.). B. Also John of Leyden, C in Meyerbeer's *Le Prophète.* H

508.21–22, Martin 205

508.22, Martin 189

508.22, minnestirring; Minnie, C in Puccini's *La fanciulla del west.* B

508.23, Clopatrick's; title C in Massenet's *Cléopâtre.* B

508.28, Pranksome Quaine; Brangäne, C in Wagner's *Tristan und Isolde.* H

508.32, Collinses; Colleen Bawn, C in Benedict's *Lily of Killarney.* G

508.34, liszted; Liszt (comp.). B

508.35, 509.1–4, watching you as watcher . . . wash . . . watching the watched watching. Vechers all. . . . watching . . . witching; "Silentium—wach' auf," A (chorus) in Wagner's *Die Meistersinger.* B

509.3, Vechers; Mrs. Vixen, C in Gay's *Beggar's Opera.* B

509.4, witching; Mrs. Vixen and Jemmy Twitcher, Cs in Gay's *Beggar's Opera.* B

509.20, coaxes; Mrs. Coaxer, C in Gay's *Beggar's Opera.* B

509.28–29, Tiffpuff up my nostril, would you puff the earthworm; Fafner, C in Wagner's *Ring.* H

509.28–29, Tiffpuff . . . puff; "Piff, paff," A in Meyerbeer's *Les Huguenots.* B, H

510.7, married on that top of all strapping; Giuseppina Strepponi (sop., became Verdi's wife). H

510.8, .16, my good watcher? . . . Awake! Come, a wake; "Silentium—wach' auf," A (chorus) in Wagner's *Die Meistersinger.* B

510.9, frohim; Froh, C in Wagner's *Das Rheingold.* H, M. See also Martin 214.

510.13, Martin 214. Also Gunther, C in Reyer's *Sigurd.* B

510.20, Normend; Bellini's *Norma* (OT). B

510.24, ehren; Ehrenreich, one name of Octavian, C in R. Strauss's *Der Rosenkavalier.* B

510.26, O'echolowing; "Ecco il leone," A in Verdi's *Otello.* B

511.13, cygncygn; Gina Cigna (sop.). H. Also swan, T in Wagner's *Lohengrin.* B

511.14, cacchinic; Giulio Caccini (comp.). H. Also Francesca Caccini (first woman opera composer). H

511.20, suckersome; Sigurd, C in Reyer's *Sigurd.* H

511.31, crocelips; Nicolino (male sop.). B

512.3, Martin 203

512.9, coaxing; Mrs. Coaxer, C in Gay's *Beggar's Opera.* B

512.9–10, musked bell of this masked ball; Verdi's *Un ballo in maschera* (OT). HW

512.12–13, Wilt . . . Wilt . . . Wilt; Marie Wilt (sop.). H

512.17, cramwell; King Mark, C in Wagner's *Tristan und Isolde.* G

513.5, Martin 203

513.7, Jorn; Karl Jörn (ten.). H

513.8, Fluteful; Mozart's *Magic Flute* (OT). H

513.8, *Ex ugola lenonem;* "Ecco il leone," A in Verdi's *Otello.* H

513.13, polcat; Polkan (Russ. general), C in Rimsky-Korsakov's *Golden Cockerel.* H-SG

513.17, ricordo; Riccardo, C in Verdi's *Un ballo in maschera.* H. Also Ricordi family, publishers of Verdi and Puccini operas. B

513.20, Poppagenua; Papageno, C in Mozart's *Magic Flute.* HW

513.21–22, *Oropos Roxy and Pantharhea;* Stravinsky's *Oedipus Rex* (OT). B

513.22, aria; aria, T in opera generally. B

513.25–26, Martin 203

513.27, virgin page; Anna Page, C in Nicolai's *Merry Wives of Windsor.* G

513.28, graunt; Carl Heinrich Graun (ten.). H

513.34, mastersinging; Wagner's *Die Meistersinger* (OT). H, M

514.2, Normand; Bellini's *Norma* (OT). H

514.2, .6, mejical . . . flugged; Mozart's *Magic Flute* (OT). H

514.22, Nubis, Thundersday, at a Little Bit of Heaven Howth; Donner's storm creating the rainbow bridge to Valhalla. T in Wagner's *Das Rheingold.* B

514.35, Scrapp; Scarpia, C in Puccini's *Tosca.* H

515.9, *rhodammum;* Radamès, C in Verdi's *Aida.* H

516.15, pyre; "Di quella pira," A in Verdi's *Il trovatore.* B. Also Siegfried's pyre, T in Wagner's *Ring.* B

516.18, wann swanns wann; swan, T in Wagner's *Lohengrin.* B. Also probably alludes to famous opera anecdote about tenor Leo Slezak, who, discovering stagehands had moved the swan away too soon, calmly inquired "Wann fährt der nächste Schwan?" (When is the next swan?). B. Also "Wahn! Wahn!" ("Madness"), A in Wagner's *Die Meistersinger.* H

516.21, Martin 215

516.23, kanes; policeman in Caruso (ten.) monkey-house incident. See chapter 5. B

516.24, Purcell's; Purcell (comp.). H

517.7, the huggornut; Meyerbeer's *Les Huguenots* (OT). H

517.17–18, Did Box . . . Cox; Sullivan's *Cox and Box* (OT). B

517.32, rosing; Vladmir [*sic*] Rosing (ten.). H

518.3–4, .6, .10, shadows . . . diabolically . . . devil's . . . . will of Whose B. Dunn; Dalua, Shadow God, C in Boughton's *Immortal Hour.* B

518.17, .18, Piff? Puff; "Piff paff," A in Meyerbeer's *Les Huguenots.* B

518.22, Scutticules; Antonio Scotti (bar.). B

518.25–28, Martin 215

518.28, Martin 189

518.29, Canniley; Maria Caniglia (sop.). H

518.33, O bella! O pia! O pura; "Morir! sì pura e bella!" A in Verdi's *Aïda*. HW

518.33, Amem; Amneris, C in Verdi's *Aïda*. H

518.33, Amem. Handwalled; Aïda and Radamès walled in, T in Verdi's *Aïda*. H

518.33, 519.5, bella . . . Dora; Dorabella, C in Mozart's *Così fan tutte*. H

519.3–4, punnermine . . . minne; Minnie, C in Puccini's *La fanciulla del west*. B. Also Mime, C in Wagner's *Ring*. H

519.10, largos life, this is me timtomtum; "Largo al factotum," A in Rossini's *Barber of Seville*. H

519.18–20, D'yu mean to tall grand jurors of thathens of tharctic on your oath, me lad, and ask us to believe you; jury, T in Gilbert and Sullivan's *Trial by Jury*. B

519.24, Markwalther; Beckmesser as marker of Walther von Stolzing's song, C in Wagner's *Die Meistersinger*. B. Also Mark, C in Wagner's *Tristan und Isolde*. B, M

520.5, stairrods; Herod, C in Strauss's *Salomé* and in Massenet's *Hérodiade* (OT). G, B

521.6, nada; Jean Nada, French professor at Zurich Conservatory, 1917, flutist, teacher of Joyce's friend Otto Luening; played principal flute in Stadttheater orchestra. B

521.11, scotty; Antonio Scotti (bar.). B

521.15, .17, moment . . . by the way . . . Dove; "Dove sono i bei momenti," A in Mozart's *Marriage of Figaro*. H

521.17–19, wizzend? . . . darty; "Vissi d'arte," A in Puccini's *Tosca*. H

521.22, tristy; Tristan, C in Wagner's *Tristan und Isolde*. B, M

521.23, freckened; Fricka, C in Wagner's *Ring*. H

521.35–36, Farewell but whenever! Buy; "Ora e per sempre addio," A in Verdi's *Otello*. H

522.7, melanodactylism; Zinka Milanov (sop.). H

522.11, you rogue, you; Farinelli (It. for "rogue"), stage name of Carlo Broschi (male sop.). B

523.8, man from Saint Yves; King Mark, C in Wagner's *Tristan und Isolde*. G

523.16, S. Samson and son, bred by dilalahs; Saint-Saëns's *Samson et Dalila* (OT). H. Also Saint-Saëns (comp.). H

525.13–16, fishery? . . . Lalia Lelia Lilia Lulia . . . Gubbernathor! . . . Spawning ova and fry; Leïla and Nadir, Cs in Bizet's *Pearl Fishers*. H

525.14, Lola; Lola, C in Mascagni's *Cavalleria rusticana*. H

525.14, Martin 215

525.14, Lulia; Lulu, C in Berg's *Lulu*. H

525.16, Parasol Irelly; Parsifal, C in Wagner's *Parsifal.* B

526.21, folley; John McCormack (ten.) under pseudonym of Giovanni Foli.
K

526.28, Corrack-on-Sharon; John McCormack (ten.). H

526.28, Rosecarmon; Bizet's *Carmen* (OT). H

526.30–32, making faces at her bachspilled likeness in the brook after and cool-
ing herself in the element, she pleasing it, she praising it; Mélisande's
reflection in fountain, T in Debussy's *Pelléas et Mélisande.* H

526.32, salices; "Salce, salce" (Willow Song), A in Verdi's *Otello.* H

527.1, Iscappellas; Pelléas, C in Debussy's *Pelléas et Mélisande.* H

527.1, Ys; Lalo's *Le Roi d'Ys* (OT). H

527.1, Gotellus; Verdi's *Otello* (OT). H

527.1–528.13, Martin 203

527.3, harrowd; Herod, C in R. Strauss's *Salomé* and in Massenet's *Hérodiade*
(OT). G, B

527.8, bombashaw; Giuseppe Bamboschek (Triestine cond.). B

527.23–24, Martin 203

527.25, Bortolo; Bartolo, C in Rossini's *Barber of Seville.* H. Also C in Mozart's
Marriage of Figaro and in Luigi and Federico Ricci's *Crispino e la comare.*
B

527.26, colombinas; Mackenzie and Hueffer's *Columba* (OT). B

527.27, Linda; Jenny Lind (sop.). H. Also Donizetti's *Linda of Chamounix* (OT).
H

527.28, My rillies; Mireille, C in Gounod's *Mireille.* H

527.29–30, Mon ishebeau! Ma reinebelle; Isolde (Isabelle), C in Wagner's *Tristan
und Isolde.* B. Also Mascagni's *Isabeau* (OT). H

528.7, .10, minne . . . meme; Mime, C in Wagner's *Ring.* H

528.12, I'll be clue to who knows you; "steh' ich treu Dir bis zum Tod" (I'll be
true to you till death; Senta's last words), T in Wagner's *Flying Dutchman.*
H

528.16–17, suora unto suora?; Puccini's *Suor Angelica* (OT). B

528.18, .26, Ding dong! . . . Dang; Ping, Pang, Pong, Cs in Puccini's *Turandot.* B

528.23, iris; Iris, C in Mascagni's *Iris.* H. Also in Handel's *Semele.* B

529.1, Hayden; Haydn (comp.). B

529.6, maternal; Amalie Materna (sop.). H

529.21, ark; *Bogen-form* (archform), T in Wagner's *Die Meistersinger.* H

529.30, pfuffpfaffing; Fafner, C in Wagner's *Das Rheingold.* H. Also "Piff, paff,"
A in Meyerbeer's *Les Huguenots.* B

529.32, fancydress nordic; Wagnerian costume, T in Wagner. H

529.32, nordic; Lillian Nordica (sop.). H

529.34, Bar; *Bar* pattern, T in Wagner's *Die Meistersinger*. H

530.19, morse-erse wordybook; "Saper vorreste," A in Verdi's *Un ballo in maschera*. H

530.20–22, Seckesign . . . Sickerson . . . Seckersen . . . Sackerson; Siegmund, C in Wagner's *Ring*. H. Also Siegfried, C in Wagner's *Siegfried*. H

530.20, van der Deckel; Vanderdecken, C in Wagner's *Flying Dutchman*. H, M

530.21, Errick; Erik, C in Wagner's *Flying Dutchman*. H, M

530.31, Wallpurgies . . . deified city; Valhalla, the Burg, T in Wagner's *Ring*. H-SG, M

530.32, Bigmesser's; Beckmesser, C in Wagner's *Die Meistersinger*. H-SG, M. See also Martin 205.

531.4, Log Laughty; Loge (Loki), C in Wagner's *Ring*. H

531.4–5, Master; Wagner's *Die Meistersinger* (OT). H

531.5, gunne; Michael Gunn (impresario). McH

531.33, archsee; *Bogen-form* (archform), T in Wagner's *Die Meistersinger*. H

531.36, Kovnor-Journal; Mussorgsky's *Khovanshchina* (OT). H

532.6, Martin 215

532.6, heil; "Heil dir, Sonne! Heil dir, Licht!" A in Wagner's *Siegfried*. H-SG

532.18, .20, verawife . . . frifrif friend; Fricka, Wotan's wife, C in Wagner's *Ring*. H

532.22, Gigglotte's; Beniamino Gigli (ten.). H

532.27, Martin 215

532.33, prize; prize song, T in Wagner's *Die Meistersinger*. H

533.3, the pu pure beauty of hers past; "Morir! sì pura e bella!" A in Verdi's *Aïda*. B

533.5, Evans's; Eva, C in Wagner's *Die Meistersinger*. H

533.7, proofpiece from my prenticeserving; prize song, T in Wagner's *Die Meistersinger*. H

533.9, Martin 203

533.16, Castrucci Sinior; Signor Pietro Castrucci (cond.). McH, B

533.16–17, De Mellos; de Mellos, who founded opera on Fishamble Street, Dublin. B

533.16–21, fourposter tunies chantreying . . . Johannes; quartet sung by Jean de Reszke (ten.), *Letters 3,* 120. B

533.19, Goosna Greene; Plunket[t] Greene (bass). B

533.20, Dodo; Dodon, C in Rimsky-Korsakov's *Golden Cockerel*. H

533.20, Martin 203

533.21, Johannes; [Jo]han[ne]s Sachs, C in Wagner's *Die Meistersinger*. H. Also Johannistag, T in Wagner's *Die Meistersinger*. H

533.28, Caulofat's; Calaf, C in Puccini's *Turandot*. H

533.32, reicherout; Theodor Reichmann (bar.). H

534.12, Pynix Park; Louisa Pyne (sop.). H

534.27, Martin 215

534.28, soffiacated green parrots; "E soffito e pareti" (and ceiling and walls), opening words of Puccini's *Madame Butterfly*. H. Also a reference to a story preserved by Colonel James Mapleson (*The Mapleson Memoirs,* 100) that during a tour of the Royal Italian Opera in 1875, Giuseppe (Carlo) Sinico fed so much parsley to Ilma di Murska's pet parrot that he killed the bird. Distraught, Mme di Murska insisted that her pet be autopsied by Glasgow doctors, whose official ruling was that the parrot had died from arsenic in the ink of green wallpaper it had eaten. Joyce may have heard the tale from his teacher in Trieste, Giuseppe Sinico, nephew of Giuseppe Carlo. B

534.31, lorking; Lortzing (comp.). H

534.33, lulul; Lulu, C in Berg's *Lulu*. H

535.2, Barktholed; *Bar* pattern, T in Wagner's *Die Meistersinger*. H

535.5, Wodin; Wotan, C in Wagner's *Ring*. H, M

535.8, pricelist; prize song, T in Wagner's *Die Meistersinger*. H

535.15, Martin 215

535.18, .36, barely . . . former; *Bar* pattern, T in Wagner's *Die Meistersinger*. H

535.25, Pass the fish; Ludwig Fischer (bass), who sang Sarastro in *The Magic Flute*. B

536.9, bonze; Alesandro Bonci (ten.). H. Also "Lo zio Bonzo," C in Puccini's *Madame Butterfly*. B

536.9, Ring; Wagner's *Ring* (OT). H

536.11, Sacks eleathury! Sacks eleathury; Hans Sachs, C in Wagner's *Die Meistersinger*. H

536.14, formed; *Bogen-form* (archform), T in Wagner's *Die Meistersinger*. H

536.21–22, zober . . . flautish; Mozart's *Magic Flute* (OT). K

536.25–32: Some day I may tell of his second storey. . . . Kanes nought . . . Give me even two months by laxlaw . . . Zerobubble Barrentone; Caruso (ten., though he had at first sung baritone parts) monkey-house incident. See chapter 5. B

536.28, I have bared my whole past; the secret of the *Bar* pattern in Wagner (see 537.10), T in Wagner. H

536.32, Barrentone; *Bar* pattern, T in Wagner's *Die Meistersinger*. H. Also Maria Barrientos (sop.). H

536.35, Harrod's; Herod, C in Strauss's *Salomé* and in Massenet's *Hérodiade* (OT). G, B

537.7, after; aftersong *(Abgesang)*, T in Wagner's *Die Meistersinger*. H

537.8, Sigismond; Siegmund, C in Wagner's *Die Walküre*. H

537.8–9, Stolterforth; Walther von Stoltzing, C in Wagner's *Die Meistersinger*. H. Also *Stollen* (stanza) form, T in Wagner's *Die Meistersinger*. H

537.10, *Ehren;* Ehrenreich, one name of Octavian, C in R. Strauss's *Der Rosenkavalier* (with his dueling foe at 538.7). B

537.10, .33, Lorencz Pattorn . . . sacret; Alfred Lorenz, *Das Geheimnis der Form bei Richard Wagner* (*The Secret of Form in Richard Wagner*), T in Wagner. H

537.24, Djamja; Djamileh, C in Bizet's *Djamileh*. H

537.30, Frick's; Gottlob Frick (bass). H. Also Fricka, C in Wagner's *Die Walküre*. H, M. See also Martin 215.

537.30, Uden; Wotan, C in Wagner's *Die Walküre*. H, M

537.35–36, mackin . . . erithmatic. The unpurdonable; "Eri tu che Macchiave," A in Verdi's *Un ballo in maschera*. H

538.3, Ledwidge; William Ludwig (bar., b. Ledwidge). B

538.3, Salvatorious; Monsalvat, T in Wagner's *Parsifal*. H

538.7, Nanenities; Nanetta, C in Verdi's *Falstaff*. B

538.7, ochtroyd; Baron Ochs von Lerchenau, C in R. Strauss's *Der Rosenkavalier*. H

538.8, Martin 203

538.8, melkkaart; Lauritz Melchior (ten.). H

538.13, Crusos; Enrico Caruso (ten.). H

538.19, choochoo chucklesome; Cio-Cio-San, C in Puccini's *Madame Butterfly*. H

538.24, covin guardient; Covent Garden Theatre, London, site of Italian opera during late nineteenth century; eventually titled "Royal Opera House, Covent Garden." Mink and B

538.27, freiung; Freia, C in Wagner's *Das Rheingold*. H

538.28–29, contey Carlow's; Verdi's *Don Carlos* (OT). H

539.1, after my both earstoear; aftersong (*Abgesang*), T in Wagner's *Die Meistersinger*. H

539.8, palmer's; Geoffrey Molyneux Palmer (comp.). B

539.8–9, I have had my best master's lessons; Sachs teaching Walther the form of the prize song, T in Wagner's *Die Meistersinger*. H

539.13, told I own stolemines; stolen gold, T in Wagner's *Ring*. H-SG, M

539.14, Hohohoho; Siegfried forging Nothung, T in Wagner's *Siegfried*. H-SG, M

539.25, bog; *Bogen-form* (archform), T in Wagner's *Die Meistersinger*. H

539.27, siegewin; Siegmund, C in Wagner's *Ring*. H. Also Wagner's *Siegfried*. (OT). B, M. See also Martin 215.

539.27, Abbot; Emma Abbott (sop.). H

539.29, soord; Nothung, T in Wagner's *Siegfried*. H

539.30, Allbrecht; Alberich, C in Wagner's *Ring*. H, M

540.1, .17, dragon worms . . . sleeping giant; Fafner the dragon, giant theme, C in Wagner's *Das Rheingold*. H, M

540.7, Labia; Fausta Labia (sop.). H. Also Maria Labia (sop.). H

540.11, *suke;* Suky Tawdry, C in Gay's *Beggar's Opera*. B

540.24, wagoners; Wagner (comp.). H, M

540.28, Been so free; "Bin ich frei!" (I'm free; Alberich's curse), T in Wagner's *Ring*. H

540.29–30, devilbobs; Meyerbeer's *Robert le diable* (OT). G, H. Also Gilbert's play *Robert le diable* (1868; not an opera). B

541.7, campaniles; Italo Campanini (ten.). H

541.14, hugheknots; Meyerbeer's *Les Huguenots* (OT). H

541.15, barthelemew; St. Bartholomew's Day massacre, T in Meyerbeer's *Les Huguenots*. B

541.21, .23, reshockle . . . Warschouw; Jean de Reszke (ten.). B

541.22, Walhalloo, Walhalloo, Walhalloo; Valhalla, T in Wagner's *Ring*. B, M. See also Martin 215.

541.24, ping on pang; Ping, Pang, Pong, Cs in Puccini's *Turandot*. B

541.24–25, Martin 215

541.26, slobodens; Oda Slobodskaya (sop.). H

541.30, sleeking beauties; Brünnhilde, C in Wagner's *Ring*. H

541.32–33, tendulcis tunes; Giusto Ferdinando Tenducci (male sop.). H

541.32–33, water parted fluted up; "Water parted from the sea," A in Arne's *Artaxerxes*. B

542.23, elisaboth; Elisabeth, C in Wagner's *Tannhäuser*. H, M

543.8–10, inchanting . . . cheoilboys so that they are allcalling on me for the song of a birtch: the more secretely bi built; aftersong (*Abgesang*) and Lorenz's *Secret of Form in Richard Wagner,* T in Wagner's *Die Meistersinger*. H

543.17, Huggin; Hagen, C in Wagner's *Die Götterdämmerung*. H. Also C in Reyer's *Sigurd*. B

543.20, drury; Drury Lane Theatre, London, site of much Italian opera in the nineteenth century. Mink and B

543.25, .27, German . . . wageearner; Wagner (comp.). H, M

544.21, ottawark; Don Ottavio, C in Mozart's *Don Giovanni.* H

545.27, seralcellars; Mozart's *Abduction from the Seraglio* (OT). H

545.28, parciful; Wagner's *Parsifal* (OT). HW, M. See also Martin 215.

545.28–29, street wauks that are darkest; "Scenes that are brightest," A in Wallace's *Maritana.* B

546.29, Taubiestimm; Richard Tauber (ten.). H

546.32, uphills . . . brunette; Brünnhilde, C in Wagner's *Ring.* H

547.2, pellmell; Debussy's *Pelléas et Mélisande* (OT). H

547.8–9, O my lors; "Shade of the Palm" ("Oh, my Dolores"), A in Stuart's *Floradora.* B

547.23, upreized my magicianer's puntpole; Wotan's spear, T in Wagner's *Ring.* H

547.25, rookwards; "Zurück vom Ringe!" (Back from the ring; last sentence, spoken by Hagen), T in Wagner's *Die Götterdämmerung.* H

547.29–31, Heaven, he hallthundred . . . strongbow; "Heda! Heda! . . . Bruder, zu mir! weise der Brücke den Weg!" (Come to me, brother. Point the way to the bridge; Donner thunders as he creates the rainbow bridge to Valhalla), T in Wagner's *Das Rheingold.* H-SG

547.33, ringstresse; Wagner's *Ring* (OT). H, M

548.6, Appia; Adolphe Appia (designer who influenced Wieland and Wolfgang Wagner's productions at Bayreuth). B. Also singer Giuseppe Appiani (Appianino). B

548.7, herr . . . amstell; "Am stillen Herd," A in Wagner's *Die Meistersinger.* H

548.33, Martin 194

549.1, Soll leve! Soll leve; "Ah! lève-toi soleil!" A in Gounod's *Roméo et Juliette.* H

549.15, marble halles; "I dreamt that I dwelt in marble halls," A in Balfe's *Bohemian Girl.* HW

549.26, .35, green . . . Joe; Verdi (comp.). B

549.28, Alta; Frances Alda (sop.). B

549.35, bargeness; *Bar* pattern, T in Wagner's *Die Meistersinger.* H

550.1, Martin 203

550.17, earth; Erda, C in Wagner's *Ring.* H

550.35, duncingk the bloodanoobs; Salomé's dance, T in R. Strauss's *Salomé.* B

551.7, Martin 203

551.9, tinsel and glitter; Humperdinck's *Hänsel und Gretel* (OT). H

551.15, evangel; Eva, C in Wagner's *Die Meistersinger*. H

551.24, minne; Mime, C in Wagner's *Ring*. H. Also Minna, Wagner's (comp.) first wife. B

551.24, minne elskede; Minnie, the beloved of Johnson (Sw. *elskede* = "beloved"), C in Puccini's *La fanciulla del west*. B

551.25, erd-; Erda, C in Wagner's *Ring*. H

552.6, arked; *Bogen-form* (archform), T in Wagner's *Die Meistersinger*. H

552.7, Astralia; Florence Austral (sop., b. in Australia). B

552.9, barkeys; *Bar* pattern, T in Wagner's *Die Meistersinger*. H

552.10, .13, truanttrulls . . . gnomes . . . gobelins; the Nibelungs, Cs in Wagner's *Ring*. B, H, M

552.12, Foley; A. J. Foli (bass, b. Foley). H. Also John McCormack (ten.) under pseudonym of Giovanni Foli. B

552.12, Smyth; Siegfried, C in Wagner's *Siegfried*. H

552.13, Hogan; Hagen, C in Wagner's *Die Götterdämmerung*. H. Also C in Reyer's *Sigurd*. B

552.16, arcane celestials to Sweatenburgs Welhell; rainbow bridge to Valhalla, T in Wagner's *Das Rheingold*. H-SG, M

552.19, Neeblow's garding; Nibelungs, Cs in Wagner's *Ring*. H

552.21, ewigs; "Ewig war ich, ewig bin ich" (Eternal I was, eternal I am), T in Wagner's *Siegfried*. H

552.25, doom adimdim adoom adimadim; twilight of the gods, T in Wagner's *Die Götterdämmerung*. H

552.29, sass; Marie-Constance Sass (sop.). H

553.1–2, vergin page . . . ana; Anne Page, C in Nicolai's *Merry Wives of Windsor*. G

553.8–9, selvage . . . carpet; "Care selve," A in Handel's *Atalanta*. H

553.9, .25, gardens . . . Guerdon, garden; Mary Garden (sop.). B. Also Covent Garden opera house, London. B

553.11–12, summiramies; Rossini's *Semiramide* (OT). H

553.13, Fra Teobaldo; Auber's *Fra Diavolo* (OT). B, HW

553.13, Nielsen; Alice Nielsen (sop.). B

553.14, Guglielmus; Guglielmo, C in Mozart's *Così fan tutte*. B

553.21, pons; Lily Pons (sop.). B. Also Lorenzo da Ponte (librettist and comp.). B

553.22, hallaw vall; "In diesen heiligen Hallen," A in Mozart's *Magic Flute*. HW. Also Valhalla, T in Wagner's *Ring*. H, M

553.27, froh; Froh, C in Wagner's *Das Rheingold*. H, M

553.29–30, Martin 189, 216

554.2, tilburys; C. Tilbury (bar.). B

554.8, .10, lalaughed . . . Luahah; "Lalaleia! Lalei!" (Rhine Maidens), T in Wagner's *Das Rheingold*. H-SG. See also Martin 216.

554.10, Marahah; King Mark, C in Wagner's *Tristan und Isolde*. G

554.10, Joahanahanahana; [Jo]han[ne]s Sachs, C in Wagner's *Die Meistersinger*. H. Also Jochanaan, C in R. Strauss's *Salomé*. B

Finnegans Wake, Book III.4:

555.1, What was thaas?; "Was ist? Isolde" (What's this? Isolde; Tristan's first words), T in Wagner's *Tristan und Isolde*. B

555.11, pallyollogass; Leoncavallo's *I pagliacci* (OT). H. Also Debussy's *Pelléas et Mélisande* (OT). B

556.1–16, Martin 203

556.3, .5, she took the veil, . . . sister; taking the veil, T in Puccini's *Suor Angelica*. B

556.6, peach; Polly Peachum, C in Gay's *Beggar's Opera*. B

556.25, henders; Roy Henderson (bar.). H

556.31, wan fine night and the next fine night; "Un bel dì," A in Puccini's *Madame Butterfly*. B

556.31, Kothereen the Slop; Kate, the maid, C in Fraser-Simon and Tate's *Maid of the Mountains*. H

556.33, veal astore; "Veau d'or," A in Gounod's *Faust*. H

557.10, fisstball; Gounod's *Faust* (OT). H. Also Berlioz's *La Damnation de Faust* and Busoni's *Doktor Faust* (OTs). B. Also Faust, C in Boïto's *Mefistofele*. B

557.13–16, each and every juridical sessions night, whenas goodmen twelve and true . . . found him guilty; jury, T in Gilbert and Sullivan's *Trial by Jury*. B

560.1, Fiammelle la; Respighi's *Fiama* (OT). B

560.2, Diva; "Casta diva," A in Bellini's *Norma*. B

560.26–27, Martin 203

560.32, Brozzo; Philip Brozel (ten.). B

560.34, tonearts; *Tonart*, Ger. for "musical key." McH

561.4, boytom; Boïto (comp.). H

561.8, Halosobuth; Elisabeth, C in Wagner's *Tannhäuser*. B, M. Also Elisabeth de Valois, C in Verdi's *Don Carlos*. B

561.8, Martin 193

561.9, Martin 221

561.12, Buttercup; Buttercup, C in Gilbert and Sullivan's *H.M.S. Pinafore.* H

561.14, drink of it filtred, a gracecup; love potion (love philter), T in Wagner's *Tristan und Isolde.* H, M

561.15, lottiest daughterpearl; Lotte Lehmann (sop., b. at Perleberg). B

561.16, auntybride; Isolde as Tristram's aunt. McH

562.2–4, Rose . . . wed ma Biddles . . . barytinette she will gift . . . maidenly; Rose Maybud weds the baronet (Sw. *gift* = "wed"), T in Gilbert and Sullivan's *Ruddigore.* H

562.9–11, Martin 193

562.9–10, Martin 203

562.32, Martin 189

563.17–18, Martin 203

563.30, Blech; Leo Blech (cond.). H

564.2, Martin 204

564.4, meseedo; as mi-si-do, opening notes of "Heil dir, Sonne! Heil dir, Licht!" A in Wagner's *Siegfried;* also of the "Preisleid," "Morgenlich leuchtend," A in Wagner's *Die Meistersinger.* Also of "Dites-lui, qu'on l'a remarqué distingué," A in Offenbach's *La Grande-Duchesse de Gérolstein.* Also of "Que veulent dire ces colères," A in Offenbach's *La Périchole.* Also of "Si l'amour sur ma route ce soir," A in Thomas's *Mignon,* and of "Love that no wrong can cure," A in Gilbert and Sullivan's *Patience.* B

564.21, pappasses for paynims; Papageno, Papagena, and Pamina, Cs in Mozart's *Magic Flute.* B

564.23, tonobloom; Tonio, C in Leoncavallo's *I pagliacci.* H-SG. Also in Donizetti's *La Fille du régiment.* B

564.23, marks; King Mark, C in Wagner's *Tristan und Isolde.* G

564.25, sylvious; Silvio, C in Leoncavallo's *I pagliacci.* H-SG

564.26, rustic cavalries; Mascagni's *Cavalleria rusticana* (OT). H-SG

564.30, Talkingtree and sinningstone; Tristan, C in Wagner's *Tristan und Isolde.* B

564.34, Martin 216

565.2, Holl Hollow; Valhalla, T in Wagner's *Ring.* H-SG, M

565.2, guttergloomering; Wagner's *Die Götterdämmerung* (OT). H-SG, M. See also Martin 189.

565.3, wankyrious; Wagner's *Die Walküre* (OT). H-SG, M

565.5, woodensdays; Wotan, C in Wagner's *Ring.* H-SG, M

565.8, Martin 204

565.17, Thunner; Donner, C in Wagner's *Das Rheingold.* B

565.20, .24, Opop opop capallo . . . pap pap pappa; Papageno, C in Mozart's *Magic Flute.* H

565.21, malchick; Mozart's *Magic Flute* (OT). H

565.22, Lublin; Germaine Lubin (sop.). H

565.29, magic; Mozart's *Magic Flute* (OT). B

565.31, elvery; Elvira, C in Verdi's *Ernani,* in Bellini's *I puritani,* in Rossini's *L'italiana in Algeri,* and in Mozart's *Don Giovanni.* H

566.26–27, *Maldelikato;* Walter Malde, C in Verdi's *Rigoletto.* H

567.4, yeoman's yard; Gilbert and Sullivan's *Yeomen of the Guard* (OT). HW

567.10, roofstaff; Falstaff, C in Verdi's *Falstaff,* Nicolai's *Merry Wives of Windsor,* and Holst's *At the Boar's Head.* G, B

567.12, Bemark; King Mark, C in Wagner's *Tristan und Isolde.* G

567.13, .15, queen . . . Nan; title C in Donizetti's *Anna Bolena.* G, B

567.13–15, queen . . . Nanetta; Queen of the Night, C in Mozart's *Magic Flute.* B. Also Nanetta, C in Verdi's *Falstaff.* H-SG

567.16, mellems the third and the fourth of the clock; "Mentre le due e le tre," A in Verdi's *Falstaff.* H-SG

567.18, knechts; knights, T in Verdi's *Falstaff.* H-SG

567.27, Eccls! What cats' killings; "Ecco il leone," A in Verdi's *Otello.* B

567.28, widows; widows, T in Verdi's *Falstaff.* H-SG

567.28, Quick; Mistress Quickly, C in Verdi's *Falstaff.* H-SG

568.10, Cloudia Aiduolcis; "Pur ti riveggo, mia dolce Aïda," A in Verdi's *Aïda.* H

568.14, Fool pay the bill; Falstaff's bill, T in Verdi's *Falstaff.* H

568.32, alfi; Alfio, C in Mascagni's *Cavalleria rusticana.* H

569.1–2, joking up with his tonguespitz to the crimosing balkonladies; Falstaff in the buckbasket, T in Verdi's *Falstaff.* H-SG

569.4, gluckspeels; Gluck (comp.). H. Also Alma Gluck (sop.). G

569.4–5, ring . . . Rng rng! Rng rng; Wagner's *Ring* (OT). H

569.4–5, 11–12, ring . . . Rng rng! Rng rng! chimant . . . tingaling pealabells; bells and chimes, T in Mozart's *Magic Flute.* H

569.5, Mark; King Mark, C in Wagner's *Tristan und Isolde.* B

569.8, Paull-the Aposteln; William Paull (bar.). B

569.10, Molyneux; Geoffrey Molyneux Palmer (comp.). B

569.10–11, Martin 193

569.14, Agithetta; Agathe, C in Weber's *Der Freischütz.* B

569.21, *Benedictus benedicat;* Benedict (comp.). B

569.25, Poppop; Papageno, C in Mozart's *Magic Flute.* B

569.25, Martin 216

569.29, Pamelas; Pamina, C in Mozart's *Magic Flute.* H

569.34, strave; Stravinsky (comp.). H

569.36, Thou traitor slave; Radamès and Aïda, Cs in Verdi's *Aïda.* B

570.12, Ys; Lalo's *Le Roi d'Ys* (OT). B. Also Isolde, C in Wagner's *Tristan und Isolde.* B

571.2, Seekhem seckhem; Siegfried, C in Wagner's *Siegfried.* B. Also Siegmund, C in Wagner's *Die Walküre.* B

571.6–7, the leaves incut on trees! Do you can their tantrist spellings?; "Connais-tu le pays?" ("Kennst du das Land?"), A in Thomas's *Mignon.* B

571.7, .10, tantrist . . . trysting; Tristan, C in Wagner's *Tristan und Isolde.* B, M

571.8, Martin 204

571.10, .14, trysting . . . triste to death . . . ivytod; "Mild und leise" ("Liebestod"), A in Wagner's *Tristan und Isolde.* B, H-SG, M

571.13, my soul dear; Isolde, C in Wagner's *Tristan und Isolde.* B

571.24, saarasplace; Sarastro, C in Mozart's *Magic Flute.* H

571.35, 572.1, our netherworld's . . . nagging firenibblers; Nibelungs, Cs in Wagner's *Ring.* B, H, M

572.31–573.29 passim, Anita; Fanny Anitúa (sop.). B

572.33, .35, Gillia . . . Gillia; Gilda, C in Verdi's *Rigoletto.* H

572.34, Barnabas; Barnaba, C in Ponchielli's *La gioconda.* H

572.36, Poppea; Monteverdi's *L'incoronazione di Poppea* (OT). H

572.36, Arancita; Giannina Arangi-Lombardi (sop.). B

573.1, Marinuzza; Gino Marinuzzi (comp.). B

573.7, .13, Sullivani; Sir Arthur Sullivan (comp.). B. Also John Sullivan (ten.). B

573.21, Gerontes; Geronte de Ravoir, C in Puccini's *Manon Lescaut.* H

573.24, Guglielmus; Guglielmo, C in Mozart's *Così fan tutte.* H

573.30, Canicula; Maria Caniglia (sop.). B

574.1, .9, .32, D'Oyly . . . Doyle . . . doyles; Richard D'Oyly Carte, of D'Oyly Carte Opera Company. G, B

574.10–576.8, jury references and trial scene; jury, T in Gilbert and Sullivan's *Trial by Jury.* B

575.6–7, 11 Ann . . . bollion; title C of Donizetti's *Anna Bolena.* G, B

575.6–7, .32, Doyle . . . Doyle's . . . Doyle . . . Doyler; Richard D'Oyly Carte, of D'Oyly Carte Opera Company. B

576.3, Calif; Calaf, C in Puccini's *Turandot.* H

576.6, Una Bellina; Bellini (comp.). B. Also title C in Donizetti's *Anna Bolena.* G, B

576.6–8, Pepigi's pact was pure piffle . . . pango with Pepigi; Papageno/Papagna (*pianissimo* duet), A in Mozart's *Magic Flute*. H

576.8, pango; Ping, Pang, Pong, Cs in Puccini's *Turandot*. B

577.8, slam; Mrs. Slammekin, C in Gay's *Beggar's Opera*. B

577.13, voguener; Wagner (comp.). H, M

577.14, humpered; Humperdinck (comp.). B

577.14, Urloughmoor; Jacques Urlus (ten.). H

577.14, Miryburrow; Meyerbeer (comp.). B

577.17, hodinstag; Wotan, C in Wagner's *Ring*. H, M

577.17, fryggabet; Fricka, C in Wagner's *Ring*. H, M

577.22, Hearths; Erda, C in Wagner's *Ring*. H

577.22, Skittish Widdas; Lehár's *Merry Widow* (OT). H

577.30, convent garden; Covent Garden Theatre, London, site of Italian opera during the late nineteenth century; eventually titled "Royal Opera House, Covent Garden." Mink, B. Also Mary Garden (sop.). B

577.34, leperties'; Leporello, C in Mozart's *Don Giovanni*. H

578.19–20, Donauwatter; Donner, C in Wagner's *Das Rheingold*. H

578.22–23, naughtygay frew; the nightingale *Fru* (Sw. *Fru* = "married woman), Jenny Lind (sop.). B

578.23, rhaincold; Wagner's *Das Rheingold* (OT). HW, M. See also Martin 216.

578.25, Pont; da Ponte, comp. and librettist, G. Also Lily Pons (sop.). B

578.25, Delisle; Dalila, C in Saint-Saëns's *Samson et Dalila*. B

578.28, brennt; Charlotte Brent (sop.). H

578.34, vixendevolment; Mrs. Vixen, C in Gay's *Beggar's Opera*. B

579.14, miracles; Doctor Miracle, C in Offenbach's *Tales of Hoffmann*. B. Also Bizet's *Le Docteur Miracle* (OT). B

580.1, ponted; da Ponte, comp. and librettist. G. Also Lily Pons (sop.). B

580.13–15, himmertality . . . hour; Boughton's *Immortal Hour* (OT). H

580.17, tour d'adieu; Turridu, C in Mascagni's *Cavalleria rusticana*. B

580.18, Isad Ysut; Isolde, C in Wagner's *Tristan und Isolde*. B, M. Also Lalo's *Le Roi d'Ys* (OT). B

581.4, sullivan's; John Sullivan (ten.). B

581.6, swanee; swan, T in Wagner's *Lohengrin*. B

581.8–9, Martin 204

582.3, coaxing; Mrs. Coaxer, C in Gay's *Beggar's Opera*. B

582.30, Sidome; as si-do-me (HCE, according to Dalton), opening notes of "O amore, o bella luce del core," A in Mascagni's *L'amico Fritz*. B

582.32, prey; Gilbert-Louis Duprez (ten.). B

583.14, Persia's; Fanny Persiani (sop.). B

583.18, dragon; Fafner, C in Wagner's *Ring.* B

584.2–3, it tickled her innings to consort pitch at kicksolock in the morm; battle over pitch in nineteenth-century England. B

584.10, and teste his metch! Three for two will do for me; the castrato Tenducci (male sop.), nicknamed Triorchis because he was rumored to have three testicles. B

584.16, pinafore; Gilbert and Sullivan's *H.M.S. Pinafore* (OT). B

585.8, chinchin dankyshin; Cio-Cio-San, C in Puccini's *Madame Butterfly.* B

585.8, dankyshin; Massenet's and other composers' *Don Quixote* (OT). B

585.11, paratonnerwetter; Donner, C in Wagner's *Das Rheingold.* H

585.16, chargeleyden; John of Leyden, C in Meyerbeer's *Le Prophète.* H

585.22, Humperfeldt; Humperdinck (comp.). H

585.23–24, whiskered beau; whisker disguise, T in Mozart's *Così fan tutte.* H

585.24, donahbella; Dorabella, C in Mozart's *Così fan tutte.* B

585.24, Totumvir and esquimeena; Escamillo, C in Bizet's *Carmen.* B

586.8–9, Martin 205

586.28, pollysigh; Polly Peachum, C in Gay's *Beggar's Opera.* B

586.28, Seekersenn; Siegfried, C in Wagner's *Siegfried.* B

587.1, Faurore; Jean-Baptiste Fauré (bar.). H. Also Gabriel Urbain Fauré (comp.). B

587.8, Theoatre Regal's; Theatre Royal, Dublin, site of Dublin opera 1821–80; later rebuilt. Mink and B

587.13–14, cuirscrween loan; "Cruiskeen Lawn," A in Benedict's *Lily of Killarney.* B

587.27, .30, twitch . . . Jimmy; Jemmy Twitcher, C in Gay's *Beggar's Opera.* B

588.12, .14, *oloroso* . . . dolour, O so mine; "Shade of the Palm" ("Oh, my Dolores"), A in Stuart's *Floradora.* B

588.24, Izzy's; Isolde, C in Wagner's *Tristan und Isolde.* B

588.28, Martin 216

588.29–32, Martin 204

589.5, forged; forging of Nothung, T in Wagner's *Siegfried.* H

590.1, sinflute; Mozart's *Magic Flute* (OT). B

590.5, Lloyd's; Edward Lloyd (ten.). B

590.7–10, rote . . . falseheaven colours from ultraviolet to subred . . . to march through the grand tryomphal arch. His reignbolt's; entrance via rainbow bridge to Valhalla, T in Wagner's *Ring.* B, M. See also Martin 216.

590.17, Martin 216

590.24, Two me see; as do-me-si (CEH, according to Dalton), opening notes of "Veille sur eux toujours, Mère, mère," A in Meyerbeer's *L'Etoile du nord.* B

590.24, gunne; Michael Gunn (impresario). McH

590.27, Ring; Wagner's *Ring* (OT). H

Finnegans Wake, Book IV:

594.8–9, Heliotropolis, the castellated; Valhalla, T in Wagner's *Ring.* B

594.12, warful dune's; Valhalla, T in Wagner's *Ring.* B

594.18, Martin 204

594.19, Lugh; Loge (Loki), C in Wagner's *Ring.* B

594.23, peneplain; title C in Fauré's *Penelope.* G, B

594.25, frohn; Froh, C in Wagner's *Das Rheingold.* H, M

594.25–26, Martin 217

595.3–4, nachasach . . . lamusong; Hans Sachs, C in Wagner's *Die Meistersinger.* B. Also prize song, T in Wagner's *Die Meistersinger.* B

595.4, strauches; Strausses (comps.). H

595.32, Fill stap; Falstaff, C in Verdi's *Falstaff,* Nicolai's *Merry Wives of Windsor,* and Holst's *At the Boar's Head.* G, B

596.2, hundering; Hunding, C in Wagner's *Die Walküre.* B, H

596.3, blundering dunderfunder; Donner, C in Wagner's *Das Rheingold.* B

596.4, fincarnate; "Finch'han dal vino" (Champagne Aria), A in Mozart's *Don Giovanni.* H

596.8, aranging; Giannina Arangi-Lombardi (sop.). H

596.13, Martin 217

596.15, Gunnar; Gunther, C in Wagner's *Die Götterdämmerung* and in Reyer's *Sigurd.* B

596.17, benedicted; Benedict (comp.). B

597.14, Martin 217

597.19, Shavarsanjivana; Mozart's *Don Giovanni* (OT). HW

597.26, a coranto of aria, sleeper awakening; "Silentium—wach' auf," A in Wagner's *Die Meistersinger.* B

597.34, fresco; Fiesco, C in Verdi's *Simon Boccanegra.* H

598.6, Alberths; Alberich, C in Wagner's *Ring.* H

598.11, destady. Doom is the faste; Verdi's *La forza del destino* (OT). B

598.18–19, Panpan . . . Tamal; Papageno and Tamino, Cs in Mozart's *Magic Flute.* H, B

598.22, Martin 204

598.33, madamanvantora of Grossguy; "Madamina, il catalogo," A in Mozart's *Don Giovanni.* B

599.5, harruad; Herod, C in Strauss's *Salomé* and in Massenet's *Hérodiade* (OT). G, B

599.23, Tamotimo's; Tamino, C in Mozart's *Magic Flute.* H

600.2, drury world; Drury Lane Theatre, London, site of much Italian opera in the nineteenth century. Mink and B

600.5, Saras; Sarastro, C in Mozart's *Magic Flute.* H

600.11, accorsaired; Verdi's *Il corsaro* (OT). B

600.12, Allbroggt; Alberich, C in Wagner's *Ring.* H

600.20, There an alomdree begins to green; "Connais-tu le pays?" ("Kennst du das Land?"), A in Thomas's *Mignon.* B. Also "Di provenza il mar," A in Verdi's *La traviata.* B

600.28, alfred; Alfred, C in J. Strauss II's *Die Fledermaus.* H. Also Alfredo, C in Verdi's *La traviata.* H

600.31, swan; swan, T in Wagner's *Lohengrin.* B

600.34, communial; Teatro Comunale Giuseppe Verdi, Trieste, where Joyce heard opera. B

601.2, frondest leoves; "Scuoti quella fronda di ciliego" (Flower Duet), A in Puccini's *Madame Butterfly.* H

601.3, kuru salilakriyamu; Enrico Caruso (ten.). B

601.3, salilakriyamu; *Una furtiva lagrima,* A in Donizetti's *L'elisir d'amore.* B

601.3, Pfaf; Fafner, C in Wagner's *Ring.* H. Also "Piff, paff," A in Meyerbeer's *Les Huguenots.* B

601.4, loke, our lake; Loge (Loki), C in Wagner's *Ring.* B, H

601.5, lemanted; Helen Lemmens-Sherrington (sop.). H

601.5, citye of Is; Lalo's *Le Roi d'Ys* (OT). H

601.20, clangalied; Klingsor, C in Wagner's *Parsifal.* H

601.24, Vestity's; "Vesti la giubba," A in Leoncavallo's *I pagliacci.* B

601.28 trema; "Io tremo" (I tremble), T in Mozart's *Don Giovanni.* B

601.29, Prayfulness! Prayfulness; "Gioca, gioca" ("Play, play"—Butterfly's last words to her son—becomes "Pray, pray" with l/r change in Japanese), T in Puccini's *Madame Butterfly.* B

601.34, Wallaby; Erda (= Wala), C in Wagner's *Ring.* H

602.14, solence; "Solenne in quest'ora," A (duet) in Verdi's *La forza del destino.* H

603.15, hydes of march; Walter Hyde (ten.). H

603.34, Martin 221

604.17, waggonwobblers; Wagner (comp.). H

605.4, .12, .17, .19–20, .28, ysland . . . Yssia . . . Ysle . . . Yshgafiena . . . Yshgafiuna . . . ysletshore; Lalo's *Le Roi d'Ys* (OT). B. Also Isolde, C in Wagner's *Tristan und Isolde.* B

606.10, seraphic; Tullio Serafin (cond.). B

606.20, franklings; David Franklin (bass). H

606.26–27, Martin 204

606.32, sukes; Suky Tawdry, C in Gay's *Beggar's Opera.* B

606.33, gamesy . . . flickars; Ladies of the Town (Sw. *flickar* = "girls"), Cs in Gay's *Beggar's Opera.* B

607.25, Hail, regn of durknass; Queen of the Night, C in Mozart's *Magic Flute.* H

607.27, hollow; Valhalla, T in Wagner's *Ring.* B

607.31, Dyk; Ernest Van Dyck (ten.). H

607.31, Isoles, now Eisold; Isolde, C in Wagner's *Tristan und Isolde.* B. See also Martin 204.

608.1, Martin 204

608.8–9, Billyhealy, Ballyhooly and Bullyhowley; Valhalla, T in Wagner's *Ring.* B

608.10, Sigurd Sigerson; Siegfried, C in Wagner's *Siegfried.* H

608.19–20, ching chang; "Chin Chin Chinaman," A in Jones's *Geisha.* HW

609.3, lloydhaired; Edward Lloyd (ten.). B

609.4, gwendolenes; Gilda (g-d-l), C in Verdi's *Rigoletto.* B. Also Chabrier's *Gwendoline* (OT). H

609.5, dolores; "Shade of the Palm" ("Oh, my Dolores"), A in Stuart's *Floradora.* HW

609.11, Rosina; Rosina, C in Rossini's *Barber of Seville.* H

609.12, flowerfruityfrond Sallysill or Sillysall; "Scuoti quella fronda di ciliego" (Flower Duet), A in Puccini's *Madame Butterfly.* B

609.16, Sassondale; Commendatore, statue ("l'uomo di sasso," or "man of stone"), C in Mozart's *Don Giovanni.* H

609.18, Wallhall; Valhalla, T in Wagner's *Ring.* H, M

609.18, Hoojahoo; "Hohoje," A in Wagner's *Flying Dutchman.* H

609.19, the thingaviking; Daland, C in Wagner's *Flying Dutchman.* B

609.20, .32, risen sun . . . Chrystanthemlander (= Japan); Japanese setting, T in Puccini's *Madame Butterfly.* B

609.24, .28, fumusiste . . . Dies; "Un bel dì . . . un fil di fumo," A in Puccini's *Madame Butterfly.* B

609.28, commandant; Commendatore, C in Mozart's *Don Giovanni.* H

609.30–34, Martin 217

609.31, who ever they wolk; "Where'er you walk," A in Handel's *Semele.* B

609.33, .35, Bonzos . . . Banza; "Lo zio Bonzo," C in Puccini's *Madame Butterfly.* B

609.35, Pongo da Banza; Sancho Panza, C in Massenet's and other composers' *Don Quixote.* B

609.36, one piece tall chap; Don Quixote, C in Massenet's and other composers' *Don Quixote.* B

610.4, rearrexes; Arne's *Artaxerxes* (OT). B

610.6, Rhedonum; Radamès, C in Verdi's *Aïda.* H

610.21, Piabelle et Purabelle; "Morir! sì pura e bella!," A in Verdi's *Aïda.* HW

611.5, chinchinjoss; "Chin Chin Chinaman," A in Jones's *Geisha.* HW

611.10: all him monkafellas; Caruso monkey-house incident. See chapter 5. B

612.9, maledictive; "la maledizione," T in Verdi's *Rigoletto.* H

612.14, chowchow; Cio-Cio-San, C in Puccini's *Madame Butterfly.* H

612.15, Ebblybally; Princess Eboli, C in Verdi's *Don Carlos.* H

612.31–32, Martin 217

613.1, Martin 217

613.2, Halled they. Awed; Valhalla, T in Wagner's *Ring.* B

613.12, Martin 217

613.20, skullhullows; Valhalla, T in Wagner's *Ring.* B, M

613.22, theas thighs; Massenet's *Thaïs* (OT; nicknamed "Thighs" in opera world). B

613.22–23, onegugulp; Sigrid Onegin (contra.). H

614.1, bonding; Marianna Bondini (sop.). H

614.28, Mamma Lujah; Mamma Lucia, C in Mascagni's *Cavalleria rusticana.* H. Also "Voi lo sapete, O mamma," A in Mascagni's *Cavalleria rusticana.* H

614.29, Marky; King Mark, C in Wagner's *Tristan und Isolde.* G

614.35, heroticisms; Herod, C in Strauss's *Salomé* and Massenet's *Hérodiade* (OT). G, B

615.3, .31, Margaret . . . margarseen; Marguérite, C in Gounod's *Faust.* H, B. Also C in Berlioz's *La Damnation de Faust* and Meyerbeer's *Les Huguenots.* Also Margherita, C in Boïto's *Mefistofele.* B

615.24, Martin 204

615.27–28, That was the prick . . . dreamland; Brünnhilde sleeping, T in Wagner's *Ring.* B

615.31–32, Thinthin thinthin; "Chin Chin Chinaman," A in Jones's *Geisha.* HW

615.32, commendmant; Commendatore, C in Mozart's *Don Giovanni.* H

616.11, Peris; Jacopo Peri (comp.), composer of first opera, *Dafne*. H

616.16, .25, Wriggling reptiles . . . drag; Fafner the dragon, C in Wagner's *Ring*. B

616.32–33, Martin 221

617.19, Gilly; Dinh Gilly (bar.) and Renée Gilly (sop.). H

618.2–3, handsel for gertles; Hänsel, Gretel, and their mother, Gertrud, Cs in Humperdinck's *Hänsel and Gretel*. H

618.22, Wanterlond Road; Wanderer (Wotan), C in Wagner's *Siegfried*. B

619.5, crossmess parzel; Wagner's *Parsifal* (OT). H

619.16, Alma Luvia; Almaviva, C in Rossini's *Barber of Seville* and in Mozart's *Marriage of Figaro*. H

619.16, Luvia, Pollabella; Polly Peachum and Lucy Lockit, Cs in Gay's *Beggar's Opera*. H

619.20, Lsp; "Lust" (desire; Isolde's and opera's last word), T in Wagner's *Tristan und Isolde*. H

619.23–24, the woods . . . robins; Weber's *Der Freischütz* (OT). H

619.29, Norvena's; Eidé Norena (sop.). H

619.30, silve me solve; Silvio, C in Leoncavallo's *I pagliacci*. B. Also Silva, C in Verdi's *Ernani*. B

619.33, toddy; "Mild und leise" ("Liebestod"), A in Wagner's *Tristan und Isolde*. H

620.5, Alby; Alberich, C in Wagner's *Ring*. H

620.7, wonderdecker; Vanderdecken, C in Wagner's *Flying Dutchman*. H, M

620.25, wanton; Wotan, C in Wagner's *Ring*. H

620.29–30, runaways . . . stray; Manon, C in Puccini's *Manon Lescaut* and in Massenet's *Manon*. B

620.30, gricks; des Grieux, C in Puccini's *Manon Lescaut* and in Massenet's *Manon*. H

620.35–621.3, spun . . . sleeping duties; Brünnhilde, T in Wagner's *Ring*. H

621.1–3, Phoenix . . . flame is . . . lausafire; Siegfried's funeral pyre, T in Wagner's *Die Götterdämmerung*. H. Also Brünnhilde in ring of flame, T in Wagner's *Ring*. H

621.17, Lst; "Lust" (desire; Isolde's and opera's last word), T in Wagner's *Tristan und Isolde*. H

621.18–20, Martin 204

621.20–22, .26, Give me your great bearspaw . . . Mineninecyhandsy . . . burnt in ice; Mimi's death, T in Puccini's *La bohème*. Also "Che gelida manina," A in Puccini's *La bohème*. Also "Là ci darem la mano," A in Mozart's *Don Giovanni*. Also Commendatore's icy grasp, T in Mozart's *Don Giovanni*. H-SG

621.21, fol a miny tiny. Dola. Mineninecyhandsy, in the languo of flows; as sol-me-si-do-la, the opening notes of "O Seligheit, dich fass' ich kaum," A from Weber's *Euryanthe*. B

621.25–26, hugon . . . you'd been burnt; Meyerbeer's *Les Huguenots* (OT). H

621.26, burnt in ice; riddle (ice), T in Puccini's *Turandot*. B

621.35–36, the birds start . . . yours off, high on high; Wotan's ravens fly off at end of opera, T in Wagner's *Ring*. H, M

621.36, treestirm; Tristan, C in Wagner's *Tristan und Isolde*. B, M

622.6, lodge of Fjorn na Galla of the Trumpets; Masonic lodge, T in Mozart's *Magic Flute*. H

622.7, tamming; Tamino, C in Mozart's *Magic Flute*. H

622.11, .13, mile . . . leisure; "Mild und leise" ("Liebestod"), A in Wagner's *Tristan und Isolde*. H

622.24, the moskors . . . ball; Verdi's *Un ballo in maschera* (OT). HW

622.35, Ford; Ford, C in Verdi's *Falstaff*. H. Also C in Nicolai's *Merry Wives of Windsor,* where he is also called "Fluth." B

623.4, .6, Old Lord . . . promnentory; Commendatore, C in Mozart's *Don Giovanni*. H-SG

623.6–7, door always open; open for repentance, T in Mozart's *Don Giovanni*. H

623.8, invoiced him last Eatster; "A cenar teco m'invitasti," A in Mozart's *Don Giovanni*. H-SG

623.11, graciast kertssey; Amelita Galli-Curci (sop.). B

623.22, follied; John McCormack (ten.) under pseudonym of Giovanni Foli. K

623.24, Hnmn hnmn; Humming Chorus, A in Puccini's *Madame Butterfly*. B. Also Papageno's "Hm, hm," T in Mozart's *Magic Flute*. H

623.25, benn, me on you; "Ah si, ben mio," A in Verdi's *Il trovatore*. H

623.27, .30, When the moon of mourning . . . cast ashore; "Casta diva" (aria praying to moon for peace), A in Bellini's *Norma*. B

624.6, Lss; "Lust" (desire; Isolde's and opera's last word), T in Wagner's *Tristan und Isolde*. H

624.10, Jove; Don Giovanni, C in Mozart's *Don Giovanni*. H

624.19–20, One of these fine days; "Un bel dì," A in Puccini's *Madame Butterfly*. H-SG

624.27, Grand; Grane, Brünnhilde's horse, T in Wagner's *Ring*. H

625.2, Jermyn; Germont, C in Verdi's *La traviata*. H

625.3, play; "gioca" (play; Butterfly's last word to her son), T in Puccini's *Madame Butterfly*. H-SG

625.3–4, Pharaops . . . Aeships; Pharohs, Cheops, Egypt, Ts in Verdi's *Aïda*. H

625.7, villities, valleties; Valhalla, T in Wagner's *Ring*. B

625.10, parish pomp's a great warrent; "Parigi, o cara," A (duet) in Verdi's *La traviata*. H

625.14, he'll come some morrow; "con onor muore chi non può serbar vita con onore" (he who cannot live with honor can die with honor), T in Puccini's *Madame Butterfly*. H-SG. Also "Un bel dì," A in Puccini's *Madame Butterfly*. B

625.20, .24, parshes . . . cara; "Parigi, o cara," A (duet) in Verdi's *La traviata*. H

625.25, abandoned; "Sola, perduta, abbandonata," A in Puccini's *Manon Lescaut*. H

625.30–31, To hide away the tear, the parted; "Water parted from the sea," A in Arne's *Artaxerxes*. B

625.35, Martin 217

626.1, .3, Annamores . . . adamant evar; Amneris, Radamès, Aïda, Cs in Verdi's *Aïda*. H

626.26, pray; "Gioca, gioca" ("Play, play"—Butterfly's last words to her son—becomes "Pray, pray" with l/r change in Japanese), T in Puccini's *Madame Butterfly*. H-SG. Also "preghera" (pray; Gilda's last word), T in Verdi's *Rigoletto*. H-SG

626.28, Thorror; Kerstin Thorborg (mezzo-sop.). B. Also "terror," Don Giovanni's last word. B

626.29, joy; "gioia," Violetta's last word, T in Verdi's *La traviata*. H-SG

627.1, sonhusband; incest theme, T in Charpentier's and other composers' *Medea*. (T). B

627.7–9, For she'll . . . scarce a cloud; "O patria mia . . . O cieli azzurri," A in Verdi's *Aïda*. B

627.21–23, I thought you . . . bumpkin; Cinderella story, T in Rossini's *La cenerentola*. B

627.31, stormies. Ho hang! Hang ho; Valkyries, T in Wagner's *Die Walküre*. H. Also "Heiaho!" (Brünnhilde's last word), T in Wagner's *Die Götterdämmerung*. H-SG, M

627.35, They'll never see; "Siegfried! Sieh!" (Brünnhilde's penultimate line), T in Wagner's *Die Götterdämmerung*. H-SG

628.1–2, cold father, my cold; Commendatore, statue ("l'uomo di sasso," or "man of stone"), C in Mozart's *Don Giovanni*. H

628.4, seasilt saltsick; "Siegfried! Sieh!" (Brünnhilde's penultimate line), T in Wagner's *Die Götterdämmerung*. H-SG

628.5, .8, therrble . . . taddy, like you; "O terra addio," A in Verdi's *Aïda.* H

628.5, therrble; "horreur," Marguérite's last word, T in Gounod's *Faust.* H-SG. Also "terror," last word and T in Mozart's *Don Giovanni.* H-SG

628.6, moremens more; Otello, C in Verdi's *Otello.* H-SG

628.6, Avelaval; "Ave Maria," A by Desdemona near end of Verdi's *Otello.* H-SG

628.7–8, Lff! . . . taddy; "Mild und leise" ("Liebestod"), A ending Wagner's *Tristan und Isolde.* H-SG

628.9–10, toy fair . . . Arkangels; *Teufel* (devil) of hell and angels who carry Marguérite to heaven, T in Gounod's *Faust.* H-SG

628.9–14, If I seen him bearing down on me now under whitespread wings like he'd come from Arkangels, I sink I'd lie down . . . mememormee; "Remember me!" (T) from "When I am laid in earth," A in Purcell's *Dido and Aeneas,* as well as chorus from same opera, "With drooping wings, ye cupids, come." H-SG, B

628.10–11, I sink I'd die down over his feet; "O sink hernieder," A in Wagner's *Tristan und Isolde.* H-SG

628.10–11, sink . . . down . . . washup; "versinken" (sink; Isolde speaking at end of opera), T in Wagner's *Tristan und Isolde.* H-SG. Also "Silentium—wach' auf," A (chorus) in Wagner's *Die Meistersinger.* H, M

628.14–15, Bussoftlhee, mememormee! . . . Lps; "Then You'll Remember Me," A in Balfe's *Bohemian Girl,* beginning "When other lips." HW

628.15, A way a; "Weia! Waga! . . . Wagalaweia!" (Rhine Maidens at beginning of opera), A in Wagner's *Das Rheingold.* H-SG, M

7

Alphabetical List of Composers (and Their Operatic Works), Librettists, Designers, Critics, and Conductors in *Finnegans Wake*

All opera and light opera allusions are listed with page/line number from *Finnegans Wake*.

Alphabetizing follows the conventions of musicology: Opera titles are alphabetized without regard to initial articles—a, das, der, die, gli, i, il, l', la, le, les, lo, the—but with attention to personal titles (e.g., *Les Huguenots* under *H, Prince Igor* under *P*).

Arias are alphabetized taking initial articles into consideration (e.g., "Un bel di" under *U*).

Characters with complete names have those names inverted. Characters with only one name and a title (Captain, Comte, Count, Don, Donna, Doctor, Fra, Prince, Princess, Reine, Roi are alphabetized as if inverted, by name rather than title (e.g., Don Giovanni under *G*).

The allusions are alphabetically arranged in the following format:

Composer with dates: any allusions to composer by name
> *Opera name* (date of opera): any allusions to opera by name
> > A Arias or distinctive vocal portions from that opera alluded to in *FW*
> > C Characters from that opera
> > T Themes, leitmotifs, fragments of libretto from that opera

For example:

Beethoven, Ludwig van (1770–1827): 360.8
> *Fidelio* (1805): 6.26; 58.11; 369.17; 466.26
> > A "Komm', Hoffnung, lass den letzten Stern," (act 1): 222.10–11
> > "Mir ist so wunderbar" (act 1 quartet): 446.2
> > C Don Fernando: 457.3
> > Fidelio: 80.21; 162.23

Florestan: 246.16, .18
Leonore: 246.16, .19; 344.4
Marzelline: 176.22; 456.32
Pizarro: 287.31
Rocco: 415.10
T "Gott! Welch Dunkel hier": 466.30
prison in *Fidelio* + Marzelline + Marshalsea Prison: 176.22

This indicates that Beethoven as composer is mentioned on line 8 of p. 360 of
FW; that *Fidelio* as an opera title is alluded to four times; that two arias and
seven characters from the opera are alluded to; and finally, that a line from the
libretto is quoted and the opera's prison and one character are merged in an
allusion to Marshalsea Prison.

Adam, Adolphe (1803–56)
 Le Postillon de Longjumeau (1836): 453.36
 C Chappelou as St. Phar: 452.20
Antheil, George (1900–59): 360.34
Appia, Adolphe (1862–1928), designer: 297.25; 548.6
Arditi, Luigi (1822–1903), cond.
 A "The Stirrup Cup" (song): 40.1–2
Arne, Thomas (1710–78)
 Artaxerxes (1762): 337.36; 610.4
 A "Water parted from the sea": 147.30; 371.6–9, .19–20, 31–32; 372.26–
  27; 373.10–11; 390.22, .28–30, .33; 541.32–33; 625.30–31
Auber, Daniel François Esprit (1782–1871): 466.20
 Fra Diavolo (1830): 466.19–20, .24, .27; 553.13
 C Fra Diavolo: 205.10

Balfe, Michael (1808–70), sang Papageno in first performance of *The Magic
 Flute* in English: 199.29
 The Armourer of Nantes (1863): 447.6
 Bianca (1860): 238.23; 240.18
 The Bohemian Girl (1843 in English; produced in Italian in London in 1858
  as *La zingara*): 32.35; 68.9; 170.10; 246.18; 404.26
 A "The heart bowed down" (act 2) 199.27–28; 457.34–35
  "I dreamt that I dwelt in marble halls" (act 2): 49.9; 64.4–5; 199.9–10;
   264.F2; 449.18–19; 549.15
  "The Secret of My Birth" (act 2): 38.34

"Then You'll Remember Me" ("When other lips," act 3): 88.30; 135.32–33; 170.10; 235.10–11; 245.5–6; 276.F6; 360.24; 460.34; 461.26; 508.5; 628.14–15

  C Arline: 32.35; 164.31

      Florestein: 246.16, .18

      Thaddeus: 246.16, .19; 456.30

The Bondman (1846): 435.22

The Enchantress (1845): 237.11

Satanella (1858): 232.23

The Siege of Rochelle (1835): 73.23–24

  A "My love and cottage near Rochelle": 179.32; 466.25–26

Bamboschek, Giuseppe (1890–1969). Born in Trieste, graduated from Trieste Conservatory 1907; went to the United States as accompanist in 1913 and joined the Metropolitan Opera staff in 1919. He also conducted for radio and movies after 1929 and directed opera recordings made by the Victor Symphony Orchestra: 98.13; 527.8

Bartlett, Thomas A. See Stuart, Leslie.

Beethoven, Ludwig van (1770–1827): 360.8

Fidelio (1805): 6.26; 58.11; 369.17; 466.26

  A "Komm', Hoffnung, lass den letzten Stern" (act 1): 222.10–11

      "Mir ist so wunderbar" (quartet in canon form, act 1): 446.2

  C Don Fernando: 457.3

      Fidelio: 80.21; 162.23

      Florestan: 246.16, .18

      Leonore: 246.16, .19; 344.4

      Marzelline: 176.22; 456.32

      Pizarro: 287.31

      Rocco: 415.10

  T "Gott! Welch Dunkel hier" (act 2, sc. 1, opening words): 466.30

      prison in *Fidelio* + Marzelline + Marshalsea Prison: 176.22

Bellezza, Vincenzo (1888–64), cond.: 211.14

Bellini, Vincenzo (1801–35): 6.22; 309.19; 360.7; 432.21; 576.6

Norma (1831): 117.26–27; 189.25; 264.29; 345.21; 510.20; 514.2

  A "Casta diva" (act 1): 147.24; 202.8; 350.17; 560.2; 623.27, .30

  C Norma, druid priestess: 360.25

      Oroveso: 234.4–5; 356.6; 414.27

Il pirata (1827): 463.21

  C Elvino: 215.22

      Imogene: 251.17

Bizet, Georges (1838–75): 40.7; 234.2

   Carmen (1873–74; prod. 1875): 239.24; 360.13; 448.12; 526.28

   A "Chanson Bohème" ("Les tringles des sistres tintaient," act 2): 235.32

      "Parle-moi de ma mère" (duet, act 1): 196.1–3; 410.23

      "Votre toast, je peux vous le rendre" (Toreador's Song, act 2): 60.31

   C Escamillo: 350.21; 585.24

      Don José: 472.15

      Micaëla: 153.32

   T Carmen's dance (act 1): 235.35

   Djamileh (1871, 1872)

   C Djamileh: 537.24

   Le Docteur Miracle (1856): 365.1; 384.10; 427.23; 440.2; 467.19; 579.14

   Ivan IV (1862–63; this opera was first staged in 1946; Joyce may have heard
      of it, but he never saw it produced)

   C Ivan: 138.17

   La Jolie Fille de Perth (*The Fair Maid of Perth* 1866; prod. 1867): 186.36

   The Pearl Fishers (1863)

   C Leïla: 525.13–16

      Nadir: 297.12; 525.13–16

Blech, Leo (1871–1958), cond.: 563.30

Boïeldieu, Adrien (1775–1834): 322.2

Boïto, Arrigo (1842–1918; b. Enrico); comp. and librettist (for Verdi); librettos sometimes written under name of "Tobia Gorrio": 165.29; 211.12;
   219.11; 225.08; 561.4

   Mefistofele (1868): 441.11–12

   C Faust: 74.9; 83.29; 160.29; 252.2; 288.9; 292.22; 311.31; 356.1; 557.10

      Margherita: 146.12; 164.14, .19–20; 166.30; 247.21; 249.12; 281.6,
       .14; 406.7–8; 458.10; 460.26; 495.30; 496.23; 615.3, .31

   Nerone (1924, unfinished): 177.14

Borodin, Alexander (1833–87)

   Prince Igor (completed by Rimsky-Korsakov and Glazunov; prod. 1890):
      353.19

   C Konchak: 424.9–10

Boughton, Rutland (1878–1960): 569.33

   The Immortal Hour (prod. privately 1914; London 1922): 580.13–15

   A "How beautiful they are, the lordly ones": 11.29–31

   C Dalua, lord of shadow (Shadow God): 495.24; 518.3–4, .6, .10

      Lord of the Hidden Way: 499.15

   T fairy-land: 78.13

Bülow, Hans von (1830–94), cond.: 150.15; 151.11, .32–33; as Wagner's baton: 418.34–419.8

Busoni, Ferruccio (1866–1924), and Philipp Jarnach
    Arlecchino (1917, Zurich, with his *Turandot,* when JJ was in Zurich)
    C Leandro: 203.13
    Doktor Faust (Busoni was working on this in Zurich, 1917; it was completed by Jarnach after Busoni's death): 74.9; 83.29; 160.29; 252.2; 288.9; 292.22; 311.31; 356.1; 557.10
    C Mephistopheles: 225.11; 441.11–12
        Duchess of Parma: 223.7; 461.17–18
    Turandot (1917, Stadttheater, Zurich, with *Arlecchino*); see also Puccini's *Turandot.*
    C Turandot: 236.35–36

Caccini, Francesca (1587–ca. 1640), daughter of Giulio; singer, first woman opera comp., collaborator with Michaelangelo. Her *La liberazione di Ruggiero* of 1625 was first It. opera performed outside Italy: 261.12; 511.14

Caccini, Giulio (ca. 1545–1618), rival of Jacopo Peri, q.v.: 261.12; 511.14

Carte, Richard D'Oyly (impresario): 279.F1.21–22; 574.1

Castrucci, Pietro (1679–1752), violist and violinist for Handel; came to Dublin in 1715 as leader of Handel's orchestra and died there: 533.16

Catalani, Alfredo (1854–93): 266.24–25
    Loreley (1890; revision of *Elda,* 1876, prod. 1880): 201.35
    La Wally (1852): 211.11; 333.9

Chabrier, (Alexis-) Emmanuel (1841–94), in the group of composers called *Le petit Bayreuth*
    Gwendoline (1886): 433.6; 609.4

Charpentier, Gustave (1860–1956)
    Louise (1900): 223.2
    C Louise: 147.12; 223.2

Charpentier et al.
    Medea
    C Medea: 348.7
    T incest theme: 627.1

Cilea, Francesco (1866–1950): 207.12
    L'arlesiana (1897)
    A "È la solita storia" (act 2): 117.11; 454.18–19

Cocteau, Jean (1889–1963). See Stravinsky.

Cornelius, Peter (1824–74), part of Liszt's circle at Weimar and, after 1861, of

Wagner's at Bayreuth. A Danish tenor (1865–1934) bore the same name: 98.9
Costa, Sir Michael (1808–84), cond. and director of Royal Italian Opera, Covent Garden, 1871–79: 172.22; 464.30
Coward, Noel (1899–1973)
   Bitter Sweet (1929): 170.7
Crotty, Leslie (1853–1903), impresario and singer with Carl Rosa Opera Company; husband of soprano Georgina Burns: 141.14

Daddi, João Guilherme: 431.32; 439.20; 446.13
da Ponte, Lorenzo (1749–1838; b. Emanuele Conegliano), librettist for Mozart and comp. in his own right: 178.24; 410.14; 493.29; 553.21; 578.25; 580.1
Debussy, Claude (1862–1918): 40.7; 234.3; 445.19
   Pelléas et Mélisande (1902; Debussy's only opera): 430.22; 547.2; 555.11
   C   Arkel: 186.11
        Golaud (Golo): 495.16
        Mélisande: 212.9; 238.34; 414.30; 477.30
        Pelléas: 380.25; 495.15; 527.1
   T   hair of Mélisande: 495.19
        Mélisande's reflection in fountain: 526.30–32
Delibes, Léo (1836–91)
   Lakmé (1883): 245.27
   A   "Où va la jeune Hindoue" (Bell Song): 461.32
Delius, Frederick (1862–1934)
   Irmelin (1890–92; prod. 1953): 345.1
de Mellos (?), established opera on Fishamble Street, Dublin, ca. 1715: 57.2; 422.26; 437.33; 533.16–17
de Sabata, Victor (1892–1967), cond.: 229.19
d'Indy, Vincent. See Indy.
Donizetti, Gaetano (1797–1848): 32.8
   Anna Bolena (1830)
   C   Bolena, Anna: 117.16; 313.29; 333.18; 406.13, .27; 445.24; 567.13, .15; 575.6–7, .11; 576.6
   Betly (1836): 246.33
   C   Max: 248.34
   L'elisir d'amore (1832): 133.19; 237.9
   A   "Quanto è bella" (act 1): 224.28
        "Udite, udite, o rustici" (act 1): 504.20
        "Una furtiva lagrima" (act 2): 432.25; 601.3

German, Edward (1862–1936), and Arthur Sullivan (1842–1900)

 The Emerald Isle, or The Caves of Carrig-Cleena (1901): 62.11–12; 214.21

Gilbert, W. S. (1836–1911). See *Robert le diable* under Meyerbeer.

Gilbert, W. S. (1836–1911), and Arthur Sullivan (1842–1900). See also Sullivan, Arthur

 The Gondoliers (1889): 317.15

 A "Right Down Regular Royal Queen" (act 1): 19.4–5; 108.5–6; 381.10–11; 424.35–36; 452.26

  "Take a pair of sparkling eyes" (act 2): 75.17; 396.11; 451.24–25; 462.11

  "When a man marries": 6.11

 C Casilda: 228.26

  Gianetta: 243.15

  Luiz, Marco, and Giuseppe: 243.35; 246.17

  Tessa: 243.34

  Vittoria, Giulia, and Fiametta: 242.12, .21, .34

 H.M.S. Pinafore: or, The Lass That Loved a Sailor (1878): 226.25; 297.28–29; 440.30; 453.3; 584.16

 C Buttercup: 21.33; 145.14; 321.16; 428.27; 429.19; 433.25; 561.12

  Captain Corcoran: 504.20

  Josephine: 243.35; 246.17

 Iolanthe (1882): 11.8–9

 A "Lord Chancellor's Song" ("When you're lying awake"): 180.17–30

 The Mikado (1885): 233.27

 A "Willow, Tit-Willow, Tit-Willow" (act 2): 360.2–3

 C Koko, Lord High Executioner: 36.20; 236.4, .5–6

  Nanki-Pooh: 244.20

  Pitty Sing: 242.30; 244.20

  Pooh-Bah: 224.28

 T language: 244.18–20

  town of Titipu: 225.1

 Patience (1881): 108.8–10; 253.20

 A "If you're anxious for to shine in the high aesthetic line" ("a most particularly pure young man this pure young man must be," act 1): 237.25

  "Love that no wrong can cure, Love that is always new" (act 2, no. 5): 564.4

  "Turn, turn in this direction" (act 2, no. 3): 194.4–9

 C Bunthorne, Reginald: 253.11; 254.35–36; 342.33

  Ella: 237.26

  Grosvenor, Archibald: 219.9; 230.34; 254.11

Goossens, Eugene II (1867–1958), cond. with Carl Rosa Opera Company and for the brief life of the Burns-Crotty company: 253.23–24

Goossens, Aynsley Eugene (1893–1962), cond. and comp. associated with Sir Thomas Beecham, who set several of Joyce's poems to music; grandson also of opera singer Aynsley Cook, who sang with Carl Rosa Opera Company: 253.23–24

Gounod, Charles (1818–93): 177.18

 Faust (1859): 74.9; 83.29; 160.29; 252.2; 288.9; 292.22; 311.31; 356.1; 412.9; 557.10

 A Duet: 200.9

  "Faites-lui mes aveux" (Flower Song, act 3): 23.36; 249.13

  Jewel Song ("Ah, je ris," act 2): 225.21–22, .24, .26; 432.4; 441.19; 461.10; 493.28

  "Salut, demeure, chaste et pure" (act 2): 454.16–18

  "Veau d'or" (act 2): 406.18; 438.2; 556.33

 C Faust: 83.29; 160.29; 412.9

  Marguérite: 146.12; 164.14, .19–20; 166.30; 247.21; 249.12; 281.6, .14; 406.7–8; 458.10; 460.26; 495.30; 496.23; 615.3, .31

  Méphistophélès: 225.11; 441.11–12

  Valentin: 249.4; 289.28; 439.17; 458.2

 T angels: 628.10

  devil: 628.9

  Walpurgis Nacht: 229.16

 Mireille (1864): 327.30

 C Mireille: 527.28

 Polyeucte (1878)

 A "A Vesta, portez vos offrandes" (act 1): 194.4–9

 Roméo et Juliette (1867): 350.22; 391.21

 A "Ah! leve-toi soleil!" (act 2): 549.1

  Duet (acts 2 and 4): 200.9

 C Roméo: 463.8; 481.16

  Juliette: 148.13

Gruenberg, Louis (1884–1964)

 The Emperor Jones (1933): 431.12–13

Gui, Vittorio (1885–1975), cond. associated with revival of bel canto; debuted Rome 1907 with *La Gioconda* (JJ was in Rome three months in 1907): 332.18; 360.26–27

Gunn, Michael (1840–1901), Dublin impresario: 220.24; 263.18; 531.5; 590.24

Gye, Frederick (1809–78), London impresario: 332.18; 360.26–27

Indy, Vincent d' (1851–1931): 92.20
Isola (?), codirector of Opéra-Comique, Paris, 1914–25: 209.24; 289.28; 384.31
Isola, Gaetano (1754–1813), It. comp.: 209.24; 289.28; 384.31

Janáček, Leoš (1854–1928): 457.36
    Jenůfa (1904): 233.21
    From the House of the Dead (1930): 407.35–36
Jones, Sidney (1861–1946)
    The Geisha (1896): 464.32
    A   "Chin Chin Chinaman" (act 2): 34.17; 57.3–4; 58.13; 75.8; 82.12;
            106.19; 131.34; 191.36; 272.30; 304.F2; 336.20; 465.28; 484.26–
            27; 485.28, .36; 608.19–20; 611.5; 615.31–32
        "Jewel of Asia" (act 2): 105.20
    C   Mimosa-san: 247.34, .36; 267.2; 449.10
Jouy, Etienne (1764–1846): 430.10
Julienn, Louis (1812–60), Fr. comp. and cond.; conducted in London after
    1840, attempted to organize English opera company at Drury Lane, brought
    Hector Berlioz to England as conductor, and eventually went mad: 45.25–
    26; 350.22

Korngold, Erich Wolfgang (1897–1957): 75.10

Lalo, Edouard (1823–92): 450.16
    Le Roi d'Ys (1888): 75.11; 364.27; 393.30; 527.1; 570.12; 580.18; 601.5;
            605.4–28
Lazzari, Sylvio (1857–1944), Aus.-Fr. comp. who was JJ's contemporary in Paris:
    429.6
Lecocq, Charles (1832–1918): 214.19–23
    Le Docteur Miracle (1857): 365.1; 384.10; 427.23; 440.2; 467.19; 579.14
    La Fille de Madame Angot (1872): 214.19–23
    Giroflé, Girofla (1874): 129.30
Lehár, Franz (1870–1948)
    The Land of Smiles (*Das Land des Lächelns,* 1929)
    A   "Yours is my heart alone" ("Dein is mein ganzes Herz," act 2): 412.5–
            6; 418.1
    The Merry Widow (*Die Lustige Witwe,* 1905): 457.36; 577.22
    A   Laughing Aria: 461.32
    C   Popov: 461.15

Leoncavallo, Ruggiero (1857–1919): 368.33

   I pagliacci (1892): 380.25; 495.15; 555.11

     A "Si può?" (prologue, starting on notes G, B, D): 422.22; 433.4; 437.7

       "Vesti la giubba" (act 1): 66.30; 149.26; 150.28; 338.11, .17, .21;

         447.13, .33; 466.18; 601.24

     C Canio: 225.16; 233.13–14; 338.12

       Nedda: 225.16; 325.33

       Pagliaccio: 171.15; 338.12

       Silvio: 225.16; 564.25; 619.30

       Tonio: 323.32; 564.23

     T harlequin: 221.25

   Zàzà (1900): 248.2

     C Zàzà: 68.27

   I zingari (1912): 68.9

Leoni, Michael (1770–71; b. Meyer Lyon), English male alto, sang in Dublin; part owner of a theater in Capel St. with Tommaso Giordani and of English Opera Company in Dublin, ca. 1760–96; teacher of tenor John Braham: 246.16. See also the aria "Ecco il leone" under Verdi's *Otello.*

Leroux, Xavier (1863–1919)

   La Reine Fiammette (1903)

     C Violette: 223.7

Levi, Hermann (1839–1900), first cond. of *Parsifal* at Bayreuth: 150.15; 151.32–33

Liszt, Franz (1811–86), cond. and pianist, comp. of a single opera; greatest claim to opera fame as father-in-law of Richard Wagner: 238.23; 508.34

Lortzing, Albert (1801–51): 534.31

   Cazanova (1841): 230.15

     A Nun's Chorus: 233.25; 457.29

   Der Wildschütz (1842)

     C Baculus: 365.6

   Zar und Zimmermann (1837): 349.4

     A "O sancta justitia" (act 1): 154.28

Luening, Otto (1900–), Am. comp., member of English Players in Zurich

   Evangeline (comp. 1930–32; excerpts performed in Chicago, 29 Dec. 1932): 223.19

Lully, Jean-Baptiste (1632–87)

   Amadis (1684)

     C Amadis: 86.18

MacCunn, Hamish (1868–1916), comp. and cond. of first English-language
Tristan: 376.2

Mackenzie, Alexander C. (1847–1935)
Colomba (1883): 129.31; 358.12, 361.1; 527.26

Mahler, Gustav (1860–1911): 510.15

Manners, Charles (1857–1935; b. Southcote Mansergh), singer and impresario: 102.15

Mapleson, James (1830–1901), "Colonel Mapleson," impresario of Royal Italian Opera in London, which made annual Dublin "seasons" of several weeks to a month in length: 155.25

Marinuzzi, Gino (1882–1945): 573.1

Mascagni, Pietro (1863–1945)
L'amico Fritz (1891): 420.9
A   "O amore, o bella luce del core" (act 3): 582.29–31
Cavalleria rusticana (1890, 1 act): 162.22; 234.3; 370.7; 465.16; 564.26
A   "Gli aranci olezzano sui verdi margini" (opening chorus): 226.31
"Mamma, quel vino è generoso" (just prior to duel): 60.31; 265.23, .28; 362.16, .19; 406.22–23
"Siciliana" (sc. 1): 179.34–35; 354.14
"Viva il vino" (brindisi, after intermezzo): 382.2; 437.11; 462.2–3
"Voi lo sapete, O mamma" (early in opening scene): 60.31; 614.28
C   Alfio: 568.32
Lola: 244.4, .22; 250.19, .21; 254.23; 434.23; 525.14
Mamma Lucia: 226.14–15; 239.34; 614.28
Santuzza: 243.34; 247.20; 434.23; 455.36
Turiddu: 60.31; 580.17
T   Alfio stabs Turiddu: 180.12
Turiddu begins by singing behind curtain: 467.6–7
Iris (1898): 238.32
C   Iris: 30.1; 285.27; 493.28; 528.23
Isabeau (1911): 146.17; 527.29–30

Massenet, Jules (1842–1912): 219.5; 294.25
Amadis (1895; prod. 1922 in Monte Carlo): 86.18
Le Cid (1885)
A   "O souverain, ô juge" (act 2): 243.10; 455.7
Cléopâtre (1914)
C   Cléopâtre: 104.20; 166.34; 508.23
Grisélidis (1901): 170.34

Don Quixote (some sixty others also wrote an opera of this title): 234.4; 405.6–7; 459.34; 477.22; 482.14; 585.8

C   Dulcinea: 234.23

Panza, Sancho: 234.6; 464.11; 609.35

Don Quixote: 360.36; 609.36

Hérodiade (1881)

C   Herod: 13.20; 127.11; 159.15; 275.F5; 423.8; 520.5; 527.3; 536.35; 599.5; 614.35

Manon (1884): 203.21

A   "En fermant les yeux" (act 2): 424.4–5

C   des Grieux: 11.35; 620.30

Manon (prostitute): 203.21; 260.17; 433.4; 620.29–30

Thaïs (1894): 177.25; 613.22

Werther (1892): 28.31; 241.8

A   "Des cris joyeuse": 395.32

"Pourquoi me réveiller" (Werther's song from Ossian, act 3; JJ sang this): 117.18; 385.26–27, .36

C   Charlotte: 51.35; 241.33; 504.28

Méhuel, Etienne-Nicolas (1763–1817)

Joseph (1807)

A   "Champs paternels": 478.21, .28, .34

Mendelssohn, Felix (1809–47)

Lorelei (unfin., 1847): 201.35

Mercadante, Saverio (1795–1870): 327.18; 360.8

I brigante (1836)

C   Amelia: 355.22; 410.23

Messager, André (1853–1929): 405.7

Véronique (1898): 204.30

C   Véronique (Hélène de Solanges): 458.14

Meyerbeer, Giacomo (1791–1864): 243.26; 360.7; 373.5; 484.15; 577.14

L'Africaine (1865)

A   "O paradiso" (act 4): 69.9–10; 230.6, .13; 418.1; 435.18

C   Selika: 28.26; 212.6

Vasco da Gama: 229.22; 230.6, .13

Das Brandenburger Tor (*Singspiel,* 1814): 246.6

Dinorah, or *Le Pardon de Ploërmel* (1859): 243.25

A   "Ombre légère qui suis mes pas" (Shadow Song, act 2): 495.24

C   Hoël: 143.15

"Là ci darem la mano" (act 1, sc. 3, duet): 621.20–22, .26
"Madamina, il catalogo" (act 1, sc. 2): 21.6; 117.26–27; 183.25–28;
    230.10; 409.12–13; 440.4; 451.3; 598.33
"Notte e giorno faticar" (act 1, sc. 1): 409.16
"O statua gentilissima" (act 2, sc. 2): 470.24–25; 471.28
"Questo è il fin" (finale): 221.4–5
"Vedrai, carino" (act 2): 7.3; 426.30
C Commendatore: 5.31; 93.6; 162.6; 432.26–27; 609.28; 615.32; 623.4,
    .6
    Commendatore's statue—l'uomo di sasso, or man of stone: 5.31; 471.28;
      609.16; 628.1–2
    Elvira: 565.31
    Don Giovanni: 455.11; 461.31, .33; 470.33; 624.10
    Leporello: 172.23; 338.20; 440.17; 462.24–25; 577.34
    Don Ottavio: 467.8; 544.21
T Commendatore's icy grasp: 621.20–22, .26
    terror—Don Giovanni's last word: 626.28; 628.5
    Io tremo (I tremble): 601.28
    open for repentance: 623.6–7
The Magic Flute (1791): 43.31–32; 200.35; 444.8; 451.8; 513.8; 514.2, .6;
    526.21–22; 536.21–22; 565.21, .29; 590.2
A "Der Hölle Rache" (act 2): 222.10–11
    "In diesen heiligen Hallen" (act 2, sc. 2): 553.22
    "O, Isis and Osiris" (act 3, sc. 4): 470.13, 15–20; 493.28
    Papageno/Papagena—*pianissimo* duet: 576.6–8
    "Wie, wie, wie" (quintet, act 5): 360.34
C Monostatos the Moor: 222.18
    Pamina: 64.25; 237.15; 253.24; 564.21; 569.29
    Papagena: 332.5; 463.11; 564.21
    Papageno: 65.8; 172.1–2; 332.5; 379.20; 445.17; 463.11; 484.35;
      513.20; 564.21; 565.20, .24; 569.25; 598.18–19
    Queen of the Night: 64.16, .19–20; 147.13; 222.18; 223.24; 229.16;
      241.22; 360.12–13; 497.32; 567.13–15; 607.25
    Sarastro: 223.21; 254.12; 310.8; 571.24; 600.5
    Tamino: 241.25; 404.26; 442.3; 598.18–19; 599.23; 622.7
T bells and chimes: 360.11–12; 569.4–5, .11–12
    "Hm, hm, hm" (Papageno in quintet, act 1, sc. 1): 623.24
    Masonic lodge: 622.6
    Papageno's pipes: 220.26; 237.15

The Marriage of Figaro (1786): 117.16; 421.22

A   "Cinque—dieci—venti—trenta—trenta sei—quaranta tre" (act 1, sc. 1):
403.2, .4

"Dove sono i bei momenti" (act 3): 521.15, .17

"Pian, pianin" (act 4 finale): 200.35

"Sull'aria" (Letter Duet, act 3): 346.10

"Voi, che sapete" (act 2): 450.12, .24

C   Almaviva: 244.14–15; 619.16

Bartolo: 21.35; 246.27; 247.10; 372.7; 527.25

Don Basilio: 25.9; 463.22

Cherubino: 65.28; 177.14; 258.34; 469.34–35

Figaro: 420.9–10; 421.31; 440.17; 463.5

Mussorgsky, Modest (1839–81)

Khovanshchina (1886): 531.36

C   Dosifey or Dositheus: 470.13

Sorochintsi Fair (1874–81): 451.8

Nada, Jean, French professor at Zurich Conservatory, 1917, teacher of Joyce's
friend Otto Luening; principal flutist in Stadttheater orchestra: 470.1; 521.6

Nicolai, Otto (1810–49)

The Merry Wives of Windsor (1849): 227.1–2

C   Falstaff: 6.22; 7.13; 35.27; 63.29; 96.11; 161.16; 320.20–23; 366.30;
370.13; 379.12, .18; 405.13; 406.18; 434.24; 567.10; 569.1–2;
595.32

Ford (Fluth): 622.35

Jungfer Anna Page: 289.25; 513.27; 553.1–2

Nikisch, Arthur (1855–1922), conducted Wagner in Zurich during Joyce's stay
there, 1915–1920; as student in 1872 played in first violin section under
Wagner's direction at laying of cornerstone for Bayreuth Festival Theater.
Baker's Biographical Dictionary of Musicians calls Nikisch the first of his pro-
fession to become "the conductor as hero." Appeared also in Boston, Leipzig,
London, and Budapest: 11.4; 50.35; 203.21; 365.28; 422.33

O'Dwyer, Robert (1862–1949): 446.31

Offenbach, Jacques (1819–80): 456.33

La Grande-Duchesse de Gérolstein (1867)

A   "Dites-lui, qu'on l'a remarqué distingué" (act 2): 564.4

C   Wanda: 147.14; 199.12

Orfée aux enfers (1858)

C   Orfée: 414.27, .35; 463.3
La Périchole (1868): 254.14; 369.19
A   "Que veulent dire ces colères" (act 2): 564.4
Tales of Hoffmann (1881): 359.24–25
C   Coppelius: 313.24; 363.20; 368.33; 446.24
     Dapertutto: 289.22–23; 464.24
     Giuletta: 363.20
     Doctor Miracle: 365.1; 384.10; 427.23; 440.2; 467.19; 579.14
     Hoffman and Stella: 59.1–2
     Lindorf: 469.21
     Spalanzani: 350.27, .30
T   tall stories: 427.23
Orff, Carl (1895–1982): 463.3

Paderewski, Ignacy Jan (1860–1941)
     Manru (1901): 169.18
Palmer, Geoffrey Molyneux (1882–1961): 539.8; 569.10
     Sruth na maoile: 428.21
Pergolesi, Giovanni Batista (1710–36): 360.7
     La serva padronna (intermezzo, 1733): 495.35–36
Peri, Jacopo (1561–1633): 11.9; 616.11
     Dafne (the first opera, 1597): 406.25
Piccinni, Niccolò (1728–1800): 248.5
Ponchielli, Amilcare (1834–86): 257.23
     La gioconda (1876)
A   "Suicidio!" (act 4): 462.36
C   Barnaba: 237.15; 572.34
     La Cieca: 245.21
     I promessi sposi (1856)
C   Lucia: 178.9; 239.34; 253.32; 327.5
Porpora, Nicola (1686–1768): 200.4; 351.13
Puccini, Giacomo (1858–1924): 231.21; 248.5; 376.1; 412.8; 461.13
     La bohème (1896): 170.10; 404.26
A   "Addio senza rancor" (act 3): 446.13
     "Che gelida manina" (act 1, echoed later): 621.20–22, .26
     "Mi chiamano Mimi" (My name is Lucia, but they call me Mimi, act
         1): 247.36; 249.29; 253.28, .32
     "Nei cieli bigi guardo fumar" (act 1): 6.3; 14.34–35
C   Colline: 12.21; 153.4; 224.11; 252.15

Manon Lescaut (1893): 203.21; 433.4
A   "Sola, perduta, abbandonata" (act 4): 625.25
C   des Grieux: 11.35; 620.30
    Manon (prostitute): 203.21; 260.17; 433.4; 620.29–30
    Ravoir, Geronte de: 115.12; 573.21
La rondine (1917): 239.27, .36; 359.28–29
Suor Angelica (1918): 528.16–17
C   Angelica: 233.5; 239.29; 252.31; 346.5
T   taking the veil: 556.3, .5
Il tabarro (1918): 360.26
C   Michele: 199.28
Tosca (1900): 25.26; 106.5; 427.22; 459.6
A   "E lucevan le stelle ed olezzava la terra" (act 3): 406.23–24; 407.19–20;
        426.32; 427.10–11
    "O dolce bacio" (act 3, part of "E lucevan le stelle"): 427.13
    "O dolci mani" (act 3): 427.25
    "Vissi d'arte" (act 2): 521.17–19
C   Mario Cavaradossi: 470.13–14
    Scarpia: 233.33; 253.27; 514.35
    Tosca, Floria: 25.26; 220.3; 245.1
Il trittico. See *Gianni Schicchi, Suor Angelica,* and *Tabarro.*
Turandot (1926): 232.27; 235.8; 238.1; 245.10; 251.23, .26, .28; 257.27–
        28. See also Busoni's *Turandot.*
A   "Non piangere Liù" ("Sorrow no more," act 1): 426.16–17
    "Signore, ascolta" (act 1): 223.18
    "Tu, che di gel sei cinta" (act 3): 250.16–18
C   Calaf: 233.34; 240.21, .24–25; 254.35; 255.14; 367.33; 426.13; 438.2;
        533.28; 576.3
    Liù: 236.6, .17–18; 245.6; 250.19–22; 485.30
    Ping, Pang, Pong: 58.24; 231.10–11; 233.28; 243.7; 344.22–23;
        359.26; 379.30; 528.18, .26; 541.24; 576.8
    Timur: 136.21; 227.35; 231.10–11; 233.34; 255.4; 342.35
    Turandot: 236.35–36
T   Chinese pidgin: 485.29
    eons theme: 226.36; 230.13, .17; 231.19; 236.30; 254.26
    Pekin: 240.30
    riddle theme: 240.26; *amor*/love: 255.4; Calaf's name: 254.19; 255.1;
        fire: 228.29; 231.32; *gel*/ice: 228.14; 233.36; 246.20; 621.26; hope:
        227.17; 235.4; 252.24; 621.26; *sangue*/blood: 231.16

Purcell, Henry (ca. 1659–95): 187.18; 412.22; 516.24
   Dido and Aeneas (1689): 357.15
    A "Haste, haste to town" (act 2): 450.22
       "With drooping wings ye cupids come" (act 3 chorus): 628.9–14
    C Dido: 291.F3
    T "Remember me!" (from "When I am laid in earth," end of act 3): 628.11, .14
   The Fairy Queen (semi-opera, 1692): 328.31

Respighi, Ottorino (1879–1936)
   Fiama (1934): 560.1
Reyer, Ernest (1823–1909; b. Louis Etienne Rey)
   Sigurd (1884): 233.31
    C Gunther: 67.16; 257.34; 376.18; 510.13; 596.15
       Hagen: 98.30; 201.35–36; 352.25; 543.17; 552.13
       Sigurd: 429.19; 511.20
Ricci, Luigi (1805–59) and Federico (1809–77)
   Crispino e la comare (1850)
    C Bartolo: 21.35; 246.27; 247.10; 372.7; 527.25
Richter, Hans (1843–1916), according to Shaw, the first good Wagnerian cond. in England: 231.27
Rimsky-Korsakov, Nicolay (1844–1908): 360.8; 497.28
   The Golden Cockerel (1909)
    C Dodon: 533.20
       Polkan (Russian general): 341.1; 513.13
   The Maid of Pskov (subtitle: "Ivan the Terrible," 1873): 340.25; 353.24
    C Ivan: 138.17
   Mlada (1892): 54.11
   Sadko (1898): 156.10
Rinaldo di Capua (ca. 1710–ca. 1780)
   La zingara (1753): 68.9
Rossini, Gioacchino (1792–1868): 223.6; 351.13; 359.33; 465.30
   The Barber of Seville (1816): 223.6; 348.36; 410.26
    A "Dunque io son" (duet, act 1, sc. 2): 405.6–7
       "Ecco ridente in cielo" (act 1, sc. 1): 409.12; 468.20
       "La calunnia è un venticello" (act 1, sc. 2): 25.9; 199.28–29
       "Largo al factotum" (act 1, sc. 1): 519.10
       "Una voce poco fà" (act 1, sc. 2): 407.13–14; 448.34–35
       "Zitti, zitti, piano, piano" (trio, act 1): 222.32–33; 250.12

C   Almaviva: 244.14–15; 619.16
     Bartolo: 21.35; 246.27; 247.10; 372.7; 527.25
     Don Basilio: 25.9; 463.22
     Figaro: 420.9–10; 421.31; 440.17; 463.5
     Rosina: 245.18; 609.11
La cenerentola (1817): 224.30; 331.26; 440.27
C   Angelina: 233.5; 238.10–11; 239.29; 252.31; 443.35
     Dandini: 234.16; 238.3; 247.34
     Don Magnifico: 100.14; 222.17
     Ramiro: 247.6
T   Cinderella story: 627.21–23
Le Comte Ory (1828)
C   Adèle: 234.35
     Alice: 214.24
     Le Comte Ory: 185.25; 372.32; 498.19
La donna del lago (1819): 465.36
La gazza ladra (1817): 436.6
A   "Di piacer me balza il cor" (act 1): 450.22
C   Lucia: 178.9; 239.34; 253.32; 327.5
L'italiana in Algeri (1813)
C   Elvira: 565.31
L'occasione fa il ladro (1812)
C   Berenice: 243.26
Semiramide (1823): 553.11–12
Tancredi (1813): 337.35–36
William Tell (1829): 459.36
A   "Asile héréditaire" (act 4): 172.13, .23
C   Arnold: 443.22
     Gessler: 233.11
     Jemmy: 92.25; 498.13
     Tell, who would not submit: 154.31–36

Saint-Saëns, Camille (1835–1921): 523.16
  Samson et Dalila (1877): 340.22–23; 523.16
A   "Ah! réponds à ma tendresse" (act 2): 407.27–28
     "Arrêtez, ô mes frères" (act 1): 223.19–21
     "Israël, romps ta chaîne" (act 1): 226.25–29
     "Mon coeur s'ouvre à ta voix" (act 2): 407.13, .20–21, .24, .33

Marschallin: 456.32

Octavian (a crossdress male role sung by a female soprano): 467.8; as Bonaventura: 207.26; as Ehrenreich:, 338.3; 510.24; 537.10; as Hyacinth: 86.15; 87.12; 281.14; 335.6; as Maria: 214.18; under nickname Quinquin: 221.25; 285.F6; 298.8; 305.20; 462.34; 463.21; 495.18; 496.36; 497.1

Salomé (1905): 360.27; 471.5; 497.33

C   Herod: 13.20; 127.11; 159.15; 275.F5; 423.8; 520.5; 527.3; 536.35; 599.5; 614.35

Jochanaan, or John the Baptist: 453.14–15; 554.10

Salomé: 244.26; 245.1

T   Salomé dancing: 550.35

Stravinsky, Igor (1882–1971): 189.8; 569.34

Oedipus Rex (1927–28: 30 May 1927 as oratorio in Paris; 23 February 1928 as opera in Vienna); text by Jean Cocteau: 513.21

Stuart, Leslie (1864–1928; pseud of Thomas A. Barrett)

Floradora (1899): 458.14

A   "Shade of the Palm" ("Oh, my Dolores," act 1) and Miss Douce: 3.20–21; 238.17; 274.15; 290.11, .16, .18, .F6; 457.20; 547.8–9; 588.12, .14; 609.5

Sullivan, Arthur (1842–1900): 573.7, .13. See also German and Sullivan; Gilbert and Sullivan.

Cox and Box (1867): 105.5; 308.L; 325.16; 347.29; 409.35; 517.17–18

Tate, James W. (1875–1922), brother of Maggie Teyte; husband first of Lottie Collins and later of Clarice Mayne; father of José Collins, star of *The Maid of the Mountains;* managed Carl Rosa Opera Company

The Maid of the Mountains (with Harold Fraser-Simon, 1916)

A   "Love will find a way": 215.4, .6, .10

C   Kate: 556.31

Tchaikovsky, Pyotr (1840–93): 424.6, .10; 498.15

Eugene Onegin (1879): 361.21

C   Lenski: 60.11; 464.35

Pique Dame (*The Queen of Spades,* 1890): 124.10, .23; 405.27, .30

Telemann, Georg Philipp (1681–1767): 176.36

Thomas, Ambroise (1811–96)

Hamlet (1968)

A   "O vin, dissipe la tristesse" (act 1 brindisi): 382.2; 437.11; 462.2–3

Mignon (1866): 157.33

A "Eri tu che Macchiave" (act 3): 537.35–36
  "La rivedrà nell' estasi" (act 1): 231.9
  "Saper vorreste" (act 3): 530.19
C Amelia: 355.22; 410.23
  Gustavus: 231.3; 234.33
  Oscar: 419.24
  Renato: 358.3
  Count Ribbing: 250.4
  Riccardo: 215.23; 221.27; 230.22; 513.17
  Silvano: 495.36
  Ulrica: 434.29
Il corsaro (1848): 343.3; 577.10; 600.11
Don Carlos (1867): 379.10; 538.28–29
C Don Carlos: 214.30
  Princess Eboli: 373.12; 612.15
  Elisabeth de Valois: 289.26; 561.8
Ernani (1844)
A "Evviva!" (act 1): 4.24
C Elvira: 565.31
  Ernani: 42.26; 433.31
  Silva: 113.11; 495.36; 619.30
Falstaff (1893): 366.30; 379.18
A "Mentre le due e le tre": 567.16
  "Pizzica, pizzica, pizzica": 92.19
  "Tutto nel mondo" (act 3): 287.25; 333.23
C Alice, Ford's wife: 214.24
  Falstaff: 6.22; 7.13; 35.27; 63.29; 96.11; 161.16; 320.20–23; 366.30;
    370.13; 379.12, .18; 405.13; 406.18; 434.24; 567.10; 569.1–2;
    595.32
  Ford: 622.35
  Nanetta: 117.16; 538.7; 567.15
  Mistress Quickly: 567.28
T Falstaff's bill: 568.14
  "Falstaff O la": 4.11
  "l'honore": 413.16, .19
  knights: 567.18
  Merry Wives of Windsor source: 227.1–2
  "reverenza": 249.32; 334.17
  widows: 567.28

La forza del destino (1862): 162.2–3; 413.1; 421.10; 598.11

A   "Pace, pace" (act 4): 175.16

    "Solenne in quest'ora" (duet, act 3): 602.14

C   Melitone, Friar: 446.2

Luisa Miller (1849): 236.6

C   Rodolfo: 241.8; 389.27

Macbeth (1847)

A   "Si colmi il calice" (act 2 brindisi): 382.2; 461.35; 462.2–3

T   regicide: 250.16–18

Nabucco (1842): 24.35; 103.8, .11; 177.14; 403.13; 412.29; 456.22

A   "Va, pensiero, sull' ali dorati" (act 3, sc. 2): 403.14–16

Oberto, Conte di San Bonifacio (1839): 70.9; 577.11

Otello (1887): 196.1–2; 527.1

A   "Ave Maria" (act 4): 244.14–15; 411.20; 628.6

    "Come sta oggi signor moro mio": 409.14

    "Credo in un Dio crudel" (act 2): 411.20–21

    "Ecco il leone" (act 3): 462.27; 477.33, .34; 510.26; 513.8; 567.27

    "Era la notte, Cassio dormia" (act 2): 14.8

    "Esultate!" (act 1): 66.9

    "Evviva!" (act 1): 4.24

    "Ora e per sempre addio" (act 2): 241.33; 468.28; 521.35–36

    "Salce, salce" (Willow Song, "Piangea cantando," act 4): 281.21; 526.32

    "Inaffia l'ugola" (act 1 brindisi): 382.2; 461.35; 462.2–3

C   Cassio: 281.16

    Desdemona: 281.17; 498.18

    Emilia: 410.23

    Iago: 41.2; 281.21; 417.32; 430.7–8

    Otello (Moor): 247.10; 281.21, .F4; 409.14; 410.29; 426.8; 430.7–8;

      449.31–32; 468.27; 477.29; 628.6

T   Desdemona's death: 207.3–6

    "Il fazzoletto" (handkerchief): 281.18–19

    "Una vela!" (opening words: "A sail!"): 147.14

Rigoletto (1851): 234.26

A   "Caro nome" (act 1, sc. 2): 95.6; 238.33, .35; 473.7; 502.36

    "Infelice cor tradito" (act 3 quartet): 433.4

    "La donna è mobile" (act 3): 210.30; 235.13; 292.12; 309.21; 403.9–

      10; 433.3–4 (rhythm); 454.18–20

    "La rà, la rà, la rà, la rà" (act 2): 415.11–12

    "Pari siamo" (act 1, sc. 2): 350.27

"Questa o quella" (act 1): 3.21; 61.16; 183.20–21; 360.13; 419.21

C Gilda: 147.12; 276.6; 433.6; 450.31; 572.33, 35; 609.4

  Maddalena: 211.8; 352.8

  Malde, Walter: 317.18; 566.26–27

  Duke of Mantua: 408.2; 433.6

  Rigoletto: 171.15; 319.20; 338.12

  Sparafucile: 350.27, .30; 404.21

T "Maledizione" (act 1, scs. 1 and 2): 269.F3; 439.6; 612.9

  "preghera" (Gilda's last word): 626.26

Simon Boccanegra (1857)

A "Il lacerato spirito" (prologue): 403.13, .17, 404.19

C Amelia: 355.22; 410.23

  Fiesco: 597.34

Stiffelio (1850): Trieste premiere, 301.16–18

La traviata (1853): 366.23–24; 416.31

A "Addio del passato" (act 3): 146.33–36; 446.13

  "Ah! Dite alla giovine" (act 2): 196.1–2

  "Ah, fors'è lui" (act 1): 95.6

  "Di più non lacerarmi. . . . Prendi quest'è" (recitative, act 3, sc. 8): 144.6

  "Di Provenza il mar" (act 2): 144.10; 297.24; 600.20–21

  "Libiamo, libiamo," (act 1 brindisi): 382.2; 441.9; 461.35, 462.2–3

  "Parigi, o cara" (act 3, recorded by John McCormack): 350.27–28;
    625.10, .20, .24

C Alfredo: 203.27; 600.28

  Germont: 230.32–34; 338.3; 625.2

  Violetta: 54.9; 102.26; 157.8; 203.29–30; 211.8; 223.7; 231.20; 238.5;
    261.2; 351.8; 403.15, .22; 432.31; 461.17–18

T cough: 147.12; 210.9; 444.3

  "gioia" (Violetta's last word): 626.29

Il trovatore (1853): 165.7; 173.4; 211.35; 224.25; 288.2; 289.27; 301.17;
    341.9; 366.23–24; 370.8; 411.29; 430.15; 439.9; 478.21

A "Ah si, ben mio" (act 3): 623.25

  "Ai nostri monti" ("Home to Our Mountains," act 4): 338.16–17;
    360.11; 462.32

  "D'amor sull'ali rosee" (act 4): 235.13

  "Deserto sulla terra" (act 1, sc. 2): 421.7

  "Di quella pira" (act 3): 466.9; 473.18–19; 516.15

  "Miserere" (act 4): 466.32

  "Stride la vampa" (act 2, sc. 1): 246.22; 411.31; 473.19

C   Ferrando: 457.3
    Count (Graf) di Luna: 339.23; 340.32; 464.7; 465.21; 476.24
    Manrico: 339.23
T   "Il trovatore! Io tremo": 341.9; 462.26
    lute (balaleika): 341.9; 462.25–26
    setting mother on fire: 426.3–4
I vespri siciliani (1855): 179.34–35

Wagner, Richard (1813–83): 70.4–5; 126.10–11; 149.13; 230.12; 301.14–15;
    360.8–9; 431.11; 540.24; 543.27; 553.29; 577.13; 604.17; *Bar* pattern:
    529.34; 535.2, .18, .36; 536.28, .32; 539.8–10; 543.8–10; 549.35; 552.9;
    Bogen-form: 529.21; 531.33; 536.14; 539.25; 552.6; Bayreuth: 229.34;
    241.26; 465.17; 500.24; and von Bülow: 418.34–419.8; conductors:
    150.15; 151.11, .32–33; dandyism: 166.24–26; 529.32; on diet: 441.8–10;
    and "hush": 14.6; 159.19; 334.31; 501.7; and Alfred Lorenz: 537.10, .33;
    543.8–10; and Ludwig II: 243.17; 434.21–23; 525.14; polemics on Jewish
    music: 150.26–28; *Stollen* form, see *Bar* pattern; and tubas: 290.21; 327.16;
    338.17; 412.8; and Verdi: 346.4; wife Cosima von Bülow: 151.1; wife Min-
    na: 12.25; 54.10; 189.12; 206.15–16; 238.34; 318.17–18; 508.22; 551.24;
    and Wesendonks: 229.35; 230.21; *Zukunftsmusik* (music of the future):
    407.31–32; 518.28
Die Feen (comp. 1833–34; prod. 1888): 518.27; 562.32
The Flying Dutchman (*Der fliegende Holländer,* 1843; London prod. [1870]
    was first Wagner opera in England): 314.22; 318.3–10; 319.16–17;
    323.1–8; 327.23; 362.8–9; 416.30–32; 469.19–20
A   "Hohoje" (first words of act 1): 5.9; 609.18
    "Summ' und brumm'" (chorus, act 2): 14.8; 44.19; 231.23; 336.13–14
C   Daland: 311.5; 427.17–18; 609.19
    Erik: 220.25–26; 277.23; 316.8; 359.26; 456.22; 487.15; 530.21
    Senta: 268.3; 327.22–26; 434.23; 440.19–20
    Vanderdecken: 233.11; 323.1; 530.20; 620.7
T   Cape of Good Hope: 312.19–20
    "Nirgends ein Grab! Niemals der Tod!" (act 1, in Vanderdecken's first
        speech): 202.19
    opulence: 126.16
    portrait: 232.26–233.2
    seven-year term: 312.5–8; 316.15–16; 423.22–23
    "steh' ich treu Dir bis zum Tod" (Senta's last words): 528.12
Die Götterdämmerung (1876): 14.30–31; 17.15; 37.17; 68.14; 130.4–5;

221.36; 226.4–15; 257.34; 258.2; 277.3–5; 316.17; 318.13–14; 325.25–26; 352.25; 518.25–28; 532.27; 565.2; 594.25–26; 612.31–32; 613.12; 625.35. See also *Ring.*

A "Gross Glück und Heil lacht nun dem Rhein, da Hagen, der Grimme" (act 2, sc. 3, chorus): 450.22

C Flosshilde: 213.3; 225.35

Gunther: 67.16; 257.34; 376.18; 510.13; 596.15

Hagen: 98.30; 201.35–36; 352.25; 543.17; 552.13

Siegfried, funeral pyre: 24.33; 473.18; 516.15; 621.1–3; recovers memory: 231.23–25

T "Betrug! Betrug! Schändlichster Betrug!" (Brünnhilde, act 2): 459.20–22

blood-brotherhood: 310.15–16; 323.4; 325.26; 338.9; 465.31

"Heiaho!" (Brünnhilde's last word): 627.31

Norns, winding the skein of life: 310.15; 345.21

"Siegfried! Sieh!" (Brünnhilde's penultimate line): 627.35; 628.4

twilight of the gods: 304.4; 552.25

Weltesche (Yggdrasil): 55.27–30; 131.13–14; 502.9; 506.15–18; 588.28

"Zurück vom Ringe!" (last sentence of *Götterdämmerung*, spoken by Hagen): 249.20–21; 547.25

Lohengrin (1850)

A "Einsam in trüben Tagen" (Elsa sings in act 1): 152.18–19

"Treulich geführt" (Wedding March, or Bridal Chorus, act 3): 197.17–18

C Elsa: 211.12; 213.25; 226.4–5; 246.35; 444.31; 495.25

Duke Gottfried: 198.13

Henry the fowler: 197.8

Lohengrin: 212.27; 324.16

Ortrud: 139.32; 221.15; enchants Gottfried: 548.33

T swan: 49.5–6; 113.12; 139.32; 197.6; 208.19; 226.4–5; 248.23; 249.18–20; 250.19–21; 383.15; 450.2–3, .5; 511.13; 516.18; 581.6; 600.31

"Mein lieber Schwan" (act 3, sc. 3): 113.12; 384.31–32

Die Meistersinger von Nürnberg (1868): 151.13; 508.21; 513.34; 531.4–5

A "Am stillen Herd" (act 1, sc. 3): 548.7

"Das Blumenkränzlein aus Seiden fein" (act 1, sc. 2): 194.12–14

"Hört ihr Leut' und lasst euch sagen, Die Glock' hat Zehn geschlagen" (nightwatchman's song, act 2, sc. 5): 403.1–22

"Morgenlich leuchtend" ("Preislied," act 3, sc. 2): 79.21, .22, .28; 564.4

"Silentium—wach' auf" (act 3, sc. 5): 44.4; 427.32–33; 476.8; 508.35, 509.1–4; 510.8, .16; 597.26

"Wahn! Wahn!" ("Madness," act 3, sc. 1): 72.4–5; 516.18

Das Rheingold (1869): 414.1; 578.23. See also *Ring*.

A "Weia! waga! Woge, du Welle, walle zur Wiege! Wagalaweia! Wallala
Weia! Waga! . . . Wagalaweia!" (Rhine Maidens at beginning of *Das
Rheingold*): 4.2–3; 6.35–36; 98.32–33; 197.26; 301.15; 315.26;
465.7; 475.2; 628.15

"Weialala leia / Wallala leialala" (Rhine Maidens' Song as quoted by T. S.
Eliot in "The Waste Land," lines 277–78 and 290–91): 159.16–17;
235.7–8; 525.14; 554.8–10

C Donner: 22.4; 87.32; 283.L2; 323.9; 499.33; 565.17; 578.19–20;
585.11; 596.3

Freia: 24.26; 211.4; 231.13; 246.26; 253.33; 335.15; 356.17; 510.10;
538.28

Froh: 510.9; 553.27; 594.25

Niebelung: 24.1; 134.33

T Alberich's curse ("Verfluch"): 23.25; 58.12

Alberich's curse ("Bin ich nun frei"): 113.25; 540.28

"Der Wonne, seligen Saal" (Wotan's first words in *Ring*, addressing Valhalla): 246.15

Rhine—first leitmotiv of Wagner's *Ring:* 3.1; 207.7; 242.17; 379.17

"He, he! Ihr Nicker!" (Hey, you nixies: Alberich's first words in *Rheingold*): 11.4; 422.33

rainbow bridge to Valhalla at end of *Rheingold:* 3.14; 22.28; 62.12–13;
126.10; 178.24–26; 186.28; 203.26–27; 262.3, .5, .11–12; 273.4–
5; 304.9; 323.9; 337.28; 403.6; 493.29–30; 494.1–4; 499.33; 514.22;
547.29–31; 552.16; 590.10

Rhinegold: 201.35–36; 213.5–7; 613.1

"Welle" (waves): 205.16; 209.18; 213.11

Der Ring des Nibelungen (1876): 25.30–31; 58.13; 117.5–6; 147.19; 158.25–
28; 158.31–159.1; 167.32; 225.2, .30; 226.25; 239.26; 239.36;
246.13; 268.2; 319.7; 435.30; 441.21; 459.2; 500.4; 536.9; 547.33;
569.4–5; 590.27. See also *Götterdämmerung, Rheingold, Siegfried,
Walküre.*

C Alberich: 11.5; 202.20; 539.30; 598.6; 600.12; 620.5

Brünnhilde: 13.26–27; 213.6; 246.32; 250.29–30; 399.4; 477.23;
500.21, .22, .27; 502.9; 541.30; 546.32; 620.35–621.3; in ring of
flame: 621.1–3; sleeping: 615.27–28

Erda: 17.30; 550.17; 551.25; 577.22; = Wala: 601.34; Erda wakes: 74.1–
2; 262.15; warning: 503.28

treasure guarded by Fafner: 24.33

Valhalla: 4.35; 5.6; 5.30; 19.25; 56.5–8; 62.28; 69.7–10; 91.30; 107.36;
  156.25, .32–33; 231.7, .21; 246.3–5, .14; 258.2; 348.10; 359.34;
  365.16; 379.12; 435.30; 460.32; 487.9–10; 499.8; 530.31; 541.22;
  553.22; 565.2; 569.25; 594.8–9, .12; 597.14; 607.27; 608.8–9;
  609.18, .33; 613.2, .20; 625.7; burning: 131.13–14

Siegfried (1876): 84.28; 281.20–23; 539.27. See also *Ring.*

A "Ewig war ich, ewig bin ich" (act 3): 552.21

   "Heil dir, Sonne! Heil dir, Licht!" (act 3): 189.25; 532.6; 564.4

   "Nothung! Nothung! Niedliches Schwert" (Siegfried's forging song, act
   1): 5.9

C Siegfried: 106.12; 222.29–30; 223.25–26; 231.36; 233.11; 237.31;
   243.16; 246.10; 281.20–23; 371.6; 376.36; 429.19; 471.30; 503.28;
   530.20–22; 539.27; 545.28; 552.12; 571.2; 586.28; 608.10; horn:
   245.1, .10; forges Nothung: 181.16; 231.20–22; 247.7; 305.3–4;
   431.17; 539.14; 589.5; funeral pyre: 24.33; 473.18–19; 516.15; 621.1–
   3; recovers memory: 231.23–25; wakes Brünnhilde: 74.1–2; 505.25

   Wanderer (Wotan): 229.14; 245.24; 355.33–35; 365.1; 377.13; 532.27;
   618.22. See also Wotan under *Ring.*

T Bird's song: 224.19; 250.1, .11–12; 306.20–21; 359.32; 360.2, .13–16;
   412.7–8

   Mime's interior monologue: 105.11; 254.13

   Nibelheim: 590.17

   Nothung, Siegfried's sword: 222.22; 227.34; 249.35; 250.35; 253.8;
   281.L3; 294.6; 295.18; 344.4; 379.21; 424.34; 494.14; 539.29

   Rhine: 245.1

   Siegfried forges Nothung: 181.16; 231.20–22; 247.7; 305.3–4; 431.17;
   539.14; 589.5; forging song: 5.9

Tannhäuser (1845): 113.21

A "Dich, teure Halle, grüss' ich wieder, froh grüss' ich dich" (act 2): 409.15

   "Dir, hohe Liebe, töne begeistert mein Gesang" (act 2, sc. 4): 53.18–19

   "O du, mein holder Abendstern" (act 3, sc. 2): 248.13–14; 266.27;
   267.22; 268.14–15; 312.8

   Pilgrim's Chorus ("Beglückt darf nun dich, o Heimath, ich schauen,"
   act 3; the pilgrims sing several choruses in the course of the opera, but
   this is the one known as "The Pilgrim's Chorus"): 234.20, .36;
   248.13–14

C Elisabeth: 156.34; 289.26; 328.36; 495.25; 542.23; 561.8

   Urban II: 154.20

· 8 ·

Finding List of Opera and
Aria Titles and Opera Characters in
Finnegans Wake

Operas, arias, and opera characters alluded to in *Finnegans Wake* are listed here briefly. For full information, please turn to chapter 7, where the composers alluded to in *Finnegans Wake* are listed alphabetically. (Operas alluded to are listed alphabetically under the composer's name in chapter 7, and arias and characters are listed there under the relevant opera.)

Opera titles are alphabetized without regard to initial articles—a, das, der, die, gli, i, il, l', la, le, les, lo, the—which are here omitted to save space (e.g., *Les Huguenots* is under *H*); opera titles beginning with personal titles are alphabetized under those titles (e.g., *Prince Igor* under *P* or *Don Giovanni* under *D*).

Arias are alphabetized taking initial articles into consideration (e.g., "Un bel dì" under *U*).

Characters with complete names have those names inverted. Characters with single names and titles—Captain, Comte, Count, Don, Donna, Doctor, Fra, Prince, Princess, Reine, Roi—are alphabetized as if inverted, by name rather than title (e.g., Don Giovanni under *G*).

The format is as follows:

Opera title (composer)
"Aria" (composer, opera)
Character (composer, opera)

"A cenar teco m'invitasti" (Mozart, *Don Giovanni*)
"A paradox? A paradox!" (Gilbert and Sullivan, *Pirates of Penzance*)
"A te o cara" (Bellini, *I puritani;* sung by John McCormack)
"A Vesta, portez vos offrandes" (Gounod, *Polyeucte*)
Abduction from the Seraglio (Mozart)
Acis and Galatea (Handel)

"Addio, del passato" (Verdi, *Traviata*)

"Addio, fiorito asil" (Puccini, *Madame Butterfly*)

"Addio senza rancor" (Puccini, *Bohème*)

Adèle (J. Strauss, *Fledermaus;* also Rossini, *Comte Ory*)

Adina (Donizetti, *Elisir d'Amore*)

Aennchen (Weber, *Freischütz*)

Africaine (Meyerbeer)

Agathe (Weber, *Freischütz*)

Agnes (Weber, *Freischütz*)

"Ah, che barbaro appetito." See "Già la mensa."

"Ah! Dite alla giovine" (Verdi, *Traviata*)

"Ah, fors'è lui" (Verdi, *Traviata*)

"Ah! je ris!" (Jewel Song, Gounod, *Faust*)

"Ah! lève-toi soleil!" (Gounod, *Roméo et Juliette*)

"Ah! réponds à ma tendresse" (Saint-Saëns, *Samson et Dalila*)

"Ah si, ben mio" (Verdi, *Trovatore*)

"Ah! tu dei vivere!" (Verdi, *Aïda*)

"Ai nostri monti" ("Home to Our Mountains," Verdi, *Trovatore*)

Aïda (Verdi)

Aïda (Verdi, *Aïda*)

"Alas, those chimes so sweetly stealing" (Wallace, *Maritana*)

Alberich (Wagner, *Ring*)

Alfio (Mascagni, *Cavalleria rusticana*)

Alfred (J. Strauss, *Fledermaus*)

Alfredo (Verdi, *Traviata*)

Alice (Verdi, *Falstaff;* also Rossini, *Comte Ory,* and Meyerbeer, *Robert le diable*)

Almaviva (Mozart, *Marriage of Figaro;* also Rossini, *Barber of Seville*)

"Am stillen Herd" (Wagner, *Meistersinger*)

Amadis (Lully)

Amadis (Massenet)

Amadis (Lully, *Amadis;* also Massenet, *Amadis*)

Amelia (Verdi, *Ballo in maschera;* also Verdi, *Simon Boccanegra,* and Mercadante, *Brigante*)

Amfortas (Wagner, *Parsifal*)

Amico Fritz (Mascagni)

Amina (Bellini, *Sonnambula*)

Amneris (Verdi, *Aïda*)

Amonasro (Verdi, *Aïda*)

Amore dei tre re (Montemezzi)

"Amore o grillo" (Puccini, *Madame Butterfly*)
Andrea Chénier (Giordano)
Angelica (Puccini, *Suor Angelica*)
Angelina (Rossini, *Cenerentola;* also Gilbert and Sullivan, *Trial by Jury*)
Anna Bolena (Donizetti)
Antigone (multiple operas by multiple composers)
Archibald. See Grosvenor.
Archibaldo (Montemezzi, *Amore dei tre re*)
Ariane et Barbe-bleu (Dukas)
Arianna (Monteverdi)
Arkel (Debussy, *Pelléas et Mélisande*)
Arlecchino (Busoni)
Arlesiana (Cilea)
Arline (Balfe, *Bohemian Girl*)
Armourer of Nantes (Balfe)
Arnold (Rossini, *William Tell*)
"Arrêtez, ô mes frères" (Saint-Saëns, *Samson et Dalila*)
Artaxerxes (Arne)
"Asile héréditaire" (Rossini, *William Tell*)
At the Boar's Head (Holst)
Atalanta (Handel)
Attila (Verdi)
"Ave Maria" (Verdi, *Otello*)
Avito (Montemezzi, *Amore dei tre re*)

Baculus (Lortzing, *Wildschütz*)
Ballo in maschera (Verdi)
Bánk-Bán (Erkel)
Barber of Seville (Rossini)
Barnaba (Ponchielli, *Gioconda*)
Bartered Bride (Smetana)
Bartolo (Rossini, *Barber of Seville;* also Mozart, *Marriage of Figaro,* and Luigi
    and Federico Ricci, *Crispino e la comare*)
Don Basilio (Rossini, *Barber of Seville;* also Mozart, *Marriage of Figaro*)
Bastien and Bastienne (Mozart)
Bastienne (Mozart, *Bastien and Bastienne*)
Beckmesser (Wagner, *Meistersinger*)
Beggar's Opera (Gay)
"Beglück darf nun dich." See "Pilgrim's Chorus."

"Bell Song." See "Où va la jeune hindoue."

Belmonte (Mozart, *Abduction from the Seraglio*)

Berenice (Handel)

Berenice (Handel, *Berenice;* also Rossini, *Occasione fa il ladro*)

Bertram (Meyerbeer, *Robert le diable*)

Betly (Donizetti)

Bianca (Balfe)

Bitter Sweet (Coward)

Blanche, Lady (Gilbert and Sullivan, *Princess Ida*)

Blonde (Mozart, *Abduction from the Seraglio*)

Bohème (Puccini)

Bohemian Girl (Balfe)

Bolena, Anna (Donizetti, *Anna Bolena*)

Bonaventura. See Octavian.

Bondman (Balfe)

Lo zio Bonzo (Puccini, *Madame Butterfly*)

Brandenburger Tor (Meyerbeer)

Brangäne (Wagner, *Tristan und Isolde*)

Bridal Chorus (Wagner). See "Treulich geführt."

Brigante (Mercadante)

Brindisi, any drinking song in opera, with a solo toast, after which all others respond with the same words and melody. See "Libiamo ne' lieti calici," "Si colmi il calice," "Il segreto per esser felice," "Innaffia l'ugola," and "Viva il vino spumeggiante." With a freer form, the French and German drinking songs include "Versez! que tout respire," "O vin, dissipe la tristesse," and "Lass mich Euch fragen."

Brogni (Halévy, *Juive*)

Brünnhilde (Wagner, *Ring*)

Bunthorne, Reginald (Gilbert and Sullivan, *Patience*)

Buttercup (Gilbert and Sullivan, *H.M.S. Pinafore*)

Calaf (Puccini, *Turandot*)

Canio (Leoncavallo, *Pagliacci*)

Caramello (J. Strauss, *Eine Nacht in Venedig*)

"Care selve" (Handel, *Atalanta;* recorded by John McCormack)

Don Carlos (Verdi, *Don Carlos*)

"Caro nome" (Verdi, *Rigoletto*)

Carmen (Bizet)

Casilda (Gilbert and Sullivan, *Gondoliers*)

Caspar (Weber, *Freischütz*)

Cassio (Verdi, *Otello*)

"Casta diva" (Bellini, *Norma*)

Cavalleria rusticana (Mascagni)

Cavaradossi, Mario (Puccini, *Tosca*)

Caves of Carrig-Cleena. See *Emerald Isle.*

Cazanova (Lortzing)

"Cease your funning" (Gay, *Beggar's Opera*)

"Celeste Aïda" (Verdi, *Aïda;* recorded by John McCormack)

Cenerentola (Rossini)

Champagne Aria. See "Finch'han dal vino."

"Champs paternels" (Méhul, *Joseph;* recorded by John McCormack)

"Chanson bohème." See "Les tringles des sistres tintaient."

Chappelou (called St. Phar; Adams, *Postillon de Longjumeau*)

Charlotte (Massenet, *Werther*)

"Che gelida manina" (Puccini, *Bohème;* recorded by John McCormack)

Chénier, Andrea (Giordano, *Andrea Chénier*)

Cherubino (Mozart, *Marriage of Figaro*)

"Chin Chin Chinaman" (Jones, *Geisha*)

Cid (Massenet)

"Cinque—dieci—venti—trenta—trenta sei—quaranta tre" (Mozart, *Marriage of Figaro*)

Cio-Cio-San (Puccini, *Madame Butterfly*)

Clemenza di Tito (Mozart)

Cléopâtre (Massenet)

Cléopâtre (Massenet, *Cléopâtre*)

Coaxer, Mrs. (Gay, *Beggar's Opera*)

Colleen Bawn (Benedict, *Lily of Killarney*)

Colline (Puccini, *Bohème*)

Colomba (Mackenzie)

"Come sta oggi signor moro mio" (Verdi, *Otello*)

Commendatore and his statue (Mozart, *Don Giovanni*)

Comte Ory (Rossini)

Conchita (Zandonai)

"Connais-tu le pays?" ("Kennst du das Land?" Thomas, *Mignon;* sung by John McCormack)

Constanze (Mozart, *Abduction from the Seraglio*)

Coppelius (Offenbach, *Tales of Hoffmann*)

Corcoran, Captain (Gilbert and Sullivan, *H.M.S. Pinafore*)

Corsaro (Verdi)

Così fan tutte (Mozart)

Cox and Box (Sullivan)

"Credo in un Dio crudel" (Verdi, *Otello*)

Cregan, Hardress (Benedict, *Lily of Killarney*)

Crispino e la comare (Ricci)

"Cruiskeen Lawn" (Benedict, *Lily of Killarney*)

da Gama, Vasco (Meyerbeer, *Africaine*)

Dafne (Peri)

Daland (Wagner, *Flying Dutchman*)

Dalila (Saint-Saëns, *Samson et Dalila*)

"Dalla sua pace" (Mozart, *Don Giovanni*)

Dalua, Lord of Shadow (Boughton, *Immortal Hour*)

Damnation de Faust (Berlioz)

"D'amor sull'ali rosee" (Verdi, *Trovatore*)

Dandini (Rossini, *Cenerentola*)

Dapertutto (Offenbach, *Tales of Hoffmann*)

"Das Blumenkränzlein aus Seiden fein" (Wagner, *Meistersinger*)

"Dein ist mein ganzes Herz." See "Yours is my heart alone."

"Der Hölle Rache" (Mozart, *Magic Flute*)

"Des cris joyeuse" (Massenet, *Werther*)

des Grieux (Massenet, *Manon;* also Puccini, *Manon Lescaut*)

Desdemona (Verdi, *Otello*)

"Deserto sulla terra" (Verdi, *Trovatore*)

Despina (Mozart, *Così fan tutte*)

"Di piacer me balza il cor" (Rossini, *Gazza ladra*)

"Di più non lacerarmi . . . Prendi quest'è" (Verdi, *Traviata*)

"Di Provenza il mar" (Verdi, *Traviata*)

"Di quella pira" (Verdi, *Trovatore*)

"Dich, teure Halle, grüss' ich wieder, froh grüss' ich dich" (Wagner, *Tannhäuser*)

Dido and Aeneas (Purcell)

Dido (Purcell, *Dido and Aeneas*)

Dinorah (Meyerbeer, *Pardon de Ploërmel*)

"Dir, hohe Liebe, töne begeistert mein Gesang" (Wagner, *Tannhäuser*)

"Dites-lui, qu'on l'a remarqué distingué" (Offenbach, *Grande-Duchesse de Gérolstein*)

Diver, Jenny (Gay, *Beggar's Opera*)

Djamileh (Bizet)

Djamileh (Bizet, *Djamileh*)

Docteur Miracle (Bizet)

Docteur Miracle (Lecocq)

Dodon (Rimsky-Korsakov, *Golden Cockerel*)

Doktor Faust (Busoni)

Don Carlos (Verdi)

Don Giovanni (Mozart)

Don Pasquale (Donizetti)

Don Quixote (Massenet et al.)

Donna del lago (Rossini)

Donner (Wagner, *Rheingold*)

Dorabella (Mozart, *Così fan tutte*)

Dosifey or Dositheus (Mussorgsky, *Khovanschina*)

"Dove sono i bei momenti" (Mozart, *Marriage of Figaro*)

Dreigroschenoper (Weill)

Duet (Gounod, *Roméo et Juliette*)

Dulcinea (Massenet, *Don Quixote*)

"Dunque io son" (Rossini, *Barber of Seville*)

"Durch Mitleid wissend, der reine Tor" (Wagner, *Parsifal*)

"È la solita storia" (Cilea, *Arlesiana*)

"E lucevan le stelle ed olezzava la terra" (Puccini, *Tosca;* recorded by John Mc-
Cormack)

Eboli, Princess (Verdi, *Don Carlos*)

"Ecco il leone" (Verdi, *Otello*)

"Ecco ridente in cielo" (Rossini, *Barber of Seville;* sung by John McCormack)

Ehrenreich. See Octavian.

"Eily Mavourneen" (Benedict, *Lily of Killarney;* recorded by John McCormack)

"Ein Schwert verhiess mir der Vater" (Wagner, *Walküre*)

Eine Nacht in Venedig (J. Strauss)

"Einsam in trüben Tagen" (Elsa's dream, Wagner, *Lohengrin*)

Eléazar (Halévy, *Juive*)

Elektra (R. Strauss)

Elisabeth (Wagner, *Tannhäuser*)

Elisabeth de Valois (Verdi, *Don Carlos*)

Elisir d'amore (Donizetti)

Ella (Gilbert and Sullivan, *Patience*)

"Elle ne croyait pas" (Thomas, *Mignon;* sung by JJ in recital as "In her simplicity" and recorded under that title by John McCormack)

Elsa of Brabant (Wagner, *Lohengrin*)

Elvino (Bellini, *Sonnambula;* also Bellini, *Pirata*)

Elvira (Mozart, *Don Giovanni;* also Verdi, *Ernani,* Bellini, *Puritani,* and Rossini, *Italiana in Algeri*)

Emerald Isle (German and Sullivan, *Caves of Carrig-Cleena*)

Emilia (Verdi, *Otello*)

Emperor Jones (Gruenberg)

"En fermant les yeux" (Massenet, *Manon;* recorded by John McCormack)

Enchantress (Balfe)

Enrico (Donizetti, *Lucia di Lammermoor;* also Haydn, *L'isola disabitata*)

"Era la notte, Cassio dormia" (Verdi, *Otello*)

Erda (Wagner, *Ring*)

"Eri tu che Macchiave" (Verdi, *Ballo in maschera*)

Erik (Wagner, *Flying Dutchman*)

Ernani (Verdi)

Ernani (Verdi, *Ernani*)

Escamillo (Bizet, *Carmen*)

Esmeralda (Arthur Thomas)

Esmeralda (Smetana, *Bartered Bride*)

"Esultate!" (Verdi, *Otello*)

Etoile du nord (Meyerbeer)

Eugene Onegin (Tchaikovsky)

Euridice or Eurydice. See Orfeo, Orfée.

Euryanthe (Weber)

Eva (Wagner, *Meistersinger*)

Evangeline (Luening)

"Evviva!" (Verdi, *Ernani;* also Verdi, *Otello*)

"Ewig war ich, ewig bin ich" (Wagner, *Siegfried*)

Fafner (Wagner, *Ring*)

Fair Maid of Perth. See *Jolie Fille de Perth.*

Fairy Queen (Purcell)

"Faites-lui mes aveux" (Flower Song, Gounod, *Faust*)

Falstaff (Verdi)

Falstaff (Verdi, *Falstaff;* also Nicolai, *Merry Wives of Windsor,* and Holst, *At the Boar's Head*)

Fanciulla del west (Puccini)

Faninal (R. Strauss, *Der Rosenkavalier*)

Fasolt (Wagner, *Ring*)

Faust (Gounod)

Faust (Gounod, *Faust;* also Berlioz, *Damnation de Faust,* Busoni, *Doktor Faust,* and Boïto, *Mefistofele*)

Favola d'Orfeo (Monteverdi)

Favorita (Donizetti)

Fedora (Giordano)

Feen (Wagner)

Fernand. See Octavian.

Don Fernando (Beethoven, *Fidelio*)

Ferrando (Mozart, *Così fan tutte;* also Verdi, *Trovatore*)

Fiama (Respighi)

Fiametta. See Vittoria.

Fidelio (Beethoven)

Fidelio (Beethoven, *Fidelio*)

Fidès (Meyerbeer, *Prophète*)

Fiesco (Verdi, *Simon Boccanegra*)

Figaro (Mozart, *Marriage of Figaro;* also Rossini, *Barber of Seville*)

Filch (Gay, *Beggar's Opera*)

Fille de Madame Angot (Lecocq)

Fille du régiment (Donizetti)

"Finch'han dal vino" (Champagne Aria, Mozart, *Don Giovanni*)

Fiora (Montemezzi, *Amore dei tre re*)

Fiordiligi (Mozart, *Così fan tutte*)

Fledermaus (J. Strauss)

Fliegende Holländer. See *Flying Dutchman.*

Floradora (Stuart)

Florestan (Beethoven, *Fidelio*)

Florestein (Balfe, *Bohemian Girl*)

Flosshilde (Wagner, *Rheingold;* also Wagner, *Götterdämmerung*)

Flower Duet. See "Scuoti."

Flower Song. See "Faites-lui mes aveux."

Flower Maidens (Wagner, *Parsifal*)

Flower Maidens' Song (Wagner, *Parsifal*)

Flying Dutchman (Wagner)

Ford (Verdi, *Falstaff;* also Nicolai, *Merry Wives of Windsor,* where sometimes the name is "Fluth")

Forza del destino (Verdi)
Fra Diavolo (Auber)
Fra Diavolo (Auber, *Fra Diavolo*)
Francesca da Rimini (Zandonai)
Freia (Wagner, *Rheingold*)
Freischütz (Weber)
Fricka (Wagner, *Ring* and *Die Walküre*)
Froh (Wagner, *Rheingold*)
"From Inchigela all the way" (Benedict, *Lily of Killarney*)
From the House of the Dead (Janáček)

Gama (Gilbert and Sullivan, *Princess Ida*)
Gazza ladra (Rossini)
Geisha (Jones)
Gennaro (Donizetti, *Lucrezia Borgia;* also Wolf-Ferrari, *Gioiella della Madonna*)
Genoveva (Schumann)
Germont (Verdi, *Traviata*)
Gertrud. See Hänsel.
Gessler (Rossini, *William Tell*)
"Già la mensa è preparata . . . che barbara appetito" (Mozart, *Don Giovanni*)
Gianetta (Gilbert and Sullivan, *Gondoliers*)
Gianni Schicchi (Puccini)
Gilda (Verdi, *Rigoletto*)
Gioconda (Ponchielli)
Gioiella della Madonna (Wolf-Ferrari)
Don Giovanni (Mozart, *Don Giovanni*)
Giroflé, Girofla (Lecocq)
Giuletta (Offenbach, *Tales of Hoffmann*)
Giulia. See Vittoria.
Giuseppe. See Luiz.
"Gli aranci olezzano sui verdi margini" (Mascagni, *Cavalleria rusticana*)
Glückliche Hand (Schoenberg)
Golaud (Golo) (Debussy, *Pelléas et Mélisande*)
Golden Cockerel (Rimsky-Korsakov)
Gondoliers (Gilbert and Sullivan)
"Gott! Welch Dunkel hier" (Beethoven, *Fidelio*)
Götterdämmerung (Wagner)
Gottfried, Duke (Wagner, *Lohengrin*)
Grande-Duchesse de Gérolstein (Offenbach)

Grane, Brünnhilde's horse (Wagner, *Ring*)

Gretel. See Hänsel.

Grisélidis (Massenet)

"Gross Glück und Heil lacht nun dem Rhein" (Wagner, *Götterdämmerung*)

Grosvenor, Archibald (Gilbert and Sullivan, *Patience*)

Grosvenor, Lady Jane (Gilbert and Sullivan, *Patience*)

"Groves of Blarney." See "'Tis the last rose of summer."

"Guardate ancor, padrone" (Mozart, *Don Giovanni*)

Guglielmo (Mozart, *Così fan tutte*)

Gunther (Wagner, *Götterdämmerung;* also Reyer, *Sigurd*)

Gustavus (Verdi, *Ballo in maschera*)

Gwendoline (Chabrier)

H.M.S. Pinafore (*The Lass That Loved a Sailor,* Gilbert and Sullivan)

Hagen (Wagner, *Götterdämmerung;* also Reyer, *Sigurd*)

Halka (Moniuszko)

Halka (Moniuszko, *Halka*)

Hänsel und Gretel (Humperdinck)

Hänsel, Gretel, and Gertrud (Humperdinck, *Hänsel und Gretel*)

Harriet (alias Martha) (Flotow, *Martha*)

"Haste, haste to town" (Purcell, *Dido and Aeneas*)

"Heil dir, Sonne! Heil dir, Licht!" (Wagner, *Siegfried*)

Henry the Fowler (Wagner, *Lohengrin*)

Herod (Massenet, *Hérodiade;* also R. Strauss, *Salomé*)

Hérodiade (Massenet)

Herzeleide (Wagner, *Parsifal*)

"Ho capito, signor" (Mozart, *Don Giovanni*)

Hoël (Meyerbeer, *Dinorah*)

Hoffmann and Stella (Offenbach, *Tales of Hoffmann*)

"Hohoje" (Wagner, *Flying Dutchman*)

"Home to Our Mountains." See "Ai nostri monti."

"Hört ihr Leut' und lasst euch sagen, Die Glock' hat Zehn geschlagen" (Wagner, *Meistersinger*)

"How beautiful they are, the lordly ones" (Boughton, *Immortal Hour*)

Huguenots (Meyerbeer)

Humming Chorus (Puccini, *Madame Butterfly*)

Hunding (Wagner, *Walküre*)

Hyacinth. See Octavian.

"I dreamt that I dwelt in marble halls" (Balfe, *Bohemian Girl*)

Iago (Verdi, *Otello*)

Ida, Princess (Gilbert and Sullivan, *Princess Ida*)

"If you're anxious for to shine in the high aesthetic line" ("a most particularly
   pure young man this pure young man must be") (Gilbert and Sullivan,
   Patience)

"Il lacerato spirito" (Verdi, *Simon Boccanegra*)

"Il mio tesoro" (Mozart, *Don Giovanni;* recorded by John McCormack)

"Il segreto per esser felice" (Donizetti, *Lucrezia Borgia*)

"I'm Alone" (Benedict, *Lily of Killarney*)

Immortal Hour (Boughton)

Imogene (Bellini, *Pirata*)

"In diesen heiligen Hallen" (Mozart, *Magic Flute*)

"In her simplicity." See "Elle ne croyait pas."

Incoronazione di Poppea (Monteverdi)

"Infelice cor tradito" (Verdi, *Rigoletto*)

"Innaffia l'ugola" (Verdi, *Otello*)

Iolanthe (Gilbert and Sullivan)

Iris (Mascagni)

Iris (Mascagni, *Iris;* also Handel, *Semele*)

Irmelin (Delius)

Isabeau (Mascagni)

Isola d'Alcina (Gazzaniga)

Isola disabitata (Haydn)

Isola disabitata (G. Scarlatti)

Isolde (Wagner, *Tristan und Isolde*)

"Israël, romps ta chaîne" (Saint-Saëns, *Samson et Dalila*)

Italiana in Algeri (Rossini)

Ivan IV (Bizet)

Ivan the Terrible. See *Maid of Pskov.*

Ivan (Bizet, *Ivan IV;* also Glinka, *Life for the Tsar,* and Rimsky-Korsakov, *Maid
   of Pskov*)

Jemmy (Rossini, *William Tell*)

Jenůfa (Janáček)

"Jewel of Asia" (Jones, *Geisha*)

Jewel song. See "Ah! je ris!"

Jochanaan or John the Baptist (R. Strauss, *Salomé*)

John of Leyden (Meyerbeer, *Prophète*)
Johnson (Puccini, *Fanciulla del west*)
Jolie Fille de Perth (Bizet, *Fair Maid of Perth*)
Don José (Bizet, *Carmen*)
Joseph (Méhuel)
Josephine (Gilbert and Sullivan, *H.M.S. Pinafore*)
Judge in chambers (Gilbert and Sullivan, *Trial by Jury*)
Juive (Halévy)
Juliette (Gounod, *Roméo et Juliette*)

Kate, the maiden (Fraser-Simon, *Maid of the Mountains*)
Khovanshchina (Mussorgsky)
Klingsor (Wagner, *Parsifal*)
Koko, Lord High Executioner (Gilbert and Sullivan, *Mikado*)
"Komm" (Flower Maidens' waltz, Wagner, *Parsifal*)
"Komm', Hoffnung, lass den letzten Stern der Müden nicht" (Beethoven, *Fidelio*)
Konchak (Borodin, *Prince Igor*)
Kundry (Wagner, *Parsifal*)

"La calunnia è un venticello" (Rossini, *Barber of Seville*)
"La causa è santa" ("Pour cette cause sainte," Meyerbeer, *Huguenots*)
"Là ci darem la mano" (Mozart, *Don Giovanni*)
La Cieca (Ponchielli, *Gioconda*)
"La donna è mobile" (Verdi, *Rigoletto;* recorded by John McCormack)
"La rà, la rà, la rà, la rà" (Verdi, *Rigoletto*)
"La rivedrà nell' estasi" (Verdi, *Ballo in maschera*)
Lakmé (Delibes)
Land des Lächelns. See *Land of Smiles.*
Land of Smiles (Lehár, *Land des Lächelns*)
"Largo al factotum" (Rossini, *Barber of Seville*)
"Lass mich Euch fragen" (Flotow, *Martha*)
Lass That Loved a Sailor. See *H.M.S. Pinafore.*
Laughing Aria (Lehár, *Merry Widow*)
Lauretta (Puccini, *Gianni Schicchi*)
Leandro (Busoni, *Arlecchino*)
"Légères hirondelles, oiseaux bénis de Dieu" (Thomas, *Mignon*)
Leïla (Bizet, *Pearl Fishers*)

Lenski (Tchaikovsky, *Eugene Onegin*)
Leonore (Beethoven, *Fidelio*)
Leporello (Mozart, *Don Giovanni*)
Lerchenau, Baron Ochs von (R. Strauss, *Rosenkavalier*)
"Les tringles des sistres tintaient" ("Chanson bohème," Bizet, *Carmen*)
Letter Duet. See "Sull'aria."
"Letzte Rose." See "'Tis the last rose of summer."
"Libiamo ne' lieti calici" (Verdi, *Traviata;* see also Brindisi)
"Liebestod." See "Mild und leise."
Life for the Tsar (Glinka)
Lily of Killarney (Benedict)
Linda di Chamounix (Donizetti)
Lindorf (Offenbach, *Tales of Hoffmann*)
Lionel (Flotow, *Martha*)
Lisa (innkeeper, Bellini, *Sonnambula*)
Liù (Puccini, *Turandot*)
Lockit, Lucy (Gay, *Beggar's Opera*)
Loge or Loki (Wagner, *Ring*)
Lohengrin (Wagner)
Lohengrin (Wagner, *Lohengrin*)
Loki. See Loge.
Lola (Mascagni, *Cavalleria rusticana*)
"Lord Chancellor's Song" (Gilbert and Sullivan, *Iolanthe*)
Lord of the Hidden Way (Boughton, *Immortal Hour*)
Lorelei (Mendelssohn)
Loreley (Catalani)
Lotte. See Charlotte.
Louise (Charpentier)
Louise (Charpentier, *Louise*)
"Love that no wrong can cure, Love that is always new" (Gilbert and Sullivan,
    Patience)
"Love will find a way" (Fraser-Simon, *Maid of the Mountains*)
Lucia di Lammermoor (Donizetti)
Lucia (Donizetti, *Lucia di Lammermoor;* also Rossini, *Gazza ladra,* and Pon-
    chielli, *Promessi sposi;* see also Mimi)
Lucrezia Borgia (Donizetti)
Ludmila (Glinka, *Russlan and Ludmila;* also Smetana, *Bartered Bride*)
Luisa Miller (Verdi)

Luiz, Marco and Giuseppe (Gilbert and Sullivan, *Gondoliers*)
Lulu (Berg)
Lulu (Berg, *Lulu*)
Luna, Count (Graf) di (Verdi, *Trovatore*)
Lustige Witwe. See *Merry Widow*.

Macbeth (Verdi)
Macheath, Captain (Gay, *Beggar's Opera*)
Madame Butterfly (Puccini)
"Madamina, il catalogo" (Mozart, *Don Giovanni*)
Maddalena (Verdi, *Rigoletto;* also Donizetti, *Linda di Chamounix*)
Magdalene (Wagner, *Meistersinger*)
Magic Flute (Mozart)
Don Magnifico (Rossini, *Cenerentola*)
Maid of Pskov (Rimsky-Korsakov, *Ivan the Terrible*)
Maid of the Mountains (Fraser-Simon and Tate)
Malde, Walter (Verdi, *Rigoletto*)
Mamma Lucia (Mascagni, *Cavalleria rusticana*)
"Mamma, quel vino è generoso" (Mascagni, *Cavalleria rusticana*)
Manfredo (Montemezzi, *Amore dei tre re*)
Manon (Massenet)
Manon (Massenet, *Manon;* also Puccini, *Manon Lescaut*)
Manon Lescaut (Puccini)
Manrico (Verdi, *Trovatore*)
Manru (Paderewski)
Mantua, Duke of (Verdi, *Rigoletto*)
"M'appari" (Flotow, *Martha;* recorded by John McCormack)
Marcella (Giordano)
Marcello (Puccini, *Bohème*)
Marco. See Luiz.
Mařenka (Smetana, *Bartered Bride*)
Margherita (Boïto, *Mefistofele*)
Marguérite (Gounod, *Faust;* also Berlioz, *Damnation de Faust,* and Meyerbeer, *Huguenots*)
Maria. See Octavian.
Maria di Rohan (Donizetti)
Maria di Rohan (Donizetti, *Maria di Rohan*)
Maritana (Wallace)
Mark, King (Wagner, *Tristan und Isolde*)

Marriage of Figaro (Mozart)

Marschallin (R. Strauss, *Rosenkavalier*)

"Martern aller Arten" (Mozart, *Abduction from the Seraglio*)

Martha (Flotow)

Martha, alias of Harriet (Flotow, *Martha*)

Marzelline (Beethoven, *Fidelio*)

Mat of the Mint (Gay, *Beggar's Opera*)

Max (Weber, *Freischütz;* also Donizetti, *Betly*)

Medea (Charpentier and others)

Medea (in many operas with that title)

Mefistofele (Boïto). See also Méphistophélès.

Meistersinger von Nürnberg (Wagner)

Mélisande (Debussy, *Pelléas et Mélisande;* also Dukas, *Ariane et Barbe-bleu*)

Melissa (Gilbert and Sullivan, *Princess Ida*)

Melitone, Friar (Verdi, *Forza del destino*)

"Mentre le due e le tre" (Verdi, *Falstaff*)

Méphistophélès (Gounod, *Faust;* also Berlioz, *Damnation de Faust*). See also
    Mefistofele.

Merry Widow (Lehár, *Lustige Witwe*)

Merry Wives of Windsor (Nicolai)

"Mi chiamano Mimi" (Puccini, *Bohème*)

Micaëla (Bizet, *Carmen*)

Michele (Puccini, *Tabarro*)

Mignon (Ambroise Thomas)

Mikado (Gilbert and Sullivan)

Mikleford, Lord Tristan or Tristram de (Flotow, *Martha*). See also Tristan.

"Mild und leise" ("Liebestod," Wagner, *Tristan und Isolde*)

Mime (Wagner, *Ring*)

Mimi (Puccini, *Bohème*)

Mimosa-san (Jones, *Geisha*)

Minnie (Puccini, *Fanciulla del west*)

Doctor Miracle (Offenbach, *Tales of Hoffmann*)

"Mir ist so wunderbar" (Beethoven, *Fidelio*)

Mireille (Gounod)

Mireille (Gounod, *Mireille*)

"Miserere" (Verdi, *Trovatore*)

Mlada (Rimsky-Korsakov)

"Mon coeur s'ouvre à ta voix" (Saint-Saëns, *Samson et Dalila*)

Monostatos the Moor (Mozart, *Magic Flute*)

"Morgenlich leuchtend" (Prize song, Wagner, *Meistersinger*)
"Morir! si pura e bella!" (Verdi, *Aïda*)
Musetta (Puccini, *Bohème*)
"My love and cottage near Rochelle" (Balfe, *Siege of Rochelle*)

Nabucco (Verdi)
na Coppaleen, Myles (Benedict, *Lily of Killarney*)
Nadir (Bizet, *Pearl Fishers*)
Nancy (Flotow, *Martha*)
Nanetta (Verdi, *Falstaff*)
Nanki-Pooh (Gilbert and Sullivan, *Mikado*)
Nedda (Leoncavallo, *Pagliacci*)
"Nei cieli bigi guardo fumar" (Puccini, *Bohème*)
"Nemico della patria" (Giordano, *Andrea Chénier*)
Nemorino (Donizetti, *Elisir d'amore*)
Nerone (Boïto)
Nevers, Comte de (Meyerbeer, *Huguenots*)
Nibelung (Wagner, *Ring*)
Nixies (Wagner, *Ring*)
"Noch ein Weilchen" (Smetana, *Bartered Bride*)
"Non piangere Liù" (Puccini, *Turandot*)
Norma (Bellini)
Norma (Bellini, *Norma*)
"Nothung! Nothung! Neidliches Schwert" (Wagner, *Siegfried*)
"Notte e giorno faticar" (Mozart, *Don Giovanni*)
"Nume, custode e vindice" (Verdi, *Aïda*)
Nun's Chorus (Lortzing, *Cazanova*)

"O amore, o bella luce del core" (Mascagni, *Amico Fritz*)
"O azure skies." See "O patria mia."
"O Dieu, Dieu" (Halévy, *Juive*)
"O dolce bacio" (Puccini, *Tosca*)
"O dolci mani" (Puccini, *Tosca*)
"O du mein holder Abendstern" (Wagner, *Tannhäuser*)
"O, Isis and Osiris" (Mozart, *Magic Flute*)
"O paradiso" (Meyerbeer, *Africaine*)
"O patria mia . . . O cieli azzurri" (Verdi, *Aïda*)
"O ruddier than the cherry" (Handel, *Acis and Galatea*)
"O sancta justitia" (Lortzing, *Zar und Zimmerman*)

"O Seligheit, dich fass' ich kaum" (Weber, *Euryanthe*)

"O, sink hernieder" (Wagner, *Tristan und Isolde*)

"O souverain, ô juge" (Massenet, *Cid*)

"O statua gentilissima" (Mozart, *Don Giovanni*)

"O terra addio" (Verdi, *Aïda;* recorded by John McCormack)

"O vin, dissipe la tristesse" (Thomas, *Hamlet*)

Oberon (Weber)

Oberto, Conte di San Bonifacio (Verdi)

Occasione fa il ladro (Rossini)

"Ocean, thou mighty monster" (Weber, *Oberon*)

Octavian (R. Strauss, *Rosenkavalier*)

Odabella (Verdi, *Attila*)

"Oh, my Dolores." See "Shade of the Palm."

"Ombra mai fù" (Handel, *Serse*)

"Ombre légère qui suis mes pas" (Shadow Song, Meyerbeer, *Dinorah*)

"Ora e per sempre addio" (Verdi, *Otello*)

Orest (R. Strauss, *Elektra*)

Orfée aux enfers (Offenbach)

Orfeo ed Euridice (Gluck)

Orfeo (Orpheus) and Eurydice (Offenbach, *Orfée aux enfers;* also Monteverdi, *Favola d'Orfeo*, Gluck, *Orfeo ed Euridice*, Monteverdi, *Favola d'Orfeo*)

Orlando (Handel)

Oroveso (Bellini, *Norma*)

Ortrud (Wagner, *Lohengrin*)

Comte Ory (Rossini, *Comte Ory*)

Oscar (Verdi, *Ballo in maschera*)

Osmin (Mozart, *Abduction from the Seraglio*)

Otello (Verdi)

Otello (Verdi, *Otello*)

Don Ottavio (Mozart, *Don Giovanni*)

"Où va la jeune hindoue" (Bell Song, Delibes, *Lakmé*)

"Pace, pace" (Verdi, *Forza del destino*)

Page, Anna (Nicolai, *Merry Wives of Windsor*)

Pagliacci (Leoncavallo)

Pagliaccio (Leoncavallo, *Pagliacci*)

Pamina (Mozart, *Magic Flute*)

Panza, Sancho (Massenet, *Don Quixote*)

Papagena (Mozart, *Magic Flute*). See also Papageno.

Papageno (Mozart, *Magic Flute*). See also Papagena.

Papageno/Papagena's *pianissimo* duet (Mozart, *Magic Flute*)

Pardon de Ploërmel. See *Dinorah*.

"Pari siamo" (Verdi, *Rigoletto*)

"Parigi, o cara" (Verdi, *Traviata;* recorded by John McCormack)

"Parle-moi de ma mère" (Bizet, *Carmen;* recorded by John McCormack)

Parma, Duchess of (Busoni, *Doktor Faust*)

Parsifal (Wagner)

Parsifal (Wagner, *Parsifal*)

Patience (Gilbert and Sullivan)

Peachum, Polly (Gay, *Beggar's Opera*)

Pearl Fishers (Bizet)

Pedrillo (Mozart, *Abduction from the Seraglio*)

Pelléas et Mélisande (Debussy)

Pelléas (Debussy, *Pelléas et Mélisande*)

Penelope (Fauré)

Penelope (Fauré, *Penelope*)

Perfect Fool (Holst)

Périchole (Offenbach)

"Pian, pianin" (Mozart, *Marriage of Figaro*)

"Piff, paff" (Meyerbeer, *Huguenots*)

Pilgrim's Chorus (Wagner, *Tannhäuser*)

Ping, Pang, Pong (Puccini, *Turandot*)

Pinkerton (Puccini, *Madame Butterfly*)

Pique dame (Tchaikovsky, *Queen of Spades*)

Pirata (Bellini)

Pirates of Penzance (Gilbert and Sullivan)

Pitty Sing (Gilbert and Sullivan, *Mikado*)

Pizarro (Beethoven, *Fidelio*)

"Pizzica, pizzica, pizzica" (Verdi, *Falstaff*)

"Plus blanche que la blanche ermine" (Meyerbeer, *Huguenots*)

Pogner (Wagner, *Meistersinger*)

Polkan (Rimsky-Korsakov, *Golden Cockerel*)

Polyeucte (Gounod)

Pooh-Bah (Gilbert and Sullivan, *Mikado*)

Popov (Lehár, *Merry Widow*)

Poppea (Monteverdi, *Incoronazione di Poppea*)

"Possente Phtha" (Verdi, *Aïda*)

Postillon de Longjumeau (Adam)

"Pour cette cause sainte." See "La causa è santa."

"Pour me rapprocher de Marie, je m'ensolai pauvre soldat" (Donizetti, *Fille du régiment*)

"Pourquoi me réveiller" (Massenet, *Werther*)

Prince Igor (Borodin)

Princess Ida (Gilbert and Sullivan)

Promessi sposi (Ponchielli)

Prophète (Meyerbeer)

Psyche, Lady (Gilbert and Sullivan, *Princess Ida*)

"Pur ti riveggo, mia dolce Aïda" (Verdi, *Aïda*)

Puritani (Bellini)

"Quanto è bella" (Donizetti, *Elisir d'amore;* sung by John McCormack)

"Que veulent dire ces colères" (Offenbach, *Périchole*)

Queen of Spades. See *Pique dame.*

Queen of the Night (Mozart, *Magic Flute*)

"Questa o quella" (Verdi, *Rigoletto;* recorded by John McCormack)

"Questo è il fin" (Mozart, *Don Giovanni*)

Quickly, Mistress (Verdi, *Falstaff*)

Quinquin. See Octavian.

Don Quixote (Massenet, *Don Quixote*)

Rachel (Halévy, *Juive*)

Radamès (Verdi, *Aïda*)

Raimbaut the minstrel (Meyerbeer, *Robert le diable*)

Ramiro (Rossini, *Cenerentola*)

Rance, Jack (Puccini, *Fanciulla del west*)

Raoul (Meyerbeer, *Huguenots*)

Ravoir, Geronte de (Puccini, *Manon Lescaut*)

Reginald. See Bunthorne.

Reine Fiammette (Leroux)

Renato (Verdi, *Ballo in maschera*)

Rheingold (Wagner)

Rhine Maidens (Wagner, *Ring*)

Rhine Maidens' Song (Wagner, *Rheingold*)

Ribbing, Count (Verdi, *Ballo in maschera*)

Riccardo (Verdi, *Ballo in maschera*)

"Right Down Regular Royal Queen" (Gilbert and Sullivan, *Gondoliers*)

Rigoletto (Verdi)

Rigoletto (Verdi, *Rigoletto*)
Rinaldo (Handel)
Ring des Nibelungen (Wagner)
"Ritorna vincitor" (Verdi, *Aïda*)
Robert le diable (Gilbert)
Robert le diable (Meyerbeer)
Rocco (Beethoven, *Fidelio*)
Rodolfo (Puccini, *Bohème;* also Verdi, *Luisa Miller*)
Rohan. See Maria di Rohan.
Roi d'Ys (Lalo)
Roméo et Juliette (Gounod)
Roméo (Gounod, *Roméo et Juliette*)
Rondine (Puccini)
Rosamunde (Schubert)
Rose Marie (Friml)
"Rose Marie" (Friml, *Rose Marie;* recorded by John McCormack)
Rosenkavalier (R. Strauss)
Rosina (Rossini, *Barber of Seville*)
Ruddigore (Gilbert and Sullivan)
Russlan and Ludmilla (Glinka)
Ruth. See Zorah. See also Gilbert and Sullivan, *Pirates of Penzance.*

Sachs, Hans (Johannes) (Wagner, *Meistersinger*)
Sadko (Rimsky-Korsakov)
St. Phar. See Chappelou.
"Salce, salce" (Willow Song, Verdi, *Otello*)
Salomé (R. Strauss)
Salomé (R. Strauss, *Salomé*)
"Salut, demeure, chaste et pure" (Gounod, *Faust;* recorded by John McCormack)
Samiel (Weber, *Freischütz*)
Samson et Dalila (Saint-Saëns)
Samson (Saint-Saëns, *Samson et Dalila*)
Santuzza (Mascagni, *Cavalleria rusticana*)
"Saper vorreste" (Verdi, *Ballo in maschera*)
Saphir (Gilbert and Sullivan, *Patience*)
Sarastro (Mozart, *Magic Flute*)
Satanella (Balfe)

Scarpia (Puccini, *Tosca*)

"Scenes that are brightest" (Wallace, *Maritana*)

Schwanda (Weinberger)

"Scuoti quella fronda di ciliego" (Puccini, *Madame Butterfly*)

Selika (Meyerbeer, *Africaine*)

Selim Pasha (Mozart, *Abduction from the Seraglio*)

Semele (Handel)

Semiramide (Rossini)

Senta (Wagner, *Flying Dutchman*)

Serse (Handel)

Serva Padronna (Pergolesi)

"Shade of the Palm" (Stuart, *Floradora*)

Shadow God (Boughton, *Immortal Hour*)

Shadow Song. See "Ombre légère qui suis mes pas."

"Shall I never more behold thee?" (Donizetti, *Lucia di Lammermoor*)

Shvanda the Bagpiper. See *Schwanda.*

"Si colmi il calice" (Verdi, *Macbeth*)

"Si l'amour sur ma route ce soir m'étend la main" (Thomas, *Mignon*)

"Si può?" (Leoncavallo, *Pagliacci*)

"Siciliana" (Mascagni, *Cavalleria rusticana;* recorded by John McCormack)

Siege of Rochelle (Balfe)

Siegfried (Wagner)

Siegfried (Wagner, *Siegfried* and *Götterdämmerung*)

Siegfried's forging song. See "Nothung! Nothung!"

Sieglinde (Wagner, *Walküre*)

Siegmund (Wagner, *Ring* and *Walküre*)

"Siegmund heiss' ich, und Siegmund bin ich" (Wagner, *Walküre*)

"Signore, ascolta" (Puccini, *Turandot*)

Sigurd (Reyer)

Sigurd (Reyer, *Sigurd*)

"Silentium—wach' auf" (Wagner, *Meistersinger*)

Silva (Verdi, *Ernani*)

Silvano (Verdi, *Ballo in maschera*)

Silvio (Leoncavallo, *Pagliacci*)

Simon Boccanegra (Verdi)

Slammekin, Mrs. (Gay, *Beggar's Opera*)

Slippery Sam (Gay, *Beggar's Opera*)

"Sola, perduta, abbandonata" (Puccini, *Manon Lescaut*)

"Solenne in quest'ora" (Verdi, *Forza del destino*)

Sonnambula (Bellini)

Sorochintsi Fair (Mussorgsky)

Spalanzani (Offenbach, *Tales of Hoffmann*)

Sparafucile (Verdi, *Rigoletto*)

Sperata (Thomas, *Mignon*)

"Spirto gentil" (Donizetti, *Favorita;* recorded by John McCormack)

Sruth na maoile (Palmer)

Stella. See Hoffmann and Stella.

Stiffelio (Verdi)

Stolzing. See Walther.

"Stride la vampa" (Verdi, *Trovatore*)

"Suicidio!" (Ponchielli, *Gioconda*)

"Sull'aria" (letter duet, Mozart, *Marriage of Figaro*)

Sulpice (Donizetti, *Fille du régiment*)

"Summ' und brumm'" (Wagner, *Flying Dutchman*)

Suor Angelica (Puccini)

Suzuki (Puccini, *Madame Butterfly*)

Tabarro (Puccini)

"Take a pair of sparkling eyes" (Gilbert and Sullivan, *Gondoliers*)

Tales of Hoffmann (Offenbach)

Tamino (Mozart, *Magic Flute*)

Tancredi (Rossini)

Tannhäuser (Wagner)

Tantris (the syllables of *Tristan* inverted). See Tristan.

Tawdry, Suky (Gay, *Beggar's Opera*)

Tell, William (Rossini, *William Tell*)

Tessa (Gilbert and Sullivan, *Gondoliers*)

Thaddeus (Balfe, *Bohemian Girl*)

Thaïs (Massenet)

"The Colleen Bawn" (Benedict, *Lily of Killarney*)

"The heart bowed down" (Balfe, *Bohemian Girl*)

"The Memory of the Past." See "There is a flower that bloometh."

"The Moon Has Raised Her Lamp Above" (Benedict, *Lily of Killarney;* recorded by John McCormack)

"The Secret of My Birth" (Balfe, *Bohemian Girl*)

"The Stirrup Cup" (song by opera conductor Luigi Arditi)

"Then You'll Remember Me" ("When other lips," Balfe, *Bohemian Girl,* recorded by John McCormack)

"There is a flower that bloometh" (Wallace, *Maritana;* recorded by John McCormack)

Thor (Wagner, *Ring*)

Thore (Meyerbeer, *Huguenots*)

Three kings (Montemezzi, *Amore dei tre re*). See also Archibaldo, Avito, and Manfredo.

Timur (Puccini, *Turandot*)

"'Tis the last rose of summer" ("Letzte Rose," Flotow, *Martha*)

Tonio (Leoncavallo, *Pagliacci;* also Donizetti, *Fille du régiment*)

Toreador's Song. See "Votre toast, je peux vous le rendre."

"Tornami a dir" (Donizetti, *Don Pasquale*)

Tosca (Puccini)

Tosca (Puccini, *Tosca*)

Traviata (Verdi)

"Treulich geführt" (Bridal Chorus, Wagner, *Lohengrin*)

Trial by Jury (Gilbert and Sullivan)

Tristan und Isolde (Wagner)

Tristan (Wagner, *Tristan und Isolde;* also Flotow, *Martha*)

Trittico. See *Gianni Schicchi, Suor Angelica,* and *Tabarro.*

Trovatore (Verdi)

Troyens (Berlioz)

"Tu, che di gel sei cinta" (Puccini, *Turandot*)

"Tu? tu? piccolo iddio!" (Puccini, *Madame Butterfly*)

Turandot (Busoni)

Turandot (Puccini)

Turandot (Puccini, *Turandot,* and Busoni, *Turandot*)

Turiddu (Mascagni, *Cavalleria rusticana*)

Turk. See Selim Pasha.

"Turn on, old time" (Wallace, *Maritana*)

"Turn, turn in this direction" (Gilbert and Sullivan, *Patience*)

"Tutto nel mondo" (Verdi, *Falstaff*)

Twitcher (Gay, *Beggar's Opera*)

"Udite, udite, o rustici" (Donizetti, *Elisir d'amore*)

Ulrica (Verdi, *Ballo in maschera*)

"Un bel dì" (Puccini, *Madame Butterfly*)

"Un giorno la mano me porse un donzello" (Donizetti, *Zingara*)
"Una furtiva lagrima" (Donizetti, *Elisir d'amore;* sung by John McCormack)
"Una voce poco fà" (Rossini, *Barber of Seville*)
Urban II (Wagner, *Tannhäuser*)

"Va, pensiero, sull' ali dorati" (Verdi, *Nabucco*)
Valentin (Gounod, *Faust*)
Valentine (Meyerbeer, *Huguenots*)
Valois. See Elizabeth de Valois.
Vanderdecken (Wagner, *Flying Dutchman*)
"Veau d'or" (Gounod, *Faust*)
"Vedrai, carino" (Mozart, *Don Giovanni*)
"Veille sur eux toujours, Mère, Mère" (Meyerbeer, *Etoile du nord*)
Véronique (Messager)
Véronique (Messager, *Véronique*)
"Versez! que tout respire" (Meyerbeer, *Prophète*)
Vespri siciliani (Verdi)
"Vesti la giubba" (Leoncavallo, *Pagliacci;* recorded by John McCormack)
Violetta (Verdi, *Traviata*)
Violette (Leroux, *Reine Fiammette*)
"Vissi d'arte" (Puccini, *Tosca*)
Vittoria, Giulia, Fiametta (Gilbert and Sullivan, *Gondoliers*)
"Viva il vino" (Mascagni, *Cavalleria rusticana*)
Vixen, Mrs. (Gay, *Beggar's Opera*)
Vogelweide. See Walther von der Vogelweide.
"Voi che sapete" (Mozart, *Marriage of Figaro*)
"Voi lo sapete, O mamma" (Mascagni, *Cavalleria rusticana*)
Volsung (Wagner, *Ring*)
"Votre toast, je peux vous le rendre" (Toreador's song, Bizet, *Carmen*)

Wälse (Wotan, Wagner, *Ring*)
"Wahn! Wahn!" (Wagner, *Meistersinger*)
Walküre (Wagner)
Wally (Catalani)
Walther von der Vogelweide (Wagner, *Tannhäuser*)
Walther von Stolzing (Wagner, *Meistersinger*)
Wanda (Doppler)
Wanda (Doppler, *Wanda;* also Offenbach, *Grande Duchesse de Gérolstein*)
Wanderer (Wotan, Wagner, *Siegfried*)

"Water parted from the sea" (Arne, *Artaxerxes*)

Wedding March. See "Treulich geführt."

"Weia! Waga! Woge, du Welle, walle zur Wiege! Wagalaweia! Wallala Weia! Waga! . . . Wagalaweia!" (Wagner, *Ring*)

Wellgunde (Wagner, *Ring*). See also Flosshilde.

Werther (Massenet)

"When a man marries" (Gilbert and Sullivan, *Gondoliers*)

"When first I saw." See "M'appari."

"When I am laid in earth" (Purcell, *Dido and Aeneas*)

"When other lips." See "Then You'll Remember Me."

"When you're lying awake." See "Lord Chancellor's Song."

"Where'er you walk" (Handel, *Semele;* recorded by John McCormack)

"Wie, Wie, Wie" (quintet, Mozart, *Magic Flute*)

Wildschütz (Lortzing)

William Tell (Rossini)

Willow Song. See "Salce, Salce."

"Willow, Tit-Willow, Tit-Willow" (Gilbert and Sullivan, *Mikado*)

"With drooping wings, ye cupids, come" (Purcell, *Dido and Aeneas*)

Wotan (Wagner, *Ring*). See also Wälse, Wanderer.

Wozzeck (Berg)

Wreckers (Smyth)

Yeomen of the Guard (Gilbert and Sullivan)

"Yours is my heart alone" ("Dein ist mein ganzes Herz," Lehár, *Land of Smiles*)

"Youth's the season" (Gay, *Beggar's Opera*)

Zar und Zimmermann (Lortzing)

Zàzà (Leoncavallo)

Zàzà (Leoncavallo, *Zàzà*)

Zingara. See *Bohemian Girl.*

Zingara (Donizetti)

Zingara (Rinaldo)

Zingari (Leoncavallo)

"Zitti, zitti, piano, piano" (Rossini, *Barber of Seville*)

Zorah and Ruth (Gilbert and Sullivan, *Ruddigore*)

· 9 ·

Opera Singers in *Finnegans Wake*

All page references are to *Finnegans Wake,* by page/line number. Thus, Emma Abbot is alluded to on line 12 of p. 237, lines 14–15 of p. 392, and line 27 of p. 539. First names, nationality, vocal ranges, and dates are provided where they could be ascertained.

Abbott, Emma (Am. sop., 1850–91): 237.12; 392.14–15; 539.27
Ackte, Aïno (Finn. sop., 1876–1944): 241.1
Adams, Suzanne (Am. sop., 1872–1953): 381.19
Albani, Emma (Can. sop., b. Marie Louise Cécile Lajeunesse, 1847–1930): 137.7; 463.24; 489.32
Alboni, Marietta (It. contra., b. Maria Anna Marzia, 1823–94): 137.7
Alda, Frances (New Z. sop., b. Davies, 1883–1952): 155.36; 186.10; 549.28
Althouse, Paul (Am. ten., 1889–1954): 338.20
Amato, Pasquale (It. bar., 1878–1942): 262.F4
Ancona, Mario (It. bar., 1860–1931): 467.33
Anderson, Marian (Am. sop., 1902–93): 412.23; 413.5, .14–15; 414.2
Andrade, Francisco d' (Port. bar., 1859–1921): 414.13
Andrésen, Ivar (Nor. bass, 1896–1940): 413.15
Anitúa, Fanny (Mex. sop., 1887–1968): 572.31–573.29 passim
Annibali, Domenico (It. male sop., ca. 1700–99): 337.8
Anselmi, Giuseppe (It. ten., 1876–1929): 458.29
Appiani, Giuseppe (called Appianino, 1712–42; made a short career but collected huge fees in Venice, Genoa, Milan, Vienna, and Bologna): 297.25; 548.6
Arangi-Lombardi, Giannina (It. sop., 1891–1951): 226.30–31; 572.36; 596.8
Arkor, André d' (Bel. ten., 1901–71): 186.28
Arnoldson, Sigrid (Sw. sop., 1861–1943): 443.22

Artôt, Désirée (Bel. mezzo-sop., b. Marguerite Joséphine Désirée Montagney, 1835–1907): 254.36

Austral, Florence (Austral. sop., b. Mary Wilson Favaz, 1894–1968): 50.10; 457.7; 464.27; 465.16; 552.7

Badini, Ernesto (It. bar., 1876–1937): 425.18

Baillie, Isobel (Scot. sop., 1895–1983): 448.19

Balfe, Michael (Irish bar., 1808–70): 199.29

Barrientos, Maria (Sp. sop., 1883–1946): 536.32

Beard, John (En. ten., ca. 1717–91): 443.26

Belhomme, Hypolite (Fr. bass, 1854–1923): 450.32

Belloc-Giorgi, Teresa (It. mezzo-sop., b. Maria Teresa Ottavia Faustina Trombetta, 1784–1855): 368.10, .15

Bender, Paul (Ger. bass, 1875–1947): 200.24

Benucci, Francesco (It. bass, also called Pietro Benucci, ca. 1745–1824): 473.17

Besanzoni, Gabriella (It. mezzo-sop., 1888–1962): 234.5; 432.32

Bianchi, Bianca (Ger. sop., b. Bertha Schwarz, 1855–1947): 238.23; 240.18; 321.9

Billington, Elizabeth (En. sop., 1765–1818): 47.5; 436.27

Bishop, Anna (En. sop., 1810–84): 392.14–15

Björling, Jussi (Sw. ten., shared JJ's 2 Feb. birthday, 1911–60): 471.30; 472.15

Bland, Maria Theresa (En. mezzo-sop., 1769–1838): 3.11; 57.26; 484.21

Bockelmann, Rudolf (Ger. bass-bar., 1892–1958): 388.33

Bohnen, Michael (Ger. bass-bar., 1887–1965): 238.26

Bonci, Alessandro (It. ten., 1870–1940): 408.26; 455.14; 468.36; 536.9

Bondini, Marianna (It. sop., 1780–1813): 614.1

Bordoni, Faustina (It. sop., 1700–81): 292.22

Borgioli, Armando (It. bar., 1898–1945): 152.27

Bori, Lucrezia (Sp. sop., b. Lucrecia Borja y Gonzalez de Riancho, 1887–1960): 182.28

Borosini, Francesco (It. ten., ca. 1690–after 1747): 483.11

Braham, John (En. ten., b. Abraham, 1774–1856; *Grove's* says "foreigners" often remarked, "Non c'è in Italia tenore come Braham" [There is no tenor like Braham in Italy]—*Grove's*, s.v. "Braham"): 81.7; 200.4; 284.F4; 422.26; 441.25

Brambilla family (It. singers: Amalia, sop., ?–1880; Marietta, contra., 1807–75; Teresa, sop., 1813–95; Teresina, sop., 1845–1921; also Paolo, comp., 1787–1838): 366.22

Brent, Charlotte (En. sop., ca. 1735–1802): 578.28

Broschi, Carlo. See Farinelli.

Brozel, Philip (ten., sang *I pagliacci* in Dublin 1903 or 1904, much admired by John McCormack): 560.32

Bugge (famous sop. who fell into poverty and ended in the morgue. Her cadaver was identified by a doctor who had admired her singing): 58.17

Burke, Edmund Arbrickle (Can. bass, 1876–1970): 256.12; 443.16

Burns, Georgina (En. sop., born 1860; debuted in 1877 as Anna Page in *Merry Wives of Windsor* with Carl Rosa Opera Company in Aberdeen): 223.7. See also Crotty.

Butt, Clara (En. contra., 1873–1936): 254.13; 421.4; 444.17

Calvé, Emma (Fr. sop., b. Rosa Noémie Emma Calvet de Roquer, 1858–1942): 438.2; 461.15

Campanini, Italo (It. ten., 1845–96): 541.7

Caniglia, Maria (It. sop., 1905–79): 518.29; 573.30

Capoul, Joseph-Amédée-Victor (Fr. ten., 1839–1924): 370.36

Carestini, Giovanni (It. male contra., called "Cusanino, "1705–60): 163.17

Caruso, Enrico (It. ten., 1873–1921): monkey-house incident, 46.27–31; 47.26–29; 63.7, .29; 64.16; 70.7–9; 76.25; 139.30–32; 193.32; 307.L; 491.12–13, .16–18; 516.23; 536.25–32; 611.10; and Black Hand: 495.1–3; other: 211.16; 406.15; 538.13; 601.3

Catalani, Angelica (It. sop., 1780–1849): 266.24–25

Catley, Anne (En. sop., 1745–89; celebrated in Dublin in 1760s; wore her hair plain over forehead, in even line to eyebrows, setting a new fashion when ladies had their hair "Catley-fied." JJ merges "Catley" and "cowlick"): 409.12; 485.1

Cavalieri, Lina (It. sop., b. Natalina, 1874–1944): 370.7

Chaliapin, Fyodor Ivanovich (Russ. bass, also spelled "Shalyapin," 1873–1938): 351.13–14; 467.26

Cigna, Gina (Fr.-It. sop., b. Ginetta Sens, 1900–): 511.13

Clément, Edmond (Fr. ten., 1867–1928): 154.20

Coates, Edith (En. mezzo-sop., 1908–83; sang role of the Countess in *Queen of Spades*): 325.25–26; 411.31; 447.27–28

Coates, John (En. ten., 1865–1941): 325.25–26

Cobelli, Giuseppina (It. sop., 1898–1948): 178.10

Colbran, Isabella (Sp. sop., 1785–1845): 318.31

Cook, Thomas Aynsley (En. bass, 1831 or 1836–94): 456.31

Cooke, Tom (Irish ten., 1782–1848): 424.12; 456.31

Cordon, Norman (Am. bass, 1904–64): 459.26

Cornelius, Peter (Dan. ten., b. Lauritz Peter Corneliys Petersen, 1865–1934): 98.9; 389.28

Corri, Sophia. See Sophia Dušsek.

Cortis, Antonio (Sp. ten., 1891–1952): 468.31

Crabbé, Armand (Bel. bar., 1883–1947): 257.23; 417.28

Crescentini, Girolamo (It. sop., 1762–1846; "one of the last great castrati"— Heriot, 117): 260.11; 369.9

Cross, Joan (En. sop., 1900–): 228.5; 448.8

Crotty, Leslie (Irish bar., 1853–1903, with Carl Rosa Opera Company 1875– 80, husband of Georgina Burns and manager of Burns-Crotty Opera Company, briefly, 1893): 141.14. See also Burns.

Cunningham, Robert (ten., sang Rodolfo in Carl Rosa's initial production of *La bohème* in Manchester, 1897): 95.9; 393.5; 434.12. See also William Paull, C. Tilbury.

Cusanino. See Giovanni Carestini.

Daddi, Francesco (ten.; played the mute servant Sante in the Philadelphia-Chicago Opera Company production of *Il segreto di Susanna* at the Metropolitan Opera, 13 Dec. 1912): 431.32; 439.20; 446.13

dal Monte, Toti (It. sop., b. Antonietta Meneghelli, 1893–1975): 287.25; 333.23

Dalla Rizza, Gilda (It. sop., 1892–1975): 454.21

Damcke, ? (ten.; Dubliners hooted him off the stage at their city's Theatre Royal, calling him "Donkey"): 373.4; 397.10

Darclée, Hariclea (Rom. sop., b. Haricly Hartulary, 1860–1939): 244.13; 404.1; 434.31

Davies, Edward (ten., appeared in *Faust* in Dublin, 1903–4): 391.28

Dawson, Peter (bar.): 276.19

de Angelis, Nazzareno (It. bass, 1881–1962): 405.7; 443.35

de Begnis, Giuseppe (It. bass, 1793–1849): 407.10

de Begnis, Giuseppina Ronzi (It. sop., 1800–53): 407.10

de Luca, Giuseppe (It. bar., 1876–1950): 438.30

de Lucia, Fernando (It. ten., 1860–1925): 438.30

de Paolis, Alessio (It. ten., 1893–1964): 117.24

de Reszke, Edouard (Polish bass, 1853–1917): 81.34

de Reszke, Jean (Polish ten., b. Jan Mieczyslaw, 1850–1925; made Dublin debut before 1876 as baritone under name of Jean or Giovanni di Reschi): 81.34; 155.27; 200.9; 222.10; 344.32; 408.4; 541.21, .23; as singer in quartet: 533.16–21

Delna, Marie (Fr. contra., b. Ledan, 1875–1932): 200.9; 221.13

Destinn, Emmy (Czech sop., b. Emilie [Ema] Pavlina Kittlová, 1878–1930): 413.1; 421.10; 455.17

di Murska, Ilma (Croat. sop., 1836–89): 136.1; 212.13; 251.15

di Reschi. See de Reszke.

Dorus-Gras, Julie (Bel. sop., b. Aimée-Josèphe van Steenkiste, 1805–96): 462.7

Duma, ? (female singer with Carl Rosa Opera Company in Dublin, 1894): 54.9

Dunelli. See Dunn.

Dunn, ? (bass at Theatre Royal, Dublin; called himself Dunelli): 84.36

Duprez, Gilbert-Louis (Fr. ten., 1806–96): 80.21; 228.3; 231.6; 350.25; 582.32

Dušsek, Sophia (Anglo-It. mezzo-sop., b. Sophia Giustina Corri, 1775–after 1828): 461.9

Dux, Claire (Ger.-Am. sop., 1885–1967): 8.19; 449.6

Eames, Emma (Am. sop., 1865–1952): 306.F1; 412.8

Easton, Florence (En. sop., 1882–1955): 236.8; 413.8; 447.35; 453.22; 471.11

Edvina, Louise (Fr.-Can. sop., b. Marie-Louise Lucienne Martin, ca. 1880–1948): 51.14

Elmo, Cloe (It. mezzo-sop., 1910–62): 460.17

Erb, Karl (Ger. ten., 1877–1958): 451.7

Fancelli, Giuseppe (It. ten., 1833–87): 440.21

Farinelli (It. male sop., b. Carlo Broschi, 1705–82. Farinelli was a family nick-name, meaning "rogue" or "rascal" in Italian. Broschi was also known as "Il Ragazzo" [the boy]): 151.7; 224.30; 359.19–20; 372.28; 436.6; 450.10; 522.11

Farrar, Geraldine (Am. sop., 1882–1967): 241.20; 433.7

Faucit, Helen (sop. [?], appeared Theatre Royal, Dublin, April 1875): 418.11

Faure, Jean-Baptiste (Fr. bar., 1830–1914): 587.1

Favero, Mafalda (It. sop., 1905–81): 186.10; 470.11

Fenton, Lavinia (En. sop., 1708–60): 327.12

Ferrier, Kathleen (En. contra., 1912–53): 404.19

Figner. See Mei-Figner.

Flagstad, Kirsten (Nor. sop., b. Malfrid, 1895–1962): 448.23; 473.5

Fleischer-Edel, Katherina (Ger. sop., 1873–1928): 422.3

Foli, A(llan) J(ames) (Irish bass, b. Foley, 1835–99): 243.16; 397.12; 464.5; 552.12

Foli, Giovanni (name under which John McCormack made his Italian operat-ic debut at Savona, Italy, in January 1906): 112.33; 212.13; 230.21;

Graziani, Lodovico (It. ten., 1820–85; first Alfredo in Verdi's *La traviata* and specialist in Verdi repertory): 186.31; 231.7

Greene, Plunket or Plunkett (Irish bass, 1865–1936; biographer of Villiers Stanford and mentioned in *Letters 1* [66]): 533.19

Greveuse, Louis (ten., born Douthitt): 13.7

Grisi, Giuditta (It. mezzo-sop., 1805–30): 170.34; 410.9

Grisi, Giulia (It. sop., 1811–69; companion of the tenor Mario): 170.34; 410.9; 412.33; 464.29

Gulbranson, Ellen (Sw. sop., b. Norgren, 1863–1947): 171.14

Gura, Eugen (Ger. bass-bar., 1842–1906; first King Mark in Wagner's *Tristan und Isolde* in England): 349.9

Harty. See Nicholls.

Hayes, Catherine (Irish sop., 1825–61): 397.10; 434.12

Hayes, Roland (Am. ten., 1887–1977): 397.10; 434.12

Heldy, Fanny (Bel. sop., b. Marguerite-Virginia Emma Clementine Deceuninck, 1888–1973): 229.33

Hempel, Frieda (Ger. sop., 1885–1955): 175.17

Henderson, Roy (Scot. bar., 1899–): 556.25

Hislop, Joseph (Scot. ten., 1884–1977): 422.13

Homer, Louise (Am. contra., b. Louise Dilworth Beatty, 1871–1947): 129.23; 306.L3; 445.32

Horn, Charles Edward (En. ten.-bar., 1786–1849): 39.36; 264.5–6

Hotter, Hans (Ger. bass-bar., 1909–): 406.17

Howard, Kathleen (Can.-Am. contra., 1884–1956): 242.33

Hyde, Walter (En. ten., 1875–1951): 66.17; 150.17–18; 374.21; 603.15

Isola, Anna (It. sop., fl. 1728–45): 209.24; 289.28; 384.31

Janssen, Herbert (Ger.-Am. bar., 1892–1965): 173.12

Jeritza, Maria (Czech. sop., b. Mimi Jedlitzková, 1887–1982): 257.6

Johnson, Edward (Can. ten., 1878–1959): 377.32–33

Jones, J. F. (sang role of S. Vincent in Wallace's *Maritana* at Theatre Royal, Dublin): 48.11–12

Jones, Parry (Welsh ten., 1891–1963): 431.12

Jörn, Karl (Latvian ten., 1876–1947): 142.27; 428.3; 513.7

Journet, Marcel (Fr. bass, 1867–1933): 417.34; 431.27

Juch, Emma (Am. sop., 1863–1939): 209.4; 417.30; 450.17

Kappel, Gertrude (Ger. sop., 1884–1971): 448.9

Kellogg, Clara Louise (Am. sop., 1842–1916): 456.31

Kelly, Michael (Irish ten., 1762–1826): 32.29; 199.28; 390.7; 407.16; 445.14; 456.30, .31; 484.33

Kipnis, Alexander (Russ.-Am. bass, 1891–1978): 243.22

Kirkby-Lunn, Louise (En. mezzo-sop., 1873–1930): 137.9–10

Klein, Peter (Ger. ten., 1907–): 330.24

Knote, Heinrich (Ger. ten., 1870–1953): 441.6

Kraus, Ernst (Ger. ten., 1863–1941): 404.24; 424.18

Kraus, Otakar (Czech.-En. bar., 1909–80): 404.24; 424.18

Krauss, Felix von (Aus. bass, 1870–1937): 404.24; 424.18

Krauss, Gabrielle (Aus. sop., 1842–1906): 404.24; 424.18

Kurt, Melanie (Aus. sop., 1880–1941); 100.31

Labette, Dora. See Perli.

Labia, Fausta (It. sop., 1870–1935): 540.7

Labia, Maria (It. sop., 1880–1953): 540.7

Lablache, Luigi (It. bass, of Irish-French parentage, 1794–1858): 237.33

Larsén-Todsen, Nanny (Sw. sop., 1884–1982): 75.8

Lassalle, Jean (Fr. bar., 1847–1909): 226.29

Lauri-Volpi, Giacomo (It. ten., 1892–1979; thought by Joyce to be John Sullivan's "enemy"): 4.10–11; 97.14; 223.3; 249.7; 379.24; 406.6; 413.34; 480.28

Lawrence, Marjorie (Austral. sop., 1907–79): 405.24

Lazaro, Hippolito (Sp. ten., 1887–1974): 429.6

Lazzari, Virgilio (It.-Am. bass, 1887–1953): 429.6; 484.25

Ledwidge. See Ludwig.

Lehmann, Lilli (Ger. sop., 1848–1929): 38.7

Lehmann, Lotte (Ger.-Am. sop., 1888–1976; b. at Perleberg): 38.7; 561.15

Leider, Frida (Ger. sop., 1888–1975): 42.17; 508.18

Lemmens-Sherrington, Helen (En. sop., 1834–1906): 421.2; 601.5

Leoni, Michael (En. male alto, b. Meyer Lyon; teacher of tenor John Braham; sang in Dublin 1770 or 1771; part owner of a theater in Capel St. with Tomasso Giordani [1783] and of Dublin's English Opera Company [ca. 1760–96]): 246.16; 422.26

Licette, Miriam (En. sop., 1892–1969): 440.12; 445.10

Lind, Jenny (Sw. sop., b. Johanna Maria, 1820–87; known as the "Swedish nightingale"): 180.13–14; 359.32, .35; 360.2; 438.36; 445.32; 450.17; 490.25–26; 527.27; 578.22–23

List, Emanuel (Aus.-Am. bass, b. Fleissig, 1888–1967): 238.23

Litvinne, Félia (Fr.-Russ. sop., b. Françoise-Jeanne Schütz, 1860–1936): 382.13

Lloyd, Edward (Teddy) (En. ten., 1845–1927): 373.4; 590.5; 609.3

Lubin, Germaine (Fr. sop., 1890–1979): 42.17; 565.22

Lucca, Pauline (Aus. sop., 1841–1908): 295.20; 438.30; 497.18

Ludwig, William (Irish bar., b. Ledwidge, 1847–1923): 243.17; 243.35; 246.17; 338.20; 361.21; 538.3. Bloom recalls his "stupendous success" in *The Flying Dutchman,* which he sang in Dublin in 1877; see Thornton's *Allusions in "Ulysses."*

Lunn, Louise Kirkby. See Kirkby.

Maas, Joseph (En. ten., 1847–86; famous as des Grieux in Massenet's *Manon* with Marie Roze): 165.2; 203.31; 212.8; 243.35; 246.17; 384.6; 391.8; 491.15

McCormack, John (Irish-Am. ten., 1884–1945): 222.7–8; 243.16; 359.35–36; 376.1; 380.24; 397.12; 408.11–12; 410.2; 413.15; 418.3–4, .16; 419.22; 426.7–15; 427.29; 450.25, .28; 463.22; 464.5; 526.28; and tennis partner Willingdon: 8.10–10.17; *Song o' My Heart* (film): 224.35; and Sir William Orpen (1878–1931), who painted M's favorite portrait of McCormack: 492.30. See also Foli, Giovanni.

M'Guckin, Barton (Irish ten., 1852–1913): 180.8

Malibran, María Felicità, (Sp. mezzo-sop., b. Maria-Felicita, 1808–36; she and her sister, Pauline, performed as the Garcia sisters): 423.2

Malibran, Pauline (Sp. mezzo-sop., 1821–1910; sister of María Felicità, q.v.): 423.2.

Mallinger, Mathilde (Croatian sop., b. Lichtenegger, 1847–1920): 192.5; 475.22

Malten, Therese (Ger. sop., b. Müller, 1855–1930): 228.22–23; 229.23

Manners, Charles (Irish bass, b. Southcote Mansergh, 1857–1935): 57.2–3; 443.3; 444.26; 457.14. See also Moody.

Manowarda, Josef von (Aus. bass, 1890–1942): 46.15–16

Mara, Gertrud (Ger. sop., b. Schmeling, 1749–1833): 62.5; 407.16; 460.17

March, ? (male singer with Carl Rosa Opera Company, Dublin, 1894): 282.26; 380.12

Marchesi, Blanche (Fr. sop., 1863–1940): 13.27

Marchesi, Luigi Lodovico (It. male sop., b. Marchesini, 1754–1829): 13.27

Marchesi, Salvatore (It. bar., Cavaliere de Castrone, Marchese della Rajata, 1822–1908): 13.27

Pertile, Aureliano (It. ten., 1885–1952): 422.23; 445.8

Pinza, Ezio (It. bass, b. Fortunio, 1892–1957): 417.21; 425.18; 461.15; 465.18

Plançon, Pol-Henri (Fr. bass, 1851–1914): 477.25

Pons, Lily (Fr.-Am. sop., b. Alice Joséphine Pons, 1898–1976): 98.20; 178.24; 493.29; 553.21; 578.25; 580.1

Ponselle, Rosa (Am. sop., b. Ponzillo, 1897–1981): 98.30; 173.10; 425.18

Pyne, Louisa (En. sop., 1832–1904): 221.28; 534.12

Raaff, Anton (Ger. ten., 1714–97; teacher of Ludwig Fischer, q.v.): 97.14; 136.13

Ragazzo, Il. See Farinelli.

Raisa, Rosa (Polish sop., b. Rose Burchstein, 1893–1963): 436.35

Reeves, Sims (En. ten., b. John Reeves, 1818–1900): 58.3; 197.1; 397.10; 408.21–23; 422.26; 427.29; his much applauded encore, "Turn on old time": 408.23; 426.26

Reichmann, Theodor (Ger. bar., 1849–1903): 533.32

Reining, Maria (Aus. sop., 1903–91): 332.15

Reiss, Albert (Ger. ten., 1870–1940): 210.28

Reizen [Reyzen], Mark (Russ. bass, b. Osipovich, 1895–): 210.28

Robeson, Paul (Am. bass-bar., 1898–1976): 199.29; 434.12

Robinson, Anastasia (En. sop., ca. 1695–1755): 403.11

Rode, Wilhelm (Ger. bass-bar., 1887–1959): 228.24; 369.11; 445.9

Roger, Gustave-Hippolyte (Fr. ten., 1815–79): 66.21; 373.15

Romer, Emma (En. sop., ca. 1814–68): 185.5

Rosing, Vladimir (Russ.-Am. ten., 1890–1963): 346.20; 363.10; 517.32

Rossi, Countess (sop.): 250.3; 465.30

Roze, Marie (Fr. sop., b. Hippolyte Ponsin, 1846–1926; sang with Carl Rosa Opera Company and starred in Puccini's *Manon Lescaut* opposite Joseph Maas): 204.2

Rubini, Giacomo. See Lauri-Volpi, Giacomo.

Rubini, Giovanni-Battista (It. ten., 1794–1854; sang Elvino in Bellini's *La sonnambula* and also appeared in Donizetti's *Anna Bolena* and *Lucia di Lammermoor*): 249.7; 379.24; 413.34

Ruffo, Titta (It. bar., b. Ruffo Cafiero Titta, 1877–1953): 247.10

Russ (sop.): 199.22

St. Austell, Ivan (En. ten., b. W. H. Stephens, fl. 1890s; performed with Arthur Rousbey Opera Company and named in *U*): 48.11–12

St. Just, Hilton (stage name) (En. ten., fl. 1890s; performed with Arthur Rousbey Opera Company and named in *U*): 48.11–12

Saléza, Albert (Fr. ten., 1867–1916): 142.12; 446.28

Salvini-Donatelli, Fanny (It. sop., b. Francesca Lucci or Lucchi, 1815–91):
495.36

Sammarco, Mario (It. bar., 1868–1930): 253.12

Sanderson, Sybil (Am. sop., 1865–1903): 412.23; 413.5, .14; 414.2

Santley, Charles (En. bar., 1834–1922; sang with Mapleson's Royal Italian
Opera, Carl Rosa, and other companies that appeared in Dublin; sang
title role of first London production of Wagner's *Flying Dutchman* 1870;
in company of Gaiety Theatre, 1870, in *Zampa, Zar und Zimmermann*,
and *Fra Diavolo*): 247.20; 254.33

Sass, Marie-Constance (Bel. sop., b. Sasse, 1834–1907): 240.1; 403.2; 552.29

Schack, Benedikt (Boh.-Aus. ten., b. Zak, 1758–1826): 468.33; 469.23

Schipa, Tito (It. ten., b. Raffaele Attilio Amadeo, 1888–1965): 437.16

Schlusnus, Heinrich (Ger. bar., 1888–1952): 228.14; 448.7

Schnorr von Carolsfeld, Ludwig (Ger. ten., 1836–65; chosen by Wagner to sing
first Tristan): 257.36

Schnorr von Carolsfeld, Malvina (Dan. sop., b. Garrigues, 1832–1904: sang
first Isolde): 257.36

Schorr, Friedrich (Hung.-Am. bass-bar., 1888–1953): 230.10; 266.8; 454.7

Schott, Anton (Ger. ten., 1846–1913): 230.10

Schumann-Heink, Ernestine (Aus.-Am. contra., b. Rössler, 1861–1936): 238.13

Scotti, Antonio (It. bar., 1866–1936): 412.24; 518.22; 521.11

Sheridan, Margaret (Irish sop., 1889–1958): 213.1; 256.12–13

Siems, Margarethe (Ger. sop., 1879–1952): 245.8

Slezak, Leo (Aus.-Czech. ten., 1873–1946): 516.18

Slobodskaya, Oda (Russ. sop., 1888–1970): 541.26

Smith, Frank (sang role of Vyvyan in Wallace's *Maritana* at Theatre Royal,
Dublin): 48.11–12

Souez, Ina (Am. sop., b. Rains, 1908–): 234.18

Spani, Hina (Argen. sop., b. Higinia Tuñon, 1896–1969): 255.32

Stabile, Mariano (It. bar., 1888–1968): 465.15

Stehle, Sophie (Ger. sop., 1838–1921): 460.17

Stephens, Catherine (En. sop., 1794–1892): 300.F2

Stephens, W. H. See St. Austell.

Storchio, Rosina (It. sop., 1876–1945): 255.9

Strepponi, Giuseppina (It. sop., b. Clelia Maria Josepha, 1815–97; became
Verdi's wife): 444.19; 510.7

Sucher, Rosa (Ger. sop., b. Hasselbeck, 1849–1927; first Isolde in England): 424.28

Sullivan, John (Irish ten., 1878–1955; Joyce promoted him tirelessly): 58.10; 93.30; 142.26; 222.8; 435.29; 495.1–3, .7; 573.7, .13; 581.4

Supervia, Conchita (Sp. mezzo-sop., 1895–1936, famous for singing of Rossini roles): 252.17; 268.3

Swarthout, Gladys (Am. mezzo-sop., 1900–69): 250.5

Tamagno, Francesco (It. ten., 1850–1905): 404.26; 450.23

Tamburini, Antonio (It. bar., 1800–76): 248.9; 415.9

Tauber, Richard (Aus.-En. ten., b. Ernst Seiffert Denemy, 1891–1948): 7.6; 105.9; 466.20; 546.29

Tenducci, Giusto Ferdinando (It. sop., 1736–90; sometimes known as Senesino but not the same as the great Senesino; despite being an *evirato* he eloped with the daughter of a Dublin councillor and fathered several children. One of his nicknames was "triorchis," or triple-testicled): 128.26; 371.6; 381.27–28; 541.32–33; 584.10

Ternina, Milka (Croat. sop., 1863–1941): 416.25

Tetrazzini, Luisa (It. sop., 1871–1940): 457.13

Teyte, Maggie (En. sop., b. Tate, 1888–1976; sister-in-law of music hall singer Lottie Collins): 432.11

Thill, Georges (Fr. ten., 1897–1984; principal ten. at Paris Opéra at time of writing *FW*): 409.30; 461.28

Thorborg, Kerstin (Sw. mezzo-sop., 1896–1970): 626.28

Thornton, Edna (En. contra., 1875–1964): 63.6

Tibbett, Lawrence (Am. bar., b. Tibbet, 1896–1960): 424.29; 448.23

Tichatschek, Joseph (Boh. ten., b. Josef Aloys Tichacek, 1807–86): 465.29–30

Tietjens, Therese (Ger. sop., b. Carola Johanna Alexandra, 1831–77; described in Dublin as having "a heart as big as herself"; Shaw described her as being of "immense corpulence"): 155.26; 406.23; 432.11

Tilbury, C. (bar., sang Schaunard in Carl Rosa Opera Company's 1897 production of Puccini's *La bohème*): 554.2. See also Robert Cunningham, William Paull.

Todi, Luisa (Port. mezzo-sop., 1753–1833): 60.28

Tofts, Catherine (En. sop., ?–1756; first English-born singer to sing in Italian opera in England, 1705): 277.11; 331.21

Tombesi, ? (ten.): 24.16; 27.1, .22

Traubel, Helen (Am. sop., 1899–1972): 354.29

Trebelli, Zélia (Fr. mezzo-sop., b. Gloria Caroline LeBert or Gillebert [last name anagrammed to Trebel(li)], 1834–92): 267.17; 474.10

Turner, Eva (En. sop., 1892–1990; famous Turandot): 248.7, .33; 251.23, .26, .28; 390.6; 466.9; 469.2

Unger, Georg (Ger. ten., 1837–87): 422.24; 457.7; 464.28; 465.16

Urbani, Valentino (It. contra. or counter-ten., b. Valentino Urbani, fl. 1690– 1719; known as Valentini): 249.4; 289.27–28; 439.17; 458.2

Urlus, Jacques (Dutch ten., 1867–1935; leading *Heldentenor* who sang Tristan and Parsifal): 577.14

Valanga, La ("The Avalanche," otherwise unidentified prima donna who sang in *La forza del destino* [*Letters 1,* 358]; Triestines say that the term is not Triestine dialect, so Joyce probably heard her in Rome, 1906–7): 28.9; 162.31; 240.32; 406.9

Valentini or Valentino. See Urbani.

Valentini or Valentino, Pier Francesco (It. bar., principally a comp., ca. 1570– 1654): 249.4; 289.27–28; 439.17; 458.2

Van Dyck, Ernest (Bel. ten., 1861–1923): 607.31

Velluti, Giovanni Battista (It. male sop., 1781–1861): 230.30; 313.20

Vestris, Lucia Elizabeth (En. contra., b. Bartolozzi, 1787–1856): 26.7

Viardot-Garcia, Pauline [Michèle-Ferdinande] (Fr. mezzo-sop., 1821–1910): 423.2

Vignas, Francisco (Sp. ten., b. Viñas, 1863–1933): 440.22

Vogl, Heinrich (Ger. ten., 1845–1900): 224.19

Waldmann, Maria (Aus. mezzo-sop., 1842–1920): 345.4

Walker, Edyth (Am. mezzo-sop., 1867–1950): 473.3; 476.4

Waltz, Gustavus (Ger. bass, ?–ca. 1759; was also Handel's cook): 78.32; 282.F4

Widdop, Walter (En. ten., 1892–1949): 101.4, .18

Wilt, Marie (Aus. sop., b. Liebenthaler, 1833–91; also sang as Maria Vilda): 76.27; 512.12–13

Winkelmann (Winckelmann), Hermann (Ger. ten., 1849–1912): 255.23; 413.34; 435.25

. Appendix .
Opera in Dublin, 1898–1904

STEPHEN WATT AND NONA K. WATT

Opera performances in Dublin at the turn of the nineteenth century were normally given Monday through Saturday evenings, with matinees on Monday and Saturday, totaling eight shows weekly. This meant that a single tenor, for instance, would on successive evenings sing leading roles as Faust, Lohengrin, and Manrico in *Il trovatore,* appearing on the fourth night as a weak-voiced Hardress Cregan in *The Lily of Killarney.* Singers must have been grateful that theaters were closed Sunday.

Abbreviations:
G = Gaiety Theatre; QR = Queen's Royal Theatre; TR = Theatre Royal

1898

3–29 Jan. (4 wks.)	TR	Rousbey Opera Co.
11–16 Apr.	G	D'Oyly Carte Opera Co.
22 Aug.–3 Sept. (2 wks.)	G	Carl Rosa Opera Co.
14–19 Nov.	TR	Grand English Opera Co.
5–10 Dec.	G	D'Oyly Carte Opera Co.
	TR	*The Geisha*
26 Dec.	G	D'Oyly Carte Opera Co.

1899

1–7 Jan.	G	D'Oyly Carte Opera Co.: *The Vicar of Bray*
9–28 Jan. (3 wks.)	G	Robert Cunningham's National Grand Opera Co.: *Faust, Bohemian Girl, Maritana, Tannhäus-*

STEPHEN WATT, associate professor of English at the University of Indiana, has special interests in the fields of modern drama and Irish studies, particularly Sean O'Casey and James Joyce. NONA K. WATT, M.L.S., is head of technical services at the Indiana University Law Library, Bloomington, Indiana.

er, *Lohengrin, Il trovatore, Lily of Killarney, Don Giovanni, Cavalleria rusticana, Handel* [sic] *and Gretel, The Prentice Pillar*

6–11 Feb.	G	D'Oyly Carte Opera Co.: *The Lucky Star*
20 Feb.	G	*The Greek Slave* (?)
3–15 Apr. (2 wks.)	TR	Rousbey Opera Co.: *Maritana, Lily of Killarney, Il trovatore, Bohemian Girl, Faust, Lucia di Lammermoor, La traviata, Rigoletto, Tannhäuser, Don Giovanni*
17–29 July (2 wks.)	QR	F. S. Gilbert's Opera Co.
21 Aug.–2 Sept. (2 wks.)	TR	*The Geisha*
25 Sept.–1 Oct.	G	"comic opera," *Paul Jones*
30 Oct.–11 Nov. (2 wks.)	TR	Moody-Manners Opera Co.: *Masanello, The Amber Witch, Il trovatore, Lohengrin, Lily of Killarney, The Puritan's Daughter, Maritana*
20–25 Nov.	G	D'Oyly Carte Opera Co.: *Mikado, Pirates of Penzance, Yeomen of the Guard, Gondoliers, Patience, Trial by Jury*

1900

19–24 Mar.	TR	*A Greek Slave* ("New" Roman Opera)
9–28 Apr. (3 wks.)	TR	Moody-Manners Opera Co.: *Faust, Il trovatore, Lily of Killarney, The Puritan's Daughter, Carmen, Bohemian Girl, Maritana, Tannhäuser, Lohengrin*
16–21 Apr.	G	D'Oyly Carte Opera Co.: *Gondoliers, Mikado, Yeomen of the Guard, Iolanthe, Patience*
4–9 June	G	D'Oyly Carte Opera Co.: *The Rose of Persia*
10–15 Sept.	TR	*The Geisha*
24–29 Sept.	G	Carl Rosa Opera Co.: *Maritana, Carmen, Tannhäuser, Lohengrin, Faust, At the Harbour Side*
22–27 Oct.	G	D'Oyly Carte Opera Co.: *Mikado, Gondoliers, Yeomen of the Guard, Iolanthe, H.M.S. Pinafore,*
12–17 Nov.	TR	*Floradora*
19–24 Nov.	TR	Moody-Manners Opera Co.: *Maritana, Faust, Lohengrin, The Jewess, Tannhäuser, Bohemian Girl*
26 Nov.–1 Dec.	G	D'Oyly Carte Opera Co.

1901

18–23 Feb.	TR	*La Poupée*
25 Feb.–2 Mar.	TR	*Madame Butterfly*
29 Apr.–4 May	TR	*The Geisha*
27 May–1 June	G	D'Oyly Carte Opera Co.
5–10 Aug.	QR	English Opera Co.: *Maritana*
	G	*La Cigale*
14–19 Oct.	G	D'Oyly Carte Opera Co.

25 Nov.–7 Dec. (2 wks.)	G	Carl Rosa Opera Co.: *Tannhäuser, Faust, Carmen,* etc.
	TR	*Floradora*
16–21 Dec.	TR	*The Geisha*
20 Dec.–4 Jan. (2 wks.)	TR	Moody-Manners Opera Co.: *Carmen, Bohemian Girl, Lily of Killarney*

1902

6–18 Jan. (2 wks.)	TR	Moody-Manners Opera Co.: *Faust, Il trovatore, Carmen, Bohemian Girl, Lily of Killarney*
24–29 Mar.	G	D'Oyly Carte Opera Co.
	TR	opera
11–16 Aug.	TR	*The Geisha*
22–27 Sept.	G	Carl Rosa Opera Co.
	TR	*A Greek Slave*
3–8 Nov.	TR	*Floradora*
1–6 Dec.	G	D'Oyly Carte Opera Co.

1903

12–17 Jan.	TR	Moody-Manners Opera Co.
9–14 Mar.	G	D'Oyly Carte Opera Co.
13–25 Apr. (2 wks.)	TR	opera
	QR	*Bohemian Girl* (half week)
13–18 July	QR	*Maritana*
20–25 July	QR	*Faust*
10–15 Aug.	G	*Les Cloches de Corneville*
7–12 Sept.	TR	*The Geisha*
14–19 Sept.	G	Carl Rosa Opera Co.
7–12 Dec.	TR	Irish opera
28 Dec.–2 Jan.	TR	Moody-Manners Opera Co.: *Daughter of the Regiment, Faust, Maritana*

1904

4–23 Jan. (3 wks.)	TR	Moody-Manners Opera Co.: *Daughter of the Regiment, Faust, Il trovatore, Mignon, Martha, Carmen, Lily of Killarney, Romeo and Juliette, Lohengrin, Bohemian Girl*
18–24 Apr.	G	*Mikado, H.M.S. Pinafore*
13–25 June (2 wks.)	QR	Elster-Grimes Opera Co.: *Maritana, Il trovatore, Carmen, Lily of Killarney, Bohemian Girl, Daughter of the Regiment, Faust, Satanelle*

Joyce left Ireland in the first week of October 1904

28 Nov.–3 Dec.	TR	*Floradora*
5–10 Dec.	TR	*The Geisha, A Greek Slave*
12–17 Dec.	G	Carl Rosa Opera Co.: *Rigoletto, Carmen, Tristan*

		and Isolde, Faust, Don Giovanni, Tannhäuser, Bohemian Girl
26–31 Dec.	TR	Moody-Manners Opera Co.: *Carmen, Il trovatore, Lily of Killarney, La traviata, Mignon, Daughter of the Regiment, Faust, Bohemian Girl*

Note

Information in this appendix comes from notes for Stephen Watt, *Joyce, O'Casey, and the Irish Popular Theater* (Syracuse: Syracuse University Press, 1991).

. Bibliography .

Adams, Robert Martin. *Surface and Symbol: The Consistency of James Joyce's "Ulysses."* New York: Oxford University Press, 1962.

Altmann, Wilhelm. *Frank's kurzgefasstes Tonkünstler-Lexikon,* 14th ed. Regensburg: Gustav Bosse Verlag, 1936.

Antheil, George. *Bad Boy of Music.* Garden City, N.Y.: Doubleday, Doran, 1945.

Arditi, Luigi. *My Reminiscences.* Ed. Baroness von Zedlitz. London: Skeffington and Son, 1896.

Bagnoli, Giorgio. *La Scala Encyclopedia of the Opera.* Trans. Graham Fawcett. New York: Simon and Schuster, 1993.

Baker's Biographical Dictionary of Musicians, 7th ed. Ed. Nicolas Slonimsky. New York: Schirmer; London: Collier Macmillan, 1984.

Barlow, Harold, and Sam Morgenstern. *Dictionary of Vocal Themes.* New York: Crown, 1950; London: Benn, 1956.

Baudelaire, Charles. "Richard Wagner and *Tannhäuser* in Paris." In *Baudelaire as Literary Critic: Selected Essays,* intro. and trans. Lois Boe Hyslop and Francis E. Hyslop Jr., 188–231. University Park: Pennsylvania State University Press, 1964.

Bauerle, Ruth. *The James Joyce Songbook.* New York: Garland, 1984 (1982).

———, ed. *Picking Up Airs: Hearing the Music in Joyce's Text.* Urbana: University of Illinois Press, 1993.

Beach, Sylvia. *Shakespeare and Company.* New York: Harcourt Brace and World (Harvest), 1959 (1956).

Beecham, Sir Thomas. *A Mingled Chime.* New York: Putnam's, 1943.

Benco, Silvio. "James Joyce in Trieste." In *Portraits of the Artist in Exile,* ed. Willard Potts, 47–58. Seattle: University of Washington Press, 1979.

Benson, E. F. *As We Were: A Victorian Peep Show.* New York: Blue Ribbon, 1934 (1930).

Borach, Georges. "Conversations with James Joyce." In *Portraits of the Artist in Exile,* ed. Willard Potts, 67–72. Seattle: University of Washington Press, 1979.

Borovsky, Victor. *Chaliapin: A Critical Biography.* New York: Knopf, 1988.

Brockman, William S. *Music: A Guide to the Reference Literature.* Littleton, Colo.: Libraries Unlimited, 1987.

Brockway, Wallace, and Herbert Weinstock. *The World of Opera: The Story of Its Origins and the Lore of Its Performance.* New York: Pantheon, 1941, 1962.

Brown, Carole. "Will the Real Signor Foli Please Stand up and Sing 'Mother Machree'?" *A Wake Newslitter,* n.s. 17 (Dec. 1980): 99–100.

Brown, Carole, and Leo Knuth. "More Wakean Memories of McCormack: A Centenary Tribute." *A Wake Newslitter* Occasional Paper no. 4. Colchester, England.: A Wake Newslitter Press, 1984.

———. *The Tenor and the Vehicle. A Wake Newslitter* Monograph, no. 5. Colchester, England: A Wake Newslitter Press, 1982.

Brown, James D., and Stephen S. Stratton. *British Musical Biography.* London: William Reeves, 1897.

Byrne, J. F. *Silent Years.* New York: Farrar, Straus and Young, 1953.

Caruso, Dorothy. *Enrico Caruso: His Life and Death.* New York: Simon and Schuster, 1945.

Caruso, Enrico Jr., and Andrew Farkas. *Enrico Caruso: My Father and My Family.* Portland, Ore.: Amadeus, 1990.

Césari, Giulio. "I Sinico: una famiglia Triestina di musicisti" (The Sinicos: a Triestine family of musicians). *Rivista Mensile della Città di Trieste* 5, no. 4 (Apr. 1932): 187–97.

Chorley, Henry Fothergill. *Thirty Years' Musical Recollections.* Ed. Ernest Newman. New York: Knopf, 1926.

Christiansen, Rupert. *Prima Donna.* New York: Viking, 1985.

Colum, Padraic, and Mary Colum. *Our Friend James Joyce.* Garden City, N.Y.: Doubleday, 1958.

Cone, John Frederick. *Adelina Patti: Queen of Hearts.* Ed. Andrew Farkas and William R. Moran. Opera Biography Series, no. 4. Portland, Ore.: Amadeus, 1993.

Costello, Peter. *James Joyce: The Years of Growth, 1882–1915.* New York: Pantheon, 1992.

Curran, Constantine P. *James Joyce Remembered.* New York and London: Oxford University Press, 1968.

Dalton, Jack P. "Music Lesson." In *A Wake Digest,* ed. Clive Hart and Fritz Senn, 13–16. Sydney: Sydney University Press, 1968.

Davison, J. W. *From Mendelssohn to Wagner: Memoirs of J. W. Davison, Forty Years Music Critic of "The Times."* Ed. Henry Davison. London: Wm. Reeves, 1912.

Delimata, Bozena Berta. "Reminiscences of a Joyce Niece." Ed. Virginia Moseley. *James Joyce Quarterly* 19 (Fall 1981): 45–62.

Dent, Edward J. *Ferruccio Busoni.* London: Oxford University Press, 1933.

Dizonario enciclopedico universale della musica e dei musicisti (Universal encyclopedic dictionary of music and musicians). N.p.: UTET, 1985.

Doherty, Paul. "Q. & A. with Stephen Joyce." *Irish Literary Supplement,* Spring 1991, 5.

Donington, Robert. *Opera and Its Symbols.* New Haven, Conn.: Yale University Press, 1990.

Eichelberger, Carl. " 'Words? Music? No, It's what's behind.' Verbal and Physical Transformations in 'Sirens.' " In *International Perspectives on James Joyce,* ed. Gottlieb Gaiser, 59–67. Troy, N.Y.: Whitston, 1986.

Ellis, S. M. *The Life of Michael Kelly: Musician, Actor, and Bon Viveur, 1762–1826.* London: Victor Gollancz, 1930.

Ellmann, Richard. *James Joyce,* 2d ed. New York: Oxford University Press, 1982.

Enciclopedia della musica (Encyclopedia of music). Milan: G. Ricordi, 1964.

Ewen, David. *Opera: Its Story Told through the Lives and Works of Its Foremost Composers*. New York: Franklin Watts, 1972.

———. *Musicians since 1900*. New York: H. W. Wilson, 1978.

Fahy, Catherine, compiler. *The James Joyce–Paul Léon Papers in the National Library of Ireland: A Catalogue*. Dublin: National Library of Ireland, 1992.

Farkas, Andrew. *Opera and Concert Singers: An Annotated International Bibliography of Books and Pamphlets*. New York: Garland, 1985.

Ferrer, Daniel. "Echo or Narcissus?" In *James Joyce: The Centennial Symposium*, ed. Morris Beja, Phillip Herring, Maurice Harmon, and David Norris, 70–75. Urbana: University of Illinois Press, 1986.

Fitzpatrick, Samuel A. Ossory. *Dublin: A Historical and Topographical Account of the City.* New York: Dutton, 1907.

Forbes, Elizabeth. *Mario and Grisi*. London: Victor Gollancz, 1985.

Foster, Myles Birket. *History of the Philharmonic Society of London, 1813–1912*. London: John Lane, the Bodley Head, 1912.

Frank, Nino. "The Shadow That Had Lost Its Man." In *Portraits of the Artist in Exile*, ed. Willard Potts, 73–105. Seattle: University of Washington Press, 1979.

Fuld, James J. *The Book of World Famous Music*. New York: Crown, 1971.

Gatti-Casazza, Giulio. *Memories of Opera* (title page reads "Memories of *the* Opera"). New York: Scribner's, 1941.

Geiringer, Karl. *Musical Instruments*. Trans. Bernard Miall. New York: Oxford University Press, 1945.

Giedion-Welcker, Carola. "Meetings with Joyce," In *Portraits of the Artist in Exile*, ed. Willard Potts, 253–80. Seattle: University of Washington Press, 1979.

Gilbert, Stuart. *Reflections on James Joyce: Stuart Gilbert's Paris Journal*. Ed. Thomas F. Staley and Randolph Lewis. Austin: University of Texas Press, 1993.

———. "Selections from the Paris Diary of Stuart Gilbert, 1929–34," ed. Thomas F. Staley and Randolph Lewis. *Joyce Studies Annual* 1, ed. Thomas F. Staley. Austin: University of Texas Press, 1990.

Gilbert, W. S. *Authentic Libretti of the Gilbert and Sullivan Operas*. New York: Crown, 1939.

Gillespie, Michael Patrick. "'Prying into the family life of a great man': A Survey of the Joyce/Léon Papers at the National Library of Ireland." *James Joyce Quarterly* 30 (Winter 1983): 277–94.

———. "Wagner in the Ormond Bar: Operatic Elements in the 'Sirens' Episode of *Ulysses*." In *Irish Renaissance Annual IV*, ed. Zack Bowen, 157–73. Newark: University of Delaware Press, 1983.

Gillet, Louis. "Farewell to Joyce." In *Portraits of the Artist in Exile*, ed. Willard Potts, 165–69. Seattle: University of Washington Press, 1979.

———. "The Living Joyce." In *Portraits of the Artist in Exile*, ed. Willard Potts, 170–204. Seattle: University of Washington Press, 1979.

Glasheen, Adaline: *Third Census of "Finnegans Wake."* Berkeley: University of California Press, 1977.

Glass, Beaumont. *Lotte Lehmann: a Life in Opera & Song*. Santa Barbara, Calif.: Capra, 1988.

Gobbi, Tito. *Tito Gobbi on His World of Opera*. New York: Franklin Watts, 1984.

Gollancz, Victor. *Journey towards Music: A Memoir*. New York: Dutton, 1965.

Goossens, Eugene [III]. *Overture and Beginners: A Musical Autobiography*. London: Methuen, 1951.

Graves, Charles Larcom. *Post-Victorian Music, with Other Studies and Sketches*. London: Macmillan, 1911.

Graves, Perceval. "The Moody-Manners Partnership," *Opera* 9 (1958): 558–64.

Greene, Harry Plunket. *Charles Villiers Stanford*. London: Edward Arnold, 1935; New York: Longmans, Green, n.d.

Greenfeld, Howard. *Caruso*. New York: Putnam's, 1983.

Grove's Dictionary of Music and Musicians. 3d ed. Ed. H. C. Colles. New York: Macmillan, 1942.

Hamm, Charles. *Opera*. Boston: Allyn and Bacon, 1966.

Harewood, George Henry H. L., Earl of, ed. *Kobbé's Illustrated Opera Book*. New York: Putnam's, 1989.

———, ed. *New Kobbé's Complete Opera Book*. New York: Putnam's, 1976.

Hart, Clive. *A Concordance to "Finnegans Wake."* Corrected ed. Mamaroneck, N.Y.: Paul P. Appel, 1974.

———. *Structure and Motif in "Finnegans Wake."* Evanston, Ill.: Northwestern University Press, 1962.

Hart, Clive, and Fritz Senn. *A Wake Digest*. Sydney: Sydney University Press, 1968.

Hayman, David. "Tristan and Isolde in *Finnegans Wake:* A Study of the Sources and Evolution of a Theme." *Comparative Literature Studies* 1 (1964): 93–112.

Heriot, Angus. *The Castrati in Opera*. London: Secker and Warburg, 1956; New York: DaCapo, 1974.

Hodgart, Matthew J. C. *James Joyce: A Student's Guide*. London: Routledge, 1978.

Hodgart, Matthew J. C., and Mabel Worthington. *Song in the Works of James Joyce*. New York: Columbia University Press for Temple University Press, 1959.

Holroyd, Michael. *Bernard Shaw*. Vol. 1, *1856–1898: The Search for Love*. New York: Random House, 1988.

Hughes, Herbert. *The Joyce Book*. London: Sylvan, 1933.

Hutchins, Patricia. *James Joyce's World*. London: Methuen, 1957.

Incontrera, Oscar de. "La 'Marinella' e l'inno di San Giusto" (The "Marinella" and the hymn of San Giusto). *Rivista Vecchia Trieste Teatrale*, July 1950, 7.

Johnson, H. Earle. *Operas on American Subjects*. New York: Coleman-Roos, 1964.

Joyce, James. *Dubliners*. Viking Critical Edition. Ed. Robert Scholes and A. Walton Litz. New York: Viking, 1969.

———. *Exiles*. New York: Penguin, 1977.

———. *Finnegans Wake*. New York: Viking Compass, 1959.

———. *Letters of James Joyce*. Vol. 1. Ed. Stuart Gilbert. New York: Viking, 1957.

———. *Letters of James Joyce*. Vols. 2–3. Ed. Richard Ellmann. New York: Viking, 1966.

———. "Oscar Wilde, the Poet of 'Salomé.'" In *The Critical Writings*, ed. Ellsworth Mason and Richard Ellmann, 201–5. New York: Viking Compass, 1964.

———. *Selected Letters*. Ed. Richard Ellmann. New York: Viking, 1975.

———. *Ulysses*. New York: Garland, 1984.

Joyce, Stanislaus. *Complete Dublin Diary of Stanislaus Joyce.* Ed. George H. Healey. Ithaca, N.Y.: Cornell University Press, 1971.

————. *My Brother's Keeper: James Joyce's Early Years.* Ed. Richard Ellmann. Preface by T. S. Eliot. New York: Viking, 1958; Viking Compass, 1969.

Kain, Richard M. "An Interview with Carola Giedion-Welcker and Maria Jolas." *James Joyce Quarterly* 11 (Winter 1974): 94–122.

Klein, Herman[n]. *The Bel Canto.* Oxford Musical Essays. Oxford: Oxford University Press; London: Humphrey Milford, 1923.

————. *The Reign of Patti,* 1st ed. Da Capo Press Music Reprint Series. New York: Da Capo, 1978 (1920).

Klein, Hermann. *Thirty Years of Musical Life in London, 1870–1900.* New York: Century, 1903.

Kobbé, Gustave. *The Complete Opera Book.* New York: Putnam's, 1919.

————. *The Complete Opera Book.* New York: Putnam's, 1950 (1922).

————. *Opera Singers: A Pictorial Souvenir.* Boston: Oliver Ditson, 1913.

Koestenbaum, Wayne. *The Queen's Throat: Opera, Homosexuality, and the Mystery of Desire.* New York: Poseidon,1993; repr., New York: Vintage, 1994.

Kuhe, Wilhelm. *My Musical Recollections.* London: Richard Bentley and Son, 1896.

Kupferberg, Herbert. *Opera.* New York: Newsweek, 1975.

Labat-Poussin, Brigitte. *Archives du Théâtre National de L'Opéra: Inventaire AJ¹³ 1 á 1466.* Paris: Archives Nationales, 1977.

Lahee, Henry C. *Famous Singers of To-day and Yesterday.* Boston: L. C. Page, 1898.

Lavignac, Albert. *The Music Dramas of Richard Wagner.* New York: Dodd, Mead, 1901.

Lebrecht, Norman. *The Maestro Myth: Great Conductors in Pursuit of Power.* New York: Birch Lane, 1991.

Ledbetter, Gordon T. *The Great Irish Tenor.* New York: Scribner's, 1977.

Legerman, David, ed. *A Treasury of Opera Librettos.* Garden City, N.Y.: Doubleday, 1962.

Lehmann, Lotte. *Midway in My Song.* Indianapolis, Ind.: Bobbs-Merrill, 1938.

Leiser, Clara. *Jean De Reszke and the Great Days of Opera.* Foreword by Amherst Webber. New York: Minton, Balch, 1934.

LeMassena, C. E. *Galli-Curci's Life of Song.* New York: Paebar, 1945.

Lernout, Geert. "Singing Walking Gent: Sims Reeves in VI.B.13." *A "Finnegans Wake" Circular* 3 (Spring 1988): 43–52.

————. "*Woman the Inspirer*—Wagner in VI.B.3." *A "Finnegans Wake" Circular* 6 (1990–91): 1–11.

Leslie, Peter. *A Hard Act to Follow: A Music Hall Review.* New York and London: Paddington, 1978.

Linati, Carlo. "A Visit with Joyce." Trans. Eva Millemann. *James Joyce Quarterly* 19 (Fall 1981): 39–44.

Lindenberger, Herbert. *Opera: The Extravagant Art.* Ithaca, N.Y.: Cornell University Press, 1984.

Loewenberg, Alfred, compiler. *Annals of Opera,* 3d ed. Totowa, N.J.: Rowman and Littlefield, 1978.

Long, Charles. "An Old Story: Isolde's Fall, Deception, and Oath in James Joyce's *Finnegans Wake*—A Reader's Version." *Éire-Ireland* (Summer 1989): 100–108.

Lorenz, Alfred. *Das Geheimnis der Form bei Richard Wagner* (Richard Wagner's secret of form). 4 vols. Berlin: M. Hesse, 1924–33.

Luening, Otto. *Odyssey of an American Composer.* New York: Scribner's, 1980.

Maddox, Brenda. *Nora: The Real Life of Molly Bloom.* Boston: Houghton Mifflin, 1988.

Maddox, Lucy B. "Gabriel and *Otello:* Opera in 'The Dead.'" *Studies in Short Fiction* 24 (1987): 271–77.

Mapleson, J. H. *The Mapleson Memoirs: The Career of an Operatic Impresario, 1858–1888.* Ed. Harold Rosenthal. New York: Appleton-Century, 1966.

Marek, George R. *Puccini: A Biography.* New York: Simon and Schuster, 1951.

Marks, Edward Bennet. *They All Had Glamour.* New York: Julian Messner, 1944.

Martin, Timothy. *Joyce and Wagner: A Study of Influence.* Cambridge: Cambridge University Press, 1991.

———. "Joyce, Wagner, and Literary Wagnerism." In *Picking up Airs,* ed. Ruth Bauerle, 105–27. Urbana: University of Illinois Press, 1993.

———. "Wagner's *Tannhäuser* in *Exiles:* a Further Source." *James Joyce Quarterly* 19 (Fall 1981): 73–76.

Martin, Timothy, and Ruth Bauerle. "The Voice from the Prompt Box: Otto Luening Remembers James Joyce in Zurich." *Journal of Modern Literature* 17 (Summer 1990): 35–48.

McAlmon, Robert, and Kay Boyle. *Being Geniuses Together, 1920–30.* Rev. ed., with supplementary chapters by Kay Boyle. Garden City, N.Y.: Doubleday, 1968.

"McCormack Is Soloist as Daughter Weds; London Crowds Try to Storm into Church." *New York Times,* 17 September 1933, p. 1.

McCormack, Lily. *I Hear You Calling Me.* Milwaukee: Bruce, 1949.

McGinley, Bernard. "Annotating the Life in *Dubliners.*" *James Joyce Literary Supplement,* Spring 1993, 25–26.

McGovern, Dennis, and Deborah Grace Winer. *I Remember Too Much: 89 Opera Stars Speak Candidly.* New York: William Morrow, 1990.

McHugh, Roland. *Annotations to "Finnegans Wake."* Rev. ed. Baltimore, Md.: Johns Hopkins University Press, 1991.

Mercanton, Jacques. "The Hours of James Joyce." In *Portraits of the Artist in Exile,* ed. Willard Potts, 205–52. Seattle: University of Washington Press, 1979.

Mink, Louis. *A "Finnegans Wake" Gazetteer.* Bloomington: Indiana University Press, 1978.

Mordden, Ethan. *Demented: The World of the Opera Diva.* New York: Franklin Watts, 1984.

———. *Opera Anecdotes.* New York: Oxford University Press, 1985.

———. *The Splendid Art of Opera.* New York: Methuen, 1980.

Mortimer, John. *Murderers and Other Friends.* New York: Viking, 1995.

New Grove Dictionary of Music and Musicians. Ed. Stanley Sadie. London: Macmillan; Washington, D.C.: Grove's Dictionaries of Music, 1980.

New Grove Dictionary of Opera. Ed. Stanley Sadie. New York: Grove's Dictionaries of Music, 1992.

O'Connor, Garry. *The Pursuit of Perfection: A Life of Maggie Teyte.* New York: Atheneum, 1979.

O'Connor, Ulick. *The Joyce We Knew.* Cork: Mercier, 1967.

"Oil Trial Evidence Is Ended Abruptly." *New York Times,* 12 December 1926, p. 1.

O'Neill, Michael J. "The Joyce in the Holloway Diaries." In *A James Joyce Miscellany*, 2d ser., ed. Marvin Magalaner, 103–110. Carbondale: Southern Illinois University Press, 1959.

Osborne, Charles. *The Complete Operas of Puccini*. New York: Atheneum, 1982.

———. *Dictionary of the Opera*. New York: Simon and Schuster, 1983.

Owens, Cóilín. "*Entends Sa Voix:* Eveline's Irish Swan Song." *Éire-Ireland* 28, no. 2 (Summer 1993): 37–53.

Pavarotti and the Italian Tenor. Video produced by Michael Bronson. Public Broadcasting System, Great Performances Series, 27 April 1994. Herbert Breslin, New York Center for Visual History, New York, and South Carolina Educational Communications, 1992. Also available on Decca, London Records, and Polygram Video, 1995. 440-071-268-3.

Pearce, Charles E. *Sims Reeves: Fifty Years of Music in England*. London: Stanley Paul, 1924.

Pearsall, Ronald. *Victorian Sheet Music Covers*. Detroit: Gale Research, 1972.

Pitou, Spire. *The Paris Opéra: An Encyclopedia of Operas, Ballets, Composers, and Performers*. Vol. 3 (bound as two vols.), *Growth and Grandeur, 1815–1914*. New York: Greenwood, 1990.

Pleasants, Henry. *The Great Singers*. New York: Simon and Schuster, 1966.

Potts, Willard, ed. *Portraits of the Artist in Exile: Recollections of James Joyce by Europeans*. Seattle: University of Washington Press, 1979.

Power, Arthur. *Conversations with James Joyce*. Chicago: University of Chicago Press, 1974; repr. University of Chicago Press/Phoenix, 1982.

Rabaté, Jean-Michel. "The Silence of the Sirens." In *James Joyce: The Centennial Symposium*, ed. Morris Beja, Phillip Herring, Maurice Harmon, and David Norris, 82–88. Urbana: University of Illinois Press, 1986.

Rasponi, Lanfranco. *The Last Prima Donnas*. New York: Knopf, 1982.

Rosenthal, Harold. *Two Centuries of Opera at Covent Garden*. London: Putnam's, 1958.

Rosenthal, Harold, and John Warrack. *Concise Oxford Dictionary of Opera*, 2d ed. Oxford: Oxford University Press, 1979; repr. with corrections, 1990.

Rosset, B. C. *Shaw of Dublin: The Formative Years*. University Park: Pennsylvania State University Press, 1964.

Ruggiero, Paul. "James Joyce's Last Days in Zurich." In *Portraits of the Artist in Exile*, ed. Willard Potts, 283–86. Seattle: University of Washington Press, 1979.

Santley, Charles. *Reminiscences of My Life*. New York: Brentano's, 1909; London: Isaac Pitman and Sons, 1909.

———. *Student and Singer: The Reminiscences of Charles Santley*. New York: Macmillan, 1892.

Scarry, John. "'Finnegans Wake' III.i: A Portrait of John McCormack." *Irish University Review* 3 (1973): 155–62.

———. "James Joyce and John McCormack." *Revue Belge de Philologie et d'Histoire / Belgisch tijdschrift voor Philologie en Geschiedenis* 52 (1974): 523–36.

———. "'Joan Mockcomick' and 'Jean Souslevin' in Joyce's 'Finnegans Wake.'" *Etudes Anglaises* 27 (1974): 180–84.

———. "'Poor Georgina Burns' in Joyce's 'The Dead.'" *English Language Notes* 10 (1972): 123–26.

————. "A Singer and Some New Songs in 'Finnegans Wake' III.ii." *Neophilologus* 60 (1976): 153–59.

Scholes, Robert E. *The Cornell Joyce Collection.* Ithaca, N.Y.: Cornell University Press, 1961.

Senn, Fritz. "Dublin Theatres." In *A Wake Digest,* ed. Clive Hart and Fritz Senn, 23–26. Sydney: Sydney University Press, 1968.

Shaw, Bernard. *London Music in 1888–89 as Heard by Corno di Bassetto (Later Known as Bernard Shaw) with Some Further Autobiographical Particulars.* London: Constable, 1937; New York: Dodd, Mead, 1961.

————. *Music in London 1890–94.* 3 vols., revised. London: Constable, 1932.

Slezak, Walter. *What Time's the Next Swan?* Garden City, N.Y.: Doubleday, 1962.

Song o' My Heart. Script by Tom Barry. Hollywood, Calif.: Twentieth Century–Fox, 1930; Video Artists International, P.O. Box 153, Ansonia Station, New York, N.Y. 10023.

Soupault, Philippe. "James Joyce." In *Portraits of the Artist in Exile,* ed. Willard Potts, 106–18. Seattle: University of Washington Press, 1979.

Stanford, Charles Villiers. *Interludes: Records and Reflections.* New York: Dutton, 1922.

————. *Pages from an Unwritten Diary.* New York: Longmans, Green; London: Edward Arnold, 1914.

Strong, L. A. G. *John McCormack: The Story of a Singer.* New York: Macmillan, 1941.

Suter, August. "Some Reminiscences of James Joyce." In *Portraits of the Artist in Exile,* ed. Willard Potts, 59–66. Seattle: University of Washington Press, 1979.

Svevo, Italo (Ettore Schmitz). "James Joyce." Trans. Stanislaus Joyce and John Gatt-Rutter. Appendix to Livia Veneziani Svevo, *Memoir of Italo Svevo.* Marlboro, Vt.: Marlboro, 1990.

Svevo, Livia Veneziani. *Memoir of Italo Svevo.* Trans. Isabel Quigly. Preface by P. N. Furbank. Marlboro, Vt.: Marlboro, 1990.

Taubman, Howard. *The Maestro: The Life of Arturo Toscanini.* New York: Simon and Schuster, 1951.

Thornton, Weldon. *Allusions in "Ulysses."* Chapel Hill: University of North Carolina Press, 1968.

Topia, André. "'Sirens': The Emblematic Vibration." In *James Joyce: The Centennial Symposium,* ed. Morris Beja, Phillip Herring, Maurice Harmon, and David Norris, 76–81. Urbana: University of Illinois Press, 1986.

Towers, John. *Dictionary-Catalogue of Operas and Operettas.* Morgantown, W.Va.: Acme, 1910.

Tuggle, Robert. *The Golden Age of Opera.* New York: Holt, Rinehart and Winston, 1983.

Vinding, Ole. "James Joyce in Copenhagen." In *Portraits of the Artist in Exile,* ed. Willard Potts, 137–52. Seattle: University of Washington Press, 1979.

Wagner, Richard. *The Authentic Librettos of the Wagner Operas.* New York: Crown, 1938.

Walsh, Michael. "When Tenors Were Gods." *Time,* 18 July 1994, p. 54.

Walsh, T. J. *Opera in Dublin 1705–1797: The Social Scene.* Dublin: Allen Figgis, 1973.

————. *Opera in Old Dublin, 1819–1838.* Wexford: The Wexford Festival, 1952.

Warrack, John, and Ewan West. *Oxford Dictionary of Opera.* Oxford: Oxford University Press, 1992.

Watt, Stephen. *Joyce, O'Casey, and the Irish Popular Theater.* Syracuse, N.Y.: Syracuse University Press, 1991.

. Index .

. Photo Credits .

Pictures of Luigi Arditi and Antonio Giuglini are from Luigi Arditi, *My Reminiscences* (London, 1896).

Pictures of Italo Campanini, Jean de Reszke as Roméo, James Mapleson, Euphrosyne Parepa-Rosa, Adelina Patti, Sims Reeves, Carl Rosa, and Therese Tietjens are from Hermann Klein, *Thirty Years of Musical Life in London, 1870-1900* (New York, 1903).

Pictures of Alessandro Bonci, Enrico Caruso, Jean de Reszke as Tristan, and Johanna Gadski are from Gustav Kobbé, *Opera Singers: A Pictorial Souvenir* (Boston, 1901).

Pictures of Minni Hauk and Mario in costume are from Edward B. Marks, *They All Had Glamour* (New York, 1944).

The studio portrait of Mario is from Charles Santley, *Reminiscences of My Life* (New York, 1909).

The picture of Euphrosyne Parepa-Rosa on the cover of Balfe's *Bohemian Girl* is from a libretto in the Theodore Presser Collection, Beeghly Library, Ohio Wesleyan University.

The photograph of John McCormack is from the Bauerle Collection.

The late M A T T H E W J . C . H O D G A R T, author or coauthor of the first extensive studies of Joyce's use of musical allusion four decades ago, taught at Cambridge University, the University of Sussex, and other universities in Canada, the United States, and Australia. His previous books include the seminal study *Song in the Works of James Joyce* (with Mabel Worthington), *James Joyce: A Student's Guide,* and other books on satire, English ballads, and eighteenth-century literary figures. He was made a chevalier of the Legion of Honor and awarded the Croix de Guerre for his role in World War II.

R U T H B A U E R L E, professor emerita of English at Ohio Wesleyan University, began her studies of Joyce's musical allusions three decades ago at Northwestern University. She has previously edited the *James Joyce Songbook, A Word List to Joyce's "Exiles,"* and *Picking Up Airs.* Her essays and reviews on Joyce and other modern writers have appeared in numerous collections, as well as in journals and national magazines.

. Joyce's Grand Operoar .

Matthew J. C. Hodgart & Ruth Bauerle

Joyce's Grand

OPEROAR

Opera in *Finnegans Wake*

University of Illinois Press . Urbana and Chicago

© 1997 by the Board of Trustees of the University of Illinois
Manufactured in the United States of America
1 2 3 4 5 C P 5 4 3 2 1

This book is printed on acid-free paper.

Library of Congress Cataloging-in-Publication Data

Hodgart, Matthew John Caldwell.
Joyce's grand operoar : opera in Finnegans wake /
Matthew J. C. Hodgart and Ruth Bauerle.
p.   cm.
Includes bibliographical references and index.
ISBN 0-252-02258-0 (cloth). — ISBN 0-252-06557-3 (pbk.)
1. Joyce, James, 1882–1941—Knowledge—Music.   2. Joyce, James,
1882–1941. Finnegans wake—Concordances.   3. Opera.   4. Music and
literature. I. Bauerle, Ruth, 1924–   . II. Title.
ML80.J75H6   1997
823'.912—dc20   96-4453   CIP   MN